Ultimate LLMOps with Langfuse

Instrument, Evaluate, and Operate Production-Grade LLM Applications with Langfuse

Nikhil Talreja

www.orangeava.com

First Published: May 2026

Published By: Orange Education Pvt Ltd, AVA®

Address: 9, Daryaganj, Delhi, 110002, India

275 New North Road Islington Suite 1314 London,
N1 7AA, United Kingdom

ISBN (PBK): 978-93-49887-54-1
ISBN (E-BOOK): 978-93-49887-78-7

Scan the QR code to explore our entire catalogue

www.orangeava.com

Get a Free eBook

We hope you're enjoying your recent book purchase! Your feedback is incredibly valuable to us and helps other readers discover books that truly make a difference.

If you found this book useful or enjoyable, we'd greatly appreciate it if you could leave a short review with a 5-star rating on Amazon. Your review supports our work and allows us to reach more learners worldwide.

As a thank-you, we're happy to offer you a **free digital copy of this book** plus a **30% discount code** for your next purchase on our official websites:

www.orangeava.com

www.orangeava.in (For the Indian Subcontinent).

☑ **How it works:**

Leave your review on Amazon, take a screenshot of the confirmation or use the following link to submit the claim and email it to **info@orangeava.com.** Once received the required detail, we will send your rewards within 24 hours, **along with one month free subcription to the book on AVA SkillShelf!**

Claim Form
https://rebrand.ly/4d2477

Thank you for your support—it truly means a lot to us.

Downloading the code bundles and colored images

Please follow the links or scan the QR codes to download the
Code Bundles and Images of the book:

https://github.com/ava-orange-education/Ultimate-LLMOps-with-Langfuse

The code bundles and images of the book are also hosted on
https://rebrand.ly/504937

In case there's an update to the code, it will be updated on the existing GitHub repository.

Errata

We take immense pride in our work at **Orange Education Pvt Ltd,** and follow the best practices to ensure the accuracy of our content to provide an indulging reading experience to our subscribers. Our readers are our mirrors, and we use their inputs to reflect and improve upon human errors, if any, that may have occurred during the publishing processes involved. To let us maintain the quality and help us reach out to any readers who might be having difficulties due to any unforeseen errors, please write to us at:

errata@orangeava.com

Your support, suggestions, and feedback are highly appreciated.

Dedicated to

*My Beloved Wife and Steadfast Partner, Pooja,
Whose Unwavering Love, Strength, and Encouragement
Have Been My Anchor throughout
This Journey—My True Support and Inspiration.*

And

*Our Precious Baby Girl, Emma, Whose Joyful Arrival
Filled Our Lives with Immeasurable Happiness,
Abundant Blessings, and a Sense of
Wonder I Never Knew was Possible!*

About the Author

Nikhil Talreja is a Senior AI Engineer with above 15 years of experience building and scaling real-world software. For the past few years, he has been all-in on generative AI, working hands-on to bring Large Language Models (LLMs) into products people use every day. Hence, whether it is backend engineering, cloud platforms, or making LLMs reliable, Nikhil's focus has been always on practical solutions that work at scale.

Based in Munich, Germany, he leads the development of AI-powered features for high-traffic platforms. Nikhil takes projects from the drawing board to deployment and monitoring, mostly coding in Python and Java, and integrating LLM APIs into existing systems. One of his recent highlights was building an in-house LLM translation engine, which swapped out expensive third-party services, slashed turnaround times from days to seconds, and handled multiple European languages. He has also built customer-facing chatbots and internal agents—think text-to-SQL systems or product support bots—using Retrieval-Augmented Generation (RAG) and tool integrations so that teams can interact with enterprise data in simple English.

Nikhil began his career as Senior Software Engineer where he contributed to big, distributed platforms, mentored teams, and promoted better engineering practices. He studied Computer Engineering from Mumbai University, and holds certifications in Generative AI and Data Science.

Throughout his career, Nikhil has loved bridging the gap between experimentation and production, helping teams turn ideas into reliable systems. He is a daily user of modern development tools and AI assistants, shares his insights through writing, and enjoys engaging with the tech community.

About the Technical Reviewers

Sharat Priya is a Senior Manager in the Wealth and Asset Management Technology practice at Ernst & Young (EY) United States, bringing over 22 years of progressive, hands-on experience designing and delivering complex financial platforms for global banks, custodians, insurers, and fintech firms. His career spans both industry and consulting, marked by technical leadership, architectural innovation, and client-centric product delivery.

Sharat's work sits at the intersection of technology strategy and product architecture, with a focus on building real-world platforms that modernize financial services. Currently, he advises executive leadership teams on platform modernization, AI adoption, and operating model transformation across the U.S. wealth management landscape.

Sharat also contributes as an industry reviewer and awards judge, and regularly mentors product leaders and architects. His work emphasizes building explainable, resilient, and compliant financial systems that operate at scale, where trust, precision, and impact matter most.

Archana Choudhary is a senior project and transformation leader with extensive experience driving large-scale technology, data, and AI-enabled delivery across global enterprises. She has led complex initiatives spanning infrastructure, cloud, cybersecurity, and enterprise platforms, focusing on governance, execution excellence, and value realization.

With a background as a Global PMO Lead, Agile Transformation Leader, and Program Manager, Archana has worked at the intersection of technology delivery, operating models, and leadership, helping organizations move from traditional execution approaches to data-driven, adaptive ways of working. Her work increasingly focuses on how AI, automation, and analytics reshape project visibility, decision-making, and risk management at scale.

Through her research and practical application of AI-enabled delivery and LLM observability, including tools such as Langfuse, Archana explores how organizations can bring transparency, reliability, and governance into GenAI-powered systems ensuring that AI augments human judgment, rather than obscuring it. She is particularly interested in how monitoring, traceability, and feedback loops enable responsible AI adoption in enterprise environments.

Acknowledgments

This book would not have been possible without the support of many people. First of all, I would like to thank my family for their continuous encouragement and understanding during the long writing process.

I am grateful to my colleagues, collaborators, and the broader AI engineering community for openly sharing ideas, tools, and best practices that helped shape many of the concepts in this book. I would also like to thank the Langfuse team and open-source contributors for building and maintaining a platform that makes LLM observability practical and accessible.

I also want to say a 'big thank you' to the editorial team at Orange Education Pvt. Ltd. This whole experience would not have been the same without their kindness, encouragement, and endless patience. I am so grateful for everything they all have done, and for believing in me along the way.

Preface

Large Language Models (LLMs) have moved rapidly from experimentation to production but operating them reliably remains a challenge. Unlike traditional software, LLM systems are probabilistic, continuously evolving, and deeply dependent on data, prompts, and user behavior. This book was written to help bridge the gap between building demos, and operating dependable LLM applications in real environments.

The book takes a practical approach throughout. Rather than focusing solely on models, LLM applications are treated as full systems that require observability, evaluation, prompt management, metrics, and guardrails. Using Langfuse as a central platform, the book explores how to trace workflows, evaluate quality, detect drift, manage costs, and continuously improve production behavior.

The book is organized to follow the lifecycle of an LLM application—from foundational concepts and instrumentation, through evaluation and metrics, to security, best practices, and operational playbooks. By the end, readers become well-equipped with concrete workflows and engineering patterns for building measurable, trustworthy LLM systems.

Chapter-wise Summary

Chapter 1 introduces the Large Language Models or LLMs, and the challenges of deploying them in production, framing LLM applications as evolving systems that require observability from the start.

Chapter 2 presents core monitoring principles for LLM systems, covering traces, semantic metrics, and SRE-inspired reliability concepts such as SLIs, SLOs, and error budgets.

Chapter 3 explores drift and bias in production environments, showing why continuous measurement is necessary to maintain quality and fairness over time.

Chapter 4 introduces Langfuse and its core concepts, including projects, environments, traces, and observations, establishing the platform as the foundation for LLM observability.

Chapter 5 focuses on observability in Langfuse, demonstrating how to instrument workflows, capture metadata, and debug complex LLM pipelines.

Chapter 6 covers prompt management as an engineering practice, emphasizing versioning, comparison, and controlled iteration to ensure reproducible behavior.

Chapter 7 examines evaluation workflows in Langfuse, combining automated scoring and human review to measure quality across datasets and production traffic.

Chapter 8 shows how metrics and dashboards transform traces into actionable insights, enabling teams to monitor trends in quality, cost, and performance.

Chapter 9 addresses administration, security, and guardrails, explaining how access control, auditing, and policy enforcement support safe LLM deployments.

Chapter 10 consolidates the best practices for production LLM systems, including prompt versioning, dashboard hygiene, evaluation workflows, and regression detection.

Chapter 11 presents practical playbooks for real workflows such as RAG and agentic systems, illustrating hallucination monitoring, drift detection, cost optimization, and prompt iteration.

Chapter 12 concludes with a forward-looking perspective on LLM engineering and observability, outlining emerging trends and guidance for applying these practices to the ever-evolving systems.

DID YOU KNOW

Did you know that Orange Education Pvt Ltd offers eBook versions of every book published, with PDF and ePub files available? You can upgrade to the eBook version at **www.orangeava.com** and as a print book customer, you are entitled to a discount on the eBook copy. Get in touch with us at: **info@orangeava.com** for more details.

At **www.orangeava.com**, you can also read a collection of free technical articles, sign up for a range of free newsletters, and receive exclusive discounts and offers on Print Books and eBooks.

PIRACY

If you come across any illegal copies of our works in any form on the internet, we would be grateful if you would provide us with the location address or website name. Please contact us at **info@orangeava.com** with a link to the material.

ARE YOU INTERESTED IN AUTHORING WITH US?

If there is a topic that you have expertise in, and you are interested in either writing or contributing to a book, please write to us at **business@orangeava.com**. We are on a journey to help developers and tech professionals to gain insights on the present technological advancements and innovations happening across the globe and build a community that believes Knowledge is best acquired by sharing and learning with others. Please reach out to us to learn what our audience demands and how you can be part of this educational reform. We also welcome ideas from tech experts and help them build learning and development content for their domains.

REVIEWS

Please leave a review. Once you have read and used this book, why not leave a review on the site that you purchased it from? Potential readers can then see and use your unbiased opinion to make purchase decisions. We at Orange Education would love to know what you think about our products, and our authors can learn from your feedback. Thank you!

For more information about Orange Education, please visit **www.orangeava.com**.

Table of Contents

Chapter 1
Introduction to Large Language Models and Monitoring

Introduction

Large Language Models (LLMs) are transforming the world with their ability to understand and generate human-like content. This chapter introduces the fundamentals of LLMs—how they work, their core architectures, and where they are being applied today. We will explore the challenges that arise when deploying these models into real-world systems, including performance bottlenecks, hallucinations, escalating costs, and also the risk of bias or model drift. We will learn why monitoring is essential to ensure that LLMs remain accurate, efficient, and secure over time. The chapter further outlines the LLM lifecycle—from development and fine-tuning to deployment and continuous maintenance—and where monitoring fits in each stage. Tools and platforms such as OpenAI API, LangChain and Langfuse will be introduced, setting the stage for the more hands-on chapters ahead.

Structure

In this chapter, we will cover the following topics:

- Understanding Large Language Models (LLMs)
    - A Brief History of NLP
    - Architecture and Components of LLMs
- LLM Use Cases across Industries
    - Content Generation
    - Customer Support and Knowledge Management
    - Software Engineering
    - Finance

- Healthcare
- Retail, E-Commerce and Marketing

- Challenges in Deploying LLM Applications
  - Non-Deterministic Outputs
  - Infrastructure and Performance Requirements
  - Observability Requirements
  - Ethical, Safety, and Regulatory Concerns
- Key LLM Monitoring and Observability Metrics
  - Latency
  - Cost
  - Token Usage
  - Hallucination
  - Completeness
  - Relevance
  - Correctness
- Introduction to the LLM Application Lifecycle
  - Problem Definition and Requirements Gathering
  - Data Preparation
  - Prompt and System Design
  - Prototyping and Experimentation
  - Evaluation and Benchmarking
  - Deployment and Monitoring
- Exploring the LLM Toolkit for the Book
  - OpenAI SDK
  - LangChain
  - Langfuse

Understanding Large Language Models (LLMs)

A **Large Language Model** (LLM) is a type of artificial intelligence trained on massive collections of text to understand and generate human-like content. This content can be either text, audio, images or even videos. LLMs are built on the **Transformer**

Architecture which is a type of **Artificial Neural Network** (ANN) architecture that allows them to capture context and relationships across long passages of text like how humans understand natural language. Because of this, LLMs can perform a wide range of tasks—such as answering questions, summarizing documents, generating code, or producing creative content—without requiring task-specific programming. As an ANN, an LLM **predicts the next word** in a sequence of words.

In a 2018 research paper titled *Improving Language Understanding by Generative Pre-Training*, a team of researchers at **OpenAI** proposed a two-staged model training framework which paved the way for developing the large-scale LLMs as we know them today:

- **Unsupervised Pre-training:** This involves training a Transformer based language model on a huge amount of text with the objective of predicting the next word. This step helps the model understand language syntax, semantics and world knowledge.

- **Supervised Fine-tuning:** Taking the model from stage 1, adapt the model on a specific task like summarization, question answering, sentiment analysis and so on.

This simple paradigm of pre-train + fine-tune led to the explosion of general purpose language understanding systems that are now redefining technological and human history.

Before we jump into the core architecture and components of LLMs, let us take a trip down memory lane to see how the field of **Natural Language Processing** (NLP) evolved.

A Brief History of NLP

Natural Language Processing (NLP), the field of artificial intelligence that focuses on enabling computers to understand, interpret, generate, and interact using human language has evolved significantly over the past several decades, transitioning from early rule-based approaches to the development of advanced LLMs. Each stage in this progression addressed certain challenges while presenting new ones, ultimately leading to breakthroughs such as the Transformer architecture and GPT models.

1964 – 1967: ELIZA — The First "Chatterbot"

The story of NLP starts as early as the 1950s, a major milestone came in 1966, when a Computer Scientist and MIT Professor **Joseph Weizenbaum** built ELIZA - an NLP program that used pattern matching and hardcoded rules to simulate communication between humans and machines. Its most famous script, called DOCTOR, mimicked a psychotherapist that could talk to humans as if it understood them.

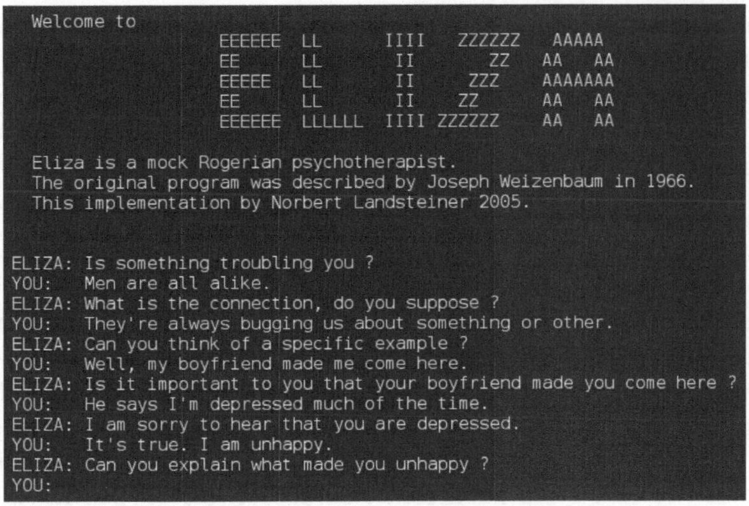

Figure 1.1: *A Conversation with ELIZA*

ELIZA essentially kicked off the **chatbot era** and raised questions about *simulation vs. true intelligence*—questions still debated with modern LLMs like GPT and Claude. Despite having no true understanding of human language, many of ELIZA's users were convinced of its capabilities and intelligence.

1990s – 2000s: NLP Starts Using Machine Learning

The earlier NLP models which were rule based were impractical. Considering the huge amount of text to be processed for every human language, this idea becomes unmaintainable quickly. Instead of manually encoding grammar or semantics, NLP started adopting early Machine Learning models that used data-driven approaches. The idea was to make models learn patterns from a big corpus of texts and make predictions based on probabilities.

These statistical models were a turning point to end the so-called **AI Winter** of the 1980s, which was a period of reduced interest (and funding) in the field. The most notable advancements during this time were:

- **N-gram Models**: These models estimate the probability of a word occurring given the preceding n-1 words. They make predictions for the next word based on how likely the word appeared in previously seen documents. While these models worked well on seen data, the biggest issue was Out-of-Vocabulary (OOV) words, which happens when the model sees a word during inference it has never seen during training. An unseen word in this model gets a zero probability, even if it is a perfectly valid word.
- **Hidden Markov Models (HMMs):** While N-gram models could predict next words, they had no understanding of parts of speech or named entities (people,

locations, organizations and so on). HMMs solved this problem by capturing relationships between sentence structure and the words. They found their way into speech recognition systems and Part-of-Speech (POS) tagging. OOV words and long texts were still a problem for these models since HMMs work under the assumption that to predict what comes next, we only need to look at the most recent step. In other words, the model remembers just one step back, as if language only had a one-word memory.

- **Recurrent Neural Networks (RNNs):** In the early 90s, researchers started experimenting with the idea of designing NLP models that could actually think and work like the human brain. This gave birth to the idea of a **Neural Network (NN)** which is a computational model inspired by the brain, made up of interconnected units ("neurons") that process and transform inputs. While NNs are a subject of its own, it would be worth mentioning a special type of NN called the Recurrent Neural Network (RNN). RNNs introduced a neural architecture capable of modeling sequences with theoretically **unlimited memory**, addressing the short-range limitations of n-grams and HMMs. RNNs were groundbreaking in showing that a neural network could, in principle, learn the sequential structure of language without explicit hard coding structure. Later innovations like **Long Short-Term Memory networks (LSTMs, 1997)** would overcome many of these limitations, setting the stage for the deep learning revolution of the 2010s.

2010s: The Rise of Neural Networks

By the early 2010s, traditional statistical NLP and early neural networks like **RNNs** showed limitations with large datasets. As digital text grew, researchers shifted to **representation learning** using improved hardware and new architectures, marking a neural renaissance in NLP. During this time, content from social media, the web, and enterprise data was exploding and created both a pressing need and an opportunity for more powerful models. Some key breakthroughs in this period were:

- **Word2Vec:** Word2Vec was a technique developed by Google AI in 2013. At its core, it represents words as dense vectors in a continuous space. This approach allowed models to capture semantic relationships between words, something traditional n-gram models could not do. In practical terms, Word2Vec enabled NLP systems to reason about meaning dramatically, improving tasks such as information retrieval, analogy solving, and sentiment analysis.

- **Encoder-Decoder Architectures:** Encoder-decoder models introduced a two-part neural framework for processing sequences: the encoder reads and compresses an input sequence into a fixed-length representation, and the decoder generates a corresponding output sequence. This approach was a major advancement in NLP because it made tasks like machine translation and text summarization feasible end-to-end without task-specific feature engineering.

- **Attention Mechanism:** The attention mechanism as introduced in the 2017 paper *Attention is All You Need* allows a model to focus selectively on different parts of the input when generating each output word, rather than relying on a single fixed representation. This fundamentally changed NLP: models could now capture long-range dependencies efficiently, scale to billions of parameters, and ultimately serve as the backbone for modern LLMs like GPT, Claude, and Llama.

2017: Attention is All You Need

The landmark paper **"Attention is All You Need"** by Vaswani et al. introduced the **Transformer architecture**, which completely reimagined how text could be processed. The Transformer's main innovation is **self-attention**, which lets the model simultaneously evaluate all words in a sequence. Unlike RNNs, Transformers process text in parallel for greater **training efficiency** and better handle **long-range dependencies**. They use **positional encodings** to maintain word order without relying on recurrence.

Transformers unified the lessons of prior neural approaches — embeddings, encoder-decoder architectures, and attention — into a single, scalable framework that has become the foundation of modern AI. In short, the Transformer made it practical to train general-purpose, highly expressive language models at a scale never before possible.

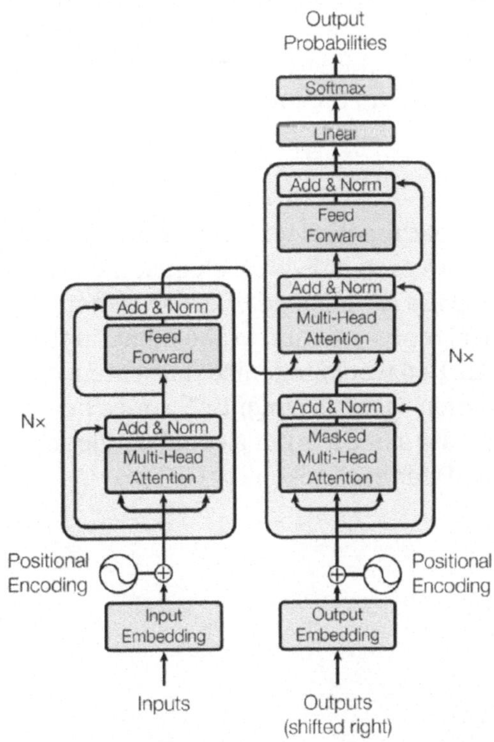

***Figure 1.2**: The Transformer - Model Architecture*
(Source – https://arxiv.org/pdf/1706.03762)

The Tipping Point: ChatGPT

The release of ChatGPT in late 2022 marked a cultural turning point. Within weeks, it had reached millions of users and entered the mainstream conversation about AI. Unlike earlier models, ChatGPT combined raw language modeling power with **instruction tuning** and **Reinforcement Learning from Human Feedback (RLHF),** making it far more aligned with user expectations.

For many people, ChatGPT was the first tangible proof that AI could converse naturally, draft essays, write code, and even brainstorm creative ideas. Its viral adoption put LLMs at the centre of public debate and business strategy.

With this history lesson we are ready to dive into the core architecture of the contemporary LLM.

Architecture and Components of LLMs

Large Language Models such as GPT, Claude, and Llama are all built on the transformer architecture that we saw in the earlier section. While implementation details differ across providers, the underlying design remains consistent. At a high level, LLMs take text as input, transform it through a series of specialized layers, and then generate the most likely output word one by one. To understand how monitoring works later, it helps to break down both the architecture (the overall structure) and the components (the building blocks) that make up the modern LLMs.

Tokenization

The inputs to an LLM are not the actual text. Text is first broken into **tokens**—which are parts of words or sometimes even individual characters. Each token is then converted into a numerical ID. These IDs are mapped to dense vectors called **embeddings**, which serve as the mathematical representation of the input. In the following figure, we can see an example of how GPT 4o would tokenize the sentence "*You are reading this book called Ultimate LLM Monitoring using Langfuse*". Notice how Langfuse is converted to three tokens: **Lang**, **f**, and **use** since it is not a standard dictionary word. The numbered list shows the numerical ID for each token for GPT4o.

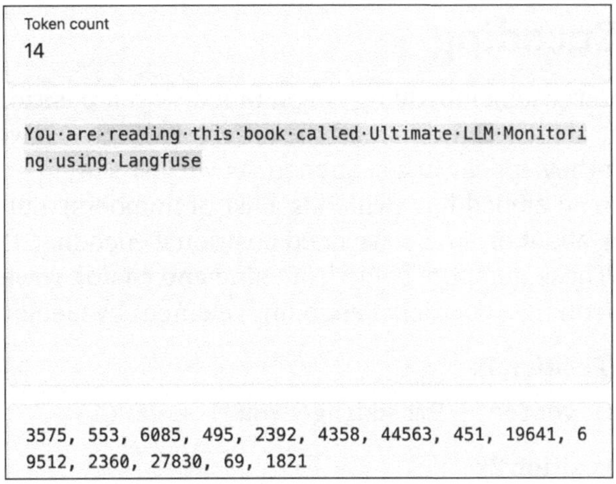

Figure 1.3: *Example of Tokenization*

Embeddings

Since computers only understand numbers, think of embeddings as the numerical equivalent of text that keeps its semantic meaning intact. This also helps the model to understand and compare meaning between texts.

- Instead of storing "You" as just text, the model represents it like:

  You as [0.12, -0.55, 0.89, ...]

- "book" might be:

  [0.33, 0.41, -0.20, ...]

- "Langfuse" might be:

  [0.02, 1.10, -0.75, ...]

Embeddings capture **meaning** and **relationships**, not just exact words.

- Words with similar meaning are close together in vector space.

For instance, "book" and "novel" as vectors will be nearby.

- Words with different meanings are far apart.

This includes "book" versus "monitoring".

These numbers come from the training stage where words that appear in similar contexts get similar vectors. Different models could use different embeddings to store the same text. Embeddings are kind of a trade secret of the model and **not universal open knowledge**. The embedding for "Langfuse" in the embedding model of OpenAI is completely different from its embedding in a Hugging Face model. The numbers are meaningful only within the context of that trained model.

Positional Encoding

To retain word order, each embedding is combined with a **positional encoding**. This gives the model the ability to understand the difference between words depending on the order in which they appear in a sequence. As we just saw, in Transformers, every word is turned into an embedding (which is a list of numbers). But vectors for words do not say anything about order. So, we need positional encoding. Positional encoding are also numbers. These numbers come from **sine and cosine waves**. We add the two vectors (word embedding + positional encoding) element by element:

- **For "You" (Position 1):**
  - `Final vector = Embedding("You") + PE (1)`
- **For "are" (Position 2):**
  - `Final vector = Embedding("are”) + PE (2)`

... and so on, until "Langfuse".

Now each word's vector not only says what the word means, but also where it is in the sentence.

Multi-Head Self-Attention

The multi-head self-attention is the heart of the transformer architecture. It lets each word look at all the other words and decide which are important for understanding it. This is represented by the following equation:

$$Attention(Q, K, V) = softmax(QK^T / \sqrt{d_k})V$$

Each word creates three vectors: *Query* (Q), *Key* (K), *Value* (V).

Similar to: "What am I asking about?" (Q), "What do I have to offer?" (K), "What info should I pass along?" (V).

Example:

- "reading" (Q) strongly matches "book" (K), so it pays a lot of attention to it.
- "Langfuse" attends to "LLM Monitoring".
- "are" attends a bit to "You" (subject) and "reading" (verb).

We have multiple sets of Q, K, V so that the model learns different perspectives:

- One head might track grammar ("subject → verb → object").
- Another might track the meaning ("LLM <-> Monitoring <-> Langfuse").

After attention, the representation of each word is updated with info from the words it cares about.

Feed Forward Network (FFN)

The FFN is a small Neural Network applied to each word separately which helps transform features into more abstract ones.

Example:

- After attention, "book" knows it is connected to "reading".
- FFN turns that into a higher-level feature: "book-as-object-of-reading".

Think of this as polishing/refining the representation.

Add (Residual) + Normalization Layers

In this architecture, **residual + normalization** acts like the **quality control system** that ensures the assembly line never breaks down.

- **Residual:** It keeps the original meaning intact at every step.
- **Normalization:** This keeps numbers stable so the next layer can process them properly.

Without these, the response of the model would quickly become unstable. One can refer to the example of our previous sentence: "*You are reading this book called Ultimate LLM Monitoring using Langfuse.*"

1. **Residual + Norm (First Time)** → This ensures that while "reading" learns from "book", it does not lose its original identity.
    - If attention overemphasized one word, normalization reins it back in.
2. **Residual + Norm (Second Time)** → Again, it prevents the FFN from distorting the signal too much.

This repeats through many layers. Each time, residual + norm guarantees that the meaning builds up gradually instead of exploding or vanishing.

Layer Stacking

If we recall the transformer diagram above, both the encoder (left) and decoder (right) stack the above layers multiple times because one pass isn't enough for the model to deeply understand language. Each layer refines and deepens the model's understanding.

- Lower layers capture local relationships (specifically "*reading* <-> *book*").
- Middle layers capture phrase-level (particularly "*called Ultimate LLM Monitoring*").

- Higher layers capture global meaning (such as "*The sentence is about a book related to Langfuse*").

After all the layers are applied to the text, it is sent to the final layer for the output.

Final Output Layer

This layer has two main operations:

- **Linear:** Projects vectors into vocabulary size of the model (for example, 50,000 possible words).
- **Softmax:** Turns them into probabilities ("next word is X with 92% chance").

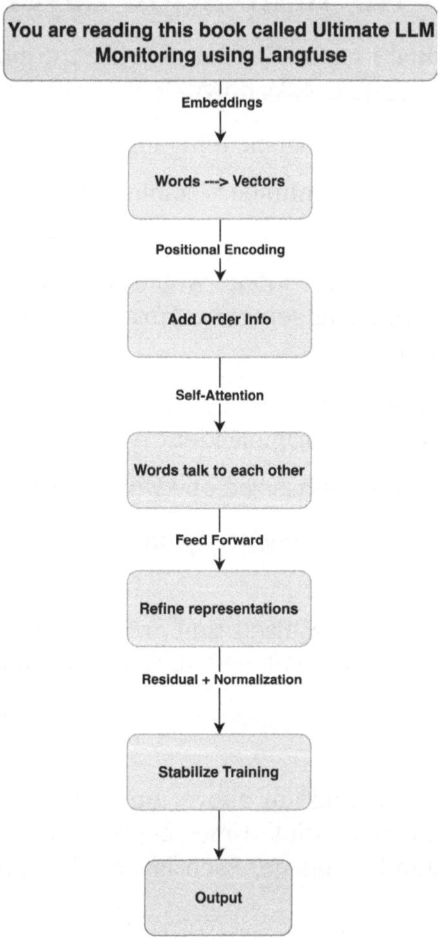

Figure 1.4: *Summary of LLM Architecture and Components*

Having reviewed the components of an LLM, let us now look at how modern LLMs are used in practice.

LLM Use Cases across Industries

Large Language Models are having a significant impact across various sectors of the society and technology. Before we examine the uses of LLMs in these fields, let's look at what LLMs can generally do today and then go in depth for some of the industry specific examples.

One of the most niche skills of an LLM is to perform NLP tasks at a scale and level which is either humanly not possible or would take weeks/months of effort. This includes: **summarization** of large texts across domains, finding **similarity** between texts, **translating** texts between different languages and **classifying** texts (for example, sentiment analysis). Of course, even when we don't have text to start with, LLMs can **generate text** too. The most notable example of this is **code generation**, which till date is one of the most widely used features of ChatGPT. Most LLMs are also **instruction-based**, meaning that users can simply prompt them to generate various types of text as they wish for.

Besides text, there are now hundreds or even thousands of models that can solve **Computer Vision** problems such as: **Image Classification, Object Detection, Image Segmentation, and** converting **Image-to-text** and vice versa. The list does not end with imagcs; **audio classification, automatic speech recognition and text-to-speech** models are also now widely used in the industry.

One of the more recent advancements in LLMs is the development of so-called **Multimodal** models which can simultaneously work with more than one type of media for example: **Document Question Answering** which can help answer questions about the content of a document or **Image text-to-text** which can answer a question about an image.

As we can see here, the possibilities are endless and this list is only growing. Let us now look at some of the more common uses of LLMs today.

Content Generation

Since LLMs are advancements in the NLP field, one of their most popular uses is to generate textual content. This includes but is not limited to blog posts, product descriptions for e-commerce websites, social media content, and creative writing. After using ChatGPT or any similar app, we have experienced this firsthand. It's amazing how these tools can generate engaging and detailed content on almost any topic with only a few lines of prompting.

Content Generation does not stop at text only. Image generation using AI is now finding its way in every field too. Tools like **Midjourney** and **DALL-E** are able to generate high-resolution and artistic images by simply prompting them. The advancement does not end here either; video generation AI platforms such as **Veo** from Google and **Sora** from OpenAI have exhibited exceptional proficiency in producing realistic videos, all initiated through prompts.

Customer Support and Knowledge Management

AI-Powered **Chatbots** and Virtual Assistants are rewriting the rules of Customer Support systems. LLMs enable conversational agents that are adept at interpreting natural language queries and providing contextually appropriate responses. These chatbots provide **24/7 customer support**, reduce wait times, and can handle high volumes of repetitive queries.

Companies and e-commerce platforms deploy LLM-based chatbots for troubleshooting, account inquiries, and order tracking. These assistants can escalate complex queries to human agents seamlessly. In more advanced cases, LLMs can analyse incoming support tickets to determine urgency, category, and optimal agent assignment.

LLMs can also automatically create, update, and summarize knowledge base articles, FAQs, and documentation. Companies can then integrate AI tools that auto-suggest solutions from documentation when support tickets are logged. This technique along with the ability of LLMs to identify trends, sentiment, and recurring issues can feed insights to product teams to help them develop new features or address customer complaints quickly.

Software Engineering

Generative AI using LLMs has permanently transformed software coding. AI streamlines software development by cutting boilerplate, automating testing and documentation, and boosting team speed and productivity. LLMs can assist developers by suggesting code snippets, completing functions, or even generating entire programs from natural language descriptions. AI tools like **GitHub Copilot** and **Cursor IDE** act as intelligent coding partners, helping developers brainstorm solutions, debug faster, and learn on the fly.

LLMs can review codebases to detect bugs, recommend solutions, and provide explanations for error messages using straightforward language. LLMs can produce unit tests, integration tests, and edge cases based on code or requirements descriptions.

LLM-based tools like **vanna.ai** can generate SQL statements for databases simply by asking it questions in plain language. This makes data more accessible to people who are not SQL native, reduces dependency on specialists, and accelerates analytics workflows.

AI powered tools like **mintlify.com** can convert code repos into talking documentation in a matter of minutes. It can keep documentation updated and reduces the overhead in engineering teams who are always struggling to keep their code docs up to date.

Finance

LLMs are steadily transforming the financial sector. By streamlining research, enhancing compliance, and improving customer interactions, AI is becoming an essential part of how modern finance operates. The advent of LLMs in finance is not a recent thing. In March of 2023, Bloomberg announced **BloombergGPT**, a 50-billion parameter LLM aimed specifically for the finance industry. Bloomberg trained this model on its own data sources (one of the largest in the domain). This model outperformed other general purpose LLMs on financial tasks by a huge margin. While BloombergGPT itself is not a public product, Bloomberg integrates its capabilities into the **Bloomberg Terminal** and related services.

Organizations are employing artificial intelligence solutions to oversee billions of daily transactions, effectively identifying potential indicators of fraud. LLMs are reshaping Anti-Money Laundering (AML) and financial crime prevention by improving tasks that depend on language and unstructured data. They enhance sanctions and name screening with better multilingual matching, streamline KYC by interpreting documents and spotting inconsistencies, and make adverse media monitoring faster through classification and summarization.

LLMs power robot-advisors that provide customized portfolio recommendations, retirement planning, and tax optimization. **However, it is important to note**—these models may provide simplistic or inaccurate suggestions because they do not possess financial judgment and may not consider every aspect of the financial circumstances or regulations of an individual. They are intended as decision-support resources rather than substitutes for certified financial advisors.

Healthcare

Generative AI with LLMs is starting to streamline healthcare administration, enhance patient communication, and assist clinical decisions. Though careful regulation is needed, early results suggest it can ease clinician workloads and boost patient outcomes.

Microsoft Dragon Copilot is an AI-powered clinical assistant made specifically for healthcare professionals. The tool can automatically generate clinical notes, draft referral letters, and create post-visit summaries from patient conversations.

LLMs enable professionals to rapidly access key information from medical databases and accelerate clinical decisions.

And even if someone is not a professional, LLMs can simplify complex medical terminology into clear, friendly explanations for information and educational purposes.

LLMs show promise in healthcare, but errors can be dangerous. They might hallucinate, overlook key details, or give misleading advice. Therefore, regulatory oversight and rigorous human validation are crucial.

Retail, E-Commerce, and Marketing

In all the industries we have seen so far, the impact of LLMs and AI is perhaps the most profound in the Retail, e-Commerce and Marketing space. This is also accelerated by the fact that online platforms are racing towards providing more and more AI features to their customers. Since this is such a broad domain there are limitless applications of AI here.

LLMs generate product titles, descriptions, and advertising copy designed to improve **Search Engine Optimization (SEO)**. This has massively reduced manual effort in content optimization and also gives a consistent tone to the catalogue of products.

The use of AI based chatbots is more prominent on e-tailers websites than anywhere else. From **personalized shopping** recommendations to query resolution, these chatbots are able to manage everything between converting customers to reducing call centre loads in the customer service department.

Behind the scenes, LLMs process customer reviews, feedback, and social media to detect trends, assess emerging needs, and observe changes in brand perception. This helps companies react quickly to changes and adapt their marketing strategies.

Thanks to multimodal LLMs, it's now even possible to search for similar products by uploading a photo of another product using visual search capabilities.

While LLMs are already transforming industries, deploying a system that uses them in real-world environments is far from straightforward. Understanding the challenges such as reliability, scalability, security, and ethical risks is essential and will be the focus of the next section.

Challenges in Deploying LLM Applications

Deploying LLM-based applications involves complexities that are distinct from those found in traditional Software-as-a-Service (SaaS) applications. While both types of applications share common concerns—like uptime, scaling, and security—LLM-based applications present unique challenges due to their reliance on **probabilistic models**, high computational requirements, and dynamic behaviour. Understanding these differences is critical for aiming to deliver robust and reliable LLM-powered solutions in production.

Non-Deterministic Outputs

As we have seen earlier, the output of an LLM is essentially a prediction (based on probability) of what the next word (or token) might be having seen the earlier words in a sentence. Considering that human language is vast, the answer to the question "*What should the next word be?*" has theoretically infinite possibilities. This makes the very nature of the output of LLMs **non-deterministic.** This is different from something like an API which would usually give a deterministic response for the same query. If you have ever used ChatGPT or any other LLM- based AI app, you would have experienced this already. In most of these applications, business logic cannot be explicitly defined, and the possible output paths could be too big to explicitly handle every edge case. Applications such as AI chatbots, summarizers, or recommendation engines must include additional layers—such as output validation, ranking, or human-in-the-loop review—to ensure reliability. Additionally, large models sometimes generate outputs that appear reasonable but contain inaccurate or irrelevant information. **Hallucinations,** as they are called, continue to be one of the trickiest problems to monitor and mitigate in LLMs.

Infrastructure and Performance Requirements

Whether we choose to host our own model or rely on proprietary APIs like GPT, Claude, or Gemini, infrastructure considerations play a central role in determining cost, latency, and scalability.

If we are implementing open-source LLMs (such as Llama, Falcon, or Mistral) we will encounter significant operational challenges. These models require substantial GPU resources and specialized hardware with high memory capacity to deliver acceptable latency. Supporting multiple simultaneous users necessitates advanced orchestration strategies, including batching requests, managing GPU allocation, and distributing workloads across clusters. Scaling inference frequently involves investment in costly GPU infrastructure, distributed serving solutions, and technical optimizations such as quantization and model distillation. In the absence of these approaches, we may experience increased latency, reduced throughput, and escalating costs.

While proprietary APIs abstract away model hosting and GPU infrastructure, this does not eliminate performance challenges; it merely shifts them to a different layer of the stack.

- **Latency:** Even with optimized inference, **API calls can take seconds**. Applications that need real-time responses must adapt UX flows—showing typing indicators, streaming partial outputs, or managing user expectations.
- **Throughput and Limits:** Providers enforce strict **rate limits** and concurrency caps. If usage spikes, applications can hit ceilings on requests per minute or tokens per second, leading to degraded user experience. Scaling is not simply a matter of adding more servers; it requires careful workload management and sometimes direct negotiation with the provider.

- **Cost-Performance Tradeoffs:** Token-based pricing means that performance is inseparable from cost. Long prompts, multi-turn conversations, and rich outputs like images/videos drive up expenses quickly.

Observability Requirements

Observability for LLM applications involves tracking multiple aspects, including performance metrics, output quality, correctness, safety, and bias. Detecting drift or degradation typically requires ongoing evaluation using benchmarks or human-reviewed data. Monitoring outputs that may vary at scale presents operational challenges.

We will see in the next section the observability metrics that are important for LLM applications in detail.

To monitor these applications, teams often build **evaluation pipelines**: capturing model outputs in production, sampling them, and reviewing against benchmarks, custom metrics or human feedback.

In the later chapters, we will see how Langfuse helps in building these pipelines end-to-end.

Ethical, Safety, and Regulatory Concerns

The next challenge is quite unique to LLM applications. Outputs from an LLM may be biased, harmful, or offensive, even unintentionally. If left unmonitored, even a single bad interaction can undermine user trust or expose an organization to legal and reputational damage.

Safety features for applications must be implemented from the beginning of development and not added as an afterthought.

The concept of **guardrailing** is a common practice when designing applications with LLMs. *Guardrailing* refers to the techniques and systems that constrain or monitor an LLM's behaviour to ensure safe, reliable, and compliant outputs. Guardrails filter responses from the model before sending them to the user. The filters can score responses on toxic or biased content and also implement some domain level or rule based constraints.

Guardrailing is also never perfect and cannot be used as a replacement for continuous monitoring of an LLM.

Across all these challenges—whether infrastructure complexity, latency and cost trade-offs, safety risks, or regulatory pressures—one thing is clear: **monitoring is indispensable**. Let us now look at some of the key metrics in LLM observability.

Key LLM Monitoring and Observability Metrics

Before we start monitoring, it is important to understand what metrics matter for an LLM-based application. It is evident that LLMs represent a significant advancement beyond previous technologies, necessitating the development of specialized metrics to accurately assess their performance. Having said that, the metrics we will see here are not an exhaustive list but the most useful and common ones that we will be inclined to use when working with LLMs. We will also see in later chapters how Langfuse can help to monitor and trace these metrics.

Latency

Latency in general refers to the total time between sending a request and receiving the **first meaningful** response. This metric is kind of a no-brainer when it comes to monitoring. Fast responses are crucial in any system and latency should be one of the first things we should monitor when working with an LLM-based application.

We have not discussed this in detail in the architecture section, but LLMs usually **stream** responses, which means they produce output word by word (or rather token by token). We may have noticed how ChatGPT shows words one by one when answering. This is nothing but streaming of the response.

In this context, latency for an LLM means the **time until the first token** is generated. This is different from the response time which is a general term used to measure the total time taken for the entire response to be seen. For an LLM, response time will be the **time until the last token** is seen.

The lower the latency, the faster the user gets the first feedback. Latency is usually measured in milliseconds.

Cost

Just like latency, cost is another basic metric that we would also want to track from the very beginning. In the case of LLMs, **every token counts** whether we use open-source models or the proprietary ones, cost is one thing we cannot ignore in our monitoring profile.

Most commercial LLMs like GPT, Claude or Gemini offer a *pay as you use* pricing model. Although the costs may seem trivial at first glance (for instance, GPT-5 costs $1.25 for a million input tokens and $10 for a million output tokens), these numbers can add up very fast. If we are developing an LLM application, it is not uncommon to try tens or even hundreds of different prompts across a handful of models. Add that up and we are spending real money even before we land on a working prototype.

Even if we choose to work with open-source models from Huggingface or Llama which do not cost by token usage, GPU inference costs could be high or even more costly, depending on the hardware we are using.

Since LLM usage is token based, costs will scale up with traffic. In such situations, even a slightly longer prompt could cause big expenses when multiplied by high no. of user hits. Long story short, cost monitoring is imperative for an LLM powered application.

Token Usage

Token usage and cost would most likely go hand in hand. Since cost is a direct function of token usage in most LLMs, by monitoring one of these metrics, we are implicitly monitoring the other one as well. Token usage like cost is also split between input token usage and output token usage.

However, there are some nuances where monitoring token usage independent of cost/latency can be insightful and necessary. By keeping our prompts the same, a jump in input token usage could indicate longer questions or queries by the users. This can also help detect unnecessary addition to context that might be sent to the LLM.

More output tokens mean longer inference time. Token usage can help explain spikes in latency/response times. In many cases, more output tokens could indicate verbose responses by the LLM which could be counterproductive if the goal is to keep the output concise.

Prompt injection is an attack where a user deliberately crafts input text to manipulate an LLM into ignoring its original instructions or policies and instead follow the instructions of the attacker. The first sign of this would be an unusual number of input tokens.

In summary, token usage is not just about costs but could be an early indicator of efficiency and security of our application.

Hallucination

The metrics we have seen so far are quantitative in nature and in the case of LLMs, monitoring quality is the crux of ensuring reliability, trustworthiness, and real-world usefulness of the system.

Hallucination refers to instances where an LLM generates content that is **not grounded in factual information** or strays from the context provided. These fabricated or misleading outputs can undermine the reliability of our application, especially in scenarios where accuracy is critical. Hallucination is, till date, one of the biggest challenges for LLMs and while significant improvements have been made to mitigate it, a “Hallucination free” application is very unlikely. By knowing when or where hallucination occurs in our system, appropriate steps can be taken to prevent our LLM from hallucinating.

We will see in later chapters how an LLM itself can infer if the output of another LLM is exhibiting signs of hallucination and can warn developers even before this hits the ground.

Completeness

Completeness measures if the response of LLM fully covers every part of the query of the user, not just a portion. In many cases, missing information can be as harmful as incomplete information. Especially in domains like health, legal or finance, the response generated by an LLM should not leave anything behind or open the possibility for the user to use their imagination.

This metric is closely tied to accuracy, where accuracy answers the question, *Is the answer correct?* Completeness covers *Does the answer cover everything that was asked for.*

Relevance

While we want the LLMs response to be complete, it will not be useful if the answer is not focused on the query of the user. The basic definition of Relevance is whether the LLM answered the question without getting distracted by unrelated, unnecessary or off-topic content.

LLMs are trained on massive amounts of information so inherently they are very brainy. This makes them susceptible to being verbose in their responses and including more information than what was asked for.

This is not always desirable, especially when a concise answer is all that is needed.

Relevance is a crucial metric in LLM systems which are based on **Retrieval Augmented Generation (RAG)**. In RAG based apps, relevance is two-tiered:

1. *Were the relevant documents retrieved to answer the question?*
2. *Does the final response stay relevant based on the retrieved documents?*

If the retrieved documents are not relevant, the answer may be off. However, if the generation part hallucinates, the answer may still be wrong even if the retrieval was correct.

Correctness

Correctness is quite self-explanatory. It measures if the LLM's responses **are factually correct**. In a traditional Machine Learning system, we may use accuracy as a metric for this. However, for an LLM the concept of accuracy could be very broad or not even applicable in some cases. For example, if we ask ChatGPT: "*Help me plan a trip to New York city*", there is no accurate answer to this question, and responses could vary a lot.

This does not mean that correctness is not widely used for judging the LLMs performance. Correctness is often the **core quality metric** for evaluating LLM usefulness. If our application has the notion of a correct answer, or a ground truth, correctness can be simply measured by comparing the response of the LLM with the ground truth.

It is not uncommon for AI applications to have the concept of a **model answer** instead of a correct one. To understand this, we can consider an example: In a translation tool, a text could be translated in many different ways and all of them could technically be "correct". If an ideal translation is known, correctness can be measured by checking how close the generated response is to this desired answer.

Although **Hallucination**, **Completeness**, **Relevance**, and **Correctness** are quality metrics, they can be quantified into numeric representation to compare, monitor and evaluate an LLM. We will see in *Chapter 7, Evaluating LLMs in Langfuse*, how the LLM-as-a-judge feature of Langfuse can help doing exactly this. Before we jump to the next section, let us see a short summary of these metrics:

Metric	Short Definition	When to Use
Latency	Time to first/last token	When user experience depends on fast responses (such as chat, search).
Cost	Money spent per request/token	When scaling usage and keeping AI expenses predictable is critical.
Token Usage	Number of tokens consumed	When optimizing prompts or detecting inefficiencies.
Hallucination	Incorrect/fabricated information	When factual reliability and trust are crucial (healthcare, legal, finance).
Completeness	Coverage of all required aspects	When tasks require full coverage of instructions (summaries, lists, reports).
Relevance	Staying on-topic to the query	When answers must stay aligned with user intent or retrieved context (RAG).
Correctness	Factual accuracy of the answer	When factual truth matters.

Table 1.1: *Summary of Key LLM Metrics*

Introduction to the LLM Application Lifecycle

Before we jump into monitoring, let us try to understand some of the common stages that an LLM application might go through. Developing an LLM-powered app involves more than prompt-response exchanges; it needs a structured approach that blends testing, solid engineering, user focus, and ongoing enhancement. Although there is

no one universal lifecycle for this kind of application, the succeeding figure shows the typical steps that LLM applications could follow. We can see how Langfuse can be used in almost all of these stages. In later chapters, we will go into more details about each of these topics.

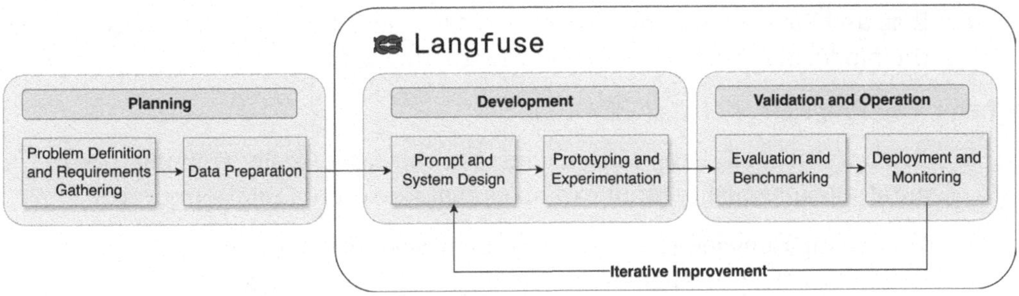

Figure 1.5: *A Typical Lifecycle of an LLM Application*

Problem Definition and Requirements Gathering

This stage focuses on defining the problem the application will address, ensuring it aligns with business or user needs. Teams set scope, success criteria, and constraints like latency, cost, compliance, and so on. At this stage, we also need to assess If an LLM is the right tool for this problem. Sometimes a traditional ML model or even a SaaS application like an API could be enough. In these cases, an LLM could even be an overkill.

A good rule of thumb in deciding whether our solution needs an LLM is, if our problem involves **understanding or generating natural language in a flexible way**, and can tolerate some uncertainty if outputs are monitored, validated, or improved with continuous iterations. If the problem is highly deterministic, structured, or safety-critical, a non-LLM solution should be our first choice.

A clear **problem statement and success metrics** are the expected outcome of this stage.

Data Preparation

LLMs rely heavily on the **quality and relevance of data provided**. The approach to data preparation differs depending on whether we are working with a foundational/self-developed LLM or a proprietary, API-based model like GPT from OpenAI.

For Foundational Models:

- **Large-Scale Dataset Collection**: We need vast, diverse, and domain-relevant corpora to train or fine-tune the model.

- **Cleaning and Pre-Processing**: Remove duplicates, normalize, and remove low-quality or harmful text. Ensure consistent formatting.
- **Domain Adaptation**: Curate specialized datasets based on domain-specific performance.
- **Bias and Safety Filtering**: Proactively filter sensitive or biased content, since the model inherits patterns from the training data.

When Using Proprietary LLMs (like GPT):

- **Prompt-Focused Preparation**: Instead of large-scale training, focus on curating high-quality input examples that represent real user queries.
- **Grounding Knowledge**: Organize domain-specific data (databases, documents, FAQs) for Retrieval-Augmented Generation (RAG) if applicable.
- **Few-Shot Examples**: Prepare representative demonstration prompts (few-shot examples) to guide the model's behavior.
- **Validation Datasets**: Build evaluation sets to test how well the proprietary LLM uses our data during prompting or retrieval.

Prompt and System Design

The prompt is essentially one of the core components in an LLM application. It is the primary input that the LLM needs to produce any output. This makes prompt designing critical to the overall functioning of the application.

Typically, designing the prompt(s) for our application would be a major chunk of effort in the overall lifecycle. **Prompt Engineering** involves designing inputs for LLMs to shape their responses. Well-crafted prompts can significantly enhance the accuracy, quality, and consistency of outputs without altering the model itself. Prompts are often broken into **system messages** (defining overall behavior), **user messages** (the task at hand), and **few-shot examples** (demonstrating the desired format or reasoning).

In theory, there are an infinite number of ways in how a prompt can be written, which makes it difficult to find the perfect prompt that will maximize the output quality of our application. Prompt design needs to be tightly coupled with experimentation, evaluation and benchmarking to iteratively reach the best possible outcome over several iterations. In modern applications, it is very common to even version control prompts like code and maintain a log of success metrics for each of the versions.

Since Prompt Engineering is a huge subject by itself, we will not go into the details here. In *Chapter 7, Evaluating LLMs in Langfuse*, we will see how Langfuse enables **prompt management** and versioning which allows us to use prompts directly in applications without having the need to maintain prompts in code.

System Design principles apply to LLM applications like they apply to any software-based system. As the name suggests, System Design defines the **architecture** for a system. LLM applications may be a new genre in application development, but foundationally they are governed by the same pillars that go into designing any robust, scalable and maintainable system which delivers quality output as required by its users. These include but are not limited to:

- **Modularity:** Breaking down a system into smaller, independent, reusable components.
- **Scalability:** Systems should perform reliably under increasing loads.
- **Availability:** The system should be available and accessible when needed.
- **Reliability:** The system's ability to give consistent results over time.
- **Performance:** The speed and responsiveness of the system.

Here are some key design decisions that are specific to the current LLM applications:

1. **Data and Context Handling:**
    - How will external knowledge be integrated — via Retrieval-Augmented Generation (RAG), fine-tuning, or API calls?
    - What caching or pre-computation strategies can reduce repeated calls and cost?
2. **Reliability and Safety:**
    - How will inputs/outputs be validated?
    - What moderation or filtering layers are needed to handle unsafe, biased, or irrelevant content?
3. **User Experience:**
    - Should the application return streaming responses for faster perceived performance?
    - How will the system handle ambiguous queries?
4. **Scalability and Cost Efficiency:**
    - Will smaller models handle simple queries, reserving larger models for complex ones?
    - Can batching or rate-limiting be used to optimize performance at scale?
5. **Monitoring and Feedback Loops:**
    - What metrics should be logged (latency, token usage, cost and so on)?
    - How will user feedback feed into prompt refinement or fine-tuning?

Prototyping and Experimentation

With the previous stage we are now already in the iteration phase. Once the problem is defined, the data prepared, and the initial prompt/system design outlined, the next step is to validate assumptions through prototyping. In LLM application development, prototyping is about testing how the model behaves in realistic scenarios and uncovering gaps before committing to a final solution.

Prototyping should typically be done in an **offline** fashion, that is, before going live with an iteration of the application. It's more efficient to test prompts, retrieval pipelines, and outputs in lightweight experiments than to build full systems upfront. Prototypes are able to simulate interactions and provide initial feedback on the usefulness, reliability, and quality of responses.

What Experimentation looks like:

- **Prompt Comparison:** Compare different types of prompts with different structures and styles.
- **Models:** Test different LLMs (some of which includes GPT, Llama, Claude) to balance cost, speed, and accuracy.
- **Context Strategies (if Applicable):** Evaluate how different knowledge sources impact performance.
- **Output Comparison:** Try different output (JSON schemas, bullet points, summaries and so on) to see what yields the best result in terms of usability.

Once we have some evidence that the prototype works, we can move onto evaluation, otherwise we refine the prototype.

Evaluation and Benchmarking

Now that we have a prototype, it is time to see how it performs in a real-world like environment. The success metrics we defined in the first stage form the backbone of the evaluation and benchmarking stage. In the Data Preparation stage, we also have our validation dataset which will be used to make equal comparisons of different evaluation stages.

It is important to re-iterate that choosing the **right success metrics** is crucial. Building the right application but tracking the wrong metrics could lead to a final product that does not fulfil the user's needs and cause unnecessary wastage of resources due to impeding rework.

While automatic evaluation may be the fastest and the most scalable option if the volume of the test is huge, it might also be the perfect time to get **Human-in-the-loop** at this stage. Depending on the application, a human evaluation could be necessary if the system is being designed for a critical domain like health, finance or legal. Business needs and security requirements could also mandate this.

The perfect blend of automatic and human evaluation can also be achieved where the first round of evaluations is automatic (sort of a screening based on basic metrics like cost, latency and so on) and the then a subset of this sample is sent to human review for checking things like factual correctness, compliance, ethical safety and so on. This dual level of evaluations is also a trademark feature of Langfuse, which we will cover in detail in *Chapter* 8.

A basic framework for an evaluation and benchmarking report could look like this:

1. **Comparison of Options:** Cross-checking which combination of prompt, model, context and retrieval strategy (if applicable) gives the best result for each of the success metrics.

2. **Balancing Trade-Offs:** It is likely that no option ranks number one in all success metrics. For example, the best performing model for correctness might also be the most expensive one or the prompt that makes the LLM hallucinate the least is also the slowest of the lot. In these cases, the winning combo could be selected by objectively prioritizing the success metrics depending on the needs of the system.

3. **Errors and Failures:** Try to identify reasons (if) and why certain options failed. Does a model hallucinate a lot? Is a certain prompt never leading to a correct answer? Are irrelevant documents being picked up for RAG. This kind of analysis helps uncover system design/prompt design problems and also influence choice of models.

4. **Recommendations:** Decide on the best configuration for deployment based on the metrics and trade-offs. Have a mitigation strategy in case the best option does not work in production.

Deployment and Monitoring

Once our application has been evaluated and chosen for production, the focus shifts to deployment and monitoring. This stage is not the end of the lifecycle but the beginning of the system's real-world journey, where it is monitored and tested continuously.

While our prototype was being run in offline mode, our actual application will be in **online** mode. The first thing to have in place for an online application is **Observability.** It means we capture interactions between the system and the user, set up alerts for application downtime and monitor all critical system parameters in real time.

Online evaluation should at least cover evaluating all success metrics for all requests or a sample of request (say 20%) if the volume is too huge. In a live application, it's also possible to monitor and gather real user feedback in addition to preset metrics. User feedback is the most valuable take away at this stage.

This feedback and evaluation complete our loop of a single iteration of the lifecycle of LLM application. Based on the results there could be several more rounds of Development/Validation/Deployment; each of which lead to a better end product.

In the next and final section of this chapter we will introduce the frameworks and tools that we will be using throughout this book. This will include some basic introductions and code blocks to help us get familiarized with integrating Langfuse in our LLM applications.

Exploring the LLM Toolkit for the Book

Now let us explore the frameworks and libraries we will use throughout the book. The LLM development landscape changes rapidly and there are new tools and frameworks almost every day. Our focus in this book is Langfuse which itself supports dozens of integration options but to keep the content on subject, we chose a subset of libraries to work with. This will keep things concise but also open up opportunities to experiment with a different tech stack. We will try and stick to Open-Source Software (OSS) where possible so that readers can freely learn about Langfuse without having to make monetary investments upfront.

Our choice of programming language in the book is **Python 3.12**. Although Langfuse also supports JavaScript/TypeScript, we will not be covering them in the book. Code examples shown in the book are easily adaptable to JS/TS with minimal effort. Having said that, readers should be familiar with coding in Python and install Python 3.12 as a pre-requisite. We will be working with virtual environments in python in this book. Official documentation is here: **`https://docs.python.org/3/library/venv.html`**. *We suggest creating a single virtual environment for the entire course of the book.*

OpenAI SDK

Our first library is the OpenAI Python SDK. The creators of ChatGPT have created this SDK to offer programmatic access to the underlying OpenAI REST API. It uses simple http-based calls and is the easiest way to get started with GPT based models.

We will start by creating a virtual environment to work with. In the terminal or shell, run:

```
python3 -m venv /path/to/environment # for Linux/Mac based systems
python -m venv C:\path\to\environment # for Windows
```

Then activate the environment by running:

```
source /path/to/environment/bin/activate # for Linux/Mac based systems
C:\> path\to\environment\Scripts\activate.bat # for Windows
```

To install the Open AI SDK in a Python application, use the command (in terminal/shell):

```
pip install openai python-dotenv
```

We will also install another python package called **python-dotenv** which is used to load environment variables. This is a pretty standard way to set up variables like API keys in the application. The package can be installed from here - **https://pypi.org/project/python-dotenv.**

This OpenAI API is a *pay as you go* service, and we need to buy credits before we can get started. We will also need an API key and purchase credits to use this model. We can do both things here - **https://platform.openai.com/settings/organization/apikeys.**

The API key needs to be added to a file named **".env"** in the root directory of the project like this:

```
OPENAI_API_KEY=<your_api_key>
```

After this, we can start using the API client to make calls to GPT.

```
from dotenv import load_dotenv
load_dotenv()

from openai import OpenAI
client = OpenAI()

response = client.responses.create(
    model="gpt-5-nano",
    input="Write a short introduction about Langfuse, the LLM
Engineering Platform"
)

print(response.output_text)
```

This will print an output similar to the following code (although the response could possible vary):

```
Langfuse is an LLM engineering platform designed to help teams build,
deploy, and govern production-ready language-model applications. It
provides end-to-end tooling for prompt and chain management, evaluation,
monitoring, and governance—so you can ship faster with confidence. With
versioned prompts, test suites, real-time observability dashboards
(latency, accuracy, errors, costs), and guardrails, Langfuse makes it
easier to iterate on models while maintaining safety and reliability.
It integrates with major LLM providers and data systems, enabling
seamless collaboration across engineering, product, and data science
teams.
```

In this basic example, we have used the GPT-5-nano model, but we can use any of the GPT models supported by Open AI.

Another common usage of this SDK is to use the **Chat Completions API** which simulates a conversation like ChatGPT. We will use this API frequently in the book.

```
completion = client.chat.completions.create(
    model="gpt-5-nano",
    messages=[
        {"role": "system", "content": "You are an expert in Langfuse,
the LLM Engineering Platform"},
        {
            "role": "user",
            "content": "What are the top 3 features of Langfuse?",
        },
    ],
)

print(completion.choices[0].message.content)
```

Output:

```
Langfuse is an LLM engineering platform that focuses on production-grade
management of LLM services. The top features users commonly highlight are:

   -  End-to-end LLM orchestration and lifecycle management
   -  Unified workflow for deploying, routing, and versioning prompts and
      models
   -  Fine-grained control over routing policies, multi-model
      ensembles, and A/B tests
   -  Observability baked in metrics, traces, and dashboards for prompt
      variants, latency, and accuracy
   -  Deployment, monitoring, and reliability tooling
   -  Seamless deployment to multiple environments and providers with
      versioned models
   -  Real-time monitoring and alerts for latency, errors, and model
      drift
   -  Proven reliability features like retries, fallbacks, and circuit
      breakers to keep production endpoints healthy
   -  Observability and measurement at scale
   -  Detailed telemetry for prompts, completions, and user
      interactions
   -  Evaluation hooks to compare model performance, safety, and
      alignment across versions
```

```
-  Data-driven optimization through dashboards, dashboards, and
   event-level insight to improve prompts and routing logic
```

Although this SDK has a lot of other features, we will not cover them in detail. The official GitHub page for the SDK is here: **https://github.com/openai/openai-python**

LangChain

We are going to be using **LangChain (https://www.langchain.com/langchain)** as the main development framework in this book. LangChain is an open-source, orchestration framework that provides a standard interface for every model, tool, and database. **LangChain** provides so-called **chains** which are sequences of steps where the LLM processes input, calls tools or APIs, and generates outputs. It works very well for retrieval-augmented generation (RAG) applications, chatbots, AI Agents, and many other types of LLM-based workflows.

One of its most powerful features is the **`plug and play`** of components which makes it very easy to swap models, databases or even prompts without re-writing the whole application.

To Install:

```
pip install langchain langchain_openai
```

To perform exactly the same operation as the Chat Completions API, the LangChain equivalent would be:

```
from langchain.chat_models import init_chat_model
from dotenv import load_dotenv
load_dotenv()

model = init_chat_model("gpt-5-nano", model_provider="openai")
model_response = model.invoke(
    input=[
        {
            "role": "system",
            "content": "You are an expert in Langfuse, the LLM
Engineering Platform",
        },
        {
            "role": "user",
            "content": "What are the top 3 features of Langfuse?",
        },
    ]
)
print(model_response.content)
```

The **`init_chat_model,`** method from LangChain automatically takes care of creating the appropriate model client from the provider's implementation (in this case OpenAI SDK). The **`invoke`** method will also format the prompt messages into the required structure as needed by the OpenAI API.

Hypothetically speaking, if we wanted to switch GPT with another model say, Google Gemini, this could be done very easily in LangChain with just one line of change:

```
model = init_chat_model ("gemini-2.5-flash", model_provider="google_genai")
```

The rest of the code will remain the same. We will additionally need to provide our **`GOOGLE_API_KEY`** instead of OpenAI API key. This swapping also works for most components in the chain and makes LangChain as one of the developers' favorite libraries to build LLM applications. Many of the examples we will see in the book will also use LangChain. **LangChain is not a pre-requisite for this book, and we will cover the necessary learning as we go along.**

Langfuse

Finally, we will be using a lot of **Langfuse (https://langfuse.com/)** as this is the main subject of the book. Langfuse is an open-source **LLM Engineering Platform** for LLM-based applications. It provides developers and ML engineers with powerful tools for tracing, prompt management, evaluation, and performance monitoring—all in one place.

We have made several mentions of Langfuse throughout the book, most notably in the section about the LLM application lifecycle where we saw how it can be used for the full development, evaluation, benchmarking and monitoring flow. Langfuse is also compatible with any LLM and supports a variety of integrations.

We will not cover any code examples in this section, but rest assured, they will be covered in much detail starting from *Chapter 4, Introduction to Langfuse.*

The next couple of chapters will deep dive a bit more into the conceptual parts of monitoring of LLMs and topics like Model Drift and Bias, setting the stage for the sections of the book dedicated to Langfuse.

Conclusion

This chapter introduces Large Language Models (LLMs), tracing their evolution from early NLP systems like ELIZA to modern Transformer-based architectures. It details the components and industry applications of LLMs, explores deployment challenges—including performance, cost, and ethical risks—and highlights the necessity of monitoring key metrics like latency, cost, token usage, and output quality. The chapter also outlines the LLM application lifecycle and presents essential tools such as OpenAI

SDK, LangChain, and Langfuse for effective development and observability. In the next chapter, we will deep dive into monitoring concepts for LLMs including the core principles and various dimensions of monitoring. We also see how we can create a robust monitoring strategy for typical LLM applications.

References

- **Improving Language Understanding by Generative Pre-Training**: https://cdn.openai.com/research-covers/language-unsupervised/language_understanding_paper.pdf
- **ELIZA - A Computer Program for the Study of Natural Language Communication Between Man and Machine**:

  https://engineering.purdue.edu/~ece495nl/protected/weizenbaum1966.pdf
- **N-gram models**:

  https://towardsdatascience.com/introduction-to-language-models-n-gram-e323081503d9/
- **Attention is All You Need**: https://arxiv.org/pdf/1706.03762
- **NLP Tasks**: https://huggingface.co/tasks
- **Vanna AI**: http://vanna.ai
- **Mintlify**: https://mintlify.com
- **Bloomberg GPT**:

  https://www.bloomberg.com/company/press/bloomberggpt-50-billion-parameter-llm-tuned-finance/
- **Fraud detection in Finance**:

  https://www.businessinsider.com/mastercard-ai-credit-card-fraud-detection-protects-consumers-2025-5
- **Microsoft Dragon Copilot**:

  https://www.microsoft.com/en-us/health-solutions/clinical-workflow/dragon-copilot
- **Open AI SDK**: https://github.com/openai/openai-python
- **LangChain docs**: https://python.langchain.com/docs/introduction/
- **Langfuse**: https://langfuse.com/

CHAPTER 2
LLM Monitoring Principles

Introduction

Monitoring LLMs involves more than verifying their operation; it ensures they consistently deliver outcomes that align with accuracy, efficiency, and security goals. This chapter presents the foundational principles of LLM monitoring and describes how these practices differ from conventional software observability. It discusses various monitoring dimensions, such as performance, cost, safety, and ethical considerations. The chapter covers approaches to developing monitoring strategies for ongoing improvement, supporting a balance among speed, accuracy, user experience, and responsible AI implementation. By the end, readers will have a set of principles for establishing an LLM monitoring framework that can scale alongside their applications.

Structure

In this chapter, we will cover the following topics:

- Monitoring and Observability in LLMs
    - Trace and Span
- Site Reliability Engineering for LLMs
    - How SRE Applies to LLMs
    - Service Level Indicators (SLIs) and Service Level Objectives (SLOs)
    - Error Budgets
    - Managing Error Budgets in Monitoring
- Principles of Effective LLM Monitoring
    - Monitor at the Semantic Layer
    - User Feedback

- Balance Performance, Cost, and Quality Metrics
- Monitor for Drift
- Monitor Safety and Compliance Metrics

- Dimensions of Monitoring
  - Functional Monitoring
  - Non-Functional Monitoring
  - Ethical Monitoring
  - Safety Monitoring
- Monitoring Dimensions for Typical LLM Applications
  - Content Generation Systems
  - Retrieval Augmented Generation (RAG) applications
  - Chatbots
  - AI Agents

Monitoring and Observability in LLMs

Let us start this section by understanding how Monitoring and Observability differ conceptually. The short answer: *Monitoring tells us that something is wrong. Observability tells us why it is wrong.*

The realms of monitoring and observability extend beyond LLMs and are general concepts from System Engineering. Observability even dates back to the 1960s and was introduced by a Hungarian- American Engineer, **Rudolf E. Kálmán** who defined it as: ***A measure of how well internal states of a system can be inferred from knowledge of its external outputs.*** In software engineering analogy this would mean determining what is happening with our application by looking at logs, metrics, events or any other outputs. A good example of this is a stack trace seen in logs when an error occurs. It exposes the internal state of the application by showing the list of method calls that led to an error. For an LLM-based application, we not only require logs or metrics for observability but also need to complement this with LLM specific elements like prompts, retrieved documents (for RAG applications) or reasoning steps if reasoning models are involved.

Monitoring on the other hand applies more linearly to LLM applications and other software systems. It is about tracking signals that indicate how the system is behaving; the difference only being what to track. We have seen in *Chapter 1, Introduction to Large Language Models and Monitoring*, some of the signals (metrics) that make sense for LLMs – Latency, Cost, Token Usage, Hallucination, Completeness, Relevance and Correctness.

To summarize, Monitoring and Observability are **complementary**; monitoring identifies *when* an issue occurs by tracking defined indicators, whereas observability enables analysis of *why* the issue arose through root cause investigation. In combination, they support both detection and diagnosis within LLM applications.

Trace and Span

In observability, a trace can be defined as the **complete execution path** of a request as it moves through a system. A trace is then composed of several spans each of which is a **discrete**, timed operation in the request's lifecycle. Spans can even be nested within other spans. A basic example of this can be seen in web applications. When you visit a page or submit a form, this starts a new trace. This trace can contain many spans, each of which represents steps like authenticating the user, querying a database, calling an API and so on. Each span has a start and an end time, status information and can also have custom attributes. Spans can be analyzed to discover latency bottlenecks, application errors or monitor health of specific components in the system.

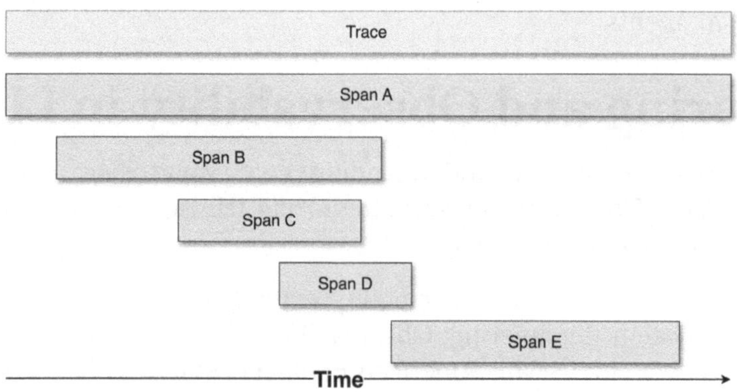

***Figure 2.1**: Trace and Span*

Here is what the spans of a trace would look like in a RAG based chatbot when the user asks a question:

```
Trace: User Query "What is the best way to get started with Langfuse?”
|
+-- Span A: Retrieve Developer Documents from langfuse.com
|     |
|     +-- Span B: Re-rank Documents based on relevance
|            |
|            +-- Span C: Construct a Prompt for the LLM using the
documents
|                   |
|                   +-- Span D: LLM Generates Answer
|                          |
|                          +-- Span E: Post-process the Output to the user’s needs
|
```

In Langfuse, Traces are the most fundamental units of observability. To make use of the Langfuse platform, the first thing that we need to do is send our application's traces to Langfuse. How this can be done will be covered in detail in Chapters 5 and 6. All the monitoring we do, will then revolve around these traces. Metrics we track will also be attached to traces.

Langfuse uses a slightly different terminology for spans. In Langfuse, spans are actually called **observations.** A trace in Langfuse is made up of several observations which give more information about the different steps in the trace. Observations can also be of different types depending on the step and there are many LLM specific observation types like **generation, retriever, tool call** and so on in Langfuse. We will cover these in more detail in *Chapter 5, Observability in Langfuse.*

Site Reliability Engineering for LLMs

Site Reliability Engineering or SRE is a discipline that originated at **Google** in 2003 as a way to monitor and enhance the availability of Software systems. Since then, it has been widely adopted by the industry to balance operational stability and development. SRE and Monitoring are deeply interconnected because monitoring provides the signals that SRE practices depend on. SRE takes those monitored signals (SLIs) and formalizes them into objectives (SLOs) and commitments (SLAs), then manages reliability through mechanisms like error budgets, alerting, and incident response. When applied to LLM-based applications, the SRE concepts are the same— but the definition of "reliability" expands from basic uptime to include semantic and behavioral correctness.

Applying SRE to LLMs

SRE was designed to keep large-scale software systems reliable without slowing innovation, and the same philosophy maps naturally onto LLM-based applications. SRE provides a structured framework for LLM monitoring by reframing abstract concerns (like hallucinations or unsafe outputs) into measurable indicators, objectives, and budgets. This helps teams balance safety and reliability with the need to innovate quickly. Applying SRE principles ensures that reliability is not defined only by infrastructure health but also by the quality and trustworthiness of model outputs. An LLM system may be "up" and responsive, but if it is hallucinating facts, leaking sensitive information, or producing biased outputs, it is fundamentally unreliable. SRE practices can be adapted to define and track reliability metrics like output consistency, semantic correctness, and user engagement to maintain the trustworthiness of an LLM-based application.

Service Level Indicators (SLIs) and Service Level Objectives (SLOs)

Within SRE, the idea is that reliability must be quantified in some form. This is done by using **Service Level Indicators (SLIs)** and **Service Level Objectives (SLOs)**. An SLI is a specific, measurable metric that reflects the quality of a service from the **perspective of the user**—for example, request latency, error rate, or system availability. An SLO is the target or threshold set for that SLI, such as "*99.9% of requests should complete within 200 milliseconds*." Together, SLIs and SLOs provide a common understanding between engineering and business teams: SLIs capture the metric, SLOs define expectations, and together they can drive operational decisions.

As we saw in the introduction of this section, the idea of reliability broadens in LLMs. This means SLIs for LLMs must capture qualities like hallucination, grounding success in RAG, or the percentage of safe responses free from toxic or harmful content. Correspondingly, SLOs become statements such as "*95% of responses must cite a retrieved source*" or "*fewer than 1% of outputs should trigger the toxicity filter*." Similarly, for a customer-facing chatbot, an SLO can be defined as "*at least 90% of sessions should resolve the customer query without needing a human agent*."

The combination of SLIs and SLOs gives us a concrete way to measure reliability and opens up the path to prioritization between experimenting and maintaining stability in the system. When SLOs are being met, teams can safely experiment with new prompts or model versions; when they are missed, stability takes precedence.

Error Budgets

Error Budgets may sound confusingly similar to cost but in SRE they are defined as the **allowed margin of failure.** When we say "*99% of the model's responses will not be toxic*", we also effectively mean that 1% of the time this might not be the case. So here, the 1% becomes the error budget for this SLI. The reason why this is seen as a "budget" is because it restricts how much we can experiment with new features without breaking the bank of stability that we have committed to. In LLM-based applications, an "error" could be a hallucination, an unsafe response, a failure to ground in retrieved content, or even a cost overrun.

Error budgets can vary by the use case. For content generation in the creative domain, this number could even be more than 5%, although not for every SLI. While for things like critical customer-facing chatbots, this could be much lower. Error budgets are always tied to a time window (for example, per week, per month). This ensures that they get evened out over time rather than pausing experimentation for long periods.

Managing Error Budgets in Monitoring

Before measuring or tracking Error Budgets, we should clearly define them for easy understanding. This means knowing in advance the SLIs and SLOs of the system. For an LLM application, this translates to determining **what constitutes a failure** (besides downtime, latency and so on) on the semantic level. Is Hallucination the biggest risk to your application? Or is it the incorrect retrieval of a document from the knowledge base? All these failures should be quantified that can be later measured and tracked.

Imagine we run an LLM-powered summarization API used by enterprise customers to convert long internal documents like reports, audits, research papers into concise summaries. We define an **SLO**: "*96% of summaries must be accurate, faithful to the source document, and generated in under 4 seconds.*"

To support this SLO, we track three **SLIs**:

- **Faithfulness Score:** How closely each summary matches the source document (measured via semantic similarity or LLM-based scoring).
- **Coverage Score:** Whether the summary includes all key points users expect.
- **Latency:** How long does the summarization endpoint take to respond.

If at the end of the month the service only meets the SLO 92% of the time, it has consumed a significant portion of its error budget. Perhaps a prompt change made the summaries more creative, reducing faithfulness; or, a recent model upgrade increased load time by a second. Either way, the system now requires stability work (tuning prompt templates, caching, smaller model variants) before shipping new features.

We will see in later chapters how Langfuse can combine monitoring with dashboard creation so that teams can continuously track how much of the error budget has already been spent. If we see the budget is consumed, we could freeze new feature rollout and prioritize stabilizing the SLIs.

Principles of Effective LLM Monitoring

We will now look at some guiding principles that can be applied to LLM monitoring. By now it's clear that LLMs are complicated. Monitoring LLM applications requires moving beyond the playbook of traditional software systems. Latency, uptime, and error codes are still important, but they only tell part of the story. What truly matters in LLM-based systems is whether the model produces **accurate, safe, cost-effective, and user-aligned outputs**. To achieve this, monitoring must be guided by a set of principles that expand observability into the semantic and behavioral layers unique to AI. The following principles outline how to design monitoring systems that not only detect failures but also explain *why* they happen and how they impact both users and the business.

Monitor at the Semantic Layer

When working with NLP, semantics or the meaning of the text are the most important thing. In LLM systems, even if the service is "healthy," the model can produce semantically incorrect outputs (hallucinations). This means our monitoring recipe is only half-baked by measuring metrics like CPU/memory usage, latency and uptime. Effective monitoring must extend into the semantic layer and directly look into content quality. Semantic monitoring should include:

- **Factual Accuracy:** Check whether the responses are grounded in reality by cross-verifying against reliable data sources or human reviews.
- **Relevance:** A good response can also be considered bad if it does not directly answer the user's questions or adds irrelevant details.
- **Consistency:** Often it happens that a model may give contradictory or unstable answers over a long conversation or repeatedly asking the same question. A lack of consistency could erode customer trust and reduce reliability on the system.

User Feedback

LLMs operate in domains where correctness is often subjective or context dependent. Automated metrics are available for semantic meaning, but they don't always reflect real-world usefulness. **User interaction** is the strongest real-world signal of model quality. A core principle therefore should be to systematically capture explicit (thumbs up/down, ratings and so on) and implicit (user re-queries, escalation to human agents and so on) signals and feed them back into our monitoring system. There is no one way to gather user feedback and it really depends on the objective of the application to understand how user feedback could be captured. Even the choice of tools could be influenced by who the users are and in what form we intend to collect their feedback. In essence, a good user feedback should include:

- **Quality of Outcome:** Did the user actually like the response? This could be a simple thumbs up/down or even a numeric rating system (1-5, 1-10 and so on).
- **Response Speed:** Most users are time conscious. They would expect responses to come in fast and slower responses could become a cause for user dissatisfaction.
- **Open Ended Response:** A free text or a comment section for the responses lets users highlight the issues or even make suggestions to improve response quality.

Monitor for Drift

Unlike other software systems, LLM applications are exposed to changing data (retrieved documents, evolving business rules) and shifting user behavior. Monitoring must include drift detection:

- **Data Drift**: Are retrievals pulling less relevant or outdated documents?
- **Behavioral Drift**: Has the model started giving longer, vaguer answers than before?

We will cover drift in much more detail in the next chapter but for now it is enough to understand that drift detection ensures system reliability over time because even if the LLM itself is stable or unchanged, external data sources that feed into the LLM at run time can change/degrade over time.

Balance Performance, Cost, and Quality Metrics

Monitoring LLMs isn't just about accuracy; cost and performance are equally critical. High-quality answers that take a long time to come or burn excessive tokens may be unacceptable in production. A principle here is to track latency, throughput, token usage, and accuracy together, since **optimizing one often degrades another**. Every system has some business constraints which it needs to operate under, and a balance needs to be struck when deciding which metrics should be optimized.

Monitor Safety and Compliance Metrics

LLMs can produce unsafe, biased, or non-compliant outputs. Monitoring must explicitly track and flag safety dimensions such as toxicity, personally identifiable information (PII) leakage, and bias across demographic groups. These should be as central as latency or cost metrics. In today's world safety should not be a post-hoc consideration; it must be monitored in real-time alongside technical KPIs.

The following table shows an example of metrics that can be tracked for each of the principles. This is **not an exhaustive list** but is presented to only give some sense of direction in designing a monitoring strategy that can suit our system's needs.

Principle	Metrics to Monitor
Semantic Layer	Hallucination, Relevance, Faithfulness to sources.
User Feedback	Thumbs up/down, Re-queries, Escalation rate to humans, User satisfaction.
Drift Detection	Document freshness (age of retrieved documents), Answer length trends, Query topic distribution.
Performance and Cost Balance	Latency, Token usage, Cost.
Safety and Compliance	Toxicity, Bias, PII exposure, Jailbreak attempts, Prompt injection attempts.

***Table 2.1**: Metrics to Monitor for Each of the Monitoring Principles*

Dimensions of Monitoring

When designing our LLM monitoring strategy, it helps to split metrics between the different areas of effect where the metric applies. In a real-life application, the list of metrics we want to monitor could be huge. Grouping them makes them more manageable and also when the time comes to visually present them, we can categorically see how our system is performing across each of the dimensions. Together, these four dimensions are intended to provide a comprehensive monitoring framework.

Functional Monitoring

This is monitoring 101 – it ensures that the system is delivering the correct outputs for the respective inputs. In other words, is the system **doing what it is supposed to do?** This dimension focuses on monitoring the quality, accuracy, and relevance of outputs relative to the task at hand. We need to monitor functionality metrics from the moment our system is conceived. Most of the indicators of correct functionality are visible from the first output itself. Even when designing a Minimum Viable Product (MVP), this type of monitoring is a must have. Typical examples of functional monitoring include:

- Monitoring whether a code generation LLM produces syntactically correct code that can run without errors.
- In an e-commerce application, does the search assistant help find products that match the intent of the user.
- When researching on a subject, whether or not the LLM retrieves the most relevant content on the subject.
- If a text needs to be translated into one or more languages, does the LLM produce translations which are accurate for the target language.

Non-Functional Monitoring

Non-functional monitoring focuses on **system qualities** rather than output correctness. These qualities include performance (speed or resource usage), scalability, and cost-efficiency. Although non-functional metrics may appear to be in the background, they are no longer an optional set of metrics that can be ignored until the later iterations of an application.

Correctness is important, but in practice, many LLM applications will produce equally correct answers. What separates an excellent system from an average one often lies in the non-functional characteristics: speed, efficiency, cost, and scalability. For instance, a chatbot that responds in less than 2 seconds creates a vastly better user experience than one that takes 10 seconds—even if both give equally good answers. Likewise, two RAG systems may generate equally good summaries, but the one that costs 50% fewer tokens will be far more attractive for enterprise adoption. These metrics matter because they directly affect **usability**, **customer satisfaction**, and **long-term sustainability.**

If non-functional monitoring is ignored for a long time, application quality can silently degrade, and our application can even become unavailable under increased load. Cost overruns could even derail projects and make them financially unsustainable.

Ethical Monitoring

The next dimension on the list is trademark to LLMs. Ethical monitoring is necessary in LLMs because these models are trained on vast amounts of human created text. These texts have a proportion that is sometimes not comprehensible even by the creators of these models. This training data includes content from the internet, books or even social media and is not always safe and inherently contains biased or untrue information. When using LLMs in applications, it is up to the developers of these applications to make sure the system behaves in line with human values. Metrics in this dimension are more challenging to automate but can include bias scores, fairness, and the collection of user feedback on perceived ethics. Ethical monitoring is essential to build trust with users and to comply with organizational or regulatory standards.

This type of monitoring may not apply to every LLM system, but a thorough review should be done before deciding against having them. If we are designing a system that works with or screens information about real people or operates in critical domains like education, healthcare or legal, ethical monitoring should be used to make sure the system does not distort facts or produce biased content against anyone.

Safety Monitoring

While closely related to ethics, safety focuses more on direct risks such as harmful content, security vulnerabilities, and misuse. The guiding question is: "Is *the system safe to use under real-world conditions?*" Safety monitoring is critical especially in conversational applications where users are directly engaged with the system and the chance of producing unsafe content rises on the input or the output side. Safety monitoring might track the rate of toxic or abusive language generated, attempts to obtain sensitive data, or successful prompt injection attacks. In many cases, it also includes monitoring for risks, such as leaking Personally Identifiable Information (PII). Safety monitoring is non-negotiable in the current advanced usages of LLMs, and is the key to protect organizations from reputational or legal damage.

We will briefly look at **Guardrails** in *Chapter 9, Administration, LLM Security and Guardrails* when discussing LLM security. Guardrails act as safety nets around the model, ensuring that even if the underlying LLM tries to generate something risky, the system intercepts, filters, or redirects the response before it reaches the user.

Here is a quick summary of the four dimensions we have seen:

Dimension	Goal	Key Metrics	Risks of not monitoring
Functional	Ensure outputs are correct, relevant, and useful.	Accuracy, Relevance, Hallucination.	Users receive misleading or useless answers.
Non-Functional	Ensure performance, scalability, and cost-efficiency.	Latency, Token Usage, Cost.	The system feels slow, expensive, or unusable even if outputs are correct.
Ethical	Ensure fairness, inclusivity, and alignment with values.	Bias, Fairness.	The model amplifies bias or excludes groups, leading to reputational or legal risk.
Safety	Prevent harm, misuse, or compliance violations.	Toxicity, PII leakage, Jailbreak/Prompt injection attempts.	Users exposed to harmful content, sensitive data leaks, security breaches.

Table 2.2*: Summary of Monitoring Dimensions*

Monitoring Dimensions for Typical LLM Applications

Now that we have understood the dimensions of LLM monitoring, let us see how to apply this to different types of LLM applications that we may build. We will not be covering every single type but at least the most typical ones are mentioned here.

Content Generation Systems

Let us start with a simple LLM application. Producing text or generating content is the basis of all LLM usage. The concept of these systems is simple: We take an LLM and give it an instruction (prompt) to produce any type of content. This can range from creating product descriptions, suggesting an itinerary for a vacation or even the code for a project we are working on. In all of these situations, outputs are open-ended and subjective. Monitoring therefore involves a mix of functional and non-functional aspects.

Functional Monitoring

- **Accuracy and Fluency**: Track whether generated text is grammatically correct for the respective language, logically structured, and readable.
- **Task Adherence**: Monitor whether outputs align with the instruction of the user.
- **Originality**: Ensure content is not overly repetitive or plagiarized.

Non-Functional Monitoring

- **Latency**: Measure how quickly outputs are produced.
- **Token Usage**: Monitor average tokens per output versus intended length.
- **Throughput**: Track performance especially when handling bulk content requests.
- **Cost per Item**: Ensure that content creation remains cheaper than human alternatives.

Ethical Monitoring

- **Bias**: Monitor outputs for stereotypes, exclusionary language, or unbalanced representation.
- **Inclusivity**: Track if generated content is culturally appropriate and avoids offensive phrasing.
- **Transparency**: Ensure that the generated text is labeled as AI-produced when required.

Safety Monitoring

- **Toxicity Filters**: Monitor outputs for profanity, hate speech, or harmful content.
- **IP and Plagiarism Risks**: Track whether generated content too closely matches copyrighted materials.
- **Guardrails**: Prevent content generation that promotes harmful activities or talks about sensitive topics.

Retrieval-Augmented Generation (RAG) Applications

RAG is one of the earliest techniques developed to complement LLMs. It has one single objective, *to help* ***retrieve*** *and* ***augment*** *new information* to the existing knowledge of the model, which the model had acquired from its pre-training or fine-tuning stage.

Even today, RAG is widely used to help build personalized LLM powered apps that can answer questions about specific topics or proprietary topics. This information can never really be available during the earlier stages of a model's development due to either being privately held or because the information was only very recently made available. The following figure shows RAG components in the simplest form:

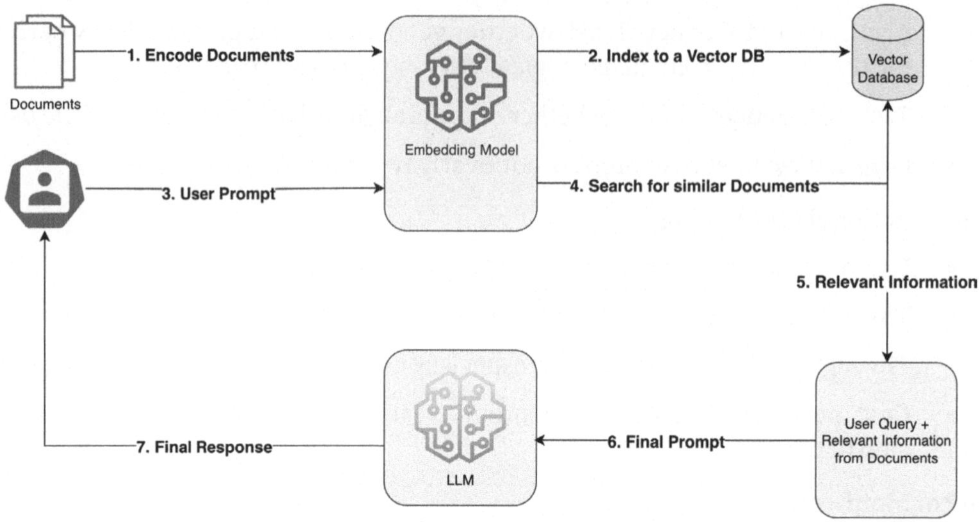

Figure 2.2: *Retrieval-Augmented Generation*

As we can see here, RAG has many steps, and each of the steps is crucial to get the final answer. Besides, RAG itself could be a component in the overall application. From a monitoring perspective, this is a lot of loops to cover. There is a two-tier monitoring needed here:

1. **Retrieval:** Making sure the correct documents were fetched. Retrieval itself could be a multi-step process of fetching documents, re-ranking them and post-processing to compress the context before sending it to the LLM.
2. **Generation:** This checks if the LLM generated the correct response by using the documents that were fetched.

Let us now see, how each of the four dimensions of monitoring can be applied here:

Functional Monitoring

- **Grounding/Faithfulness Checks**: Generated response should be based on the documents fetched and be factually correct at the same time.
- **Retrieval Relevance**: Track whether the documents retrieved actually help in answering the question.
- **Context Precision**: Monitor if retrieved documents cover the breadth of the query of the user.

- **Answer quality**: Use automated evaluation metrics or human-in-the-loop evaluation to assess accuracy and completeness.

Non-Functional Monitoring

- **Latency**: Measure latency separately for retrieval and generation to identify bottlenecks in the overall pipeline.
- **Token Usage**: Excessive retrieval can cause token usage spikes. We need to monitor usage to assess if adding extra context helped get better answers from the LLM.
- **Scalability under Load**: Track throughput for retrieval to make sure the vector DB is scaling under load.
- **Cost monitoring**: RAG based applications also incur extra costs for indexing documents besides the regular costs of using the LLM itself.

Ethical Monitoring

Bias in sources: Monitor whether retrieval disproportionately favors certain viewpoints, leading to skewed outputs. Bias can arise from the retrieval and/or the generation part.

- **Explainability**: Track whether the system can produce citations or document sources for accountability.
- **Fairness across query types**: Check if the system answers queries equally well across different demographics or regions.

Safety Monitoring

- **Prompt injection defenses**: Monitor queries for attempts to override retrieval or bypass safeguards (such as "ignore the documents and do X" type of queries).
- **PII leakage monitoring**: Ensure sensitive information in the knowledge base is not being retrieved or exposed.
- **Toxicity filters**: Monitor for toxic or harmful language in retrieved docs and generated answers.
- **Compliance risks**: Track whether restricted or confidential content is being exposed outside of intended scope.

Chatbots

Chatbots are among the most widely deployed LLM applications. Chances are that by now you have already either used or worked with some form of chat-based application that uses LLM as the engine. The recent AI chatbots are very different from a few years ago in that they could only answer questions based on certain pre-defined paths. In other cases, they would either fail or escalate to a human. Now, chatbots are able to have almost human-like conversations and can even express emotions like empathy and excitement if instructed to do so. Hence, the success of a chatbot depends on its ability to handle multi-turn interactions, maintain context, and provide a smooth conversational experience.

In most cases, chatbots are **customer-facing** and must go beyond correctness; users judge them on tone, speed, empathy, and ability to resolve queries. This makes monitoring across all dimensions equally critical. A chatbot that is factually correct but slow, biased, or toxic can do more harm than good.

Functional Monitoring

- **Intent recognition accuracy**: Track how often the chatbot correctly understands user intent.
- **Context retention**: Monitor whether the chatbot can maintain conversation history across multiple turns without contradiction.
- **Resolution rate**: Measure how often the chatbot resolves the query without escalation to a human agent.
- **Answer accuracy and helpfulness**: Use automated scoring or human feedback.

Non-Functional Monitoring

- **Latency per turn**: Monitor response times, especially in multi-turn sessions.
- **Cost**: Track tokens per full conversation, not just per message, since cost can balloon in long sessions.
- **Scalability**: Monitor throughput for concurrent conversations that happen with the chatbot.
- **Uptime**: Ensure chatbot is consistently available during service hours.

Ethical Monitoring

- **Tone and inclusivity**: Monitor whether the chatbot uses respectful, inclusive, and culturally appropriate language.
- **Bias detection**: Track if responses differ unfairly by demographic or user group.
- **Transparency**: Ensure chatbot discloses that it is an AI, not a human, in contexts where users expect this clarity.

Safety Monitoring

- **Toxicity**: Monitor for inappropriate, offensive, or harmful responses.
- **Prompt injection/jailbreak attempts**: Track when users attempt to trick the chatbot into revealing sensitive information.

- **Sensitive data protection**: Monitor whether users are inputting PII and ensure the chatbot does not store or use it improperly.

Sometimes, chatbots could also be RAG based, in which case it would make sense to monitor the RAG part separately by using the guidelines from the previous examples.

AI Agents

AI Agents are basically upgraded versions of standalone LLMs. By giving an LLM a set of powerful tools that can access information on the fly, write code or open browsers, we create an even more powerful entity called an AI Agent. These agents are now able to plan, think and reason like humans and even take autonomous decisions to perform a task using a multi-turn approach. But, ***with great power, comes great responsibility***; the responsibility to monitor the agent's action as it interacts with its environment. All this tool calling and decision making makes their behavior harder to predict. Monitoring AI Agents includes keeping track of the actions they take, the side effects of those actions, and the results they produce.

Functional Monitoring

- **Task Completion Success**: Measure how often agents successfully achieve the assigned goal.
- **Reasoning Trace Correctness**: Track the chain of thought and intermediate steps.
- **Tool Invocation Accuracy**: Monitor whether agents call the right tools with correct parameters.
- **Multi-Step Consistency**: Check that the actions of the agent across multiple steps align toward the intended outcome.

Non-Functional Monitoring

- **Latency across Steps**: Monitor not only total response time, but also per-step latency.
- **Resource Usage**: Track token consumption since agentic workflows can become expensive quickly.
- **Scalability**: Monitor performance for single versus multi-agent workflows.
- **Efficiency Trade-offs**: Compare success rate versus cost (such as does the agent consistently overspend tokens for only marginal improvements?).

Ethical Monitoring

- **Bias**: Track whether agent actions are skewed by bias of any form.
- **Transparency of Reasoning**: Ensure agents expose their reasoning traces to allow auditing of decisions.

- **Fairness**: Monitor if agents systematically favor one type of outcome over another in ways that affect users unequally.

Safety Monitoring

- **Tool Misuse Detection**: Ensure agents do not misuse or wrongly use the tools they have access to.
- **Guardrails for External Actions**: Monitor whether agents try to use tools they are not authorized to use.
- **Data Security**: Ensure sensitive information is not being passed to untrusted tools or external services.
- **Unsafe Tool Usage**: Detects if users attempt to manipulate the agent into unsafe tool calls.

Conclusion

In this chapter, we have introduced the foundational principles of monitoring LLM-based applications, emphasizing the distinction between monitoring (detecting issues) and observability (understanding root causes). It outlines the importance of tracking both technical and semantic metrics, including accuracy, latency, cost, hallucination, safety, and user feedback. The chapter explains how Site Reliability Engineering (SRE) concepts like SLIs, SLOs, and error budgets can be adapted to LLMs to balance reliability and innovation. Four key monitoring dimensions are presented: functional (correctness and usefulness of outputs), non-functional (performance, cost, scalability), ethical (bias, fairness, inclusivity), and safety (toxicity, PII leakage, compliance). Practical monitoring approaches are described for typical LLM applications—content generation, RAG systems, chatbots, and AI agents—highlighting the need to monitor across all dimensions to ensure trustworthy, efficient, and safe LLM deployment. In the next chapter, we will dive deeper into detecting drift and bias in LLMs which will conclude theoretical concepts, opening the way to learning about Langfuse.

References

- **R.E. Kalman, On the general theory of control systems, IFAC Proceedings Volumes, Volume 1, Issue 1:**

  https://www.sciencedirect.com/science/article/pii/S1474667017700948

- **What is Retrieval Augmented Generation?:**

  https://research.ibm.com/blog/retrieval-augmented-generation-RAG

- **What is Site Reliability Engineering (SRE)?:**

  https://aws.amazon.com/what-is/sre/

Chapter 3
Detecting Model Drift and Bias in LLMs

Introduction

Building on the monitoring foundations elaborated in the previous chapter, this chapter focuses on drift detection—spotting changes in LLM behavior before they impact accuracy or trust. LLMs face unique forms of drift such as prompt drift, data drift, feedback drift, and usage drift. These shifts may result from evolving facts, changing user behavior, or shifts in prompt phrasing, leading to degraded output quality and unintended bias. While the emphasis here is conceptual, we'll also preview how Langfuse can help track trends in model performance, surface early warning signals, and support bias monitoring—paving the way for more hands-on chapters ahead.

Structure

In this chapter, we will cover the following topics:

- Introduction to Drift
    - Drift in Machine Learning versus LLMs
    - How Drift Impacts Trust and Performance
- Types of Drift
    - Data Drift
    - Prompt Drift
    - Feedback Drift
    - Usage Drift
    - Knowledge Drift

- Drift Detection for LLMs
  - How Langfuse Can Help Detect Drift
- Bias and Fairness in LLMs
  - Some Real-World Examples of Bias in LLMs
  - Sources of Bias
  - Detecting Bias
  - Best Practices to Deal with Bias in LLM Applications

Introduction to Drift

Drift in general is defined as a **gradual** change in the behavior of a system over a **long period** of time. As the **environment** around a system evolves, its outputs begin to change even without any obvious changes to the system itself. We experience drift when a system that once worked well loses effectiveness, not because it was poorly designed, but because the **conditions around it shifted**. As human beings we experience drift almost constantly. Whether it is the change in our food preferences or shopping habits, or the gadgets and apps we use, our choices continuously shift towards newer or different options even when the older options do not seem to have changed at all.

This exact phenomenon is also observed when working with LLMs. An application might start producing less accurate, less relevant, or less fair outputs over time, even if the model itself has not been retrained or modified. In this case, the environment i.e. data, user behavior, expectations, or context has changed. It is impossible to avoid drift in a changing world, but with early detection, we can stop it before its impact is magnified and prevent our users from migrating to other systems due to lack of trust. Early detection of drift allows us to either rewrite prompts, update knowledge sources to the LLM or even retrain or change the LLM when external changes do not remedy the drift.

Let us go a bit deeper into the topic of drift to know why it happens and how it impacts the system.

Drift in Machine Learning versus LLMs

Drift is not a new concept in the field of machine learning. In traditional ML, models are trained on limited data (much less compared to training data used for LLMs) with pre-defined features and labels and the model essentially learns the patterns from the data it sees. The assumption is that the statistical properties of inputs will be similar to the data used in training. If the model is then made to make predictions on inputs which do not have similar characteristics, to speak statistically, the output of the model will start becoming less accurate.

Drift in ML is often about **data distributions changing over time** and the assumptions of the model which are not being held true anymore. There are well-established methods for detecting and correcting drift in ML models which include statistical tests, monitoring pipelines, and retraining strategies.

It is somewhat also easy to see the onset of drift in these models by knowing when newer features would be available on the data or when the distribution of labels has changed. For LLM's this is not very straightforward. While the underlying principle is the same—the environment around the LLM has changed, the ways drift shows up are more subtle and harder to measure. There are several factors that come into play:

- **Natural Language Inputs:** With LLMs, inputs are often natural language prompts, which vary in form and style. A small change in how users phrase a question can yield a dramatically different output, even if the underlying intent is the same. Over time, as users adapt their prompting habits, this prompt drift can cause a model to appear inconsistent or unreliable.

- **Open-Ended Ground Truths:** LLM outputs are often open-ended, subjective, and depend on context. For many cases, there is not always a single right answer, but there are many acceptable ones. This makes it harder to detect when drift has occurred, since quality often depends on user feedback, business context, or other norms that themselves evolve.

- **Knowledge Gaps in the LLM:** LLMs are trained on snapshots of data. Even the latest versions of models may be months or years behind current events. This leads to knowledge drift, that is, the training data of the model becomes outdated, and its responses diverge from reality. Updating the knowledge of an LLM is very complex and resource-intensive and not something that can be done on a very frequent basis.

- **Human Feedback:** Many LLM systems rely on user ratings to guide improvements. This introduces a new form of drift called feedback drift. If feedback becomes inconsistent, the model may start optimizing for metrics that no longer reflect the original goals of the system. For example, users who once valued detailed, step-by-step answers might later prefer brevity, making past optimization choices misaligned.

- **Expanding Scope:** LLMs are mostly general-purpose and often find new uses beyond their original scope. If a model built to answer FAQs may gradually be used for tasks like customer care, it creates usage drift where the system is used in contexts it was not originally designed for.

By comparing drift in ML and LLMs, we see that while drift is a challenge in machine learning, LLMs face a more dynamic and unpredictable form of it. In classical ML, drift can often be detected by monitoring input data distributions and performance metrics. With LLMs, drift is tied to language, human expectations, and evolving knowledge—of which are harder to quantify. Early signs of drift in LLMs do not manifest dramatically. Sometimes it appears as a slow erosion of trust, where responses feel slightly less relevant or aligned until users quietly migrate to alternatives.

A paper published in 2023 titled **"*How Is ChatGPT's Behavior Changing over Time?*" by *Lingjiao Chen, Matei Zaharia, James Zou*** highlighted that LLMs can exhibit significant drift even without explicit retraining. Comparing GPT-3.5 and GPT-4 across March and June 2023, they found substantial shifts in accuracy, verbosity, instruction-following, and safety responses—showing that LLMs change behavior over time in ways that can impact reliability, usability, and trust.

Understanding how drift affects LLMs sets the stage for the rest of this chapter. We will see the specific **types of drift** that appear in LLMs, examine their causes, and explore how they impact system performance and user trust.

How Drift Impacts Trust and Performance

As more and more people start using AI in different walks of life, they expect these systems to be trustworthy across time. Whether they use AI for writing assistance, coding, customer support, or knowledge lookup—they assume the system will **behave consistently over time**. Drift can undermine this expectation. If a user receives helpful, well-structured answers one week but vague, or incorrect responses the next, they begin to doubt the reliability of the system. As the 2023 study demonstrated, a sudden drop in instruction-following can feel like the system is behaving differently and this can build distrust in the users.

In traditional software, bugs are seen as deterministic problems that can be identified and fixed within a specified amount of time. However, the perception of instability in LLM systems could be alarming for professional use cases. If an LLM exhibits dual personalities which cannot be predicted by its users, they would be hesitant to use them in situations where predictability of answers is crucial.

Drift also shows lack of transparency which is particularly damaging because updates to underlying models are often opaque. Model Providers may improve safety, adjust prompts, or optimize costs in ways that alter outputs. Users notice the difference but rarely receive an explanation, which makes them see LLM systems as black boxes which could have hidden goals about which the users are unaware.

The most direct impact of drift is on performance, no matter how it is being measured. Whether we measure performance through accuracy, relevance or coherence, drift can cause small or big changes in how an LLM answers questions. Accuracy is impacted when the knowledge of LLM is not updated to reflect the latest facts. This can cause a sudden spike in hallucination because without new information, the model could tend to make up things and deliver outdated or wrong answers more frequently.

A lot of systems require the LLM's output to be in a certain way to process downstream tasks. This could include hard constraints like JSON outputs or a bullet list of points. This kind of output format is mostly instruction based when users add instructions like "*You must respond in* JSON" or "*Please explain in three bullets*" in the prompts to force the model to respond in a certain format. In the 2023 paper, researchers had found that GPT-4's ability to follow instructions over time had decreased and this drift explained its corresponding performance drop. This means that after switching models, we could experience some key instructions not being followed or intermittently missed which can affect other components of a system that depend on this output.

Model providers also adapt safety and regulation standards within the model to be compliant and/or make the model secure against misuse. This can sometimes result in the model adding restrictions to its own output (kind of self guardrailing) or refusing to answer questions that violate safety standards. In the worst case, things can also go the other way where a model may start giving risky or inappropriate answers which degrades performance and trust of the system.

In summary, drift can reduce predictability in performance. When accuracy or formatting is inconsistent, it may lead users to evaluate the overall reliability of the system.

Types of Drift

We already briefly mentioned the different types of drift that can happen in an LLM system. Understanding the different origins of drift is key to designing a monitoring strategy that can do early detection of drift and prevent performance degradation. These categories are not rigid—many drifts overlap or reinforce one another—but they provide a practical framework for monitoring and mitigation. **Data drift** refers to changes in the information the model is exposed to, while **prompt drift** describes shifts in the way users make their requests. Similarly, **feedback drift** captures how user reactions shape future outputs, **usage drift** reflects changes in how and why the system is being used, and **knowledge drift** highlights the drop of factual accuracy as the knowledge sources of an LLM change.

Each of these types has distinct causes and consequences. Some happen gradually, such as when the knowledge of a model becomes outdated. Others can happen rather quickly, for example if users suddenly adopt a new style of prompting or if model providers alter how instructions are interpreted. Together, they explain why an LLM that appears trustworthy and helpful today may behave differently tomorrow.

Data Drift

Data is at the heart of any AI system. Data drift which is seen in traditional ML systems, is also a common and unavoidable phenomenon in LLMs. Data drift occurs when the

data that the model is exposed to during usage is different from the one it was trained on. In simpler terms: the inputs the model receives do not quite look like the inputs it was designed to handle.

How Data Drift Appears in LLMs

For LLMs, data can be:

- **User Inputs:** The natural language queries, prompts, or documents provided to the system.
- **External Knowledge Sources:** If the LLM is using RAG or connected to APIs, the data it receives may change over time.
- **Feedback Signals:** In cases where Reinforcement Learning from Human Feedback (RLHF) or online learning is applied, user-provided data can subtly shift what the model prioritizes.

Over long periods of time, all of these inputs naturally evolve. The way people ask questions may change, new concepts may emerge, or the type of topics might shift significantly. If the model is not updated to reflect this new landscape, its responses can feel out of step with what users expect. Some of the causes of data drift include:

- **Shifting Topics:** A system originally trained to handle one set of common requests may face very different questions as user needs evolve. The types of inputs gradually shift away from the training the model received.
- **Changing Vocabulary:** Over time, new terms, expressions, or references become common. If the model was never exposed to them, it may misinterpret their meaning or ignore them entirely.
- **Evolving Structures:** Input text can change in style—longer queries, shorter prompts, or a preference for lists instead of paragraphs. These structural shifts can make the model less effective at extracting intent.
- **Information Gaps:** When the world itself changes the training data of the model no longer reflects reality. Even if the wording of questions stays the same, the answers may drift out of date.

Consequences of Data Drift

With data drift, the consequences show up in several ways:

- **Lower Accuracy:** The model gives answers that feel outdated, irrelevant, or outright wrong.
- **Misunderstood Queries:** If user input shifts in style or vocabulary, the LLM may misinterpret the intent of a request.

- **Reduced User Trust:** Users quickly notice when the system does not get it anymore, and confidence in the model erodes.

Data drift in LLMs often feels like the system is stuck in the past while the world moves forward. Because natural language is so dynamic, some level of data drift is inevitable. Unlike in traditional ML models, retraining an entire LLM frequently is not feasible. Some of the other remedies may include:

- **Fine-tuning** with newer data, if resources allow.
- Use **Retrieval-Augmented Generation (RAG)** to supplement the model with up-to-date knowledge sources.
- **Adjusting prompts** or dynamically routing queries to specialized systems can help manage input variability.

The challenge of data drift is that it is not easy to see it coming. Input patterns evolve gradually through new vocabulary, different query structures, or shifts in topics and the impact on performance may only become clear over time. Monitoring helps detect these changes early, giving us the chance to adjust before they lead to declines in relevance or accuracy. With the right monitoring in place, data drift can become a manageable part of operating LLM systems rather than cause frustration for users.

Prompt Drift

Prompt drift refers to changes in **how users make their requests** to an LLM. Unlike data drift, which is often about external information changing, prompt drift is about the language and style of interaction itself. Since LLMs are highly sensitive to phrasing, even small shifts in how users write their inputs can significantly alter the quality of responses.

Prompt drift can happen in several ways. For example, users might start using more informal language, abbreviations, or even emojis in their prompts, which can affect how accurately the LLM interprets their intent. Alternatively, they may switch from asking direct questions to issuing commands or providing incomplete information, leading the model to generate less precise or relevant outputs. Initially, users might provide short, one-line questions. Over time, they may add extensive context, bullet points, or explicit formatting instructions. Users also switch between models and providers and carry the same style of prompting from one model to another. Prompt drift therefore is a natural consequence of users experimenting and adapting their interaction styles over time. Monitoring prompt drift involves *highlighting changes in how prompts are written and by linking those changes to output quality.*

How Prompt Drift Appears in LLMs

Prompt drift can happen for several reasons:

- **Changing User Habits:** As users gain experience with LLMs, they often change how they phrase questions moving from vague, conversational queries to more structured prompts.
- **Community-Driven Patterns:** Users learn from each other. For example, if a new best practice prompt format becomes popular, it can rapidly change the style of inputs across many users.
- **Provider-Side Updates:** Internal changes to how models interpret instructions may shift the effectiveness of certain prompting styles, forcing users to adapt their queries.

Consequences of Prompt Drift

- **Reduced Effectiveness of Old Prompts:** Prompts that once produced good results may stop working as well if the model is tuned differently or if new prompting habits dominate.
- **Inconsistent Outputs:** If some users adopt new prompting conventions and others do not, the system may produce answers of highly variable quality.
- **User Dissatisfaction:** When users do not get the results they expect, they may attribute it to the model being unreliable even though the root cause is a change in how inputs are written.

At first glance, data drift and prompt drift can sound similar, since both involve changes in what the model receives as input. The key difference lies in the nature of those changes. Data drift is about shifts in the content of inputs: new topics, emerging terminology, or evolving external knowledge. It changes **what users are asking about**. Prompt drift, on the other hand, is about shifts in the style or **how users ask questions**, how much context is provided, or whether role-based prompting conventions are used. While both types of drift are fairly common, they often emerge gradually. This makes monitoring them essential. By tracking patterns in user queries, their structure, and their evolving subject matter, we can identify whether a decline in performance is due to the model not keeping up with new information (data drift) or changes in how people are phrasing their requests (prompt drift).

Feedback Drift

Feedback drift occurs when the perceptions of the user of the output of an LLM change. Unlike data drift or prompt drift, feedback drift is about **shifts in user expectations and evaluation criteria**. Over time, what users consider helpful, accurate, or satisfactory can evolve, creating a new target for the performance of the model.

In the earlier versions of ChatGPT, many users gave very positive feedback simply because it could produce coherent, fluent text on almost any topic. Today, those same kinds of answers might receive neutral or even negative ratings, because users now expect depth, factual accuracy, up-to-date knowledge, and citations. This drift in feedback signals is particularly challenging because it can blur the picture of model performance.

How Feedback Drift Appears in LLMs

Feedback drift can occur in different forms:

- **Changing Expectations:** As users become more familiar with LLMs, they may demand higher-quality answers than they did when the system was new.
- **Evolving Standards:** External factors such as new regulations, cultural sensitivities, or organizational guidelines can change how responses are judged.
- **Inconsistent Signals:** If different users have a different understanding of a subject, the same output might be rated positively by some and negatively by others.
- **Feedback Fatigue:** Over time, users may provide less feedback or give ratings that are less reflective of true quality, leading to noisier signals.

Consequences of Feedback Drift

- **Reduced Reliability of Metrics:** Metrics like satisfaction scores or acceptance rates may decline, not because the model worsened, but because the definition of "good" shifted.
- **Difficulty Diagnosing Issues:** Without clarity on feedback drift, we may misinterpret declining ratings as a model performance issue rather than a shift in expectations.
- **Erosion of Trust:** If users feel the system is not improving in line with their evolving expectations, they may perceive it as stagnant or unresponsive.

Feedback drift actually has nothing to do with the LLM itself but is defined by user expectations, which change over time. Monitoring feedback trends is therefore essential and should include not only tracking scores and ratings but also analyzing shifts in the language of written feedback, differences across user groups, and patterns of feedback engagement. With this visibility, we can separate genuine performance issues from evolving expectations and make better decisions about iterating the system. Monitoring ensures that as the definition of "good" evolves, the system evolves with it.

Usage Drift

Over time, users often discover new ways of using an LLM, or they may adopt it for tasks the system was not originally designed to handle. Usage drift happens when changes occur in **how a model is used.** One interesting example of usage drift can again be seen in ChatGPT. When ChatGPT was first released, the majority of users used it for casual purposes. Prompts often revolved around light experimentation asking for jokes, generating poetry, or exploring its conversational ability. Over time, usage shifted to cover more cases:

- **Professional Productivity:** Within months, users began employing ChatGPT for drafting emails, summarizing documents, and brainstorming professional content.
- **Specialized Tasks:** Developers discovered its ability to assist with coding and debugging, turning ChatGPT into a programming assistant.
- **Workflow Integration:** Businesses started embedding ChatGPT into customer support tools, knowledge bases, and team collaboration platforms, moving it from casual use into critical workflows.
- **Longer Interactions:** Early sessions often involved quick back-and-forth exchanges; later, users began relying on ChatGPT for long, multi-step problem-solving sessions and project-level assistance.

Consequences of Usage Drift

- **Loss of Accuracy:** The model may not have been tuned, evaluated, or monitored for the new types of use, increasing the likelihood of errors in some scenarios.
- **Increased Operational Risks:** When an LLM is suddenly applied to critical tasks, even small inaccuracies may have big consequences, compared to its original use case.
- **Metrics Misalignment:** Usage drift can cause evaluation frameworks to lose relevance. For example, speed and creativity may have been key metrics early on, but later users may value reliability more.
- **Resource Strain:** As usage intensifies, infrastructure and monitoring systems may face performance bottlenecks, impacting latency and user experience.

At first glance, changes in how people use an LLM might seem harmless since it looks like users are just getting creative. In practice, usage drift changes how an LLM must be run, measured, and governed. How a model is used determines the metrics that matter, and the operational requirements. When usage drifts, the risk profile and resource needs of the system change too. What was once low-risk, exploratory usage (like in the example for ChatGPT) can become high-risk when users adopt the model for professional or critical tasks (drafting emails or code generation). Small errors that were acceptable before now have business, legal, or safety consequences.

Higher volume and longer sessions increase compute, latency, and cost. A lot of applications now use multi-step workflows or RAG which multiply the usage of resources the system is built on. This could also in turn require complimentary optimization strategies like caching, but this requires new infrastructure to store and manage cached results.

As adoption of an LLM grows, the user base often expands beyond the original group of early adopters. Each new group brings its own needs and definitions of quality. Professional users expect the system to deliver consistent outputs, predictable formatting, and reliable performance. They also expect SLAs that define uptime, latency, and error boundaries, because the tool becomes part of their workflow. Besides reliability, they require explainability and transparency in how outputs are generated, so that they can justify or audit the responses of the model in compliance-sensitive contexts like law, finance, or healthcare.

By tracking how usage patterns shift over time, segmenting by user cohorts, and correlating those shifts with performance, we gain the visibility needed to adapt the system. Monitoring helps distinguish early experimentation from broader adoption, ensures infrastructure and costs scale sustainably, and guides the evolution of evaluation metrics to match new expectations. At the end of the day, usage drift is simply a sign that users are finding new value in the system. This can be a good thing but only if development teams are ready to keep up, otherwise the system risks becoming out of sync with the users it was meant to serve.

Knowledge Drift

Knowledge drift was discussed in a leading academic paper from 2024 titled: *Understanding Knowledge Drift in LLMs through Misinformation* by Alina Fastowski and Gjergji Kasneci. The paper shows that even well-performing LLMs can have their knowledge subtly shifted when fed repeated false or misleading statements in the context of questions. In their experiments, they inject false information into the prompt or random unrelated information alongside a factual question. They measure how the uncertainty of the model and answer correctness behave under these conditions and find that repeated exposure to the same false information sometimes lowers uncertainty in the model about its (incorrect) answer, essentially causing it to believe the false statement more over time.

What is noteworthy is that knowledge drift here is not caused by retraining or explicit model updates, but by **adversarial or manipulative user inputs** during inference time.

The authors of the paper tested several models (such as GPT-4o, GPT-3.5, Mistral-7B, LLaMA-2) using a closed-book QA setting based on TriviaQA which is a large scale distantly supervised dataset for reading comprehension. They introduce false information prompts (embedding incorrect facts alongside the question) and random information prompts (irrelevant content), then compare the models' answer correctness and measures of uncertainty (entropy, perplexity, token probability). They observe that an initial injection of misleading content raises model uncertainty by as much as **56.6%**, but repeated exposure can actually lower uncertainty even for incorrect answers by **52.8%** suggesting the models become more confidently wrong.

When false information is repeated 10 times in the prompt, accuracy drops up to **~80.9%** relative to baseline for LLaMA-2-13B. The paper also reports that for GPT-4o and GPT-3.5, accuracy under false prompt injections declines from ~98.7% baseline to ~92.1% and ~78.1% respectively.

The findings highlight knowledge drift: models can be nudged toward believing false information, losing their factual reliability over time. This means that models even when frozen are prone to evolving internal belief states based on what they see. For monitoring systems, this implies we need to track not just correctness but also model confidence, and flag cases where a model becomes more certain about wrong answers.

Consequences of Knowledge Drift

- **Factual Inconsistency:** The most obvious risk of knowledge drift is that the model starts giving false or outdated answers with high confidence, undermining credibility.
- **Hallucination Risk:** The model may become more certain about incorrect statements over time, making it hallucinate with time.
- **Propagation of Misinformation:** In some systems this drifted knowledge becomes part of what the system knows, and future users may receive and further wrong information.
- **Difficulty in Detection:** Because the model may continue giving fluent, plausible-sounding answers, changes in knowledge can be subtle or hidden.

<table>
<tr><th>Drift Type</th><th>What Changes</th><th>Examples</th></tr>
<tr><td>Data Drift</td><td>The content of inputs changes — new topics, terminology, or domains.</td><td>• A travel assistant begins receiving queries about a newly popular destination not covered during fine-tuning.
• A legal summarizer suddenly processes documents referencing new regulations introduced this year.</td></tr>
<tr><td>Prompt Drift</td><td>The style or structure of prompts changes — how users phrase their queries.</td><td>• Users shift from full sentences to task-tag prompts like “Summarize: ...”
• Users adopt new prompting conventions (“Act as an expert...”) that alter model behavior.</td></tr>
</table>

Drift Type	What Changes	Examples
Feedback Drift	The *signals indicating quality* change — ratings, corrections, or satisfaction patterns.	• Acceptance rates drop because user expectations rise after a product update. • More advanced users join, leading to stricter feedback patterns and higher rejection rates.
Usage Drift	The *purpose or workflow* of the system evolves — new tasks or user segments.	• A FAQ chatbot is increasingly used to draft documents and longer content. • Session lengths grow as users shift from one-off queries to multi-step workflows.
Knowledge Drift	The *factual correctness* of the model shifts over time — answers change or degrade.	• The model continues giving outdated answers about CEOs or product releases as facts change. • Repetition of misinformation in user queries subtly pushes the model toward incorrect answers with higher confidence.

Table 3.1: *Summary of Drift Types in LLMs*

Monitoring knowledge drift requires combining multiple strategies: regularly testing the model against a set of fact-based queries, tracking shifts in uncertainty or confidence levels, and running controlled prompt experiments to capture misleading information. Together, these practices create a feedback loop that makes knowledge drift visible and manageable rather than hidden.

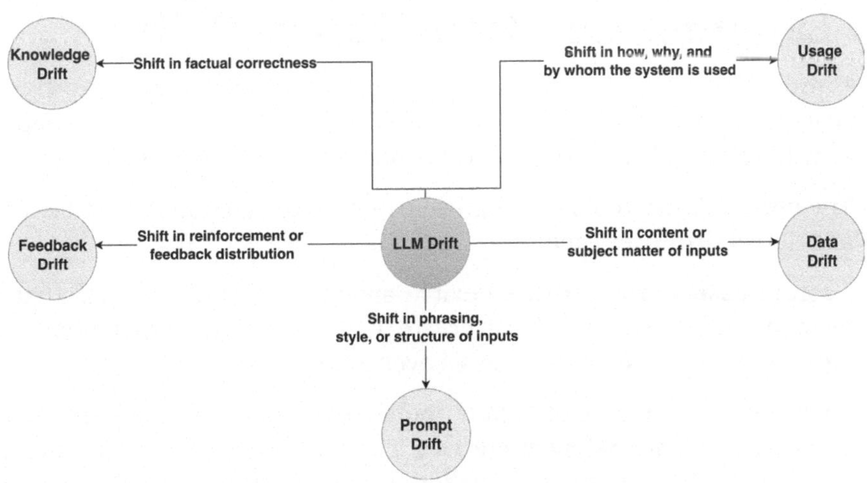

Figure 3.1: *Concept Map for Drift in LLMs*

Drift Detection for LLMs

Up to this point, we have looked at different forms of drift—data, prompt, feedback, usage, and knowledge. This section is about how we actually catch drift when it happens. Drift detection is the practice of continuously monitoring inputs, outputs, and user interactions to spot changes before they degrade performance. Different types of drift occur in different ways, so monitoring should align with the drift categories we've discussed:

- **Data Drift:** Compare the vocabulary, topics, or embeddings of incoming queries against some baselines. Tools like clustering or cosine similarity can reveal when the semantic space of queries is shifting.
- **Prompt Drift:** Track metadata about prompts like average length, formatting patterns, or use of role-based structures. A change may indicate users adopting new prompting conventions.
- **Feedback Drift:** Monitor acceptance/rejection rates, thumbs-up/down signals, or satisfaction scores over time. Sudden changes may indicate that user expectations have shifted, even if the core outputs of the model have not.
- **Usage Drift:** Look at session length, query frequency, and task diversity.
- **Knowledge Drift:** Periodically benchmark the model against a stable set of factual queries. Track not only correctness but also confidence of the model. As the 2024 paper on misinformation shows, models may become more confident in wrong answers over repeated exposures, making this one of the trickiest drifts to catch.

How Langfuse Can Help Detect Drift

Langfuse provides several key features to help detect and monitor drift in LLMs through comprehensive observability and analytics capabilities. In later chapters, we will see how to effectively use these features but here is a concise summary:

- The **observability tools** of Langfuse can monitor incoming data distributions and detect drift over time.
- **Custom dashboards** provide flexible analytics to track metrics that matter most for drift detection. We can create personalized views that monitor quality metrics and user behavior analysis over time.
- To evaluate the quality of LLM outputs and detect drift, Langfuse enables us to define and **track relevant metrics**. These include model-based evaluations, user feedback, and manual labeling. Collecting these metrics lets us track quality, gauge user interactions, and improve models over time.
- The tracing capabilities of Langfuse capture detailed execution paths within applications. Tracing requests and responses helps developers spot bottlenecks, detect errors, and understand component interactions. This detailed monitoring helps track latency, throughput, and error rates to ensure everything runs smoothly.

- We can have validation **datasets** in Langfuse which can be used to benchmark new models and prompts to make continuous improvements to the system.

These features work together to provide a comprehensive drift detection system, allowing us to monitor model performance changes, identify when outputs deviate from expected patterns, and take corrective action before drift significantly impacts the effectiveness of our application.

Detecting Data Drift

Data drift shows up when the content of inputs changes—new topics, new terminology, new external context. With Langfuse we can detect data drift using:

- **Logging Traces and Embedding Tracking**: Each prompt and response can be logged, and embeddings can be generated to map semantic space. Comparing embeddings over time highlights when input shifts.
- **Dashboards for Topic Trends**: Langfuse dashboards can visualize clusters of queries by topic, showing when certain terms or domains suddenly spike.
- **Alerts on Distribution Shifts:** Although alerting is an upcoming feature in Langfuse, using an alternative alerting mechanism, we can configure thresholds over metrics indicating data drift and inform maintainers/developers in a timely manner.

Detecting Prompt Drift

Prompt drift is about changes in how users phrase questions, not necessarily what they ask. With Langfuse:

- **Prompt Metadata Tracking:** Add metadata such as prompt length, formatting style, or use of system/role tokens to traces. Langfuse allows filtering queries by these attributes.
- **Cohort Analysis:** Segment traces by prompt styles and track performance differences between them.
- **Visualization:** A dashboard could show average prompt length over time. If it climbs steadily, that signals prompt drift.

Detecting Feedback Drift

Langfuse supports capturing different types of user feedback that can help detect drift patterns:

- **Explicit Feedback**: Direct user ratings, likes/dislikes, scales, or comments.
- **Implicit Feedback**: User behavior metrics like time spent on a page, click-through rate, or accepting/rejecting model-generated outputs.

User feedback is captured as scores in Langfuse, which can be numeric (including 1-5), categorical (similar to thumbs up/down) or binary (particularly accept/reject). Langfuse can aggregate this feedback over time, so a sudden drop in acceptance for one task type (say, summaries) becomes visible. Like other drifts, dashboards can also be created for feedback results to detect drifts early.

Detecting Usage Drift

Usage drift occurs when the system is used for different purposes than originally planned. With Langfuse:

- **Session Tracking:** By logging session lengths, query frequency, and sequences of actions, Langfuse reveals whether workflows are becoming more complex.
- **Task Categorization:** Labels or tags in Langfuse can bucket queries by type (FAQ, writing, coding and so on). Tracking how proportions change over time shows when usage is expanding.
- **Cost and Latency Monitoring:** Langfuse integrates latency and token usage metrics. If sessions grow longer and more expensive, Langfuse can show this operational dimension of drift as well.

Detecting Knowledge Drift

Langfuse offers several options that can detect if misinformation is causing performance degradation in the system:

- **Benchmark Datasets:** We can define a set of factual questions and expected answers relevant to our system. Prompt/Model experiments can then be run on these datasets to make sure the factual understanding of the system does not alter over time.
- **Answer Comparison:** Langfuse enables tracking responses to the same prompt over time, so we can see if factual answers change.
- **Audit Trails:** By preserving historical traces, Langfuse provides an audit of how the model's answers to key factual questions evolve.

Drift detection for LLMs is about maintaining clear visibility as the environment around the model changes. This could mean shifts in user input, variations in prompt styles, updated feedback, new usage trends, or even changes in the knowledge base itself. By systematically tracking key signals using benchmarks, feedback mechanisms, and logging we can identify when the performance of a model begins to move off course, often before users notice any issues. While monitoring cannot completely prevent drift, it equips us with the evidence needed to make informed adjustments, ensuring that our system continues to meet real-world needs as contexts evolve.

Bias and Fairness in LLMs

LLMs are trained on massive datasets which include content from the internet, books, code, and many other sources. These datasets contain the same stereotypes, and gaps in representation that exist in human language and society. When models learn from such data, they also inherit biases. Bias in LLMs is not always obvious. Sometimes it shows up as stereotypical-sounding associations, such as linking certain professions more strongly with one gender than another. At other times, it can be more damaging, like producing offensive outputs, under-representing certain perspectives, or making recommendations that consistently proves to be a disadvantage to particular groups. Bias also undermines trust that is harder to measure than accuracy alone. Users may sometimes accept factual mistakes, but if they feel that a model systematically favors, stereotypes, or ignores their perspective, confidence in the system goes down. This is a very sensitive topic especially, when reputational risks and regulatory expectations around fairness are rising.

Fairness comes into play because of the impact of bias. What might feel like a small issue in one context can translate into exclusion or harm in another. A model that works well for English speakers, for example, might underperform for non-native speakers. Similarly, a model that seems helpful for casual use might fail when used in a professional or regulated environment where consistency and neutrality are critical.

Addressing bias is a tedious but critical issue given the complexity of language. Our goal here is to measure where and how bias shows up in our system, monitor its effects, and put safety checks in place so that applications remain trustworthy. Just as drift detection helps us adapt to changing environments, bias monitoring ensures that models serve users fairly, regardless of their background or context.

Some Real-World Examples of Bias in LLMs

The following examples show that bias in LLMs and multimodal models is a recurring pattern that manifests in language, imagery, and even domain-specific tasks. The issue spans across demographics, geography, culture, and professional representation, often in subtle but consequential ways. Understanding these patterns is essential to address them effectively.

- A recent paper "*Gender and Positional Biases in LLM-Based Hiring Decisions: Evidence from Comparative CV/Résumé Evaluations*" (Rozado, 2025) examined 22 different LLMs. The authors presented matched CV pairs (same qualifications, different gendered first names) and asked the models to choose the more suitable candidate. Despite equal qualifications, *every single* LLM showed a preference for female-named candidates across 70 professions. They also found that when an explicit gender field was added, the preference increased.

- The paper "*Large Language Models are Geographically Biased*" by Rohin Manvi et al. (2024) shows that LLMs exhibit systemic bias when making judgments about regions, especially in subjective domains. Locations with lower socioeconomic conditions are rated unfavorably relative to more affluent regions. The authors quantify this bias: for objective topics there is strong correlation (up to 89%), but for sensitive subjective topics, the bias is significant (up to 70%).
- The "*Hidden Bias in the Machine: Stereotypes in Text-to-Image Models*" paper (2025) generated over 16,000 images across prompts involving occupations, attributes, actions, and so on. They find that generated images often reinforce stereotypes in terms of race, age, and body type. For instance, prompts for certain professions may disproportionately show people of a particular race or age, or exist with certain stereotypical attributes (specifically associating certain actions or traits with specific demographic groups).

In the next section, we will look at some of the sources of bias ranging from training data and labeling practices to model architectures and deployment contexts. By tracing bias, we gain a clearer picture of how to monitor, mitigate, and design for fairness.

Sources of Bias

Bias in LLMs arise from choices made across the lifecycle of model development: from the data collected to how it is labeled, structured, and optimized, all the way through to how the model is deployed and used in real-world contexts. By breaking down the sources of bias, we can begin to see where monitoring can be effective.

Training Data Bias

LLMs are only as representative as the data they are trained on. Since most are trained on internet-based corpora, they inherit the distribution of what is available online: English-dominant, Western-centric, and often skewed toward certain demographics. This means voices from underrepresented languages, regions, or communities are scanty from the start.

Tracking the geographic, linguistic, or topical distribution of user queries against the training data domain can reveal where the model is more likely to produce biased or incomplete outputs.

Labeling and Annotation Bias

For models that incorporate supervised fine-tuning or Reinforcement Learning from Human Feedback (RLHF), the labels and preferences provided by annotators introduce bias. Annotators bring their own cultural, social, and personal perspectives to the task, consciously or unconsciously. In RLHF, annotators may prefer shorter, more polite answers, leading models to undervalue directness or culturally different communication styles.

Representation Bias

Representation bias is present when particular groups, topics, or perspectives are either more or less frequently included in the training data. This does not just affect fairness but also accuracy, as the model builds an incomplete picture.

Tracking how often certain demographic categories, professions, or geographic regions appear in generated content can expose imbalances.

Contextual Bias

Bias also arises when models are deployed in contexts that differ from their training assumptions. A model trained or fine-tuned in one cultural or domain context may struggle when applied elsewhere not due to language limitations, but because of differences in norms, expectations, or domain-specific practices.

Usage drift (as discussed earlier) interacts directly with contextual bias. Observing where user satisfaction drops geographically or demographically can signal that context mismatch is becoming a bias issue.

Algorithmic and Architectural Bias

Even before deployment, the way models are architected and optimized shapes outcomes. For example, certain tokenization methods disproportionately disadvantage non-English languages, fragmenting words into many sub-tokens and making generation less fluent. Similarly, optimization for efficiency may lead to trade-offs that impact fairness or inclusivity.

Interaction and Feedback Bias

Finally, bias evolves with how users interact with the system. Popular prompts, repeated queries, and feedback loops amplify certain behaviors. If most users upvote casual, conversational outputs, the model may underperform when asked for formal or technical content. Continuous tracking of user interactions, prompt styles, and feedback scores is critical to prevent reinforcing narrow usage patterns at the expense of diversity and fairness.

Bias Type	Example
Training Data Bias	A model trained mostly on English web data produces weaker, less fluent results for under-represented languages.
Labeling and Annotation Bias	Annotators over-flag certain dialects as "toxic," causing the model to penalize those dialects.
Representation Bias	A text-to-image or résumé system disproportionately depicts or ranks certain demographic groups for specific roles.

Bias Type	Example
Contextual Bias	A model tuned for one cultural or domain context gives answers that are irrelevant or unsuitable in another.
Algorithmic and Architectural Bias	Tokenization that fragments words in morphologically rich languages leads to poorer fluency and higher error rates for those languages.
Interaction and Feedback Bias	If users predominantly upvote short, casual answers, the model may drift toward brevity, giving a disadvantage to users who need detailed explanations.

***Table 3.2**: Examples of Bias in LLMs*

Detecting Bias

Detecting bias in applications built using LLMs involves a mix of automated and manual techniques to uncover unfair patterns or systemic errors in outputs, data, or model behavior. Langfuse detects bias in applications by enabling us to observe and evaluate LLM outputs for fairness and equal treatment. Without going into deeper details here, these are the main features of Langfuse that can help detect bias:

- **Capturing LLM Outputs and Traces** Langfuse records every interaction, including the input, output, and metadata for each LLM call. By capturing this data, we can later analyze responses for biased patterns or unfair behavior.

  Example: Suppose our application asks an LLM to summarize job applicants' resumes. Langfuse will log each summary, the input resume, and related metadata as a trace. This allows us to later review whether certain groups are consistently described differently.

- **Defining and Tracking Evaluation Metrics** We can set up evaluation metrics in Langfuse, such as fairness or bias scores. These can be generated through model-based evaluations, user feedback, or manual labeling.

  Example: Add a bias score to each trace, where human reviewers or automated evaluators judge if an output is potentially biased (including a language that favors one demographic over another).

- **Analyzing and Visualizing Trends** Langfuse dashboards help us visualize bias-related metrics over time. We can filter traces by specific user groups, prompts, or outputs to detect if bias appears in certain contexts.

  Example: Use analytics dashboards to spot if the LLM more frequently produces gendered language when asked about certain professions.

- **Feedback Loops and Continuous Improvement** Langfuse supports integrating user or stakeholder feedback directly into traces. When users report biased results, we can track these incidents, analyze their root causes, and refine our model or prompts accordingly.

Example: Users flag a chatbot response as biased. The feedback is attached to the trace, and we can review it alongside similar traces to identify and address patterns.

- **Model-Based and External Evaluations** Langfuse allows us to set up model-based evaluations or use external pipelines to programmatically check outputs for bias or fairness.

  Example: Set up an automated evaluator that checks if responses include stereotypes or unfair assumptions and log these scores for ongoing monitoring.

By combining trace capture, metric tracking, dashboards, feedback, and automated evaluation, Langfuse gives us a structured way to detect and address bias in our LLM-powered applications.

Best Practices to Deal with Bias in LLM Applications

While there are many techniques or ways available now to mitigate bias in the model itself, it is important to acknowledge that in most cases, when building with LLMs, we cannot control the internals of the model. We cannot re-train, re-weight, or edit components of the model itself. Since the subject of the book is monitoring, instead we will focus on how to deal with bias at the **application level** through monitoring, feedback and guardrails. Here are some best practices specifically for LLM applications:

- **Prompt and Context Design**
  - Provide consistent context, role definitions, or guardrails in prompts to reduce assumptions in how the model interprets user inputs.
  - Explicitly instruct the model to use neutral or inclusive language.
  - Add clarifications, disclaimers, or reference text to reduce reliance on the default associations of the model.
- **Monitoring Outputs for Bias**
  - Use rules, classifiers, or embeddings to flag outputs that may reflect biased or unfair patterns.
  - Collect structured feedback (such as ratings, comments) to identify outputs that users perceive as biased.
  - Continuously test the system with controlled prompts designed to reveal potential biases and track results over time.
- **Human-in-the-Loop**
  - For sensitive tasks (similar to healthcare, and financial advice), route model outputs through human review when bias or harm potential is detected.

    - Regularly sample outputs across user groups and task types to check for disparities in tone, quality, or inclusivity.
    - Involve reviewers from different backgrounds to catch biases invisible to a single demographic.
- **Transparency**
    - Make clear to end users that outputs are generated by an AI system that may reflect biases.
    - Offer short explanations or references when outputs may be influenced by biased priors.
    - Allow users to flag or correct biased outputs, feeding that data back into monitoring pipelines.
- **Continuous Monitoring with Langfuse**
    - **Trace logging:** Capture input, output, and metadata to analyze bias patterns over time.
    - **Feedback capture:** Store explicit and implicit user feedback, enabling trend analysis of where bias affects satisfaction.
    - **Custom dashboards:** Track bias-related metrics in one place.
    - **Benchmark datasets:** Periodically re-run a set of standardized test prompts designed to surface potential biases and compare the outputs against previous results to track if patterns of bias are appearing or changing over time.

Here is a summary of the above-mentioned best practices with some examples:

Best Practice	Example
Prompt and Context Design	• Instead of "Describe a typical nurse," use "Describe a nurse, avoiding stereotypes. • Add "Use inclusive language" when asking for job descriptions. • Provide balanced context in a travel prompt: "Suggest destinations across different budget ranges."
Monitoring Outputs for Bias	• Flag when the model defaults to male pronouns for "doctor" or "engineer". • Detect summaries that consistently highlight Western sources but ignore others. • Benchmark by asking "Describe a leader" or "Describe a family" periodically to catch stereotype drift.

Best Practice	Example
Human-in-the-Loop	• Route financial planning answers to review when income levels differ significantly across user queries. • Sample outputs from customer support bots to check tone differences between regions. • Include evaluators from multiple cultures to spot subtle bias in product recommendations.
Transparency	• Add disclaimers like "This is AI-generated and may reflect biases". • Add a "Report response" button for users to flag biased or unfair content.

Table 3.3: *Summary of Best Practices to Deal with Bias*

Conclusion

This chapter explores the concept of drift and bias in LLMs, detailing how changes in data, prompts, feedback, usage, and knowledge can affect model accuracy, reliability, and fairness. It outlines monitoring strategies and introduces some Langfuse features for detecting drift and bias. Real-world examples and best practices are provided to help mitigate bias at the application level, emphasizing the importance of continuous monitoring, human oversight, and transparency to maintain trustworthy AI systems. From the next chapter onwards, we will jump into Langfuse, the star concept of this book and will shift from theory to practice showing how Langfuse provides the infrastructure to monitor, experiment and improve LLM applications. We will see how Langfuse can help us track, detect, and manage issues we have seen so far in real-world applications.

References

- Knowledge Drift - https://arxiv.org/pdf/2409.07085
- How Is ChatGPT's Behavior Changing over Time? - https://arxiv.org/pdf/2307.09009
- TriviaQA: https://arxiv.org/abs/1705.03551
- Alerts in Langfuse: https://github.com/orgs/langfuse/discussions/3997
- Gender and Positional Biases in LLM-Based Hiring Decisions: Evidence from Comparative CV/Résumé Evaluations - https://arxiv.org/abs/2505.17049
- Large Language Models are Geographically Biased - https://arxiv.org/abs/2402.02680
- Hidden Bias in the Machine: Stereotypes in Text-to-Image Models - https://arxiv.org/abs/2506.13780

CHAPTER 4
Introduction to Langfuse

Introduction

We have covered a lot of conceptual ground in the previous chapters and by now you should have a solid foundational understanding about monitoring LLM-powered applications. It is time now to discover the main focus of the book, Langfuse — an open-source LLM observability platform. Conceived during Winter 2023 of Y Combinator, Langfuse addresses a crucial need: making LLM-powered systems easier to debug, optimize, and scale in production. While many observability tools focus on infrastructure or model metrics, Langfuse takes a holistic approach capturing the entire LLM interaction lifecycle, from prompt design to final output. In this chapter, we shall explore the platform's core concepts and how to get started with Langfuse.

Structure

In this chapter, we will cover the following topics:

- Introduction to Langfuse
  - Need for Specialized Tools to Monitor LLM Applications
- Langfuse's Commitment to Open Source
- Langfuse versus LangSmith
- The Core Capabilities of Langfuse
  - Observability
  - Prompt Management
  - Evaluation
- Getting Started with Langfuse
  - Langfuse Technical Architecture
  - Langfuse Cloud

- Self-Hosting Langfuse
- Setting up Environment Variables for Self-Hosting
- Langfuse Features Included in Self-Hosting
- Enterprise Edition (Paid) Features

Introduction to Langfuse

Langfuse is an **open-source** observability and analytics platform built specifically for applications powered by LLMs. Unlike traditional monitoring systems designed for deterministic software like APIs, Langfuse is created to tackle the challenges of working with AI systems. It provides teams with visibility into how their LLM applications behave in real-world usage, offering structured insights into prompts, responses, evaluations, and performance metrics.

At its core, Langfuse acts as a **black box recorder** for LLM-driven applications. Every interaction between our application and the model whether it's a simple query, a multi-step reasoning chain, or an orchestration involving multiple tools can be traced, analyzed, and evaluated. This level of observability not only helps diagnose issues but also empowers teams to iterate rapidly on prompts, assess quality, and optimize costs. Being open source, Langfuse is flexible in deployment so that developers can self-host it for full control and data governance or use managed offerings for convenience. Its design is meant to complement existing MLOps and monitoring stacks, bridging the gap between traditional metrics-based observability and the requirements of generative AI systems.

Langfuse provides visibility into every interaction between users and LLMs, enabling teams to:

- **Trace** model calls and multi-step reasoning chains including RAG and chatbots.
- **Version and manage prompts** as artifacts.
- **Evaluate outputs** with human and automated feedback loops.
- **Track performance metrics** such as latency, cost, and quality.

As teams begin to deploy LLM applications into production it becomes necessary to get a clear view of how AI features are being used by users. With Langfuse, teams can track every step in the process and generate performance metrics to improve user satisfaction. By examining these metrics, it is possible to detect issues, adjust, and monitor the performance of features.

Need for Specialized Tools to Monitor LLM Applications

In *Chapter 1, Introduction to Large Language Models and Monitoring*, we saw some unique challenges that we face when it comes to deploying LLM-based applications to production. Each of those challenges highlight why conventional logging and monitoring are not enough for LLM systems. The need for specialized tools arises from several characteristics of LLM systems.

Randomness of Outputs

- **Traditional software** like APIs, work on deterministic inputs and will process the request in the same way every time for a given input.
- **LLM-driven systems,** on the other hand, will even for the same input give answers that may differ in phrasing, completeness, or even correctness.

This unpredictability means developers need tools that can capture and compare all of the responses, not just single instances. Langfuse enables teams to **log multiple outputs**, analyze variability, and quantify the stability of responses.

Prompt Sensitivity and Multi-Step Workflows

Prompts are often referred to as the "source code" of LLMs. Small changes in wording can lead to vastly different results. Applications rarely involve a single prompt–response pair. Instead, they orchestrate multiple steps, such as:

- Taking a user query;
- Retrieving relevant documents from a knowledge base (RAG);
- Passing the retrieved context into a model; and,
- Formatting and returning the final response.

Each step introduces potential failure points. Without proper observability, debugging becomes nearly impossible. The tracing functionality of Langfuse allows developers to **record the full chain** of events, making it easier to pinpoint whether an issue stemmed from retrieval, prompt formatting, or model output.

Evaluating Outputs beyond Accuracy

As we had seen in *Chapter 2, LLM Monitoring Principles and Metrics*, with LLMs, that evaluation is multi-dimensional. Consider a customer support agent built on top of an LLM. Its responses must be:

- **Factually correct** (no hallucinations);
- **Helpful** (addresses the intent of the user);
- **Polite and safe** (avoids toxic or biased language);
- **Efficient** (delivered with low latency); and,
- **Cost-effective** (optimizing token usage).

No single metric captures all of these. Dedicated tools must allow for:

- Automated evaluation (such as similarity scores against ground truth).
- Human-in-the-loop feedback (thumbs up/down scoring).
- Custom evaluators tied to domain-specific goals.

Langfuse integrates these **evaluations into a single platform**, helping teams measure quality in a structured way.

Monitoring Drift

LLM providers frequently update their models. For example:

- OpenAI may release a new version of GPT with improved reasoning but different phrasing.
- A smaller model may change its default system prompt behavior.

These updates can silently degrade application performance. Without monitoring, teams may not notice until users complain. Similarly, drifts that we saw in *Chapter* 3, *Detecting Model Drift and Bias in* LLMs, can expose weaknesses.

Langfuse helps detect drift by **tracking performance trends over time**, alerting teams when quality or reliability falls below acceptable thresholds.

Cost and Latency Metrics

In LLM-powered systems, every token (input or output) processed translates into cost. At scale, even minor changes can add up significantly. Latency is equally critical: a slow AI assistant can frustrate users and reduce adoption.

Observability tools must therefore include:

- Token-level usage metrics to analyze cost.
- Latency distributions to identify bottlenecks.
- Insights into trade-offs between quality, cost, and speed.

Langfuse's **metrics dashboard** enables teams to optimize these trade-offs, balancing user experience against budget constraints.

Supporting Collaboration and Iteration

LLM application development is highly iterative. Prompts evolve, evaluation criteria are refined, and orchestration logic changes. Teams require:

- **Prompt versioning** to track changes over time.
- **Comparison tools** to assess whether a new prompt performs better.

- **Shared dashboards** for cross-functional collaboration between developers, product managers, and domain experts.

Langfuse embeds these **collaborative features**, turning observability into an active part of the development workflow.

After this brief introduction we will see how Langfuse's true Open-Source nature makes it one of the best LLM observability tools.

Langfuse's Commitment to Open Source

Although Langfuse started in 2023, it was not completely open-sourced from the beginning. It offered a paid Pro version and many of its core features were not available to self-host. However, in June of 2025 this changed dramatically in a move that the team at Langfuse called **"Doubling Down on Open Source".**

As part of this initiative, Langfuse open sourced all its product features which were only available in the Pro version as a major boost to the community and to get faster feedback on how to grow Langfuse as a product. This list of features included **LLM-as-a-judge evaluations, annotation queues, prompt experiments and the playground** all of which make Langfuse one of the most comprehensive and openly available LLM observability platforms.

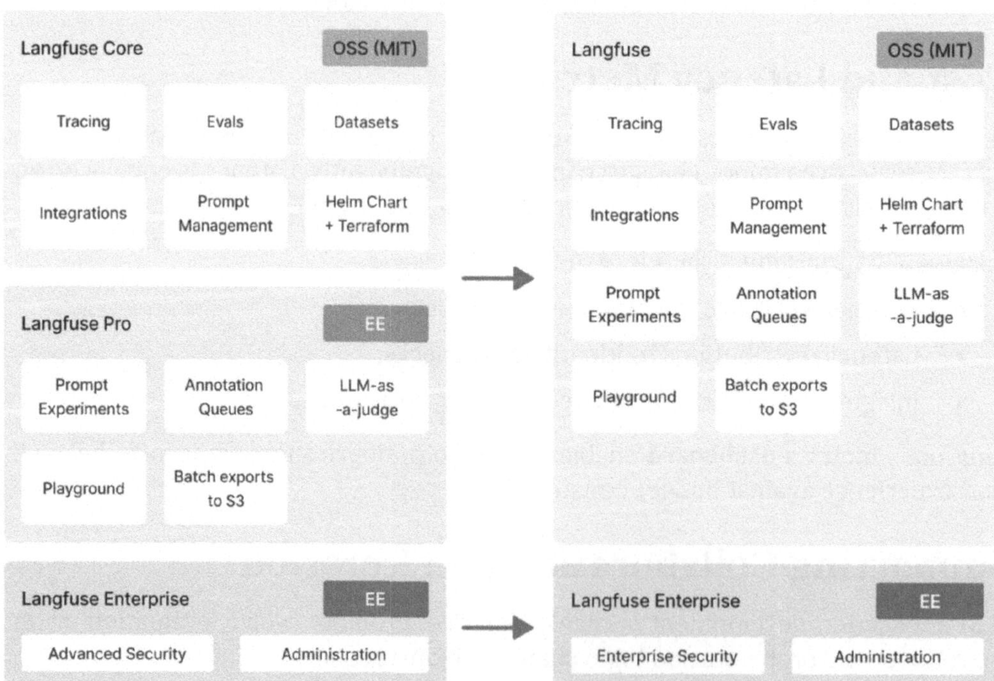

Figure 4.1: *The Open-Sourced Features of Langfuse*
(*Source – https://langfuse.com/blog/2025-06-04-open-sourcing-langfuse-product*)

Motivation behind the Decision

Langfuse lays out several key reasons for this shift:

- **Trust and Community Engagement**: They believe that removing commercial barriers builds deeper trust with developers and invites collaboration on contributions.
- **Feature Parity with Market Expectations**: Certain features (such as "LLM-as-a-judge," evaluation tooling, playground) are becoming market standards. The team argues that these capabilities should not be hidden behind paywalls but must be widely accessible to move the ecosystem forward.
- **Faster Iteration and Feedback**: With features fully in the open, both adoption and feedback cycles accelerate, making the product more responsive to real-world needs.
- **Refocusing Commercial Effort**: After open sourcing these formerly commercial features, Langfuse will concentrate its commercial efforts on cloud and enterprise features (some of which includes platform scaling, advanced security, and enterprise support) while leaving the core product fully open.

Langfuse began as an open-source project from the start, founded on principles such as:

- Users having full access to their data;
- Being model-agnostic and stack-agnostic in integrations; and,
- Allowing extensibility and customization for unique workflows.

With this announcement, they **removed the commercial boundary** and opened more of the product to even more users.

Langfuse already has a robust footprint: over **15 million monthly SDK installs**, over **6 million Docker pulls**, and **8,000+ monthly active self-hosted instances**.

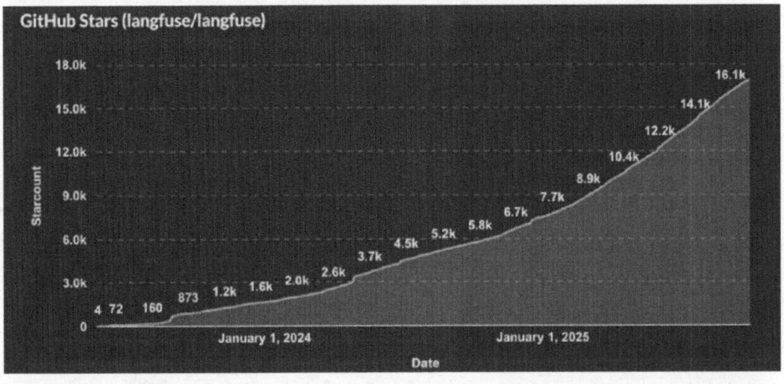

***Figure 4.2:** GitHub Stars for the Langfuse Project on https://github.com/langfuse/Langfuse*
Source – https://langfuse.com/blog/2025-06-04-open-sourcing-langfuse-product

Even today, Langfuse is one of the most popular and preferred choices of the developers in the LLM Engineering domain, having more than 24,000 stars on its GitHub project and more than a 100 contributors.

The community support to Langfuse is also very engaging with more than 1000 on-going discussions on its GitHub discussions page including ideas for future development and support to existing users. Langfuse also has a very fast development cycle with new features and fixes rolling out every other day and till date has active contributions being made by its founders, the CEO and founding members of the team.

With this in mind, let us briefly look at LangSmith, to which Langfuse is an open-source alternative.

Langfuse versus LangSmith

To understand LangSmith, it is essential first to understand the broader **LangChain** ecosystem. We introduced LangChain in *Chapter 1* already as an orchestration framework. LangChain began as one of the earliest and the most popular frameworks for building applications powered by LLMs. It provides a composable structure for chaining together multiple components—prompts, models, retrieval functions, tools, and agents—into complex reasoning pipelines.

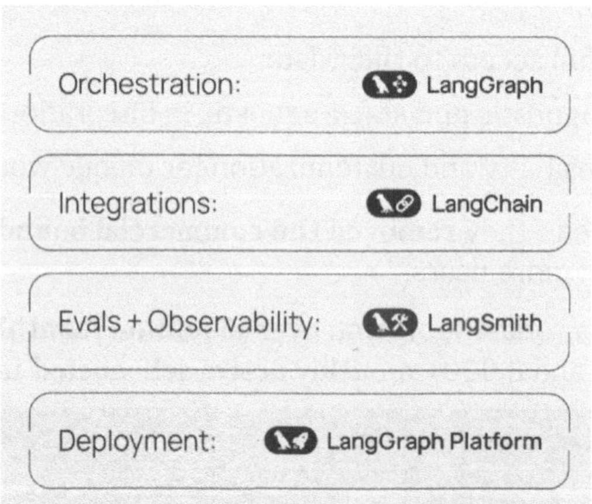

Figure 4.3: *The LangChain Ecosystem*

Building on this foundation, another one of its complimentary frameworks, **LangGraph**, introduces a graph-based orchestration model that represents an LLM application as a dynamic workflow of interconnected nodes. Each node may perform reasoning, retrieval, or decision-making, while the edges define the flow of data and control.

Within this ecosystem, **LangSmith** serves as the observability, debugging, and evaluation layer. It was created by the same team behind LangChain and LangGraph to provide developers with a platform for:

- **Tracing and visualizing chains or graphs** as they execute.
- **Recording and replaying runs** for debugging and optimization.
- **Comparing model outputs** for A/B testing.
- **Evaluating performance** with both automated and human-scored metrics.

Because LangSmith is **natively integrated** with LangChain and LangGraph, it can automatically capture detailed metadata about every chain execution, tool call, and model response offering insights into how an application behaves.

LangSmith is, however, a commercial product. It is offered through a hosted, paid service operated by LangChain Inc., with usage-based pricing tiers. While it simplifies setup and provides advanced visualization tools out of the box, self-hosting is not officially supported. This makes LangSmith ideal for teams already committed to the LangChain ecosystem who prefer managed infrastructure and enterprise-grade reliability.

Here is a comparison summary between the two platforms:

Feature / Capability	LangSmith	Langfuse	Notes / Comments
Tracing and Chain / Graph Visualizations	✔	✔	Both platforms support capturing execution traces of LLM chains and workflows.
Prompt Versioning / Experimentation	✔	✔	The ability to version prompts, run A/B experiments, and manage prompt history is present in both.
Evaluation & Scoring (LLM-as-judge, rubric templates)	✔	✔	Automated evaluation with built-in templates or custom evaluators is a core feature in both.
Human Annotation / Manual Labeling	✔	✔	Both allow human feedback or annotation of model outputs within the UI.
Metrics: Latency, Cost, Token Usage	✔	✔	Monitoring of latency, cost (token consumption), and performance over time is supported by both.
Dataset & Data Management	✔	✔	Facilities for managing datasets tied to evaluations, trace filtering, and versioning are included.
Playground / Interactive Testing	✔ (but limited)	✔	Both include "playground" or testing UIs, though feature richness may differ in edge cases.

Feature / Capability	LangSmith	Langfuse	Notes / Comments
Model-agnostic / multi-framework support	–	✔	Langfuse is built with integration flexibility for many frameworks (beyond LangChain).
Self-hosting / Data ownership	– (enterprise only)	✔	Self-hosting and full data control is a strong design point for Langfuse; LangSmith's self-hosting is limited by licensing.
Extensibility / Custom Evaluators	✔ (to some extent)	✔	Both platforms allow extension, though Langfuse's open-source nature provides greater flexibility.
Enterprise Features (RBAC, audit logs, security)	✔	✔ (or via paid add-ons)	Premium security, role-based access control, and audit logging likely require higher tiers in both systems.

Table 4.1: *Table Showing Comparison between LangSmith and Langfuse. Source – https://astralinsights.ai/wp-content/uploads/2024/06/AI-Comparison-White-Paper-June-2024.pdf*

In practice, the choice between Langfuse and LangSmith depends less on feature comparison and more on the context of the application.

LangSmith is most effective when:

- We build primarily with LangChain or LangGraph.
- Seamless integration is favored over cross-framework flexibility.
- We prefer a managed service that minimizes operational overhead.
- Data governance policies permit sending traces to a hosted environment.

Langfuse is particularly suitable when:

- Applications span multiple frameworks or custom pipelines.
- Data privacy or compliance requirements mandate on-premises storage.
- We wish to extend or customize observability logic, namely on building custom evaluators.
- We want to avoid vendor lock-in and maintain long-term control over the observability stack.

In some organizations, both tools may even coexist. Developers building quick prototypes in LangChain might rely on LangSmith for immediate feedback, while production systems integrate Langfuse for full observability and self-hosted control.

The Core Capabilities of Langfuse

Langfuse gives developers complete visibility and control over how their LLM applications behave in real-world environments. As LLM systems evolve from prototypes into production-ready solutions, developers face growing complexity due to multi-step workflows, external data sources, prompt variations, model versioning, and dynamic user interactions. Managing these components effectively requires a robust observability framework. Langfuse as an eco-system offers the following features collectively under its Products and Platform umbrella.

- **Observability** provides the tracing capabilities to help us see what is happening inside our application.
- **Prompt Management** brings version control and prompt optimization.
- **Evaluation** for systematic quality measurement through automated and human assessments.
- **Metrics** quantify application performance, enabling data-driven decisions.
- **API and Data Platform** for encapsulating different workflows and customizations using a unified API.

In the following sections, we will explore each of these core capabilities and examine how Langfuse implements them, and how they collectively improve the reliability and interpretability of AI systems.

Observability

Observability is at the heart of Langfuse. It enables developers to trace and visualize the end-to-end flow of the system – from user input through intermediate reasoning steps and API calls, to the final response. In *Chapter 2, LLM Monitoring Principles and Metrics*, we defined a "trace" which is the central unit of observability in Langfuse. Each trace captures key metadata such as model name, latency, token usage, intermediate outputs, and any chained calls made to vector databases, tools, or APIs. This level of visibility allows us to:

- Debug complex reasoning chains and multi-step agents.
- Identify failure modes or unexpected behaviors.
- Correlate latency and cost metrics with performance outcomes.
- Understand how model parameters and prompts influence outputs.

While Langfuse offers native SDKs for Python and JavaScript/TypeScript, its observability model is **framework-agnostic**. It integrates not only with LangChain but also with custom-built pipelines. Developers can instrument traces manually or automatically, making Langfuse adaptable to any system architecture – from small

RAG prototypes to large-scale enterprise AI agents. For languages other than Python/JS, Langfuse offers a public API which we will see later in the chapter.

One of the most compelling features of Langfuse is its ability to integrate with any LLM providers, framework and tools. This design makes it extremely flexible to integrate Langfuse in any LLM engineering project without making changes to the underlying tech stack. The image below shows some of the examples of the broad range of integration options available. The full exhaustive list can be found at **https://langfuse.com/integrations.**

Figure 4.4: *Langfuse Integration Examples.*
(Source: https://langfuse.com/integrations)

Under observability, Langfuse offers a ton of features to work with LLM traces. We will deep dive into these features in *Chapter 5, Observability in Langfuse* with concrete code examples but here is a list of the most commonly used ones:

- **Sessions** group traces together to give a holistic view of the entire interaction. Traces can be clubbed under a common `sessionId` just like HTTP sessions and then viewed as a complete user journey.
- Speaking of **users**, Langfuse also lets us add a `userId` to the traces which can easily distinguish between different users of the system. The definition of user is also quite flexible, and users can simply be identified based on the `userId`.

- Another option to organize traces is using **Environments** and **Tags.** Environments can separate context between production, staging or development and tags can categorize traces which could then later be used as filters.
- **Token and Cost Tracking** is an essential part of LLM observability and Langfuse by default adds this information to the traces. For many popular models like GPT, Claude of Anthropic or Google Gemini, this information is pre-populated for the traces without any extra effort. For customized models or models with non-standard pricing, Langfuse offers the option to add our own cost and token usage model either via the UI or even programmatically using the API/SDK.
- Finally, observability data should be easy to visualize and share with relevant stakeholders. For this, Langfuse allows us to create **customized Dashboards** which use its flexible query engine and rich visualization options. Data from these dashboards can also be downloaded as CSV files. This way, users have the option to do data analytics either within Langfuse itself or with external platforms.

In summary, the observability features of Langfuse turn the inner workings of an LLM into practical insights. They help teams replace trial-and-error development with a clear, evidence-based process where each model action can be understood and refined accordingly.

Prompt Management

The behavior of an LLM is largely governed by how prompts are structured, phrased, and parameterized. As applications grow in complexity, **managing prompts** systematically becomes just as important as managing source code and hence any observability platform is incomplete without the feature of prompt management.

Over time, developers experiment with numerous prompt variants to improve accuracy, tone, or reasoning. Without proper organization we can lose track of which version produced which result, or why one prompt outperformed another. Langfuse provides a dedicated product for creating, versioning, testing, and deploying prompts, so that prompt engineering becomes a controlled, reproducible process.

Prompts are not only written by developers, but even by **non-technical users**. Product managers, content designers, and domain experts often have valuable insights into tone, clarity, and factual correctness. Langfuse enables these users to participate directly in prompt development through a user-friendly and intuitive UI. From the UI, users can view, edit, and test prompts without writing code. This helps organizations bring linguistic and domain expertise directly into the optimization loop.

Langfuse decouples prompts from application logic by hosting them externally and serving them dynamically through the SDK/API. This means we can edit and **update prompts in Langfuse without redeploying the application**. We can simply reference the prompt by name, version and a label and get a prompt at runtime. This decoupling shortens iteration cycles enabling faster experimentation and reduced engineering overhead. If a newly deployed prompt leads to unexpected behavior, teams can instantly roll back to a previous version with a single action from the UI itself. Langfuse ensures that prompt management introduces no latency or availability impact on production applications. Prompts are fetched and cached locally by the client SDK, meaning updates propagate seamlessly in the background.

Langfuse's approach to prompt management combines teamwork, safety, and flexibility. It allows non-technical team members to fine-tune prompts using an intuitive visual interface, enables developers to update them independently of release cycles, and gives us complete version control without affecting runtime performance.

Chapter 6, Prompt Management in Langfuse, will be completely dedicated to Prompt Management, and we will see in detail all the advanced features of this product.

Evaluation

Under its evaluation product, Langfuse provides an integrated framework that supports multiple evaluation methods, enabling developers to assign scores to traces, sessions, or observations. **Scores** are the primary data object for evaluating outputs where every evaluation results into a consistent scoring model. The system supports built-in evaluators (for dimensions such as hallucination, relevance, toxicity, helpfulness) via **LLM-as-a-Judge** templates, which comes with best-practice prompt patterns for assessing output quality.

LLM evaluation boosts language model accuracy and reliability, leading to better user experience and trust in our AI application. The evaluation framework of Langfuse enables teams to maintain high-quality and trustworthy AI applications by systematically detecting inaccuracies, measuring performance, and tracking improvements over time. Through structured metrics, developers can monitor response quality, enhance reliability, and prevent issues before deployment and ultimately building user confidence and minimizing operational risks. LLM evaluation can be divided into 2 main segments:

Offline Evaluation:

- Evaluating the application before deployment using pre-defined test datasets.
- Used during development to measure improvements / regressions.
- It is repeatable and allows for clear accuracy measurement with available ground truth.

Online Evaluation:

- Evaluating the application in a live, real-world environment in production.
- Used to track success rates, user satisfaction scores, or other metrics.
- Can collect actual user feedback and be used to run A/B tests.

The following figure shows the continuous loop between offline and online evaluations for improving the quality of outputs. For a comprehensive evaluation, a combination of online and offline evaluations is often applied.

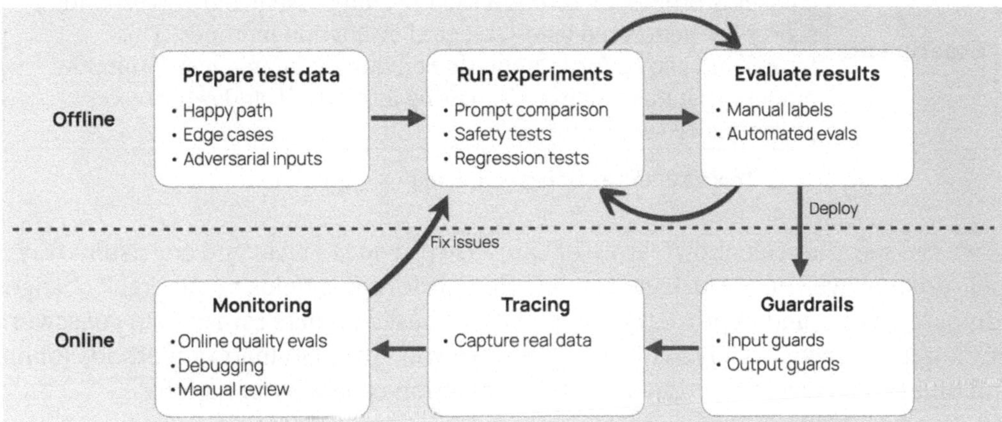

Figure 4.5: *How to Continuously Improve LLM Products Evidently by AI*
Source -https://www.youtube.com/watch?v=x9mfMkBWwCY

Langfuse includes the following core concepts in its Evaluation:

Concept	Explanation
Scores	Scores form the foundation of Langfuse's evaluation system. They are data entries that record assessment results and can be linked to different Langfuse objects such as traces, sessions, or observations. Each score is a measurable performance aspect like accuracy or relevance and helps standardize how model quality is tracked and compared over time.
Evaluation Methods	These represent the procedures or tools used to generate scores. Evaluation methods may range from automated rule-based scripts to advanced *LLM-as-a-Judge* techniques, where another model rates outputs according to defined criteria. Langfuse also supports external or custom evaluators through its API, allowing flexible integration into existing workflows.

Concept	Explanation
Datasets	In Langfuse, datasets act as structured collections of test inputs paired with expected outputs that serve as benchmarks for evaluation. They enable consistent testing across multiple models or prompt versions, ensuring that comparisons are fair, reproducible, and data driven. Datasets can be reused across experiments to monitor performance trends over time.
Experiments	Experiments are the practical execution phase of evaluation, where a dataset is processed through the LLM application and corresponding scores are generated using selected evaluation methods. This framework allows for systematic benchmarking between prompts, model variants, or releases, creating a traceable and repeatable performance testing process.

Table 4.2: *Core Concepts in Langfuse Evaluation*

As we can see, the evaluation feature of Langfuse provides a clear and consistent way to measure how well our LLM-based application performs. It helps teams track changes, compare results, and improve their applications based on data rather than guesswork. In *Chapter 7, Evaluating LLMs in Langfuse*, we will cover evaluation methods (online and offline) and drift detection using the Evaluation capability of Langfuse.

Getting Started with Langfuse

This section explores the different ways to use Langfuse, helping us choose the approach that best fits our technical environment, organizational needs, and security requirements. We introduce the two main paths: **Langfuse Cloud**, a managed, scalable solution hosted by Langfuse, and **Self-Hosted Langfuse**, which gives organizations full control over their infrastructure and data. The section discusses the operational, security, and cost considerations of each path and highlights the trade-offs between ease-of-use, control, and compliance. We will gain a clear understanding of scenarios in which each usage model is preferable, to make informed decisions when setting up Langfuse. Let us start by looking at the high-level view of the system architecture of Langfuse.

Langfuse Technical Architecture

Keeping in line with its true Open-Source nature, Langfuse only uses open-source frameworks and components in its design which makes it possible to deploy it locally or on any cloud infrastructure (either provider based on private cloud).

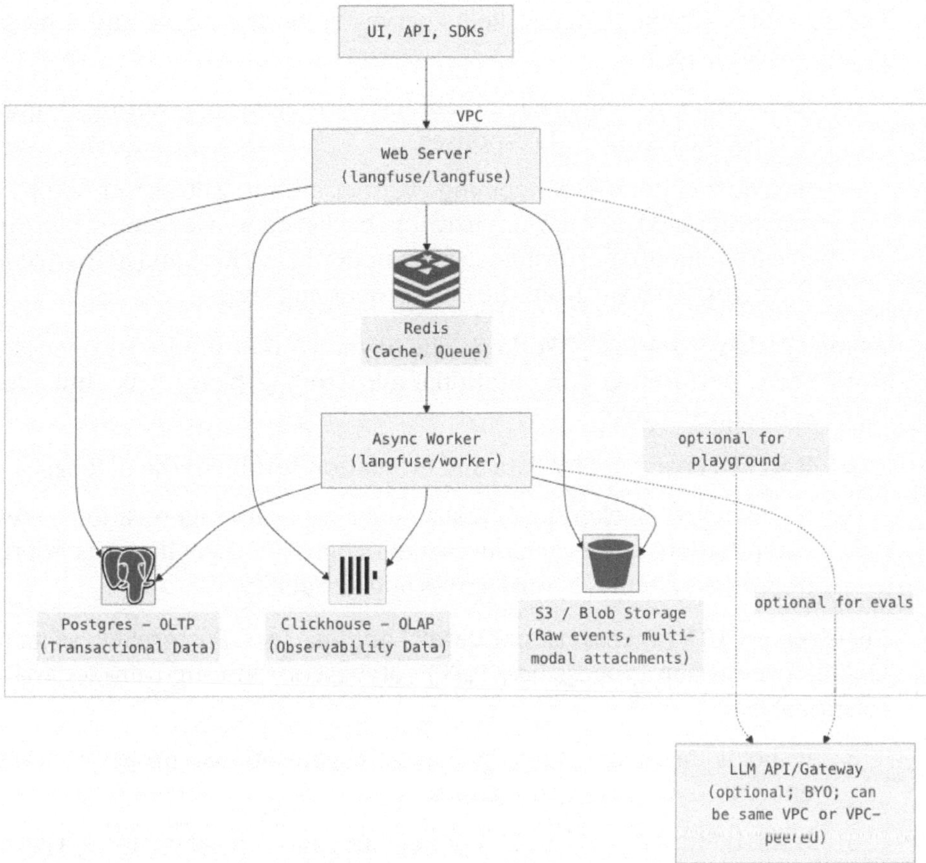

Figure 4.6: *Langfuse System Architecture. Source https://langfuse.com/self-hosting*

The architecture of Langfuse is designed for reliability, scalability, and maintainability, enabling it to handle large volumes of LLM application data efficiently. The system follows a modular and distributed design that separates concerns between data collection, storage, processing, and visualization. Each component plays a well-defined role, ensuring the system remains performant and fault tolerant.

- **Web Server (Langfuse/Langfuse):** The Web Server is the central entry point to the Langfuse system. It handles incoming requests from the UI, API, and SDKs, and acts as a gateway for both user interactions and data ingestion. It is deployed within a Virtual Private Cloud (VPC) for secure and controlled access.
    - It validates and routes data from clients to the backend.
    - It interacts directly with Redis for caching and queueing operations.
    - It communicates with databases (Postgres and ClickHouse) for storage and retrieval.

- **Redis/Valkey (Cache, Queue):** Redis serves as both a cache and a message queue within Langfuse.
    - As a cache, it helps reduce latency by temporarily storing frequently accessed data and API responses.
    - As a queue, it buffers incoming events from the web server before they are processed asynchronously by background workers. This design ensures smooth performance even under heavy load and helps decouple the ingestion layer from the data processing layer.
- **Async Worker (Langfuse/Worker):** The Async Worker processes queued jobs from Redis, performing computational and storage-heavy tasks outside the main web request cycle.
    - It writes observability data and evaluation results to the databases.
    - It manages background tasks such as data aggregation, metrics computation, and evaluation scheduling. This asynchronous approach improves system responsiveness and scalability.
- **Postgres – OLTP (Transactional Data):** Langfuse uses PostgreSQL as its main Online Transaction Processing (OLTP) database for storing transactional and relational data.
    - It holds metadata such as users, organizations, projects, datasets, encrypted API keys and settings.
    - Data integrity and ACID compliance make it ideal for structured, relational operations and administrative tasks.
- **ClickHouse – OLAP (Observability Data):** For analytics and high-volume observability data, Langfuse uses ClickHouse, a columnar Online Analytical Processing (OLAP) database.
    - It stores large-scale trace data, logs, and metrics for fast aggregation and real-time analytics.
    - The optimized columnar format of ClickHouse ensures low-latency queries on millions of records, supporting the dashboards and visualizations of Langfuse efficiently. This division between Postgres and ClickHouse ensures that transactional and analytical workloads remain isolated and optimized.
- **S3 / Blob Storage:** Langfuse integrates with AWS S3-compatible object storage to store raw event data and multi-modal attachments (such as files, images, or model inputs/outputs).
    - It is particularly useful for retaining large or binary artifacts that are impractical to store in a relational database.

 - S3 storage is also used optionally for the playground feature, which allows users to test prompts and experiments with real data.

- **LLM API / Gateway (Optional):** Langfuse can optionally connect to an LLM API or Gateway — either within the same VPC or through VPC peering.
  - This connection enables direct integration with model-serving endpoints for evaluations or real-time tracing.
  - It can be user-provided ("bring your own" setup), allowing flexible deployment across different environments and compliance requirements.

Data Flow Overview

1. Client applications (UI, API, or SDKs) send traces and evaluation data to the **Web Server.**
2. The Web Server caches requests and pushes them to **Redis**, ensuring no data loss during high traffic.
3. **Async Workers** consume these tasks, process them, and write results into **Postgres**, **ClickHouse**, or **S3**, depending on data type.
4. Metrics and traces are then aggregated and visualized through the Langfuse UI, accessible to developers and analysts.

Architectural Advantages

- **Scalability:** Asynchronous processing and separate OLTP/OLAP systems handle increasing data volume efficiently.
- **Resilience:** Redis queues buffer traffic spikes, thereby ensuring stability.
- **Performance:** Caching and columnar analytics deliver low-latency responses for both ingestion and querying.
- **Flexibility:** Optional integrations (S3, LLM gateways) make it adaptable for different use cases and infrastructure setups.

Optimizations in the Architecture of Langfuse

Irrespective of whether we use Langfuse Cloud or self-host it, it runs the exact same codebase. The only difference between the two approaches is that in the latter, we have to bring in our own infrastructure. Langfuse itself hosts the cloud version, which is the most widely used option, serving tens of thousands of teams in a production environment. This is made possible only because of its optimized and highly available architecture that is able to scale to the needs of its users. Here is a list of the most powerful optimizations:

- **Batched Trace Processing:** Incoming traces are collected in batches by the Langfuse Web Server and first saved to S3. A reference is added to Redis for queueing, and the Worker later processes and loads them into ClickHouse. This approach prevents slowdowns or errors during traffic spikes.
- **Fast API Key Lookup:** API keys used by LLMs are stored in Redis memory, allowing the system to verify requests quickly without repeatedly checking the database. This reduces load and speeds up authentication.
- **Efficient Prompt Caching:** Prompts are cached locally by the SDKs/API and refreshed in the background. They're also stored in Redis, so frequently used prompts can be fetched instantly without database queries.
- **Dedicated Analytics Database:** Analytical and read-heavy queries are handled by ClickHouse, which provides fast responses even when working with large amounts of observability data.
- **Support for Large Files:** Traces from multi-model models containing large files, such as videos or other media, are uploaded directly from the client SDKs to S3 or compatible storage systems for efficient handling.
- **Reliable Event Storage:** All tracing and evaluation data is saved to S3 or blob storage before being written to the main database. This ensures that data is never lost, even if the database is temporarily unavailable.
- **Non-Disruptive Upgrades Using Background Migrations:** Long-running database migrations required during system updates are processed as background tasks, minimizing downtime and keeping regular operations running smoothly. These tasks may involve adding or backfilling columns or migrating data between storages. Background migrations start when the worker container launches and continue in the background until they finish or fail.

With this in mind, let us jump into the two options we have for using Langfuse. Both approaches have their pros and cons, and our objective here is to give the readers an open and fair comparison between the two.

Langfuse Cloud

The quickest way to get started with Langfuse is by using its cloud version. This is completely managed by the team at Langfuse and is also the easiest way to start using. Although this way is free to start it may require upfront costs if usage exceeds beyond the free limits. We recommend starting with a **Hobby** account in the learning stage to get a feel of Langfuse and later migrate to a paid version (or self-host) depending on the usage.

To get started with Langfuse, we will create a free account at: **`https://cloud.langfuse.com/auth/sign-up`**

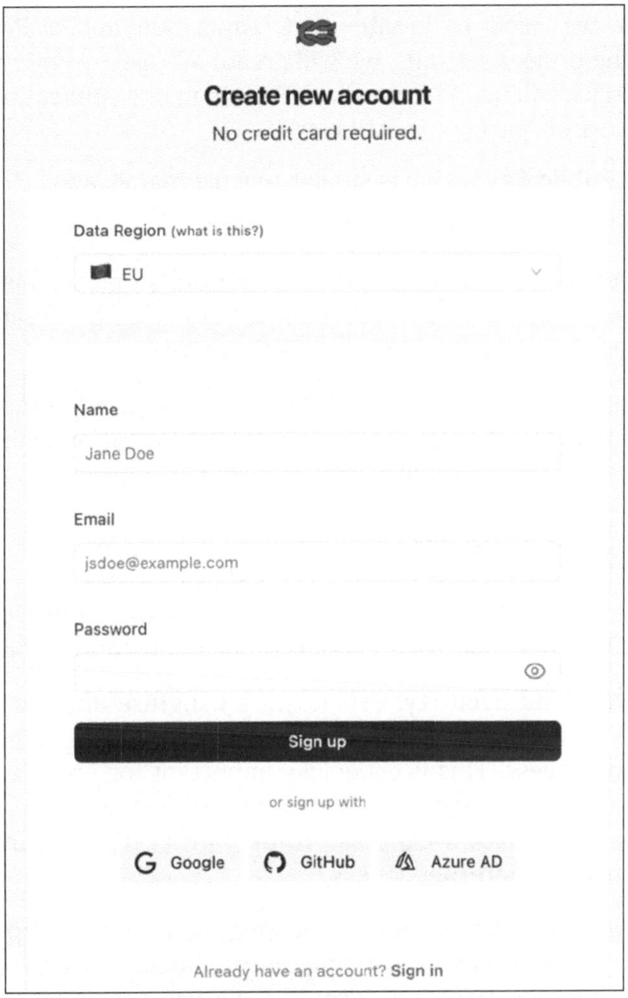

***Figure 4.7**: Langfuse Signup Page*

Besides the basic details like **`Name`**, **`Email`**, and **`Password`**, we need to choose a **Data Region**. This is very crucial since it will determine in which of the geographical locations our data will be stored. Langfuse Cloud uses Amazon Web Services (AWS) for data storage. At the time of writing, there are 3 options available:

- **US:** Oregon (AWS us-west-2)
- **EU:** Ireland (AWS eu-west-1)
- **HIPAA:** Oregon (AWS us-west-2) - HIPAA-compliant region (available only in paid plans)

Ideally, we should choose a location which is closest to our physical location and complies with data protection laws and regulations.

After signing up, we need to create an Organization and a Project within the organization. In the project settings, we will create a Project API Key. This is basically the authentication we will need to use the SDK/API in our applications to send traces to Langfuse. There are 2 parts of an API key:

- **Langfuse Public Key** which is similar to a username; and,
- **Langfuse Secret Key** which is the password.

Secret keys can only be viewed once after creation, so please make sure they are copied in a secure location. Any number of API keys can be created for a project. Deletion of API keys is permanent and cannot be undone.

If you plan to use Langfuse Cloud for this book, we suggest completing this setup before moving on to the next chapters. Besides the signing up and creation of API keys, there is no other setup required (for a Hobby account) to get started with Langfuse.

Self-Hosting Langfuse

Users may opt to self-host Langfuse instead of using the cloud version for several reasons, ranging from data control and compliance to customization and scalability.

- **Data Privacy and Security:** Self-hosting Langfuse ensures that all sensitive data stays within a user's own infrastructure, providing full control over data storage and access. This is especially important for organizations with strict compliance requirements or regulations that mandate local data residency. Self-hosting also allows Langfuse to operate in high-security environments without requiring internet access.

- **Control and Customization:** Self-hosting allows for in-depth customization and direct integration with existing internal tools and APIs. Users can modify or extend the open-source core of Langfuse without vendor constraints, building custom features or workflows on top of the platform.

- **Scalability and Performance:** There are no arbitrary usage or scalability limits when self-hosting; users can deploy the same horizontally scalable architecture that powers Langfuse Cloud, supporting anything from small tests to massive production environments processing billions of events.

- **Compliance and Enterprise Requirements:** Enterprises can self-host Langfuse to meet internal security and compliance policies, support advanced audit requirements, or ensure compatibility with internal authentication and networking practices.

- **Cost Considerations:** For organizations with substantial infrastructure or operational expertise, self-hosting can be more cost-effective over the long run especially at large scale since there are no ongoing managed service fees.

When self-hosting Langfuse, we need to build the same infrastructure that we saw in the architecture in the previous section. This means before we can self-host, we need to be ready to provide the following components:

- **Postgres**: For transactional storage like users, organizations and projects.
- **ClickHouse**: OLAP database for traces, observations, and scores.
- **Redis/Valkey cache:** For queue and cache operations.
- **AWS S3:** For all incoming events, multi-modal inputs, file exports.

All of these components can either be self-managed or be used from cloud vendors directly. The main requirement is that we have full access to these components so that Langfuse can use them without interruptions.

For self-hosting, the recommended **minimum requirements** are:

ClickHouse

Langfuse supports ClickHouse versions >= 24.3. For production setups, the minimum recommended configuration includes:

- **Replicas**: At least 3 replicas for production setups.
- **Resources**: Set `resourcesPreset` to **large** or more for larger deployments.
- **Storage**: Start with a large volume (100Gi) to prevent early resizing.

The ClickHouse user must have the following grants (Replace 'user' with your actual ClickHouse username):

```
GRANT INSERT ON default.* TO 'user';
GRANT SELECT ON default.* TO 'user';
GRANT ALTER UPDATE, ALTER DELETE ON default.* TO 'user';
GRANT CREATE ON default.* TO 'user';
GRANT DROP TABLE ON default.* TO 'user';
```

Postgres Database

Postgres serves as the main database for transactional workloads. Langfuse supports Postgres versions >= 12 and uses the ***public*** schema in the selected database. Langfuse does not specify exact minimum requirements for this database.

Redis/Valkey Cache

Redis/Valkey is used as a fast in-memory data structure store for queue and cache operations **Langfuse does not support Redis/Valkey Cluster Mode** - any replica would only serve as a stand-by instance. For production we will need at least 1.5 GB of memory to start with.

Docker

Langfuse uses Docker to containerize the application. There are two containers:

- **Langfuse Web**: The web server that serves as the frontend and hosts the UI.
- **Langfuse Worker**: The application that handles backend tasks.

For production environments, it is recommended to use at least 2 CPUs and 4 GB of RAM for both containers, at least two instances of the Web container for high availability. If using auto-scaling, add instances once the CPU utilization exceeds 50% on either container.

LLM API / Gateway

Although optional but highly recommended is to set up connections to the LLM providers we plan to use in our applications. For features like the **Playground, LLM-as-a-judge** and **Prompt Experiments,** these connections are mandatory, and the book covers these topics heavily. This means you need to have access to the LLM models for either one of the following:

- OpenAI (used in this book)
- Azure OpenAI
- Anthropic
- Google Vertex
- Amazon Bedrock

Once our infrastructure is ready, we can start deploying Langfuse.

Local or Non-Production Deployment Using Docker

Docker setup can be used for a quick try out before we are ready to use self-hosted Langfuse in production. It is sort of the Hobby account for the self-hosted version. We can do this on a local computer or a Virtual Machine (VM) inside a cloud provider like AWS, GCP or Azure. Docker setup can be done in 3 easy steps:

1. Clone the official Langfuse repository from GitHub.
2. Update the secrets in the **`docker-compose.yml`.**
3. Start the docker container.

You can also use this code block on your local machine:

```
git clone https://github.com/langfuse/langfuse.git
cd Langfuse
docker compose up
```

This will deploy Langfuse with all the infrastructure on your machine (or VM) using the default docker setup for each of the components. To browse the UI, simply go to **http://localhost:3000.**

While this setup is easy to start with, it is **not recommended** for advanced usage or production. This is mainly because this setup has very low availability due to all components running locally and will not scale beyond very simple usage as it lacks any backup functionality. We should use docker only if we wish to play around with the setup and are curious about running Langfuse on our personal computers. This is also a good, low-cost option for learning purposes.

Production Deployment Using Kubernetes or Terraform

For production or real usage, we can choose one of the two options:

Kubernetes (Helm)

- Deploy Langfuse on any Kubernetes cluster using the official Helm chart.
- Requires access to a Kubernetes cluster and Helm installed locally.
- By default, it deploys application containers and data stores (PostgreSQL, ClickHouse, Redis) but should be over-ridden by point to the infrastructure we have deployed.

The Helm chart supports configuration for sizing, external databases, and storage providers including S3. The list of values that should be updated is mentioned here:

https://github.com/langfuse/langfuse-k8s/blob/main/README.md.

In this file, we can see the full list of values that need to be customized and updated before we can deploy Langfuse. We will not go into the details of the values since it is out of scope for the book. The README file above has a good explanation of how to update chart values for the Kubernetes deployment

After updating the values, we can run:

```
helm repo add langfuse https://langfuse.github.io/langfuse-k8s
helm repo update
helm install langfuse langfuse/langfuse -f values.yaml
```

Terraform

By default, the Terraform modules will provision the necessary infrastructure for the application containers and data stores. We should configure the module to use existing infrastructure resources.

AWS (Terraform)

- Uses the official Terraform module **https://github.com/langfuse/langfuse-terraform-aws.**
- Deploys on Amazon Elastic Kubernetes Service (EKS) with managed services for databases and storage.
- Minimal configuration requires only a domain URL.

Azure (Terraform)

- Uses the official Terraform module **https://github.com/langfuse/langfuse-terraform-azure.**
- Deploys on Azure Kubernetes Service (AKS) with Azure Database for PostgreSQL, Redis Cache, and Storage Account.
- Creates complete stack with Virtual Network, Application Gateway with Web Application Firewall (WAF), and private endpoints.

GCP (Terraform)

- Uses the official Terraform module **https://github.com/langfuse/langfuse-terraform-gcp.**
- Deploys on Google Kubernetes Engine (GKE) with Cloud SQL PostgreSQL, Memorystore Redis, and Cloud Storage.
- Includes VPC setup, TLS certificates, and Cloud DNS configuration.

All production deployments follow the same architecture with:

- **Application Containers**: Langfuse Web (UI/APIs) and Langfuse Worker (async processing).
- **Storage Components**: PostgreSQL (transactional), ClickHouse (analytics), Redis/Valkey (cache/queue), S3/Blob Store (events/exports).
- **Optional LLM API/Gateway** for certain features as mentioned in the last section.

These deployments are optimized for production environments with high availability, scaling capabilities, and security features. In the final section of this chapter, we will see the environment variables that are required to self-host any instance of Langfuse.

Setting up Environment Variables for Self-Hosting

Setting up Langfuse requires a lot of configuration via environment variables. Whether you are using the Docker/Kubernetes/Terraform setup, these variables need to be known and filled out in the configuration where applicable to make sure the setup works. The full list of variables is available at **https://langfuse.com/self-hosting/configuration.** The tables below show a summary of the variables that are mandatory.

Postgres / Database

Name	Explanation	Required?
`DATABASE_URL`	Connection string for the Postgres database. Instead of **`DATABASE_URL`** we can separate the variables into **`DATABASE_HOST`** **`DATABASE_USERNAME`** **`DATABASE_PASSWORD`** **`DATABASE_NAME`** **`DATABASE_ARGS`**	**Yes**

Table 4.3: *Database env Variables*

ClickHouse

Name	Explanation	Required?
`CLICKHOUSE_MIGRATION_URL`	Migration URL (TCP) for ClickHouse (pattern clickhouse://<host>:(9000/9440)).	**Yes**
`CLICKHOUSE_MIGRATION_SSL`	Set to true to use SSL for ClickHouse migrations (default false).	No (optional)
`CLICKHOUSE_URL`	HTTP(S) URL of the ClickHouse instance (pattern http(s)://<host>:(8123/8443)).	**Yes**
`CLICKHOUSE_USER`	ClickHouse username (needs **`SELECT/ALTER/INSERT/CREATE/DELETE`** grants).	**Yes**
`CLICKHOUSE_PASSWORD`	Password for ClickHouse user.	**Yes**

Table 4.4: *Clickhouse env Variables*

Redis / Cache

Name	Explanation	Required?
`REDIS_CONNECTION_STRING`	Connection string for your Redis instance	**Yes**

Table 4.5: *Redis/Cache env Variables*

Storage / S3 / Blob (Events, Media, Exports)

Name	Explanation	Required?
`LANGFUSE_S3_EVENT_UPLOAD_BUCKET`	S3 bucket name where event/tracing data is uploaded.	**Yes**
`LANGFUSE_S3_MEDIA_UPLOAD_BUCKET`	Bucket for uploading media or multi-modal attachments.	**Yes**

Table 4.6: *S3/Storage env Variables*

Authentication / Secrets / Security

Name	Explanation	Required?
NEXTAUTH_URL	Public URL of your Langfuse web deployment (like https://yourdomain.com).	**Yes**
NEXTAUTH_SECRET	Secret to validate login session cookies (We can generate this using the command `openssl rand -base64 32`).	**Yes**
SALT	Salt used for hashed API keys (We can generate this securely using the command `openssl rand -base64 32`).	**Yes**
ENCRYPTION_KEY	256-bit key (hex, 64 chars) used to encrypt sensitive data (We can generate this securely using the command with `openssl rand -hex 32`).	**Yes**

Table 4.7: *Authentication/Secrets/Security env Variables*

Langfuse Features Included in Self-Hosting

When self-hosting, Langfuse offers additional features that help teams customize Langfuse deployments to match their infrastructure, compliance, and workflow needs. Whether it's configuring custom caching layers, securing data through encryption, setting up email alerts, or monitoring system health, these features can be configured using environment variables. Below are brief overviews of the main additional features available for self-hosted Langfuse deployments:

Caching

Langfuse includes built-in caching options for API keys and prompts to reduce latency. By caching frequently accessed objects in Redis, applications can respond faster and maintain smooth performance under high load. The cache configuration is fully adjustable through environment variables, with control over Time-to-Live (TTL) and cache enablement for specific components.

Name	Description
LANGFUSE_CACHE_API_KEY_ENABLED	Enables or disables caching for API keys (default: true).
LANGFUSE_CACHE_API_KEY_TTL_SECONDS	Sets the cache duration (TTL) for API keys in seconds (default: 300).
LANGFUSE_CACHE_PROMPT_ENABLED	Enables or disables caching for prompts (default: true).
LANGFUSE_CACHE_PROMPT_TTL_SECONDS	Sets the cache duration (TTL) for prompts in seconds (default: 300).

Table 4.8: *Caching env Variables*

Custom Base Path

The custom base path feature allows users to host Langfuse behind a reverse proxy or serve it under a sub path (for example, **yourdomain.com/langfuse**). This is particularly useful in large organizations or multi-app environments, where services are grouped under a shared domain. Configuring a base path ensures that all routes, static assets, and API endpoints remain correctly resolved even when Langfuse is not hosted at the root domain.

Name	Description
NEXT_PUBLIC_BASE_PATH	Defines a custom base path when Langfuse is served under a subdirectory (like /langfuse).
NEXT_PUBLIC_WEBAPP_URL	The full public URL of the Langfuse web interface, including protocol and base path.

Table 4.9: *Custom Base Path env Variables*

Encryption

Encryption settings allow sensitive information—such as API keys, secrets, or stored payloads—to be encrypted using a secure key before persisting to the database. This feature protects against data leakage and ensures compliance with security standards. The encryption mechanism is transparent to developers, requiring only an **ENCRYPTION_KEY** and **SALT** variables to enable encryption.

Logging

Langfuse provides configurable logging so that administrators can define log levels, specify log formats (text or JSON), and propagate HTTP headers into logs for correlation with external systems like Datadog or Grafana.

Name	Description
LANGFUSE_LOG_LEVEL	Sets log verbosity (trace, debug, info, warn, error, fatal; default: info).
LANGFUSE_LOG_FORMAT	Defines log output format (text or json; default: text).
LANGFUSE_LOG_PROPAGATED_HEADERS	Lists HTTP headers (comma-separated) to include in logs for correlation.

Table 4.10: *Logging env Variables*

Transactional Emails

Langfuse supports sending transactional emails, such as organization invites, password resets, and user onboarding notifications. Email delivery is configured via SMTP environment variables, allowing integration with services like SendGrid, SES, or custom SMTP servers. This capability enhances the self-hosted experience by enabling full user account lifecycle management.

Name	Description
`EMAIL_FROM`	Default "from" address used in transactional emails (including invites, password resets).
`EMAIL_SMTP_HOST`	SMTP server hostname or IP address.
`EMAIL_SMTP_PORT`	Port number for SMTP (usually 465 for SSL or 587 for TLS).
`EMAIL_SMTP_USER`	Username for SMTP authentication.
`EMAIL_SMTP_PASSWORD`	Password for SMTP authentication.
`EMAIL_SMTP_SECURE`	Enables secure (SSL/TLS) SMTP connections (true/false).
`EMAIL_SMTP_ALLOW_INVALID_CERT`	Allows invalid SSL certificates (should be used only for testing).

Table 4.11: *Transactional Emails env Variables*

Health and Readiness Checks

To ensure smooth operation in containerized or cloud-native deployments, Langfuse provides dedicated health and readiness endpoints. These checks monitor core components like the database, cache, and queue systems. By integrating with orchestration platforms (e.g., Kubernetes or Docker), the system can automatically restart or reschedule containers when dependencies become unavailable, ensuring high availability and stability.

Name	Description
`LANGFUSE_HEALTH_CHECK_PORT`	Port where health and readiness endpoints are served (default: 8080).
`LANGFUSE_HEALTH_CHECK_PATH`	Path for the health endpoint (default: `/healthz`).
`LANGFUSE_HEALTH_CHECK_INTERVAL_SECONDS`	Frequency (in seconds) for internal health probes (default: 30).

Table 4.12: *Health Check env Variables*

Enterprise Edition (Paid) Features

So far, the features we have seen are available on the self-hosted version without any limitations. All core Langfuse features and APIs are available under the open-source MIT license, with no limits on scale or functionality. However, Langfuse also offers additional customizable features mainly for organizations which are looking to get a full-scale experience for their users. The Enterprise Edition (EE) features require a separate license key that needs to be purchased through the sales team at Langfuse.

- **Project-Level Access Roles:** Enables fine-grained access control at the project level to better manage permissions across teams. Users in Langfuse will inherit the role of the organization they are part of. By using this feature, we can differentiate user access on a project level within the same organization.
- **Data Retention Policies:** Allows administrators to configure automatic data deletion based on retention periods for compliance and cost control. By default, Langfuse stores event data forever but with this EE feature the retention time can be reduced to a minimum of 3 days.
- **Audit Logs:** Keeps a detailed record of user and system actions for traceability and compliance audits.
- **UI Customization:** Let organizations tailor the Langfuse interface, including branding and appearance.
- **Organization Creators:** Restricts who can create new organizations within a self-hosted deployment.
- **Organization Management API:** Provides programmatic access to create, update, and manage organizations and projects.

To activate these features in a self-hosted deployment, add the following environment variable to your setup:

```
LANGFUSE_EE_LICENSE_KEY=<your-license-key>
```

Conclusion

This chapter introduced **Langfuse** in a comprehensive way. We discussed the need for specialized tools to track model performance, the open-source commitment of Langfuse, and how it compares with LangSmith within the broader LLM ecosystem. The chapter elucidated upon the core capabilities of Langfuse—observability, prompt management, and evaluation—and further, explored its architecture, deployment options, configuration settings, and enterprise features. In the next chapter, we shall take a deeper look at Observability in Langfuse along with a lot of code examples and hands-on experience of the UI of Langfuse.

References

- **Langfuse v/s LangSmith -** https://astralinsights.ai/wp-content/uploads/2024/06/AI-Comparison-White-Paper-June-2024.pdf
- **Remberg Use case of Langfuse -** https://langfuse.com/faq/all/ai-transparency-remberg-langfuse
- **Langfuse doubling down on Open Source -** https://langfuse.com/blog/2025-06-04-open-sourcing-langfuse-product
- **Langfuse GitHub discussions** - https://github.com/orgs/langfuse/discussions
- **Langfuse Home Page -** https://langfuse.com/
- **Langfuse Observability Overview** - https://langfuse.com/docs/observability/overview
- **Langfuse Prompt Management Overview -** https://langfuse.com/docs/prompt-management/overview
- **Langfuse Evaluation Overview** - https://langfuse.com/docs/evaluation/overview
- **How to continuously improve LLM products**? By Evidently AI https://www.youtube.com/watch?v=x9mfMkBWwCY
- **Langfuse Metrics Overview** - https://langfuse.com/docs/metrics/overview
- **Langfuse Self-hosting** - https://langfuse.com/self-hosting
- **Langfuse Self-hosting deployment containers** - https://langfuse.com/self-hosting/deployment/infrastructure/containers
- **Langfuse Self-hosting ClickHouse** - https://langfuse.com/self-hosting/deployment/infrastructure/clickhouse
- **Langfuse Self-hosting Docker**- https://langfuse.com/self-hosting/deployment/docker-compose
- **Langfuse Self-hosting AWS** - https://langfuse.com/self-hosting/deployment/aws
- **Langfuse Self-hosting Azure** - https://langfuse.com/self-hosting/deployment/azure
- **Langfuse Self-hosting GCP** - https://langfuse.com/self-hosting/deployment/gcp
- **Langfuse Self-hosting Configuration guide** - https://langfuse.com/self-hosting/configuration
- **Langfuse EE features** - https://langfuse.com/self-hosting/license-key

Chapter 5
Observability in Langfuse

Introduction

Observability is the center piece of reliable LLM applications, and we have seen how Langfuse provides a purpose-built platform for gaining deep visibility into how prompts, models, and responses behave in production. This chapter introduces the observability capabilities of Langfuse, explaining how metrics—such as latency, token usage, cost—can be collected, analyzed, and acted upon. This chapter sets the stage for hands-on prompt management and evaluation and will include several code examples on how to get started.

Structure

In this chapter, we will cover the following topics:

- Understanding the Observability Data Model in Langfuse
- Sending Your First Trace to Langfuse Using the Python SDK
- The Langfuse User Interface
- Token Usage and Cost tracking
- Core Observability Features in Langfuse
    - Sessions
    - User Tracking
    - Environments
    - Tags and Metadata
- Advanced Observability Features in Langfuse
    - Observation Types
    - Log Levels
    - Versioning and Releases

  - Trace URLs
  - Sampling
- Distributed Tracing
- Masking Sensitive Data in Traces

Understanding the Observability Data Model in Langfuse

Before we start sending data to Langfuse, let us quickly revise the fundamentals of observability in the context of Langfuse. The Observability Data Model is the core structure by which Langfuse represents and organizes all traceable events and workflows in our LLM applications. It is inspired by OpenTelemetry but extended to support LLM-specific constructs and use cases.

Langfuse SDK is based on OpenTelemetry which is an open-source observability framework that provides a standardized way to collect and export telemetry data — such as traces, metrics, and logs from software systems. It helps developers understand how their applications behave by offering a common data model and APIs for instrumenting code and analyzing performance across distributed systems.

Here are the main components of the data model and how they relate:

	Description	Role / Purpose
Trace	A top-level record representing a single operation or request.	Captures the full lifecycle of that operation, from input → internal steps → output + metadata.
Observation	A finer-grained record within a trace, representing a step, event or sub-operation (which includes calling a tool, invoking an LLM, retrieval, and the list continues). In traditional observability this is a span. Many observations can be nested inside a Trace.	Allows us to break down "what happened inside" the trace into meaningful pieces.
Sessions	Optional grouping of multiple traces under a higher level (for example, a conversation session).	Useful for multi-turn chat or workflows, so we can see all relevant traces for a user interaction in one place.
Scores	Flexible "score" objects attached to traces, sessions, or dataset runs.	These capture evaluation results (numeric, categorical, Boolean) and optionally link to specific observations.

Table 5.1: *Langfuse Observability Data Model*

Langfuse supports specialized types of observations, beyond generic spans/events. Examples include *generation, agent, tool, chain, retriever, embedding, guardrail*, and so on. These types allow capturing domain-specific data (such as prompt, tokens, cost) for LLM workflows. We will see later in the chapter how to specify the observation type when sending traces to Langfuse.

Langfuse tracks usage (for billing) by counting **Billable Units.**

Billable Units = Traces + Observations + Scores

If we are using Langfuse Cloud, the plan usage is largely defined by how many traces, observations, and scores we ingest.

Sending Your First Trace to Langfuse Using the Python SDK

We are now ready to start sending our first trace to Langfuse. As a prerequisite for the upcoming code example and pretty much the rest of the book, please make sure to complete these steps:

- Set up a Langfuse Cloud account (starting with Hobby) or Self-host Langfuse (Refer to the section on Getting started with Langfuse in *Chapter 4, Introduction to Langfuse*).
- Setup a python environment. Refer to the section of *Chapter 1, Introduction to Large Language Models and Monitoring* on Exploring the LLM toolkit for the book to know how to do this.
- Create a new project on Langfuse. Refer to the section on **`Getting started`** with Langfuse in *Chapter 4, Introduction to Langfuse*. This step is the same on Cloud or the Self hosted version. Add the following environment variables in the `.env` file.

```
LANGFUSE_SECRET_KEY = "sk-lf-...."
LANGFUSE_PUBLIC_KEY = "pk-lf-...."
LANGFUSE_HOST = "https://cloud.langfuse.com" # If using the EU region
# LANGFUSE_HOST = "https://us.cloud.langfuse.com" # If using the US region
# LANGFUSE_HOST = "http://localhost:3000" # If hosting locally
```

- We should also have a connection to one of the following LLM providers. These are:
  - OpenAI (used in most code examples in the book)

  - Azure OpenAI
  - Anthropic
  - Google Vertex
  - Amazon Bedrock
- Based on the LLM provider, we may need to add the necessary variables to the **.env** file as well.

Let us now send our first trace using Langfuse. We will use a very simple hello world example not using any LLM at first.

```
# Start by installing the latest version of the langfuse SDK and python-dotenv (if not installed already)
pip install langfuse python-dotenv

# We need to load the env variables from the .env file
from dotenv import load_dotenv
load_dotenv()

from langfuse import observe

@observe
def langfuse_hello_world():
    return "This is my first trace in Langfuse"

langfuse_hello_world()
```

The most straightforward way to send a trace to Langfuse is by using its **@observe** decorator. This will automatically create a span and by default capture the input and output of the method.

If everything with the setup was correct, we can see the trace on the Langfuse UI by visiting the host URL specified in **LANGFUSE_HOST** and then clicking on the Tracing option in the sidebar.

The complete URL should look something like this:

http://localhost:3000/project/cmgje7s5h0006p207p5rjnhlr/traces or **http://cloud.langfuse.com/project/cmgje7s5h0006p207p5rjnhlr/traces**

depending which Langfuse setup we have opted for.

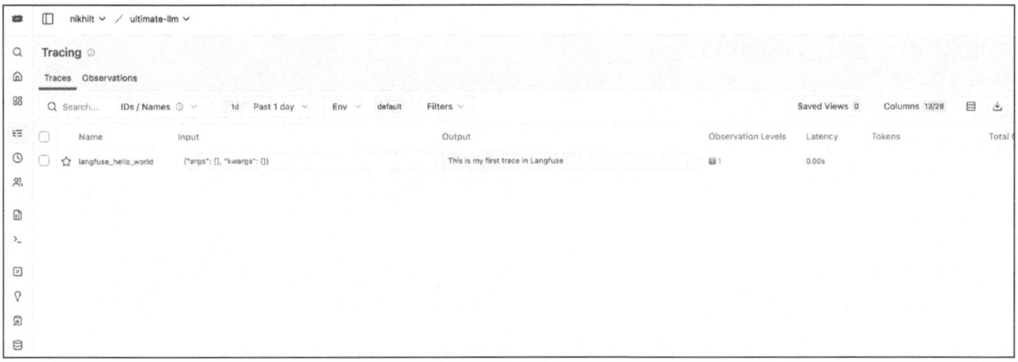

Figure 5.1: *First Trace in Langfuse*

We can get more information about the trace by clicking it which also shows additional options and the full metadata.

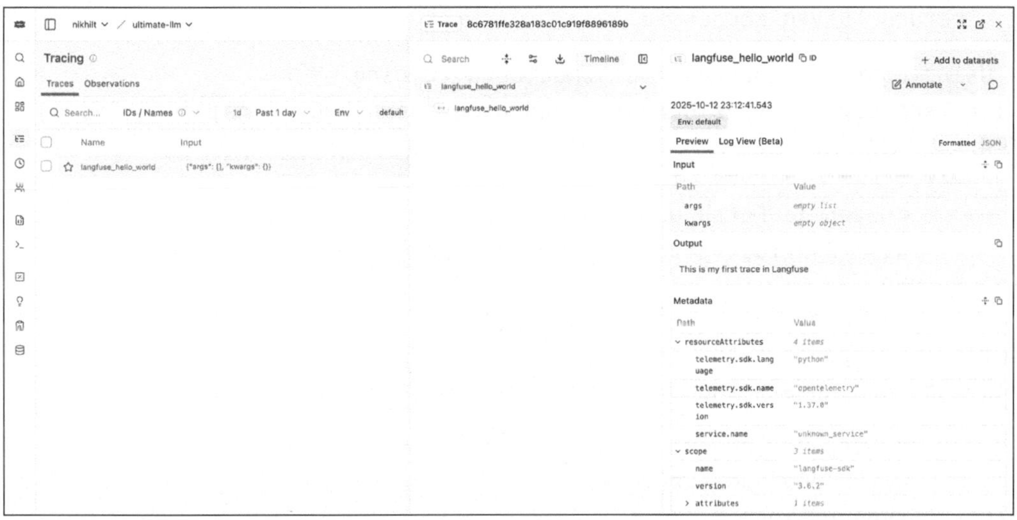

Figure 5.2: *First Trace in Detail*

When using the **`@observe`** decorator, the trace always starts when the function is called and ends when the function returns. If we want more control on when the spans should start and end, we should use the context manager option.

Here is a more elaborate example of a trace with multiple spans using context manager.

```
from langfuse import get_client
import time
import random

from dotenv import load_dotenv
load_dotenv()
```

```
langfuse = get_client()

def fetch_user_query():
time.sleep(0.2)
    return "Summarize the latest Langfuse documentation"

def call_llm_api(prompt):
time.sleep(0.5)
    # simulate LLM output
    if random.random() < 0.1:
        raise RuntimeError("LLM timeout")
    return f"Summary of '{prompt}'"

def store_result(summary):
time.sleep(0.1)
    return "Saved successfully"

# Using context managers for structured tracing
with langfuse.start_as_current_span(name="handle-user-request") as
request_span:
    try:
        # Step 1: Fetch user query
        with langfuse.start_as_current_span(name="fetch-query") as
fetch_span:
            query = fetch_user_query()
fetch_span.update(output=query)
request_span.update(input=query)

        # Step 2: Generate response using an LLM
        with langfuse.start_as_current_observation(
as_type="generation",
            name="generate-summary",
            model="gpt-4.1",
            input=query
        ) as generation:
            summary = call_llm_api(query)
generation.update(output=summary)

        # Step 3: Save results
        with langfuse.start_as_current_span(name="store-results") as
store_span:
            status = store_result(summary)
store_span.update(output=status)
```

```
request_span.update(output="Request processed successfully")

    except Exception as e:
        # Errors are automatically recorded under this trace
request_span.update(output=f"Failed: {e}")
        raise
```

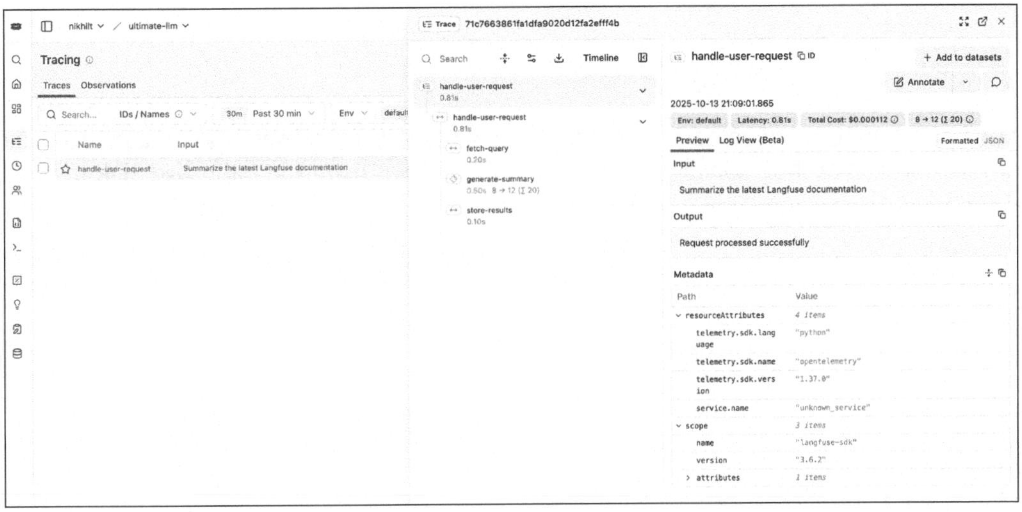

***Figure 5.3**: Capturing a Trace with Multiple Custom Spans*

This example shows a realistic LLM workflow — fetching a query, generating a response, and storing results — where each step is wrapped in its own span. This structure makes it easy to visualize execution flow, measure performance, and capture errors. Notice that in this trace, Langfuse also captures **latency, cost and token usage** based on the LLM name we provided (GPT 4.1).

Finally, let us run the code examples from chapter 1 this time with Langfuse integration.

```
# The OPENAI_API_KEY should be in a .env file which is in the root
directory of the project

# Instead of importing openai from its official package, we import it from
langfuse.openai
from langfuse.openai import openai
from dotenv import load_dotenv

load_dotenv()

completion = openai.chat.completions.create(
    model="gpt-4.1-mini",
    messages=[
        {
            "role": "system",
```

```
                "content": "You are an expert in Langfuse, the LLM
Engineering Platform",
            },
            {
                "role": "user",
                "content": "What are the top 3 features of Langfuse?",
            },
        ]
)
```

The only change we need here is that instead of importing the **openai** package from the official OpenAI Python package we use its replacement from the Langfuse SDK instead.

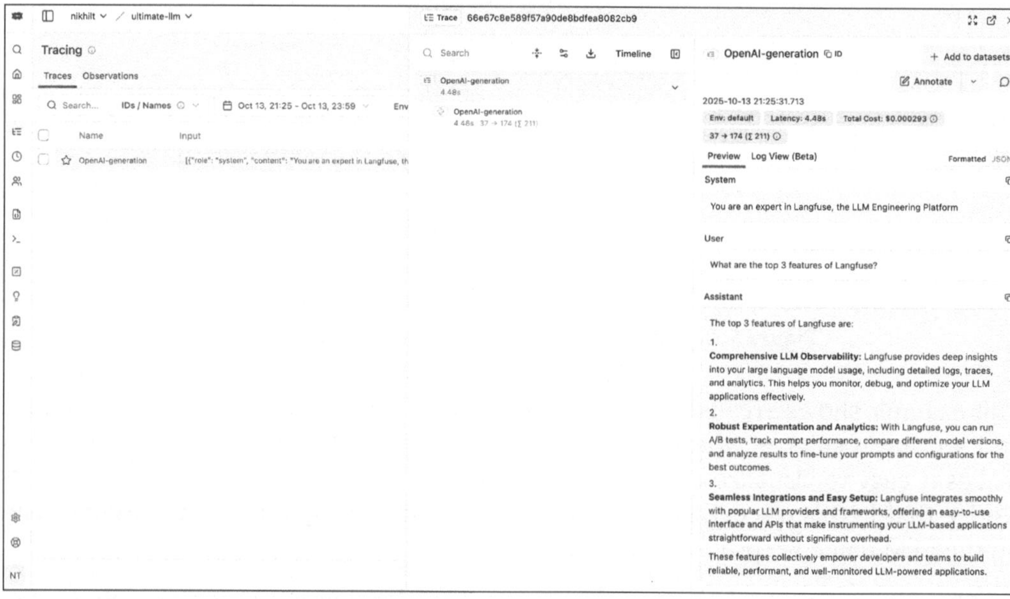

Figure 5.4: *Tracing OpenAI Calls in Langfuse*

We can see how nicely the trace is represented on the Langfuse UI. This time we have captured the real value of the latency, token usage and cost along with the input and LLM output of the trace.

These simple examples should help us get started with Langfuse and OpenAI. However, there are countless other ways in which LLM applications can be developed with the list of LLM providers and frameworks growing constantly. If we intend to use a different provider, be sure to check **https://langfuse.com/integrations** for the chosen option. No matter which framework/provider we choose, Langfuse UI provides a consistent experience with the most important information of the trace always visible on the traces page. In the next section we will look at the main features of the Langfuse UI and the different navigation options available.

The Langfuse User Interface

We have already seen the Traces tab on the Langfuse UI in the last section. The Langfuse UI is very intuitive and is meant to be used by all kinds of users, not just by tech or engineering teams.

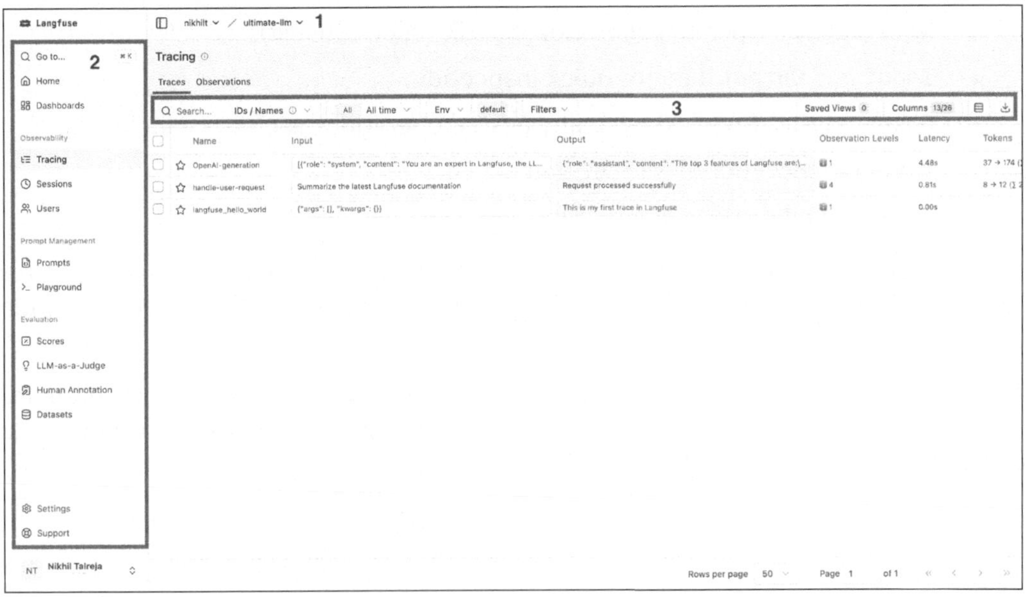

Figure 5.5: *Traces Page from the Langfuse UI*

This image above shows the **Langfuse Tracing UI**, where all recorded traces and their details are displayed.

1. **Top Navigation Bar:** This is used to navigate between organization and projects.
2. **Left Sidebar:** It is the main navigation panel. It includes key sections under Observability (Tracing, Sessions, Users), Prompt Management (Prompts, Playground), and Evaluation (Scores, LLM-as-a-Judge, Human Annotation, Datasets), along with Settings and Support.
3. **Top Filters Bar:** This provides filtering and search controls to find specific traces by name, time range, environment, or other attributes.
4. **Columns Selector:** Choose which columns/metrics to display (latency, cost, model, token count, and so on).

From this page we can also create a **`SavedView`** which can preselect columns, filters and sort order of the traces.

There is also an option to download/export the traces in CSV, JSON or JSONL format. For this option to work, batch exports need to be enabled by setting the environment variables: **`LANGFUSE_S3_BATCH_EXPORT_ENABLED`** and **`LANGFUSE_S3_BATCH_EXPORT_BUCKET`**

The main Traces table in the center lists each recorded trace with its:

- **`Name`** (such as OpenAI-generation, handle-user-request),
- **`Input`** and **`Output`** data for quick inspection,
- **`Observation levels`** (how many nested operations each trace includes),
- **`Latency`** (execution duration), and
- **`Token counts`** (usage summary).

This view gives a consolidated overview of all traced events—making it easy to monitor latency, inspect model outputs, and debug multi-step LLM workflows directly within the UI.

Another recently introduced feature on this page is the AI based search filter for traces which can help find traces based on natural language queries. This feature can construct filters for traces by simply describing what we want to filter for.

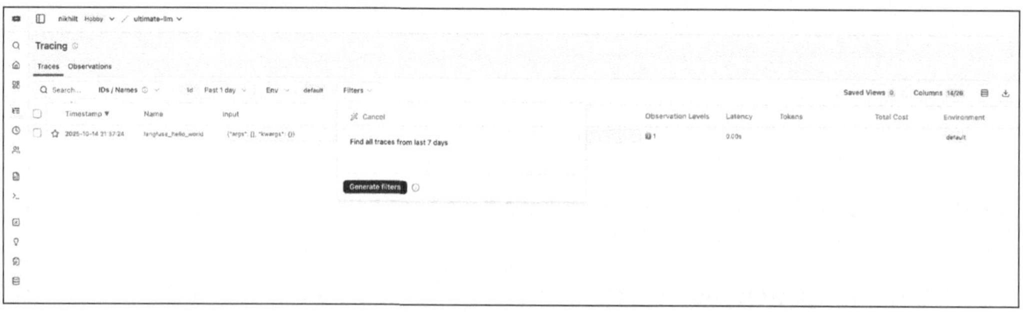

Figure 5.6: *AI Based Search Filter for Traces*

At the time of writing this feature was **only available for Langfuse Cloud**. AI features can be enabled by organization owners and admins in **`Organization Settings`** → **`General`** → **`AI Features`**.

From here we can also navigate to the **`Observations`** tab which shows every **`Observation`**, its type and extra details like model name, prompt, scores and tags where applicable. We can see the detailed view by clicking the observation.

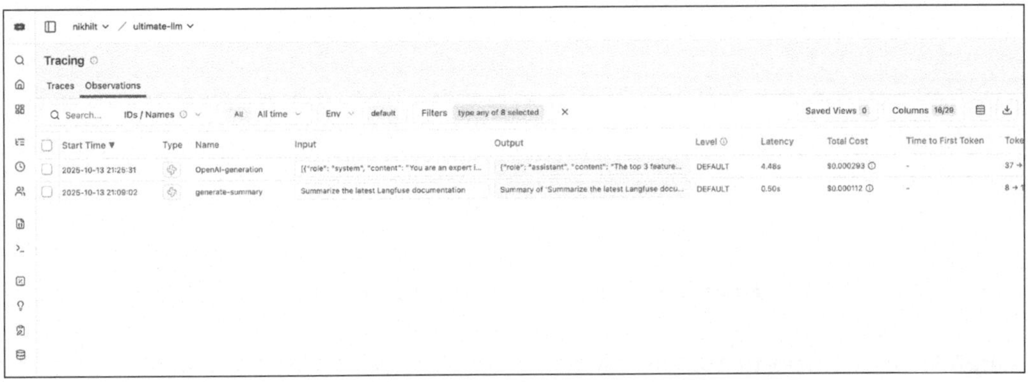

Figure 5.7: *Observations Page from the Langfuse UI*

At the bottom of the page on the right side is the navigation for quick access across pages.

Overall, this page provides a clear overview of all traced operations within the project, with key details such as inputs, outputs, and performance metrics visible at a glance.

Token Usage and Cost Tracking

Keeping track of how many tokens are used and how much we spend per call are one of the most basic observability parameters for an LLM application. As we already saw in the examples these are automatically recorded per observation which are either of type **generation** or **embedding**. By simple definition,

- **Token Usage** is the number of units (tokens) consumed; and,
- **Cost** is the cost in US Dollars ($).

With Langfuse, token usage and cost data come from two possible sources:

- **Automatically inferred**: If we use a supported model (for example, from OpenAI, Anthropic, Google) and send in the correct model identifiers, Langfuse can estimate token usage and calculate costs based on predefined pricing models. Langfuse periodically adds cost information for newer models as and when they become available.

- **Explicitly ingested**: If the LLM provider returns usage or cost data (for instance, via an API), we can feed that straight into Langfuse via the SDK or integrations. This tends to be more accurate than inference alone.

If we ingest usage information on our own, this overrides the inferred usage/cost in Langfuse. Hence, it is advised to use manual ingestion carefully.

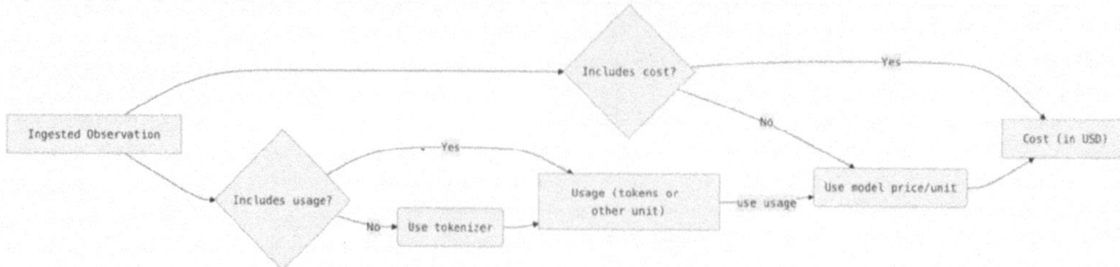

Figure 5.8: *Cost and Usage Ingestion Flowchart*

Langfuse also supports custom model definitions, so if we use models not in the built-in catalog (fine-tuned ones, self-hosted, or upcoming providers), we can add tokenizers, pricing information, and usage types (input/output, cache reads, audio/image tokens, etc.) to ensure cost tracking works correctly.

In both cases, we get per-call visibility into token counts, cost breakdowns by usage type, and aggregated metrics to monitor trends, detect anomalies, and optimize costs over time.

Here is a simple example of how to ingest usage details manually in an observation with the provided usage details of OpenAI.

```
from langfuse import get_client
import openai
from dotenv import load_dotenv

load_dotenv()

langfuse_client = get_client()

with langfuse_client.start_as_current_observation(
as_type="generation",
    name="openai-style-generation",
    model="gpt-4.1-mini"
) as generation:
    messages = [
            {
                "role": "system",
                "content": "You are an expert in Langfuse, the LLM
Engineering Platform",
            },
            {
                "role": "user",
                "content": "Summarize how cost and usage ingestion works
in Langfuse",
```

```
            },
        ]
    completion = openai.chat.completions.create(
        model="gpt-4.1-mini",
        messages=messages
    )
    # Get usage details from the completion
usage_details = completion.usage
    # Update the generation with the usage details
generation.update(
usage_details=usage_details.model_dump,
        input=messages,
        output=completion.choices[0].message.content
    )
```

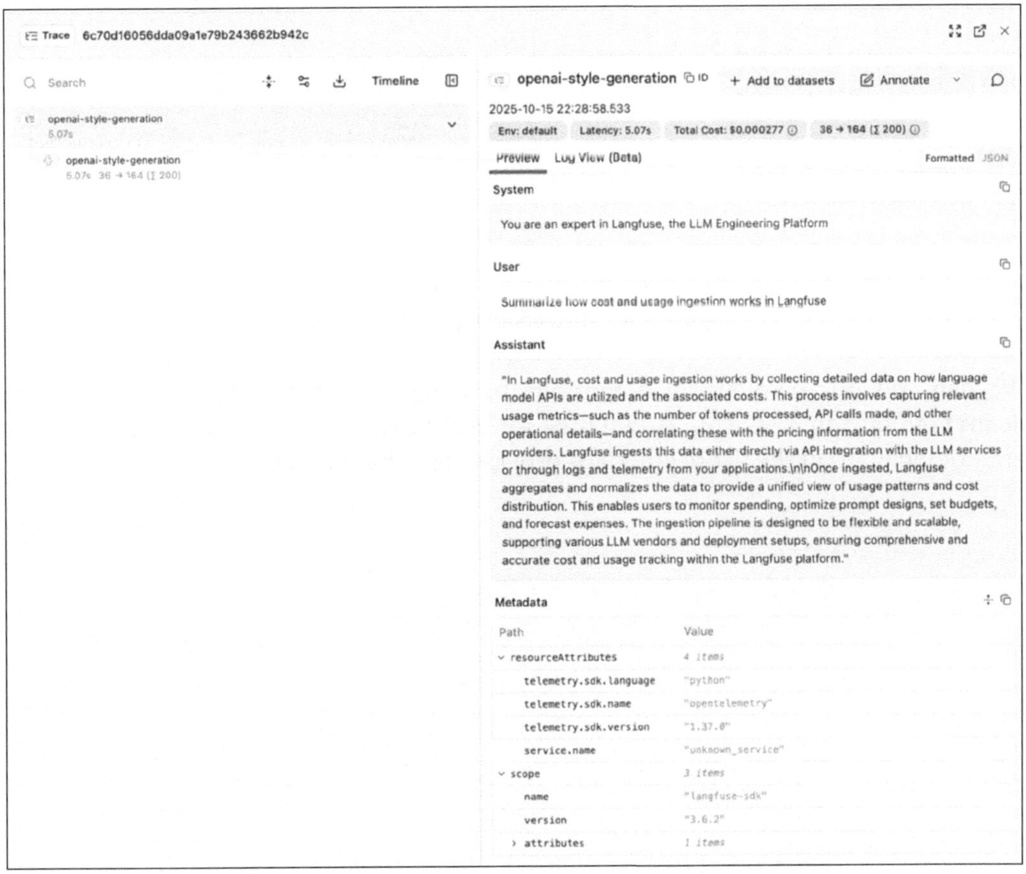

Figure 5.9: *Observation with Manually Ingested Usage Details*

If we omit the part about updating the generation with usage details, Langfuse will use its own database with pre-defined usage details. This is based on the name provided in the **`model`** parameter of the **`start_as_current_observation`** method. So, in this case *gpt-4.1-mini*. To see the list of available models go to the *Settings* page of the project and then choose *Models*.

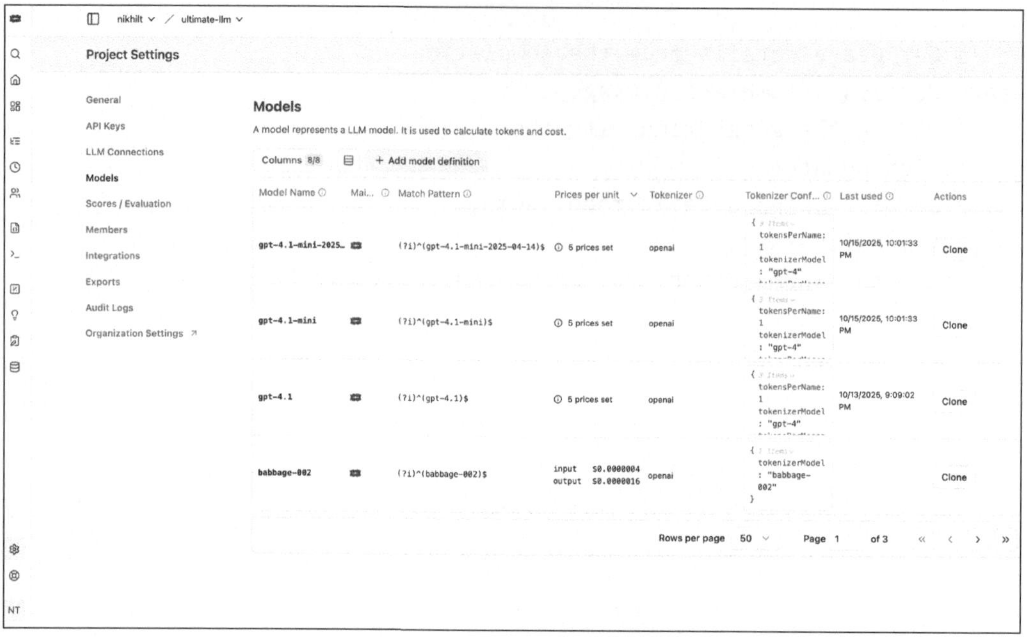

Figure 5.10: *Model Settings in the Project*

We can add our own model definitions to Langfuse by clicking the **`Add model definition`** button. This step is essential for self-hosted or fine-tuned models which are not included in the list of standard provider specific models.

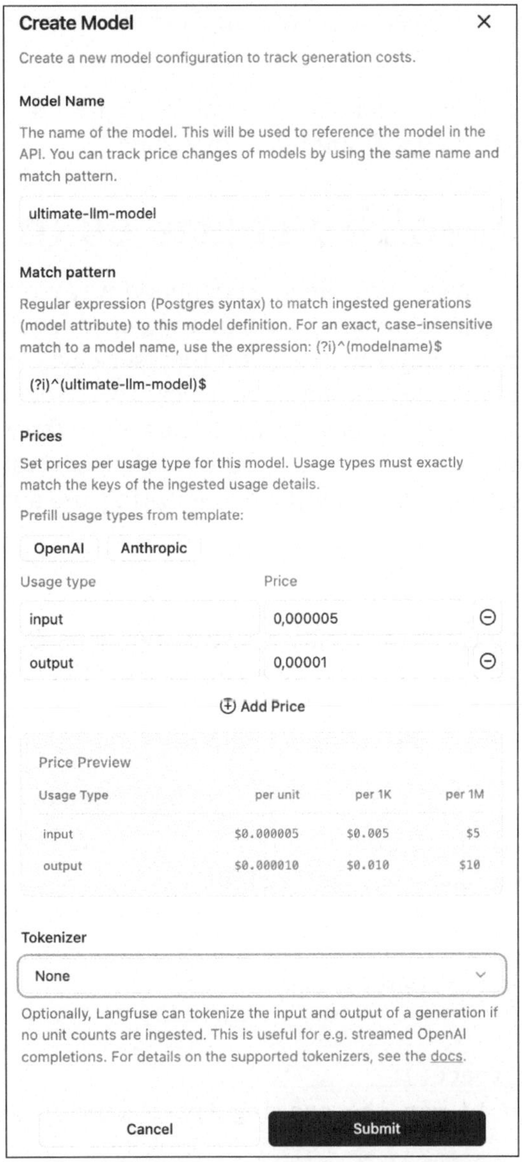

Figure 5.11: *Creating a Custom Model Definition*

For creating a custom model definition, a model name needs to be given and the pricing information should be set. Langfuse will use the regular expression in the Match pattern field to map model names to usage definitions. **User-defined models take priority over models maintained by Langfuse.** Other points to remember when creating custom model definitions.

- Model definition changes are not applied for back dated traces. The updated costs will only be applied to new generations.

- Token Usage and Cost are only applicable to generation or embedding observations.

If a standard model definition is missing, this can be requested by creating an issue on Langfuse's GitHub page - **https://langfuse.com/issue.**

Core Observability Features in Langfuse

So far in this chapter we have seen the most common ways to start sending traces to Langfuse. This is the most elementary start that we need for full observability of our applications. However, sending raw traces by themselves have little value especially for real-world applications where it might be necessary to see related traces together or track activity on a user level. By making small changes to the way we send traces, we can easily get more insights from them. Langfuse offers several built-in features that extend simple trace logging into a complete monitoring and analysis toolkit.

Sessions

The first feature on the list is the ability to create Sessions. Sessions in Langfuse are **groups of traces** that can be visualized together to cover an entire interaction with the application. Creating a session in Langfuse is very straightforward, we simply need to include a `sessionId`in the trace. All traces with the same id will be grouped together.

There are several ways in which a session ID can be passed to a trace.

```
from dotenv import load_dotenv
from langfuse import observe, get_client

load_dotenv()

langfuse_client = get_client()

@observe()
def add_session_to_trace():
    # Add a session id for the running trace when using the @observe
content manager
    langfuse_client.update_current_trace(session_id="your-unique-
session-id")

def update_session_in_span():
    """
    Adds a session id to the current span
    """
    with langfuse_client.start_as_current_span(name="another-operation"):
        # Add to the current trace
        langfuse_client.update_current_trace(session_id="another-session-id")
```

For a multi-turn conversation like a chatbot, the use of sessions is even more prominent.

```
from langfuse import get_client
from langfuse.openai import openai
import uuid
from dotenv import load_dotenv
load_dotenv()

langfuse_client = get_client()

# Create a new session for this chat
session_id = str(uuid.uuid4())

print(f"New chat session started: {session_id}\n(Type 'bye' to exit)\n")

def chat_with_bot(user_message: str):
    # Each user message is logged as a trace under the session
    with langfuse_client.start_as_current_span(name="chat-turn") as
span:
span.update_trace(input=user_message, session_id=session_id)
        try:
            # Record the LLM generation
            completion = openai.chat.completions.create(
                model="gpt-4.1-mini",
                messages=[
                    {
                        "role": "system",
                        "content": "You are a helpful and friendly
support chatbot for Langfuse",
                    },
                    {"role": "user", "content": user_message},
                ],
            )
            reply = completion.choices[0].message.content
            print(f"Bot: {reply}")
span.update_trace(output=reply)
        except Exception as e:
span.update_trace(output=f"Error: {e}")

# Run the chatbot until the user says "bye", "exit", or "quit"
while True:
user_input = input("You: ")
    if user_input.lower().strip() in ["bye", "exit", "quit"]:
        print("Bot: Goodbye! Have a great day!")
        break
chat_with_bot(user_input)
```

To browse all the sessions, we can go to the *Sessions* tab from the left navigation bar.

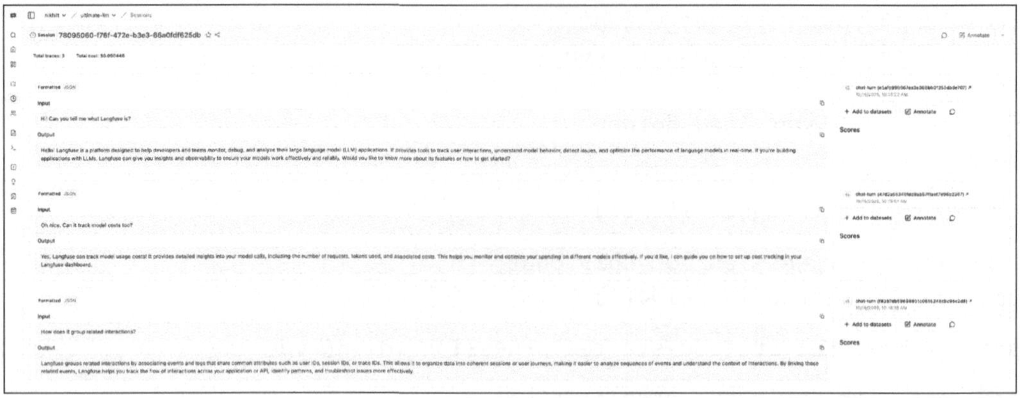

Figure 5.12: *Sessions in Langfuse*

We can also **share sessions** by clicking the share button next to the session id. This will generate a unique sharable link that can be shared with other users. **Please note that on the cloud version, this link is publicly accessible to anyone.** So be careful to not share confidential or proprietary information. This option also makes it possible for users to bookmark it in the browser.

We will see in later chapters how we can also score entire sessions or even send them for human evaluation using Annotation Queues.

User Tracking

Similar to sessions, it is also very common to track activity based on the users of a system. This helps analyze user behavior and filter interactions for a user or a group of users. In Langfuse, the definition of a user is open-ended and can be decided based on the needs of the application. A user can be identified based on a **`userId`**. Code to add a user id is also exactly the same as adding a **`sessionId`**.

```
from dotenv import load_dotenv
from langfuse import observe, get_client

load_dotenv()

langfuse_client = get_client()

@observe()
def add_user_in_trace():
    langfuse_client.update_current_trace(user_id="your-unique-user-id")

def update_user_in_span():
    """
    Adds a user id to the current span
```

```
    """
    with langfuse_client.start_as_current_span(name="another-
operation"):
        # Add to the current trace
langfuse_client.update_current_trace(user_id="another-user-id")
```

To see the list of the users, navigate to the *Users tab.*

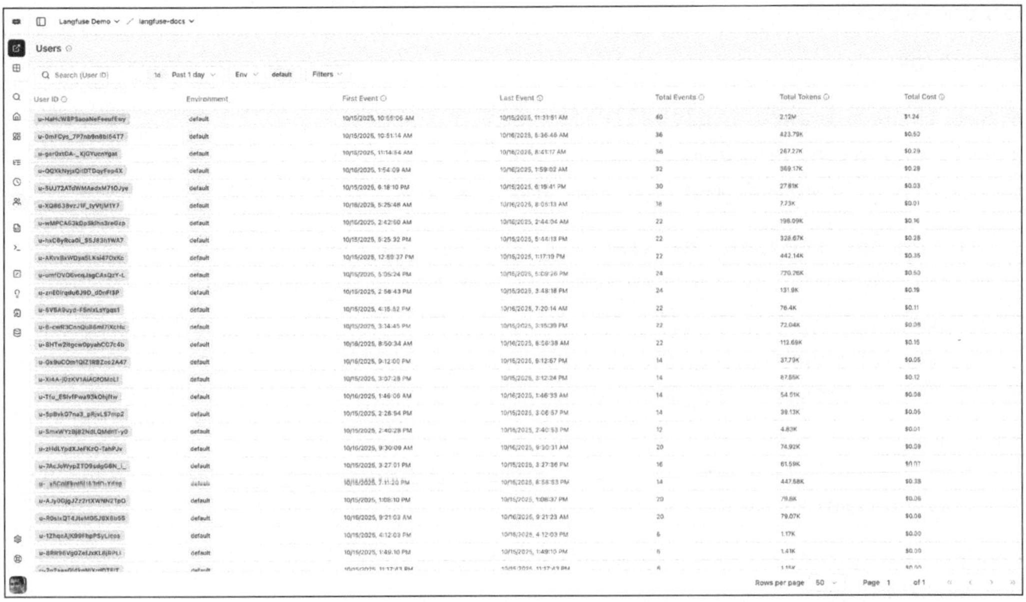

Figure 5.13: Users in Langfuse

This view shows all the users of the application along with the number of events, token usage and cost per user. To see more details about a user, we can click on the user ID to see more information.

The **`userId`** should be something unique like email or any other unique identifier to make sure traces are not wrongly linked to other users. If our application uses some form of id to identify users (like a number) it is the best option to use the same id in Langfuse for users as well. This way we can link Langfuse traces by users to other components in the application.

As of this point, Langfuse does not support addition of extra attributes like names, groups or other identifying parameters for a user.

Environments

In software applications, environments are separate setups that represent different stages of the development and deployment process. We can have environments like development, staging, beta, production etc. Typically, we would use a single instance of Langfuse for all of our stages and environments. To avoid data pollution, we can specify the environments for different Langfuse objects and organize them into the appropriate content.

Environment can be seen on: Traces, Observations, Scores, and Sessions. It should be a string that cannot start with "langfuse" and should be less than or equal to 40 characters. Besides this, it can only include lowercase letters, numbers, hyphens, and underscores.

```
import os

# Set the environment globally for all objects
# This can also be added to the .env file
os.environ["LANGFUSE_TRACING_ENVIRONMENT"] = "production"

# Set the environment on client initialization
# This will override the environment set using the env variable
from langfuse import Langfuse
from langfuse.openai import openai
from dotenv import load_dotenv

load_dotenv()

langfuse_client = Langfuse(environment="production")

completion = openai.chat.completions.create(
    model="gpt-4.1-mini",
    messages=[
        {"role": "system", "content": "You are a helpful assistant for
Langfuse"},
        {
            "role": "user",
            "content": "What is the benefit of setting environments in
Langfuse?",
        },
    ],
)
```

When we open the trace, we can see the Environment on the detail page.

Figure 5.14: *Environment in Langfuse*

In the UI, we can also filter events by environment using the environment filter in the navigation bar.

Environments in Langfuse are immutable. They are created when the first trace is ingested, and we cannot delete environments from Langfuse.

Tags and Metadata

The last core observability feature we will see is the option to add tags and metadata to traces. This is supplementary information that can be optionally added to the traces we send to Langfuse.

Tags are simple string labels that we can attach to a trace when we create or update it. A trace can have multiple tags. Tags line Environments cannot be removed once added (only augmented). Tags are meant for **categorization** and **filtering** of traces. The table below shows some examples of tags we can use for our applications.

Category	Example Tags	Description
Use Case / Workflow	*content-summarization, translation, sentiment-analysis, SQL-generation, image-search*	Label traces by the functional use case or pipeline type.
Feature / Product Area	*onboarding-flow, support-chat, recommendation-engine, data-ingestion*	Identify which product module or workflow triggered the trace.
Experiment or Model Variant	*exp-A, exp-B, gpt-4o-mini, mistral-7b, custom-rag-v2*	Differentiate traces by experiment variant or model version.
Response Outcome	*success, timeout, failed*	Mark how the trace completed for quick visual filtering.

Category	Example Tags	Description
Priority or Severity	*high, low, critical*	Useful when tracing internal pipelines or error-handling flows.
Pipeline Stage	*preprocessing, inference, postprocessing*	Tag traces to see performance of different pipeline segments.
Business Logic	*free-plan, enterprise-plan, trial-period*	Classify traces by business rules or account tier.

Table 5.2: *Examples of Tags in Langfuse*

Metadata on the other hand is an arbitrary JSON key/value data we can attach to traces or to observations/spans inside them. It can carry structured context — similar to **`{"request_id": "req-123", "user_role": "admin"},`** or model parameters, environment info, version, etc. Metadata updates are merged at the top-level key (that means adding new keys will merge with existing metadata) but we should avoid rewriting the same key multiple times. We can attach metadata at the trace level or at individual span/observation levels.

Below is a small code example to show how tags and metadata can be used to enhance traces/observations. We typically supply tags or metadata during trace creation or as updates in the application workflow.

```
from langfuse import get_client
from dotenv import load_dotenv

load_dotenv()

langfuse_client = get_client()

with langfuse_client.start_as_current_span(
    name="chat-about-langfuse",
) as span:
    # Add tags to the span
span.update_trace(tags=["chatbot", "observability", "gpt-4.1-mini"])
    with span.start_as_current_observation(
        name="llm-generation",
as_type="generation",
        # Add metadata to the observation
        metadata={"temperature": 0.7, "max_tokens": 1000},
    ) as observation:
        # Update the metadata of the observation
observation.update(
            metadata={"user_id": "user_456", "topic": "langfuse-tags-vs-
metadata"},
```

```
        )
        # Add final tag to mark session result
observation.update(tags=["completed"])
```

When to Use Tags

- When we want to label a trace with categorical labels that we often filter or group by (such as **`env:prod`**, **`experiment-A`**, **`use-case-cart`**, **`fallback-path`**).
- For quick visual toggling in UI filters (tags are visible on Traces page by default).
- When we do not need fine granularity — tags are coarse and global to the trace.

When to Use Metadata

- When we need structured context (like **`user_id`**, **`request_id`**, **`version`**, **`model_params`**) to query deeper.
- If we need to store multiple related attributes or nested data.
- When we want to associate data to specific spans/observations (not just the whole trace).
- In cases where we may need richer filtering conditions — for example, *"all traces where response_time> 500ms"* or *"where user_plan = 'premium'."*

Advanced Observability Features in Langfuse

In the previous section, we saw the basic features that Langfuse offers when sending traces. For LLM applications we may need many more options to make the monitoring more comprehensive. We will see the most important advanced features and how to use them with traces.

Observation Types

An observation in Langfuse defines the type of operation within a trace. In modern LLM applications, there are numerous different steps that can occur within an end-to-end LLM operation. So far we have mostly seen the "generation" type of observation which represents the main call to the LLM to get the response. However, this is not the only type of event that can take place inside a trace. The type of observation is either auto detected when using integrations with the SDK or we can explicitly specify them when creating traces/spans. Langfuse supports the following types of observations when using the SDK:

- **`Event`** is the root observation type under which all other observations are nested. These are automatically created for each trace.
- **`Span`** are the individual time sliced blocks within an event.
- **`Generation`** represents the observation which generates an output, considering for example an LLM call.
- **`Agent`** observation can be used when calling an AI Agent within a trace/span.
- **`Tool`** represents a tool call used mostly in connection with agents.
- **`Chain`** mostly synonymous with LangChain can include different steps which go into the entire chain of a LangChain call.
- **`Retriever`** mostly used in RAG applications, represents the data retrieval steps, such as a call to a vector store or a database.
- **`Evaluator`** can be used for a step within a trace which return a metric or a score.
- **`Embedding`** for calls to generate embeddings.
- **`Guardrail`** for guardrailing or security steps.

Here is a simple example of how to use observation types:

```
from langfuse import get_client
from langfuse.openai import openai
from dotenv import load_dotenv
import requests

load_dotenv()

langfuse_client = get_client()

# The first span is the root span of type "event"
with langfuse_client.start_as_current_span(name="weather-app") as span:
user_message = "What's the weather in Berlin today?"
span.update(input=user_message)
    # Observation type tool
    with langfuse_client.start_as_current_observation(
as_type="tool", name="weather-api", input={"city": "Berlin"}
    ) as tool_call:
tool_response = requests.get("https://wttr.in/Berlin?format=3")
tool_call.update(output=tool_response.text)

    # Calls to LLM automatically create observations of type "generation"
    completion = openai.chat.completions.create(
        model="gpt-4.1-mini",
        messages=[
```

```
            {"role": "system", "content": "You are a helpful assistant"},
            {"role": "user", "content": tool_response.text},
            {"role": "user", "content": user_message},
        ],
    )
span.update(output=completion.choices[0].message.content)
```

As we can see, Langfuse shows the trace steps with the appropriate observation types and even adds a nice graph representation of the flow.

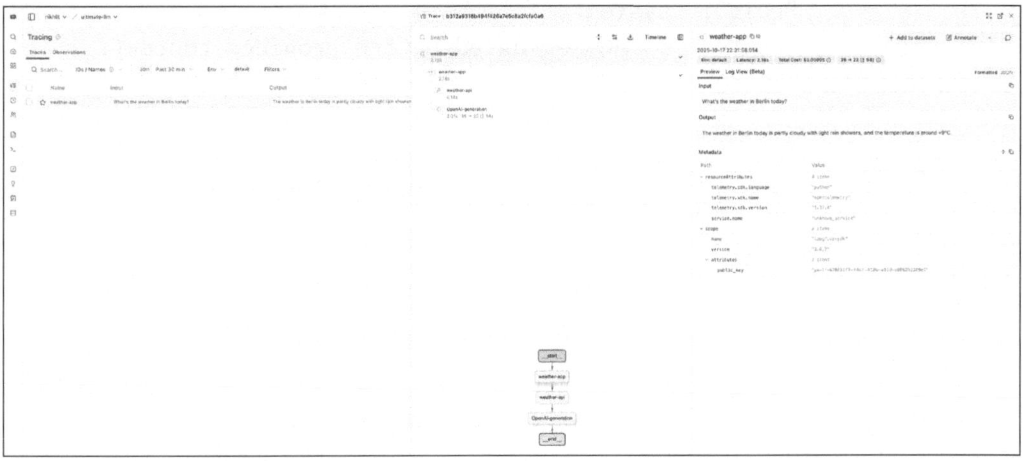

Figure 5.15: *Observation Types in Langfuse*

Adding observation types, makes the traces more expressive and visually representative of the operation. More importantly, we can also filter observations by type and then view metrics or scores for the different types.

Here is another example of observation types with a RAG based application:

```
from langfuse import get_client
from langfuse.openai import openai
from dotenv import load_dotenv

load_dotenv()

langfuse_client = get_client()

with langfuse_client.start_as_current_span(name="rag-question-
answering") as span:
    # Observation type retriever
span.update(input="What is Langfuse?")
    with langfuse_client.start_as_current_observation(
as_type="retriever",
        name="knowledge-base-search",
```

```
        metadata={"query": "What is Langfuse?"},
    ) as r:
        docs = ["Langfuse is an observability platform for LLM apps."]
r.update(output=docs)

    completion = openai.chat.completions.create(
        model="gpt-4.1-mini",
        messages=[
            {
                "role": "system",
                "content": "Answer based on the provided context.",
            },
            {
                "role": "user",
               "content": f"Context: {docs}\n\nQuestion: What is Langfuse?",
            },
        ],
    )
    answer = completion.choices[0].message.content.strip()

    # Evaluator: assessing the response quality
    with langfuse_client.start_as_current_observation(
as_type="evaluator",
        name="relevance-check",
        metadata={"criteria": "factual-correctness"},
    ) as eval:
eval.update(output="relevant and correct")
span.update(output=answer)
```

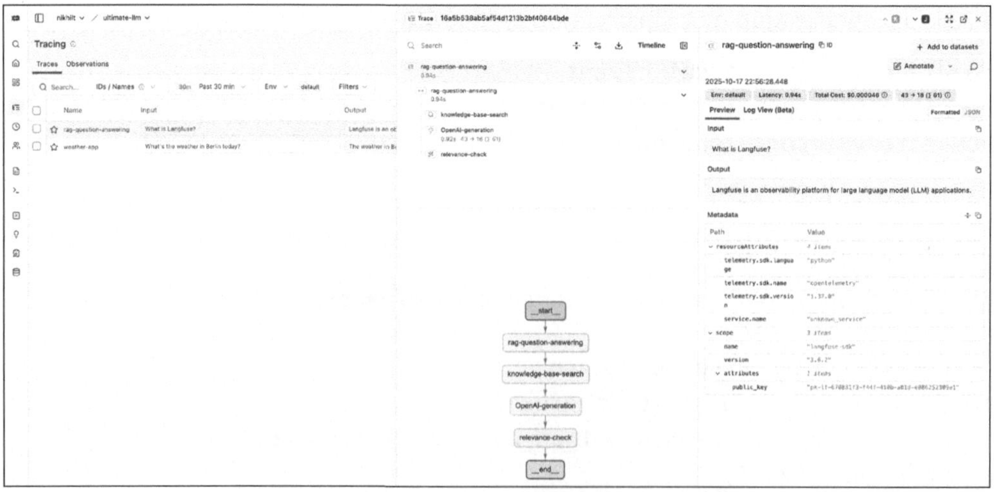

Figure 5.16: *More Observation Types in Langfuse*

Log Levels

Like application logs, observations can also have log levels as they are very similar to logs in a traditional software system. Langfuse supports the four most common log levels: **`DEBUG, DEFAULT, WARNING, ERROR.`** We can also add a log message (called **`statusMessage`**) to the observations to add further information.

By default, Langfuse does not have any levels associated with observations. When we add log levels, Observations can be filtered by levels on the UI.

```
from langfuse import get_client
from dotenv import load_dotenv

load_dotenv()

langfuse_client = get_client()

with langfuse_client.start_as_current_span(name="data-processing") as span:
span.update(output="Step 1 complete")

    with langfuse_client.start_as_current_observation(
        name="risky-step",
        level="WARNING",
status_message="This step might fail under edge cases",
    ) as risky:
        # simulate something that might go wrong
        result = None
        if result is None:
risky.update(level="ERROR", status_message="Result is unexpectedly None")

    # Update the current span at runtime
span.update(
        level="DEBUG", status_message="Finishing cleanup operations"
    )

    )
```

Versioning and Releases

Applications will evidently go through many different versions and release cycles. Langfuse offers the option add versioning to traces or observations which allows to track the effect of metrics over time. Whether it is the changes made to prompt logic, model versions, feature flags, or backend services, it is important to tie observability data back to those deployments. If we plan to do A/B tests on our application, having release versions can help compare different versions.

The release version can be set globally for an application when initializing the client.

```
from langfuse import get_client, Langfuse
from dotenv import load_dotenv

load_dotenv()

langfuse = Langfuse(release="v1.2.3")

langfuse_client = get_client()

with langfuse_client.start_as_current_span(
    name="process-user-request", version="v1.0.0"
) as span:
span.update(input="This is a versioned span")
    with langfuse.start_as_current_observation(
        name="my-versioned-observation", as_type="generation",
version="2.0.0"
    ) as observation:
observation.update(output="This is a versioned observation")
span.update(output="Done")
```

Releases and versions can be seen in the trace detail view.

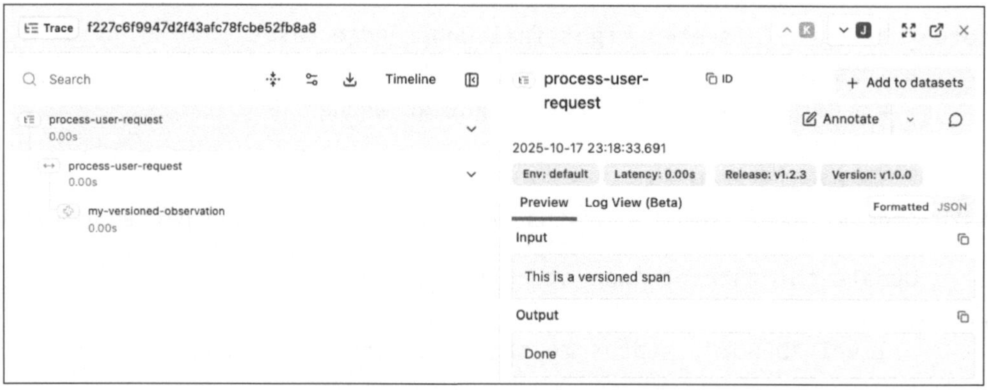

Figure 5.17: *Release and Version*

On some platforms like: Vercel, Heroku, Netlify, release versions can also be auto populated based on the available environment variables. The full list of supported variables can be seen at **`https://github.com/langfuse/langfuse-python/blob/main/langfuse/_utils/environment.py`**.

Trace URLs

In the SDK, we can programmatically generate the full URL for the trace. This can then be shared or used in other systems to directly link a trace. Using the UI, traces can also be shared publicly with other users. **Like sessions, traces can also contain sensitive information and hence should be shared with caution.**

```
from langfuse import observe, get_client
from dotenv import load_dotenv

load_dotenv()

langfuse_client = get_client()

@observe()
def get_trace_url():
    # Get the URL of the  trace
trace_url = langfuse_client.get_trace_url()
    print(f"View trace at: {trace_url}")

trace_id = langfuse_client.get_current_trace_id()
trace_url = langfuse_client.get_trace_url(trace_id=trace_id)
    print(f"View trace at: {trace_url}")
```

Running this method, produces the output:

```
View trace at: http://localhost:3000/project/cmgje7s5h0006p207p5rjnhlr/
traces/55615a3037823cf18e1800a973fd7198
View trace at: http://localhost:3000/project/cmgje7s5h0006p207p5rjnhlr/
traces/55615a3037823cf18e1800a973fd7198
```

Sampling

If our application generates a large number of traces (for example, many user requests or internal workflows), ingesting every trace can become expensive (both in bandwidth, storage, and cost). Sampling lets us control that volume by collecting only a subset of traces. Sampling can be enforced by either:

- Setting the environment variable **LANGFUSE_SAMPLE_RATE**.
- As a constructor parameter when initializing Langfuse.

```
from langfuse import Langfuse
import os

os.environ["LANGFUSE_SAMPLE_RATE"] = "0.5"

langfuse = Langfuse(sample_rate=0.5)
```

The sampling rate should be between 0 and 1. In the above example, only 50% of the traces will be ingested to Langfuse.

Distributed Tracing

In an LLM-based system we often have many different components like APIs, logging systems, Databases, web applications etc. A single user request would move across different servers or cloud functions. In such cases, it would be ideal to trace the entire workflow and not just in an individual service. Langfuse allows us to supply our own trace ID (and optionally a parent span ID / observation ID) rather than always relying on the auto-generated identifiers. This makes it possible to link together related operations across services.

When we do not supply them, Langfuse will generate a random trace ID (32 lowercase hex characters) and observation IDs of 16 hex chars (for OTEL-based SDKs). To generate our own trace ID, the trace ID must be unique within the project.

When to Use Distributed Trace IDs in LLM Apps

- When our workflow spans multiple microservices, functions, or processes (that includes retrieval service + embedding service + generation service).
- When we integrate tools and external APIs (tool calls) and want to include those in the same trace.
- When we want to correlate events from external systems (like user requests or job triggers) to the relevant trace in Langfuse.
- When we want deeper performance or cost analysis across service boundaries (for example which service is consuming most tokens or time).
- When we build agent-based systems or orchestrated workflows (such as multi-step chains) and need a full view of the flow.

```
from langfuse import get_client
from dotenv import load_dotenv

load_dotenv()

langfuse_client = get_client()

# trace ID can be passed with the trace_context parameter
with langfuse_client.start_as_current_span(
    name="my-operation",
trace_context={
        "trace_id": "abcdef1234567890abcdef1234567890"  # Must be 32 hex
chars and something unique
    },
) as span:
```

```
    # Access the trace ID of the current span
current_trace_id = langfuse_client.get_current_trace_id()
current_span_id = langfuse_client.get_current_observation_id()
    print(
f"The current trace ID is {current_trace_id} and the current span id is
{current_span_id}"
    )
```

In a real-life situation, the trace IDs could come from an upstream service or be passed to a downstream service to retain traceability even outside of Langfuse.

There are a few things to keep in mind when using distributed tracing. Developers need to ensure that every relevant process properly maintains and attaches the same trace ID. We must ensure they remain **unique** and **consistent** across distributed systems. When integrating with tools like OpenTelemetry or external APIs, we may need to generate Langfuse trace IDs as per the requirements of other systems.

Masking Sensitive Data in Traces

As the last advanced feature, we will look at Masking traces. Masking allows us to hide sensitive information before sending traces to Langfuse. This is a crucial step to protect **user privacy** or be compliant with regulatory laws. If your application works with such data, make sure to redact it before adding it to Langfuse. Langfuse maintains strong data encryption, using TLS 1.2+ for data in transit and AES-256 for data at rest. The platform adheres to recognized compliance frameworks, including SOC 2 Type II and ISO 27001, and supports GDPR. However, masking sensitive and **Personally Identifiable Information (PII)** is the responsibility of the system sending the traces to Langfuse.

To enable masking, we need to define a "**`masking_function`**" and then pass it to the Langfuse constructor. In this function we define our masking logic.

Here is a simple example of how to mask email and phone numbers from a trace.

```
from langfuse import Langfuse
from dotenv import load_dotenv
import re

load_dotenv()

def mask_pii(data: any, **kwargs) -> any:
    if isinstance(data, str):
        # Mask email addresses
        data = re.sub(r"\b[\w\.-]+?@\w+?\.\w+?\b", "[REDACTED_EMAIL]",
data)
        # Mask US-style phone numbers
```

```
        data = re.sub(r"\b\d{3}[-. ]?\d{3}[-. ]?\d{4}\b", "[REDACTED_
PHONE]", data)
    return data

langfuse = Langfuse(mask=mask_pii)

with langfuse.start_as_current_span(
    name="contact-customer", input="Email: jane.doe@example.com, Phone:
555-123-4567"
) as span:
span.update(output="Reached out to jane.doe@example.com via 555-123-
4567")
```

Langfuse will mask sensitive data on the input as well as output of the trace. Sensitive data in the metadata is also masked by default.

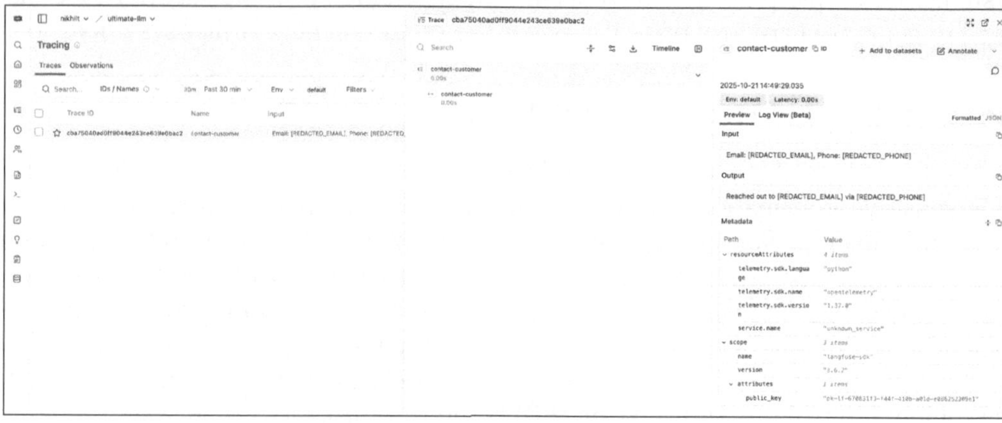

Figure 5.18: *Masking Sensitive Information in Traces*

For advanced use cases like credit card numbers, names and/or addresses, we may need to include specific libraries that can do the validation in our masking function.

Conclusion

We have covered a practical overview of observability within Langfuse for LLM applications. The chapter outlines key tools for monitoring, including the Python SDK and dashboard, describing how token usage, cost tracking, sessions, environments, and metadata are managed. Advanced capabilities such as tagging, user tracking, version management, and distributed tracing are introduced. The chapter also explains strategies for masking sensitive information, like emails and credit card numbers. In the next chapter, we shall cover one of the most interesting features of Langfuse, Prompt Management. We will further gradually see how to cover the entire lifecycle of our prompts using Langfuse including version control.

References

- Langfuse Usage and Cost Tracking - https://langfuse.com/docs/observability/features/token-and-cost-tracking
- Langfuse Sessions - https://langfuse.com/docs/observability/features/sessions
- Langfuse Users - https://langfuse.com/docs/observability/features/users
- Langfuse Environments - https://langfuse.com/docs/observability/features/environments
- Langfuse Tags - https://langfuse.com/docs/observability/features/tags
- Langfuse Metadata - https://langfuse.com/docs/observability/features/metadata
- Masking in Langfuse - https://langfuse.com/docs/observability/features/masking
- Security in Langfuse - https://langfuse.com/security
- Trace IDs - https://langfuse.com/docs/observability/features/trace-ids-and-distributed-tracing

Chapter 6
Prompt Management in Langfuse

Introduction

Prompts are the foundation of any LLM-powered application and managing them effectively is critical to building reliable and cost-efficient systems. This chapter introduces prompt management capabilities of Langfuse, which provide a structured workflow for creating, versioning, and iterating on prompts. We will learn how to organize prompts, compare versions, and roll back changes when needed—similar to software development practices like version control. We will explore how Langfuse enables prompt experimentation, making it easier to A/B test different prompt strategies, track performance metrics across variations, and ensure consistent behavior across deployments. The chapter also highlights how prompt templates, parameterization, and integration with tools like LangChain can accelerate experimentation. By the end of this chapter, we will have a strong foundation in prompt lifecycle management, preparing them for evaluation in the next chapter.

Structure

In this chapter, we will cover the following topics:

- Introduction to Prompt Engineering
- Understanding the Prompts Data Model in Langfuse
- Writing Your First Prompt in Langfuse
- Prompt Management Features in Langfuse
    - Version Control and Labels
    - Composability
    - Using Prompts in Applications
    - A/B Testing

  - Caching
  - Config
- LLM Playground in Langfuse
- Webhooks and Slack Integration

Introduction to Prompt Engineering

Before we start writing our prompts in Langfuse, we will cover a very quick introduction to the topic of Prompt Engineering. This will not be a deep dive since this is not the subject of the book but should reinforce the best practices of writing effective prompts for LLMs.

Prompt engineering is the science of designing the structured inputs we give to a generative AI so that the model produces useful, reliable, and repeatable outputs. At its core, prompt engineering answers three practical questions: *What exactly should the model do? In what format should it respond? And how will we know whether its response is acceptable*? The book *Prompt Engineering for Generative* AI (James Phoenix and Mike Taylor) captures these ideas with a small set of model-agnostic, production-minded principles that every prompt should apply. These five principles are: **Give Direction; Specify Format; Provide Examples; Evaluate Quality; Divide Labor.**

When we work with many prompts across teams or projects, small issues can quickly become big problems. Poorly written prompts lead to inconsistent results, more manual reviews, and unreliable automation. They also make debugging difficult and can reduce user trust. Langfuse helps by keeping all our prompts in one place, tracking changes, testing different versions, and monitoring performance. However, good tools alone are not enough—strong prompt design is still essential. By applying the five key principles of prompt engineering, we can make our prompts more reliable, consistent, and easier to maintain, even as models or settings change. The next sections explain each principle with simple, practical tips you can start using right away.

Give Direction

Explicitly state the task, the role or persona, constraints, and any relevant context. Leave as little ambiguity as possible about intent.

LLMs are statistical pattern matchers and ambiguous instructions lead to varied outputs. Clear direction reduces variance and aligns the probabilities of the model with your desired objective.

Practical Tips:

- Start with a short task statement: "You are an experienced product copywriter. Produce five concise product names for..."

- Include scope and constraints up front: acceptable length, tone, prohibited terms, or regulatory limits.

Specify Format

Require a strict output format when downstream systems depend on the result.

Structured formats (JSON, YAML, CSV, bullet lists with numbered headings) make parsing deterministic and reduce downstream errors.

Practical Tips:

- Provide a sample schema and an explicit "Return only" instruction, such as Return valid JSON with keys: title, bullets (array), estimated tokens (integer). No prose outside JSON.
- Use output validators as part of the prompt management pipeline—tests that run when a new prompt version is promoted.

Provide Examples

Add few-shot examples (input/desired output pairs), particularly for nuanced tasks.

Examples prime the distribution of the model toward the desired structure, style, and content. They are one of the most reliable levers for shaping output.

Practical Tips:

- Use fixed-length, representative examples that cover common edge cases.
- Distinguish positive and negative examples: show "good" and "bad" outputs and label them.

Evaluate Quality

Design explicit evaluation rules and metrics for outputs (automatic and human-in-the-loop).

Without objective checks you cannot measure regressions, compare prompts, or know when a model update changed behavior.

Practical Tips:

- **Define Pass/Fail Tests:** Format validation, factual checks, banned-term checks, semantic similarity thresholds to reference answers.
- **Instrument Prompts to Collect Telemetry:** Success rate, number of retries, user edits, and time-to-accept.

- Automate routine checks (schema, profanity, simple fact lookups) and route uncertain cases to human reviewers. Use those labels to improve prompts and examples.

Divide Labor

Split complex tasks into smaller steps or chains of prompts (planning → execution → verification) rather than asking one monolithic prompt to do everything.

Decomposing tasks reduces cognitive load on the model, improves interpretability, and makes error localization simpler.

Practical Tips:

- Use a "plan then execute" pattern: ask the model to outline steps, review the plan, then generate the final output.
- Implement prompt chains or function-calling patterns where each subtask has its own prompt and validator.
- Track each sub-prompt as an independent artifact so that you can version, test, and audit each step.

The following table shows some examples of good prompts using the above principles:

Principle	Bad Examples	Good Examples
Give Direction	"Write something about our new phone." "Explain data privacy."	"You are a tech journalist. Write a 150-word news article announcing our new smartphone, focusing on camera and battery life." "Explain data privacy to a high school student in simple, clear language with one real-life example."
Specify Format	"Summarize this article." "Extract details from this invoice."	"Summarize this article in exactly three bullet points, each under 20 words." "Extract the fields `InvoiceNumber`, `Date`, `TotalAmount`, and `VendorName` from the invoice and return only valid JSON."
Provide Examples	"Write a short product review." "Create a chatbot greeting."	"Example → Input: 'Wireless earbuds with long battery life.' Output: 'Great sound and comfortable fit. The battery lasts all day!' Now write one for: 'Noise-cancelling headphones.'" "Example → Input: 'Customer opens chat at 9 AM.' Output: 'Good morning! How can I help today?' Now write one for: 'Customer opens chat at 7 PM.'"

Principle	Bad Examples	Good Examples
Evaluate Quality	Accepting every model response without checking if it is accurate or formatted correctly.	Check that every response includes three key points, no spelling errors, and uses a friendly tone. Automatically validate JSON format and track user feedback to rate accuracy and clarity on a 1–5 scale.
Divide Labor	Write a detailed 1,000-word report on the European EV industry	Step 1: Summarize EV industry history. Step 2: List top five brands with strengths. Step 3: Write a 200-word forecast summary.

***Table 6.1**: Examples for the Five Principles of Prompt Engineering*

There are two main types of prompts we write in practice: **text-only prompts and chat-based prompts.**

A text-only prompt is a single block of text sent to the model. This was the standard format for early AI models such as GPT-3 or instruction-tuned models without chat APIs. Everything — context, role, and instruction — must be written within one message.

```
You are an expert product copywriter.
Write a short, friendly product description for a pair of wireless earbuds.
Include 3 bullet points and end with a call to action.
```

These prompts are still very useful since they are simple to construct and easy to test with parametrized templates. However, in advanced use cases, we should separate instructions by role type (system or user) especially when working with multi-turn conversations. Modern models (like GPT, Claude, or Gemini) use a **chat message format**, where multiple roles structure the conversation. This allows the model to understand who is speaking and why.

Role	Purpose	Example Content
System	Sets global behavior and identity of the model.	"You are an experienced financial analyst who writes concise, neutral summaries."
User	Provides the actual question, task, or input from the end-user.	"Summarize this quarterly report into three main points."
Assistant	Represents the model's previous responses (optional). Useful for multi-turn conversations.	"Here's your summary from last quarter..."

***Table 6.2**: Different Roles in a Prompt*

In Langfuse, we can version both text-only and chat-based prompts.

- For text-only prompts, we will usually store a single template string with parameters like **`{{product_name}}`** or **`{{tone}}`**.
- For chat-based prompts, Langfuse allows us to store system, user, and optionally assistant messages separately, making it easier to track updates and analyze performance by message type.

With this in mind, let us now look at the Prompts data model in Langfuse.

Understanding the Prompts Data Model in Langfuse

Similar to observability, Prompts too have a specific Data Model in Langfuse. The Prompts model is much more simplistic compared to the observability one and is essentially one main object called the **Prompt Object.** Let us look at the key fields of this model and understand how each contributes to reliable prompt management.

1. **Name:** The name field uniquely identifies a prompt within our Langfuse project.
    - **Purpose:** Ensures that different versions of the same logical prompt remain linked.
    - **Best practice:** Use short, descriptive names that reflect purpose, such as **`"support_reply"`**, **`"product_tagline"`**, or **`"invoice_parser"`**.
    - **Example:**
        - name: **`"product_description_v2"`**
2. **Type:** The type defines whether our prompt is a text-based or chat-based prompt. The default type is "text".
    - **Text prompts** are single-block instructions useful for summaries, classifications, or completions.
    - **Chat prompts** contain multiple messages, each with a role like system, user, or assistant, ideal for conversational or multi-turn contexts.
    - **Example:**
        - **Text:** "Write a 50-word summary of the following paragraph."
        - **Chat:** `[{"role": "system", "content": "You are a helpful tutor."}, {"role": "user", "content": "Explain Newton's laws in simple terms."}]`
3. **Prompt:** This field contains the actual prompt text or message array that the model sees. It can include placeholders (for example, **`{{product_name}}`**) for dynamic substitution at runtime.

- **For Text Prompts:** It is a single string.
- **For Chat Prompts:** It is a list of {role, content} pairs.
- **Example:**

```
[
   { "role": "system", "content": "You are an expert recruiter." },
   { "role": "user", "content": "Review this resume for {{job_title}}." }
]
```

4. **Config:** The config field holds all model-specific or behavioral parameters associated with the prompt. It is a flexible JSON object where you can define:
   - The name of the model (which includes "**gpt-4.1**", "**claude-3-haiku**").
   - Model parameters like **temperature, top_p, or max_tokens.**
   - Tool schemas or output formats (similar to JSON mode).
   - Any other settings that influence the behavior of the prompt.

   This ensures that both the text and its runtime behavior are versioned together.

   - **Example:**

```
"config": {
  "model": "gpt-4.1",
  "temperature": 0.01,
  "max_tokens": 500
}
```

5. **Version:** Every change to a prompt whether it's a small wording tweak or a new model configuration creates a new version. The version number lets Langfuse maintain a full history, allowing us to compare performance between iterations or roll back when needed. The version is automatically assigned and incremented when creating a new prompt version.
6. **Labels:** Labels act as human-readable shortcuts that map to specific versions. Instead of remembering version numbers, you can label them as "staging", "production", or "test". This allows seamless environment management: when you promote a new version to production, just move the label—no code changes required.
7. **Tags:** Tags make it easier to organize and filter prompts in the Langfuse dashboard. You can group prompts by function, product area, or owner.
   - **Example tags:** "customer-support", "email-generator", "ecommerce", "analytics"

This covers the theory part on Prompt Management. Let us now see how to create our first prompt in Langfuse.

Writing Your First Prompt in Langfuse

The simplest way to add a prompt is using the Langfuse UI. From the left navigation, under Prompt Management choose Prompts. This will show the list of existing prompts, and if no prompts are available yet, will show an option to create a new prompt. Langfuse makes it very easy for non-tech users to also do prompt management which is a key feature of the platform.

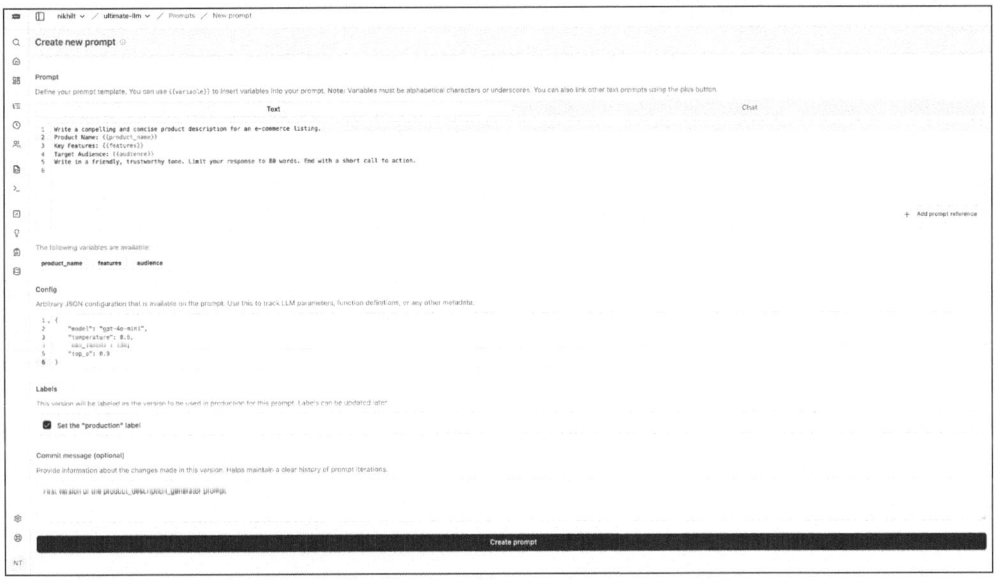

Figure 6.1: *Adding a New Prompt in Langfuse*

The fields on this page are exactly the same as the data model we saw in the previous section. Langfuse also allows us to organize prompts into folders by simply using a "/" in the prompt name. For e.g. `product/product_description_generator`. After filling out all the fields, click **Create Prompt** to create the prompt.

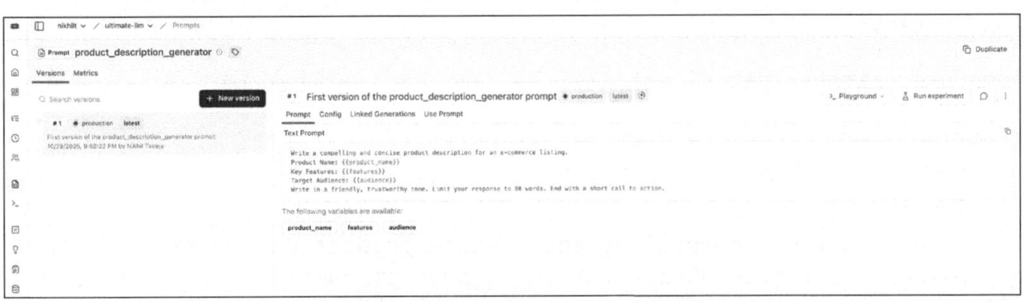

Figure 6.2: *Newly Created Prompt*

As we can see our prompt has 3 variables: **`product_name`**, **`features`**, and **`audience`** which are written inside doubly curly braces. To add tags to the prompt, we can click the tags icon next to the prompt's name and add the tags. To add a new version, click the **`New Version`** button.

Adding a chat type prompt also follows the steps, instead of choosing the **`Text`** option, we need to choose **`Chat`** instead. For a chat-based prompt, we can add different roles like system, user and assistant. These types of prompts are useful when developing applications that have conversational capabilities or when we want to keep the system and user prompts separate.

***Figure 6.3**: Chat Style Prompt*

Prompts can also be programmatically created using the Langfuse SDK.

```
from langfuse import get_client
from dotenv import load_dotenv

load_dotenv()

langfuse_client = get_client()

langfuse_client.create_prompt(
    name="product_description_generator_new",
    type="text",
    prompt="Write a compelling and concise product description for an
e-commerce listing.\n\nProduct Name: {{product_name}}\nKey Features:
{{features}}\nTarget Audience: {{audience}}\n\nWrite in a friendly,
```

```
trustworthy tone. Limit your response to 80 words. End with a short call
to action.",
    config={
        "model": "gpt-4o-mini",
        "temperature": 0.6,
        "max_tokens": 150,
        "top_p": 0.9,
    },
    labels=["staging"],
    tags=["marketing", "ecommerce", "copywriting"],
)
```

If the prompt with the same name already exists, this code will add a new version of the same prompt.

As we can see, it is very straightforward and intuitive to add new prompts in Langfuse. In the next section, we will look at some more features for prompt management and also how to make use of these prompts in our applications.

Prompt Management Features in Langfuse

So far we have seen how to create prompts in Langfuse. The examples were pretty basic and can be used as a starting point for doing prompt management. Since prompts are the building blocks of any LLM application, their lifecycle management needs a little more than just the ability to create new prompts.

As our application grows, prompts tend to evolve — we will tweak wording, add examples, adjust tone, or change how they interact with models. We would often need to know: which version is live, which one is being tested, or what changed between two edits? Langfuse helps solve this by offering **prompt management features** that give structure and control to how prompts are stored, updated, and deployed.

Prompt management in Langfuse is much like version control for code, but designed specifically for prompts. It helps us keep track of every change, experiment safely, and switch between versions without affecting main application logic. Let us explore the key features that make this possible.

Version Control and Labels

In Langfuse, every change we make to a prompt automatically creates a new version. This gives us a complete history of how our prompts have developed over time. We can view previous versions, compare them, or roll back to an earlier one whenever necessary. Versions IDs are numeric and are incremented automatically when you create a new version. Besides these IDs, prompts can also be identified based on labels such as "production", "staging" or "latest".

By default, every prompt when created for the first time, will have version ID 1 and the labels "latest" and "production". With every change to the prompt, the version number is incremented by one. Exactly one version can be labelled "production" which is the default version when requested via the SDK. For every new version, the label "latest" is applied to the most recent version.

New labels can be created via the UI or the SDK. Labels are tied to a particular prompt and can be used by any of the versions. **Labels cannot be shared between different prompts.**

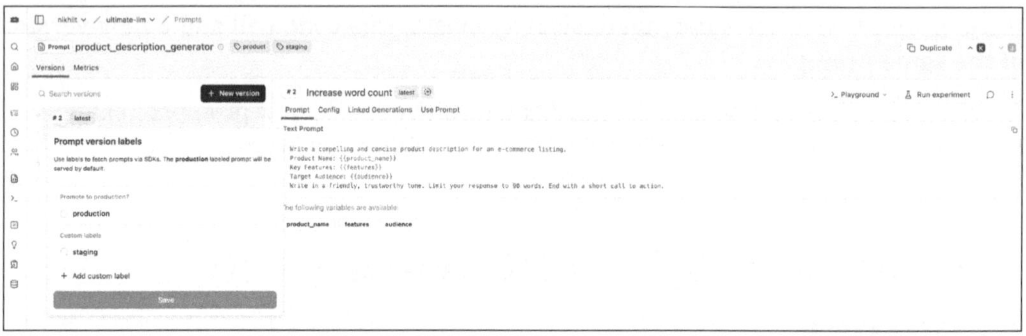

***Figure 6.4:** Adding a New Label to the Prompt*

Within the UI, we can also compare two prompt versions to check the differences.

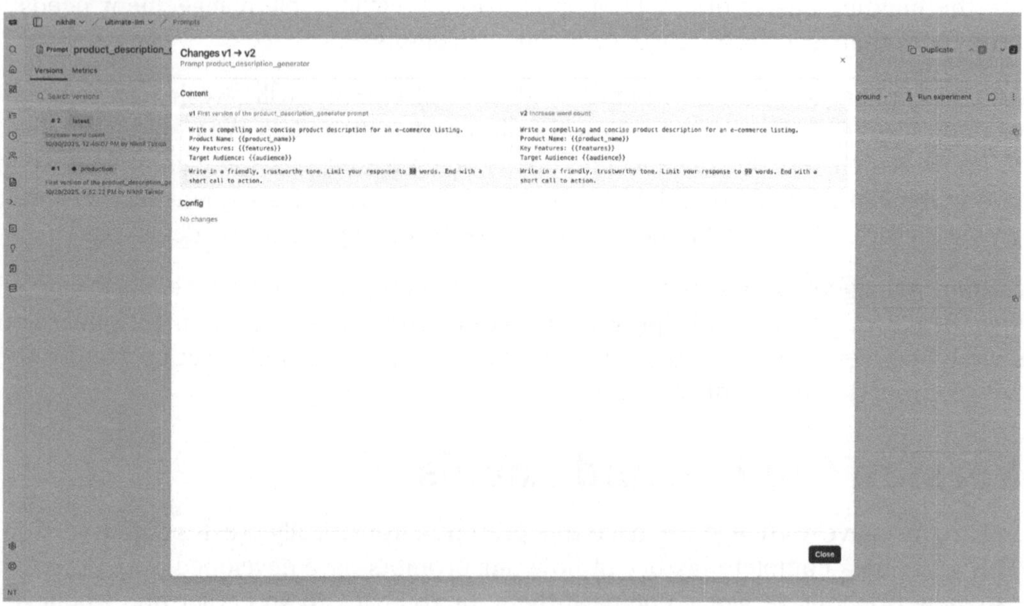

***Figure 6.5:** Comparing Two Prompt Versions*

Once we have versioned and labeled our prompt, we can retrieve it in our applications using the SDK.

```
from langfuse import get_client
from dotenv import load_dotenv

load_dotenv()

langfuse_client = get_client()

# By default the prompt with tag production is returned if no version or
label is specified
default_prompt = langfuse_client.get_prompt("product_description_
generator")

# Retrieving by label
prompt_by_label = langfuse_client.get_prompt("product_description_
generator", label="latest")

# Retrieving by version number
prompt_by_version = langfuse_client.get_prompt("product_description_
generator", version=1)

print(prompt_by_version.__dict__)
```

The returned prompt object contains all the important information about the prompt which we can use in other parts of the application. This includes the text, labels, tags and even the configuration of the prompt. We will see later in the chapter how the **config** can be used to invoke an LLM to generate a response.

```
{
  'name': 'product_description_generator',
  'version': 1,
  'config': {
    'model': 'gpt-4o-mini',
    'temperature': 0.6,
    'max_tokens': 150,
    'top_p': 0.9
  },
  'labels': ['production'],
  'tags': ['product', 'staging'],
  'commit_message': 'First version of the product_description_generator
prompt',
  'is_fallback': False,
  'prompt': 'Write a compelling and concise product description for
an e-commerce listing.\nProduct Name: {{product_name}}\nKey Features:
```

```
{{features}}\nTarget Audience: {{audience}}\nWrite in a friendly,
trustworthy tone. Limit your response to 80 words. End with a short call
to action.\n'
}
```

Retrieving prompts by version numbers should be restricted since it requires code changes and possibly the deployment of a new application version to use the new version of the prompt.

When we promote a new version to production, we do not have to modify our code. We simply move the "*production*" label to the latest version in Langfuse. This makes updates seamless, consistent, and much easier to manage across environments. However, this needs to be done with proper validation and experimentation since this can have a major impact on the functionality of our system. In case of adverse effects, we can just as easily revert to the previous working version of a prompt by labelling it back to "production".

Composability

Prompt Composability means that we can reuse prompts inside other prompts. Instead of writing each prompt from scratch and duplicating shared instructions, context, or examples, we create modular prompt components and then reference them. This avoids repetition and lets one base prompt serve many dependent prompts.

For example, we might have a prompt snippet called "*Common Instructions for Tone & Style*" that we reference in every customer-support prompt. Then if we change our company voice, we update the one snippet and all dependent prompts automatically pick up the change.

Practical Uses of Composability

- **Reduced Duplication and Easier Maintenance**: When many prompts share the same context (rules, brand voice, disclaimers), we avoid copy-pasting. If a rule changes (e.g., "use friendly tone" becomes "use professional tone"), we update one snippet instead of editing dozens of prompts manually.
- **Faster Iteration and Fewer Errors**: With modular structure, we can focus on smaller parts (just the context snippet) and know that changes ripple through dependent prompts. That means fewer opportunities for inconsistencies.
- **Better Governance and Auditability**: We can clearly identify which part of a prompt is shared, which part is unique. When something breaks, we can check the shared snippet version to see if the error stems from there.
- **Scalability for Large Teams or Many Prompts**: As we build more flows we do not explode the number of unique prompt templates blindly. We build a modular library of components.

- **Consistent Brand Voice and Rules across the Board**: Because shared context is reused, we have much greater confidence that all parts of the system are aligned with brand guidelines or regulatory requirements.

To add a composed prompt, we need to first create the individual prompt parts separately as new prompts. In the main prompt, where the composition should happen, we can click on the `Add prompt reference` button to add a prompt by label/version in the current prompt.

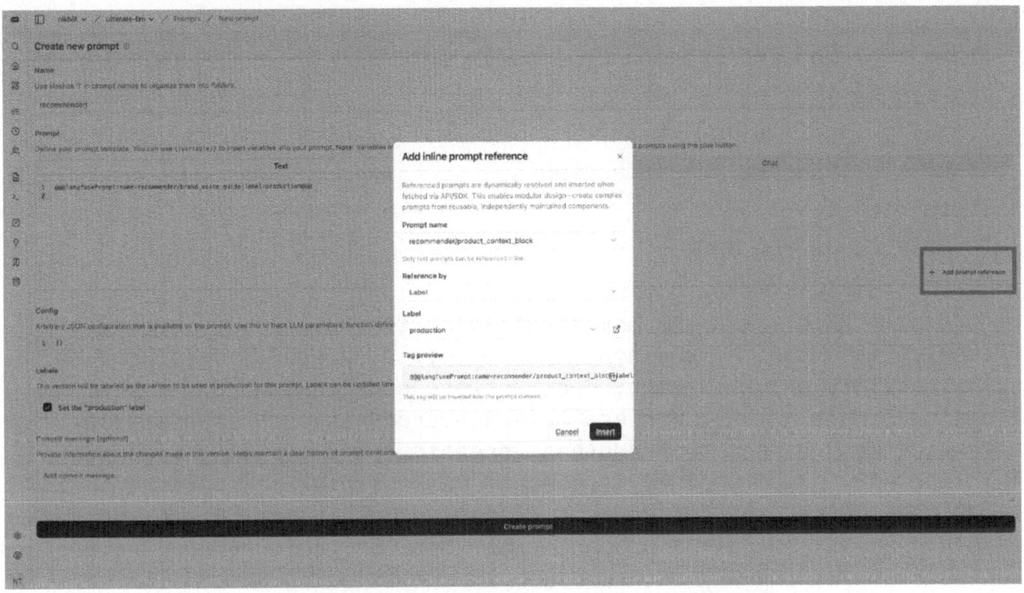

***Figure 6.6:** Composing Prompts in Langfuse*

After saving the prompt it will appear like this:

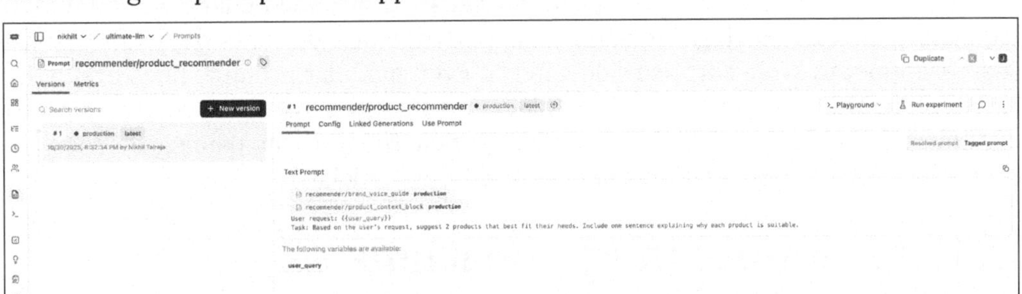

***Figure 6.7:** A Prompt Composed of Two Other Prompts*

The complete prompt can be seen by clicking the `Resolved Prompt` tab.

In the SDK, when this prompt is fetched, it returns the full resolved prompt

```
from langfuse import get_client
```

```
from dotenv import load_dotenv

load_dotenv()

langfuse_client = get_client()

prompt = langfuse_client.get_prompt("recommender/product_recommender")

print(prompt.__dict__)
```

```
{
  'name': 'recommender/product_recommender',
  'version': 1,
  'config': {},
  'labels': ['latest', 'production'],
  'tags': [],
  'commit_message': None,
  'is_fallback': False,
  'prompt': 'You are an AI assistant for a company. Always speak in a
friendly, informative, and honest tone. Avoid exaggerations. Mention
sustainability when relevant. Keep answers under 150 words. End with
a positive note.\n\nWe offer eco-friendly products such as reusable
water bottles, bamboo toothbrushes, organic cotton towels, and natural
skincare kits. Each product is sourced responsibly and supports small
local producers.\n\nUser request: {{user_query}}\nTask: Based on the
user's request, suggest 2 products that best fit their needs. Include one
sentence explaining why each product is suitable.\n'
}
```

When using references, we must manage versions and labels carefully since changing the version on a referenced prompt might cause unintended changes if an update happens without knowing. We should document which prompts depend on which shared snippet to avoid surprise side-effects. Even modular prompts need evaluation just because the base snippet updated does not guarantee every dependent prompt continues to perform well. We may need to test them. Clear naming conventions should be used so team members understand intent quickly.

Using Prompts in Applications

Now that we have created our prompts, it is time to see how we can use them in our application. We will use one of the earlier prompts we created: **`'product_description_generator'`** in a call to get a response. We will use the prompt from Langfuse to get the contents of the prompt and also the config which is tied to the prompt.

This prompt also expects 3 variables: **`product_name`**, **`features`** and **`audience`** which we need to pass to the prompt.

```
from langfuse import get_client
from dotenv import load_dotenv
from langfuse.openai import openai

load_dotenv()

langfuse_client = get_client()

# Retrieve the default prompt version (label="production")
prompt = langfuse_client.get_prompt("product_description_generator")

def generate_product_description(product_name: str, features: list[str],
audience):
    # Pass variable values to the prompt
    prompt_content = prompt.compile(
        product_name=product_name, features=features, audience=audience
    )
    # Retrieve config from the prompt and use it in the call to openai
    config = prompt.config
    completion = openai.chat.completions.create(
        model=config.get("model", "gpt-4.1-mini"),
        messages=[{"role": "system", "content": prompt_content}],
        temperature=config.get("temperature", 0.1),
        max_tokens=config.get("max_tokens", 200),
        top_p=config.get("top_p", 1),
        # Link the generation to the prompt
        langfuse_prompt=prompt,
    )
    return completion.choices[0].message.content

generate_product_description(
    product_name="PulsePro Smartwatch",
    features=[
        "Heart rate and sleep tracking",
        "built-in GPS",
        "waterproof design",
        "7-day battery life",
        "smartphone notifications",
    ],
    audience="Active professionals and fitness enthusiasts",
)
```

Variable values can be passed using the **`compile`** method on the prompt as key-value pairs. For the model parameters like **`temperature`**, **`max_tokens`** and **`top_p`** the values are also retrieved from the saved config of the prompt.

This is how the trace from the above code will look like in Langfuse.

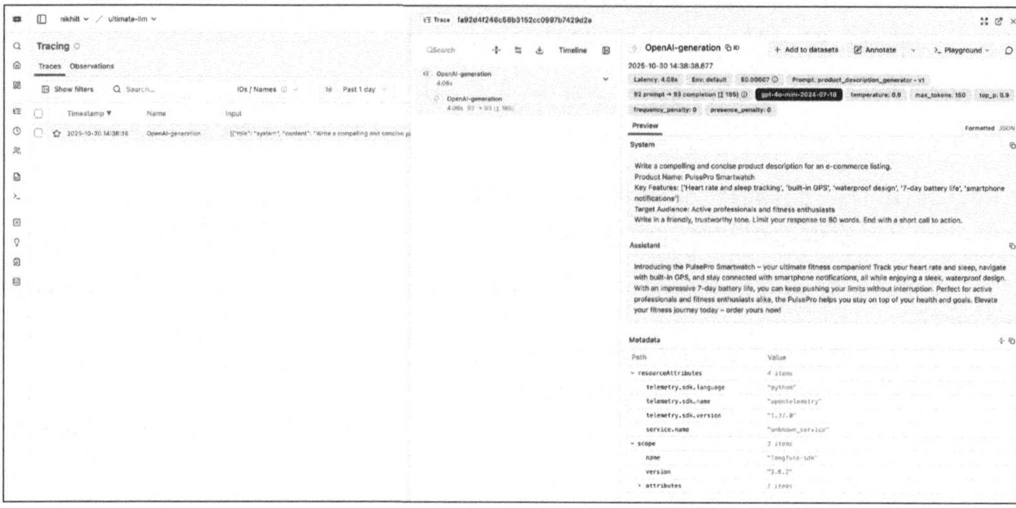

Figure 6.8: *Using Prompt from Langfuse*

By passing **`langfuse_prompt=prompt`** in the call to OpenAI, we are also able to link the prompt from Langfuse to the trace. This is a very powerful feature and allows us to track some key metrics like latency, tokens and cost on the prompt itself. After creating traces with linked prompts, we can visit the Metrics tab on the prompt, to see these metrics by prompt version.

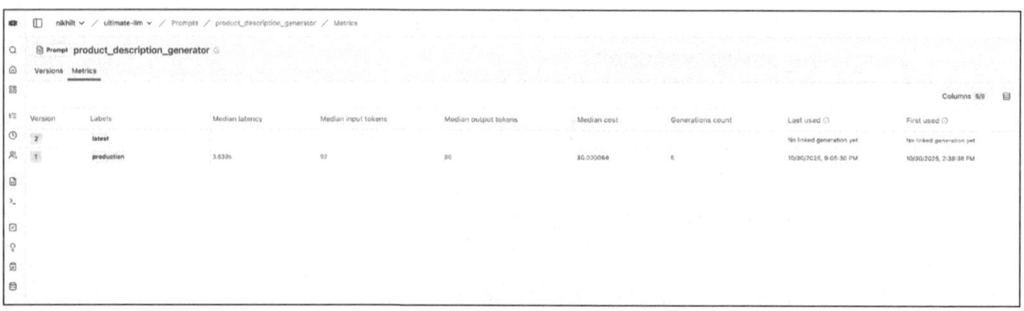

Figure 6.9: *Prompt Level Metrics*

Prompts can be linked to traces in other integrations like LangChain as well. Here is the same example using LangChain to link the prompt to the generated trace.

```
from langfuse import get_client
from dotenv import load_dotenv
from langfuse.langchain import CallbackHandler
from langchain_core.prompts import PromptTemplate
from langchain_openai import OpenAI
```

```
load_dotenv()

langfuse_client = get_client()

# Initialize the Langfuse handler for Langchain
langfuse_handler = CallbackHandler()

# Retrieve the default prompt version (label="production")
prompt = langfuse_client.get_prompt("product_description_generator")

langchain_prompt = PromptTemplate.from_template(
    prompt.get_langchain_prompt(),
    metadata={"langfuse_prompt": prompt}
)

def generate_product_description(product_name: str, features: list[str],
audience):
    llm = OpenAI()
    completion_chain = langchain_prompt | llm
    completion_chain.invoke(
        {"product_name": product_name, "features": features, "audience":
audience},
        config={"callbacks": [langfuse_handler]}
    )

generate_product_description(
    product_name="PulsePro Smartwatch",
    features=[
        "Heart rate and sleep tracking",
        "built-in GPS",
        "waterproof design",
        "7-day battery life",
        "smartphone notifications",
    ],
    audience="Active professionals and fitness enthusiasts",
)
```

Here we use **`metadata={"langfuse_prompt": prompt}`** to link the prompt with the trace.

A/B Testing

A/B testing (also known as **split testing**) is a simple but powerful method for comparing two different versions of something – for example, two website designs, two emails, or in our case, two prompt versions. Version A is presented to one group of users, while version B is presented to a different group. After collecting enough data, we compare which version performs better based on measurable outcomes, such as user satisfaction, clarity of responses, speed, or cost. This process helps us make data-driven decisions instead of relying on guesses or personal preference. A/B testing is a controlled way of testing variations directly on production on real users instead of relying completely on offline testing methods.

In Langfuse, we can label different versions of a prompt (e.g., version-a and version-b) and then split traffic between them so we can gather metrics and decide which version is better.

For example, one variant might say "Be concise and professional," while another says "Be friendly and conversational." We run both versions with actual users, measure how each performs (response quality, user engagement, cost, latency), and pick the winner.

How A/B Testing Works in Langfuse

We take a prompt and create at least two distinct versions. Then we assign labels such as version-a and version-b so we can refer to each variant clearly in code or configuration. In our application code, instead of always using the same prompt version, we randomly select between the two (or more) labelled versions. For example:

```
import random
prompt_a = langfuse.get_prompt("my_prompt", label="version-a")
prompt_b = langfuse.get_prompt("my_prompt", label="version-b")
selected = random.choice([prompt_a, prompt_b])
```

Then we call the model using **`selected`** and pass the user input. As we saw in the previous section, Langfuse records performance metrics for each prompt version: response latency, token usage, cost per call, quality / evaluation scores (if defined). This data is then available in the UI. Once we've collected enough data, we compare the two versions. Which one gave better responses (according to metrics or human feedback)? Which one cost less or was faster? Based on that, we can promote one version to production (via labels).

Running Effective A/B Testing Using Langfuse

- We need **enough traffic** so the test has meaningful results — small sample sizes may mislead.
- We should define **clear metrics** before starting (such as "percentage of sessions with no follow-up question", "response time under 800 ms", "cost per response under 0.005").
- We must manage labels and versions carefully — the version we test should be isolated and properly tracked so we know exactly which responses came from which variant.

- A/B testing is most useful when user impact is measurable and the system can tolerate variation during the test phase. If we are in a high-risk scenario we may prefer full rollout only after thorough testing.

In a later chapter, we will see a complete example of an A/B test running on Langfuse. In this example we will also leverage the feature of Evaluations to make informed decisions before choosing a prompt version.

Caching

When our application uses prompts stored in Langfuse, every time we fetch a prompt it might involve network calls and database lookups. If this happens on every request, it can add latency, impact user experience, and reduce responsiveness—especially in real-time or high-throughput applications.

Langfuse solves this by keeping a copy of the prompt locally (in memory), so subsequent requests for the same prompt avoid the full retrieval process. In Langfuse, prompt caching ensures that retrieving a prompt becomes effectively **instant**, preserving application latency while still allowing prompts to be centrally managed and updated.

How Caching Works in Langfuse

When we call the SDK method like **`get_prompt("my_prompt")`**, the first call retrieves the prompt from Langfuse's service. After that:

- The prompt is stored in the SDK's local cache with a configurable TTL (Time-to-Live) (for example, 60 seconds by default).
- On subsequent calls within the TTL, the SDK returns the cached version immediately—no network or heavy processing delay.
- If the TTL has expired, the SDK may return the **stale** version instantly and refresh the cache in the background, or it may fetch the new version directly depending on configuration. This means we rarely block on prompt retrieval.

On the Langfuse server side (particularly when self-hosting), the system leverages caching (like Redis) for prompt retrieval. This reduces database load and speeds up look-ups for frequently used prompt versions. Also, when a prompt is updated (new version created), the cache invalidates so that we do not continue serving outdated prompts.

To fetch a prompt with a fixed TTL we can use:

```
prompt = langfuse.get_prompt("product_recommender", cache_ttl_
seconds=300)
```

Similarly to disable caching, set **`cache_ttl_seconds`** to 0

```
prompt = langfuse.get_prompt("product_recommender", cache_ttl_seconds=0)
```

Practical Tips to Work with Caching

- For prompts in production, use caching with a moderate TTL (like 300 seconds).
- For prompts under active development or testing, consider a low TTL or disable caching to immediately see changes.
- On startup of your application, consider **pre-fetching** key prompts so the first user request does not have to wait for the initial network fetch. This is particularly helpful in microservices or serverless environments.
- Monitor cache hit-rates and prompt retrieval latency in logs.
- Be mindful of dependencies: if a prompt references another prompt (via composability), changes in the referenced prompt should trigger invalidation or refresh so that dependent prompts are not stale.

To fetch a prompt on startup and provide a fallback in case or errors, we can do something like this:

```
from langfuse import get_client
from dotenv import load_dotenv
from langfuse.model import TextPromptClient

load_dotenv()

langfuse_client = get_client()

fallback_prompt = (
    "Write a compelling and concise product description for an
e-commerce listing"
)

def fetch_prompt() -> TextPromptClient:
    try:
        # Fetch and cache a prompt
        langfuse_client.get_prompt(
            "product_description_generator",
            cache_ttl_seconds=300,
            fallback=fallback_prompt,
        )
    except Exception as e:
        print(f"Failed to fetch prompt : {e}")
        # We might throw an error or exit the application here
        # We can also return a fallback prompt
        return TextPromptClient(prompt=fallback_prompt, is_
fallback=True)

fetch_prompt()
```

This covers both cases of failure when either the Langfuse server is not reachable or there is an Exception while fetching the prompt.

Config

We have already seen some examples of config being used with prompts. The **config** field in Langfuse is where we store all extra settings, versioned together with the prompt itself. Besides model parameters like top_p, temperature etc., we can also store JSON schemas that can be mapped to a model response. The config is optional and is attached to a particular version of the prompt. The config can also contain metadata associated with the prompt.

Examples Where Config Can be Used

We saw in a previous code example how we can use model parameters from the retrieved prompt and use it in the call to our model:

```
completion = openai.chat.completions.create(
        model=config.get("model", "gpt-4.1-mini"),
        messages=[{"role": "system", "content": prompt_content}],
        temperature=config.get("temperature", 0.1),
        max_tokens=config.get("max_tokens", 200),
        top_p=config.get("top_p", 1),
    )
```

Now if we need to change the model or any of the parameters, we can just use the prompt config on Langfuse without changing the code.

Config can also be used to store JSON objects which map to the response structure we expect from our model.

```
{
  "model": "gpt-4.1",
  "json_schema": {
    "type": "object",
    "properties": {
      "invoiceId": { "type": "string" },
      "amount": { "type": "number" },
      "vendor": { "type": "string" }
    },
    "required": ["invoiceId","amount","vendor"]
  }
}
```

Another practical utility of the config is to store dynamic metadata for your prompt or the model call. Let us say we might have a prompt that varies by language. The config could include supported languages or the tone.

```
{
  "model": "gpt-4.1",
  "supported_languages": ["en","de","fr"],
  "tone": "playful"
}
```

If later we want to add Spanish ("es") or change tone to "formal", we update config and create a new version. This keeps behavioral changes separate from prompt text templates but still captured in one record.

With this we have covered the most useful features of prompt management in Langfuse. In the next section, we will look at how we use the Playground feature in Langfuse to do some rapid testing of prompts before we move to full-scale evaluations.

LLM Playground in Langfuse

When we start writing our prompts or refine them, we often need an interactive space to test how different phrasings, models, or settings perform. The Playground feature in Langfuse gives us exactly that: a sandbox where we can tweak prompts, experiment with variables and configurations, and instantly see how the model responds. Instead of writing a prompt, deploying, waiting, and then seeing how it behaves in real use, the Playground allows us to run the prompt directly within the Langfuse UI. We can vary the input variables, switch model parameters (**`temperature`**, **`max_tokens`**, **`top_p`**), and instantly observe different outputs.

The Playground is available on the left navigation under the heading **Playground.**

Before using this feature, we need to set up an LLM Connection. LLM Connections are used by Langfuse to connect directly to your preferred LLM providers. This is required to use the Playground and some other features. To add a new connection, we need to know all the connection parameters to the provider. This varies by provider, for e.g. OpenAI only requires an API key but other providers may require other fields. **For OpenAI Langfuse will make available all the default models to be used in the Playground.** For other providers, it is possible that we need to have one connection per model. Langfuse supports these providers for adding LLM connections:

- OpenAI
- Azure OpenAI
- Anthropic
- Google Vertex
- Amazon Bedrock

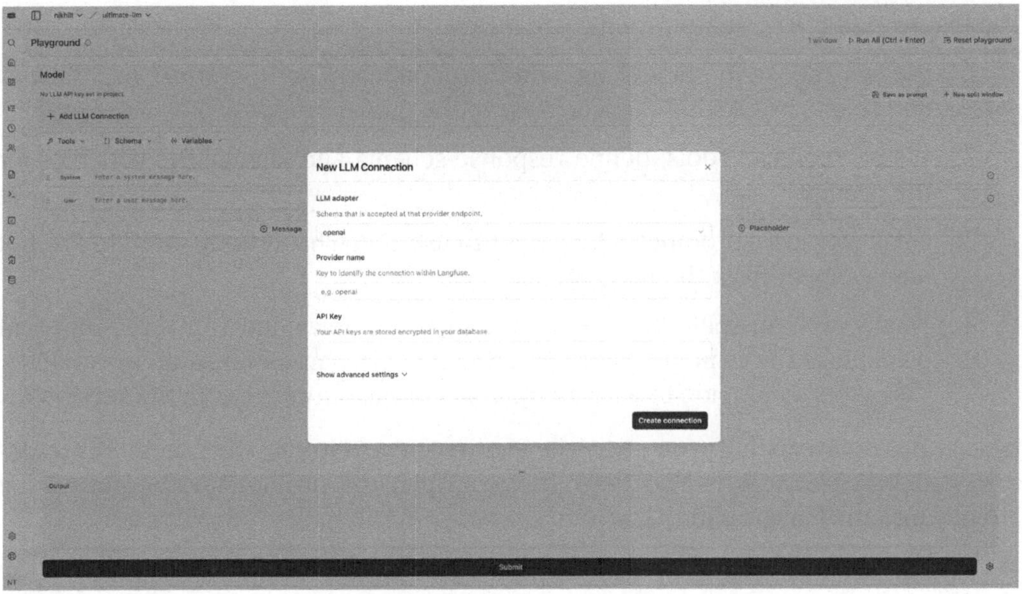

Figure 6.10: *Adding a New LLM Connection*

Once we add the connection, the Playground is ready to be used.

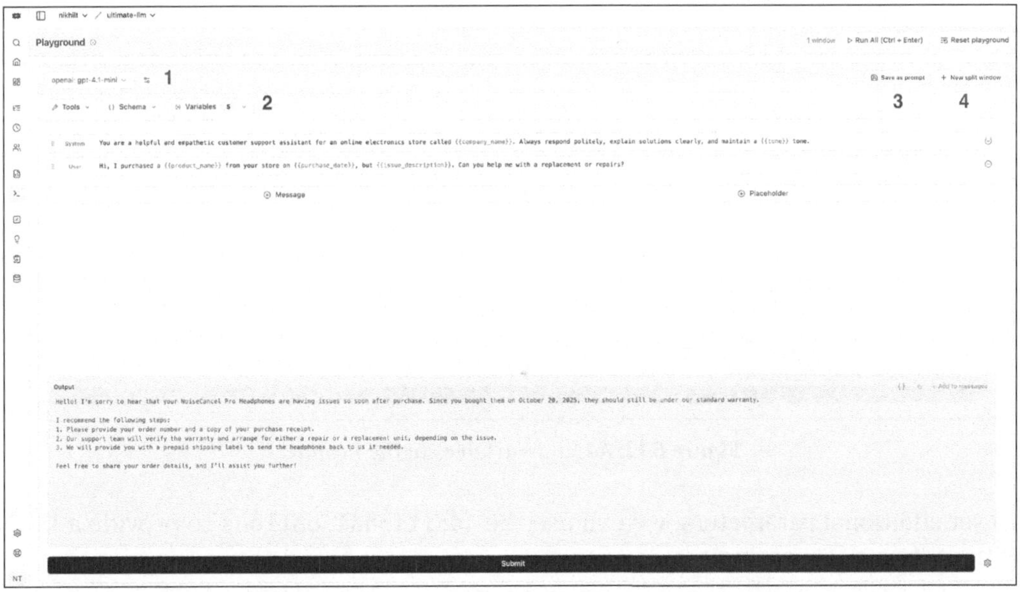

Figure 6.11: *Testing Prompts Using the Playground*

The Playground offers, some very nifty features:

1. We can choose the model and add the parameters (temperature, max tokens, and so on.) by clicking the icon next to the model dropdown.
2. We can connect tools, define response schema and change the variables for the prompt.
3. Once we have a prompt that we want to use, it can be directly saved to Prompt Management from the Playground.
4. Finally, we can split the screen into more windows and run three different prompts at the same time with different models, parameters and/or variables. This gives a nice side by side comparison of the outputs for all the versions.

We can also open existing prompts in the Playground and iterate over them. For traces with generations, there is also the option to open the prompt for the generation directly into the Playground.

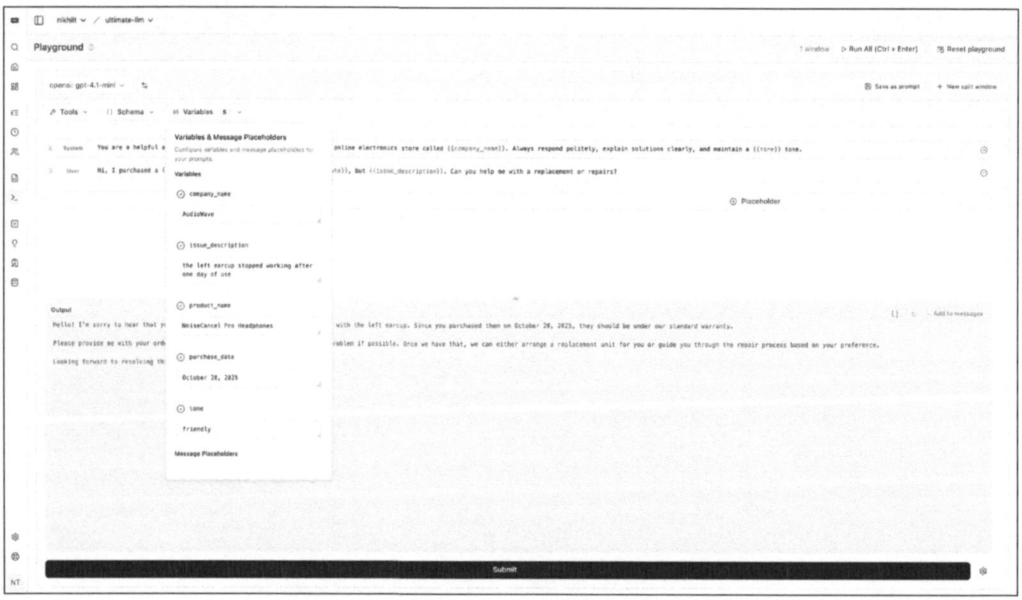

Figure 6.12: *Adding Variables to the Prompt*

To set additional parameters, we can use the **`Additional options`** to provide a JSON with other model parameters.

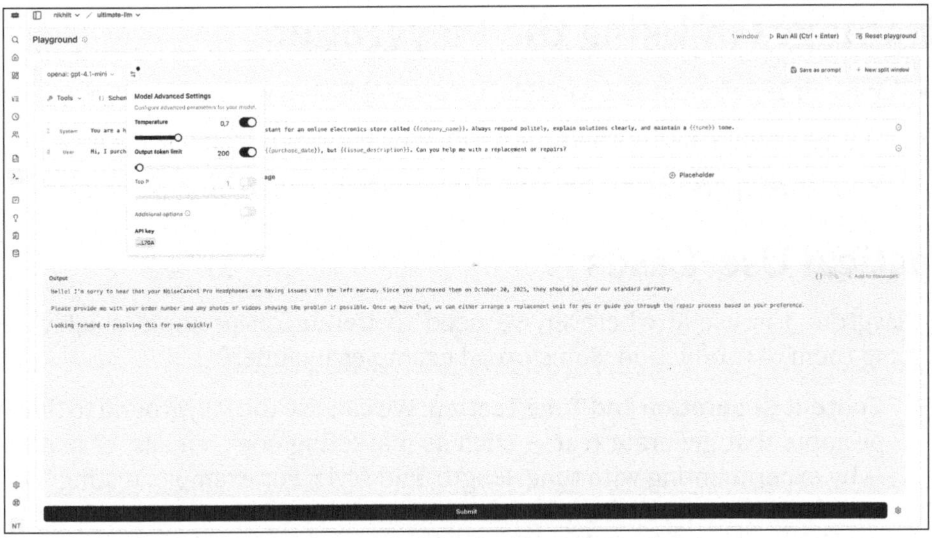

Figure 6.13: *Updating Model Parameters*

The split screen feature in the Playground makes it easier to test and refine prompts by displaying multiple versions of a prompt together. Instead of switching between separate test runs, we can view responses from different prompt variations or model configurations in one place, allowing for immediate visual and qualitative comparison.

Each setup maintains its own parameters such as model type, temperature, or system instructions so we can clearly see how individual adjustments influence the generated output. This approach helps us pinpoint which changes truly improve quality, consistency, or tone.

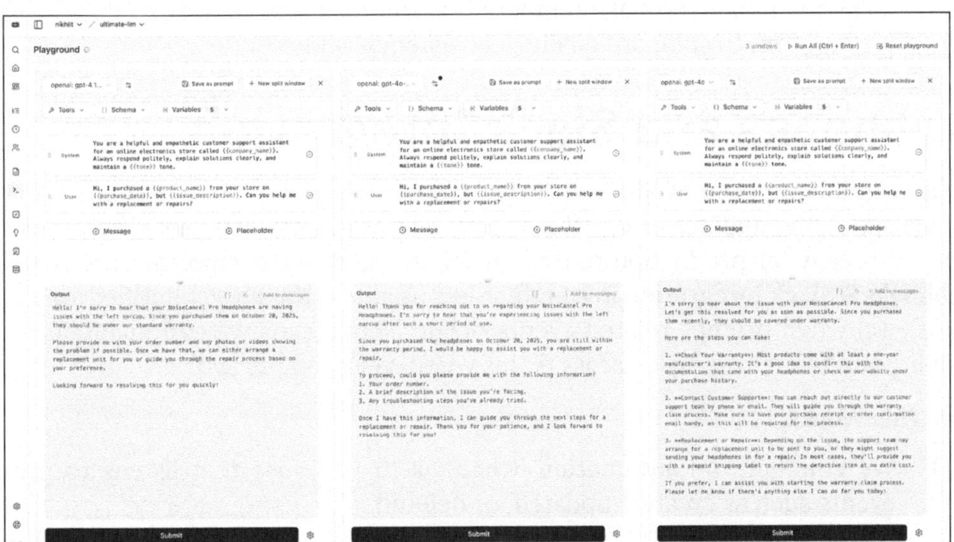

Figure 6.14: *Split Screen Feature*

Advantages of Using the Playground

- We can experiment in a sandbox before deploying widely.
- We get immediate feedback rather than waiting for production data.
- Non-developers can participate and visually compare prompt variants.

Practical Use-Cases

The Playground is useful wherever we need to iterate on prompts quickly before deploying them to production. Some broad examples include:

- **Content Generation and Tone Testing:** We can use the Playground to fine-tune prompts that generate text — such as marketing copy, emails, or summaries — by experimenting with tone, length, and style. For example, testing "concise and factual" versus "friendly and conversational" responses helps identify which tone best fits our brand voice.
- **Response Optimization for Conversational Agents:** Teams building chatbots or virtual assistants can test multiple response styles or apology patterns to find what leads to better user satisfaction.
- **Structured Output and Data Formatting:** For workflows that extract data or produce JSON outputs, we can validate prompt templates against various real-world inputs. The Playground helps ensure the model consistently follows the expected schema, even when the input data format changes.
- **Evaluating Model or Parameter Changes:** When switching to a new model or adjusting parameters like temperature and max tokens, we can use the same prompt text to compare quality, consistency, and cost.

Webhooks and Slack Integration

While maintaining prompt lifecycle in Langfuse, we can have new prompt versions, label changes, tag updates or deletions. If we do not get notified when these changes occur, it is easy for production to drift or for teams to miss important updates. The **Webhooks & Slack Integration** in Langfuse lets us automatically get notified (or trigger workflows) when prompt-related events occur. This means we can maintain better visibility and faster response across teams whenever prompts evolve.

How This Works:

1. We configure an **automation/webhook** in Langfuse that listens to prompt events such as created, updated, or deleted.

2. We provide a URL endpoint (or a Slack channel integration) that Langfuse will call whenever the event fires. The payload includes details of the prompt version, name, labels, tags, timestamp.
3. For Slack specifically, there is native support so notifications can arrive directly in chosen Slack channels, enabling real-time awareness across teams.
4. For security, each webhook call can include a signature (**`x-langfuse-signature`**) allowing the receiving service to verify authenticity.

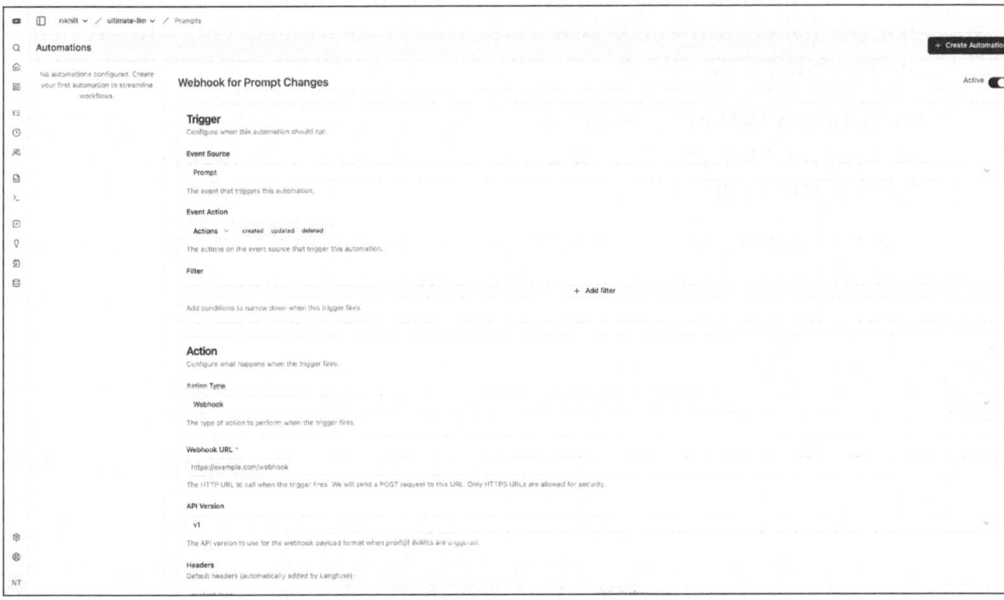

Figure 6.15: *Adding a New Webhook*

Webhooks can be added by navigating to the **Prompts** section and then clicking **Automations.**

An Automation is always created on a type of Source, for instance Prompts. We can choose the events and then filter by the Name of the prompt to only trigger the Webhook for certain prompts.

The **Webhook URL** is mandatory for triggering webhooks and if we choose slack, then we need to add a Slack Connection. For slack alerts on the self-hosted version, we need to create a new Slack app which can done using the guide at:

`https://github.com/langfuse/langfuse/blob/main/web/src/features/slack/README.md`

Besides this, we need to have these 3 env variables:

```
SLACK_CLIENT_ID=your_client_id_here
```

```
SLACK_CLIENT_SECRET=your_client_secret_here
SLACK_STATE_SECRET=your_state_secret_here
```

We can generate the **SLACK_STATE_SECRET** using:

```
openssl rand -base64 32 | tr -d "=+/" | cut -c1-32
```

Practical Usage of Webhooks

- **Production Monitoring:** We get alerted when a production prompt version changes (labels switched, new version live) so we can verify behavior and guard against regressions.
- **Team Coordination:** Instead of relying on manual communication ("Hey, I changed the prompt"), our Slack channel is automatically notified, keeping all stakeholders in the loop.
- **Workflow Automation:** We can trigger CI/CD pipelines or syncing mechanisms (such as update docs, push to GitHub) in response to prompt changes.

Conclusion

In this chapter, we have dived into Prompt Management in Langfuse, focusing on how we can build more reliable and efficient LLM applications. We explored key practices in prompt engineering—like providing direction, setting formats, and including examples—while emphasizing quality checks and collaborative workflows. We also covered the Prompts Data Model, version control, composability, A/B testing, and caching features in Langfuse, showing how these help us design and optimize prompts. Other features such as Webhooks, Slack notifications and the LLM Playground enable us to collaborate, monitor, and test prompts interactively. We have covered enough ground now to finally start evaluating our application. The next chapter is completely dedicated to this, and we will see how Evaluations work in Langfuse.

References

- Prompt Engineering for Generative AI: Future-Proof Inputs for Reliable AI Outputs Paperback English edition by James Phoenix & Mike Taylor - https://www.oreilly.com/library/view/prompt-engineering-for/9781098153427/ch01.html
- Getting Started with Prompts in Langfuse - https://langfuse.com/docs/prompt-management/get-started
- Langfuse Prompts Data Model - https://langfuse.com/docs/prompt-management/data-model

- Prompt Version Control - https://langfuse.com/docs/prompt-management/features/prompt-version-control
- Prompt Composability -
  - https://langfuse.com/docs/prompt-management/features/composability
- A/B testing prompts - https://langfuse.com/docs/prompt-management/features/a-b-testing
- Prompt Caching - https://langfuse.com/docs/prompt-management/features/caching
- Prompt Config - https://langfuse.com/docs/prompt-management/features/config
- Webhooks and Slack Integration - https://langfuse.com/docs/prompt-management/features/webhooks-slack-integrations

CHAPTER 7
Evaluating LLMs in Langfuse

Introduction

This chapter introduces the Evaluation feature in Langfuse, which allows us to assess response quality using both automated metrics and human feedback. We will cover quantitative measures such as response latency, token efficiency, and cost per query, as well as qualitative metrics such as relevance, coherence, correctness, and user satisfaction. We will also learn how to set up evaluation pipelines and collect structured feedback from end-users. The emphasis is on building an evaluation strategy that combines automation with human judgment. We will also see how we can run experiments to validate improvements and ensure that system changes lead to measurable gains.

Structure

In this chapter, we will cover the following topics:

- Evaluation of LLM Applications
- Online and Offline Evaluations in Langfuse
  - Offline Evaluation and Experimentation
  - Deployment and Live Monitoring
  - Online Evaluation and Feedback Integration
- Core Concepts of Evaluation in Langfuse:
  - Scores
  - Evaluation Methods
  - Datasets
  - Experiments
- Creating our First Dataset in Langfuse
  - What Makes a Good Dataset

  - Dataset Creation Using the UI/SDK
  - Synthetic Datasets
- Automatic Trace Scoring Using LLM-as-a-Judge
  - Benefits of Using an LLM as a Judge
  - Setting up an Evaluator
  - Accessing Scores
  - Custom Evaluators
- Manual Scoring
  - Human Annotations
  - Custom Scores
- Running Experiments in Langfuse
  - Prompt Experiments
  - Experiments Using the SDK
- Score Analytics

Evaluation of LLM Applications

In *Chapter 4, Introduction to Langfuse* we saw a small introduction to the Evaluation feature of Langfuse. Langfuse provides a robust framework for evaluating and monitoring LLM-based systems. It enables teams to collect, visualize, and analyze both quantitative and qualitative metrics across production and testing environments.

Before diving into the feature, it is important to clarify what we mean by evaluation in the context of LLM applications. Evaluation serves several purposes:

- **Performance Validation:** Ensuring that the application behaves as expected for defined use cases, such as accurately answering questions or summarizing content.
- **Reliability Measurement:** Determining how consistent the outputs of the model are across repeated queries or slight input variations.
- **Quality Assurance:** Assessing linguistic coherence, factual accuracy, and alignment with user or organizational standards.
- **Risk Mitigation:** Identifying potential failure modes such as hallucinations, bias, or unsafe outputs.
- **Optimization Feedback:** Providing actionable data to improve prompts, fine-tuned models, or system orchestration pipelines.

When we talk about evaluating an LLM application, we cannot evaluate the model in isolation. We must assess the entire system including:

- The **prompt design** and orchestration logic;
- The **retrieval or context** (if applicable);
- The **model output** itself; and,
- The **user interaction feedback.**

Evaluation should also be in line with the dimensions of monitoring: **Functional, Non-functional Ethical and Safety** monitoring.

A well-defined evaluation framework answers three fundamental questions:

1. **Is the application doing what it is supposed to do?** These tasks include – Functional adequacy, task performance and semantic accuracy.
2. **Is the application doing it consistently and efficiently keeping in consideration latency, cost, and scalability?**
3. **Is the application doing it responsibly with ethical alignment, safety, compliance, and fairness?**

Each of these dimensions requires distinct types of metrics and monitoring practices, many of which Langfuse supports through integrated evaluation pipelines, semantic scoring, and feedback collection.

By making evaluation a continuous process, we can develop systems that can do:

- **Early Drift Detection:** Identify quality regressions before users do.
- **Faster Experimentation:** Test new prompts or models with controlled metrics.
- **Data-Driven Optimization:** Replace subjective impressions with measurable trends.
- **Governance and Auditability:** Maintain traceable evidence of compliance and ethical alignment.
- **User-Centered Improvement:** Incorporate real-world feedback as part of the monitoring loop.

Online and Offline Evaluations in Langfuse

If we recall from *Chapter 4, Introduction to Langfuse*, evaluations can be broadly divided into Online and Offline evaluations which are performed before and after an application is deployed respectively.

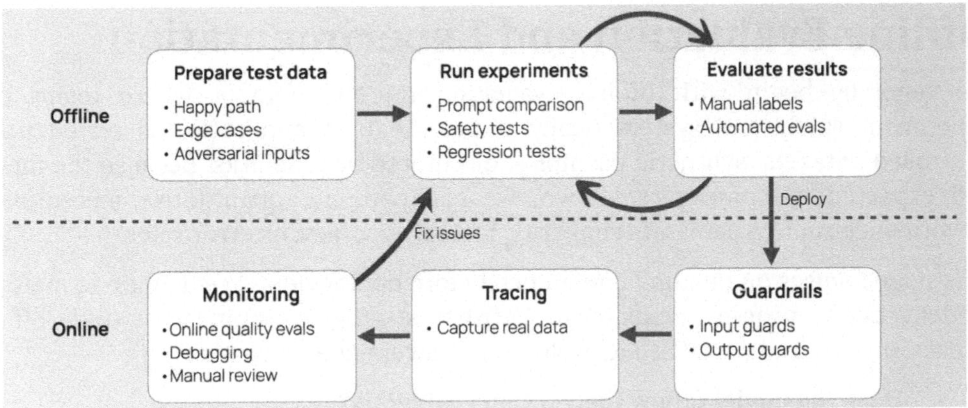

Figure 7.1: *How to Continuously Improve LLM Products Evidently by AI (Source -https://www.youtube.com/watch?v=x9mfMkBWwCY)*

This also creates a continuous loop in the LLM application development lifecycle. Langfuse uses a slightly adapted version of this process but keeping the essence of evaluation the same.

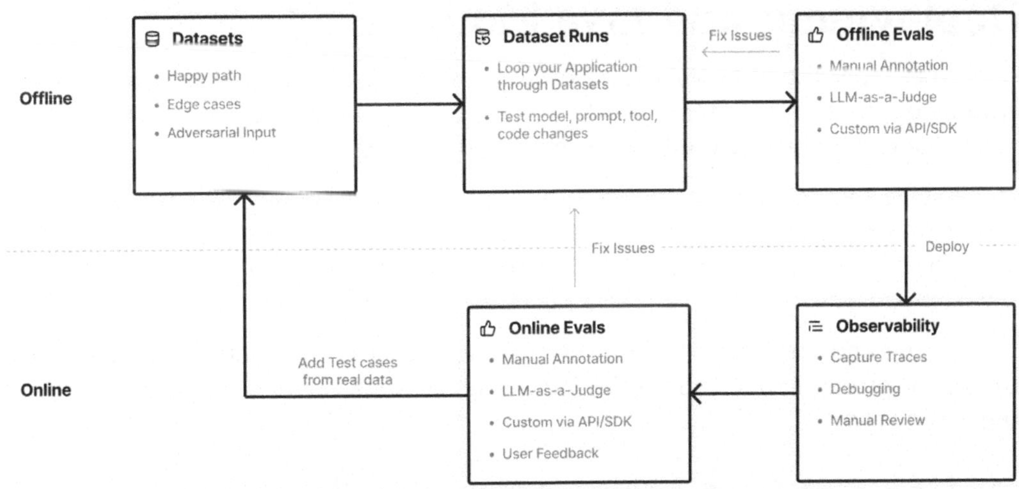

Figure 7.2: *The Evaluation Workflow in Langfuse (Source - https://langfuse.com/docs/evaluation/overview)*

The figure above illustrates a continuous feedback loop that captures how LLM applications evolve and improve over time. The diagram presents it as an **ongoing process**—a cycle that connects development, deployment, monitoring, and feedback.

This process shows how data and insights move between two major environments: **offline experimentation** and **online operation**. Together, they form a closed loop that ensures LLM systems continue to adapt as usage grows and conditions change.

Offline Evaluation and Experimentation

We generally begin with offline evaluation—an environment where teams can experiment safely and systematically. Here, the LLM application is tested using controlled **datasets**, synthetic examples, or curated benchmarks. Because the inputs and expected outcomes are known, we can compute quantitative measures of performance such as semantic similarity, factual accuracy, or error rates.

This stage focuses on building confidence before deployment. We might test multiple model versions, prompt templates, or retrieval strategies and measure trade-offs in latency, quality, and cost. Offline evaluation answers questions like:

- **Does the model follow instructions correctly?**
- **Are its responses semantically faithful to the source?**
- **Which configuration yields the best balance of quality and efficiency?**

By isolating the model from production complexity, teams can iterate quickly and identify the most promising configurations to deploy.

Deployment and Live Monitoring

Once the application shows strong offline results, it transitions to production. In production, real users interact with the application, revealing behaviors and edge cases that cannot be captured by pre-collected datasets.

At this stage, monitoring becomes central. Metrics such as latency, token consumption, and error frequency are continuously logged. More importantly, user interactions themselves become a rich source of evaluation data—through explicit ratings, implicit feedback (such as re-queries or reformulations), and session outcomes.

The tracing and observability features of Langfuse make this stage concrete: every model call, prompt input, and user response can be tracked and linked to performance and quality metrics.

Online Evaluation and Feedback Integration

The third phase closes the loop by interpreting live data as evaluation input. Unlike offline testing, which uses static benchmarks, online evaluation uses production data—real queries, real user feedback, and real-world conditions—to measure performance dynamically.

This phase serves several purposes:

- It validates whether offline assumptions hold up under true usage.
- It identifies new types of failures or drifts that were not visible in testing.
- It captures authentic user satisfaction and task success metrics.

In practice, this might involve A/B testing two prompt variants, comparing outputs from different models, or automatically scoring live responses with an evaluator LLM. The insights gathered here feed directly back into the offline evaluation phase, enriching test datasets with real examples of success and failure.

For modern LLM applications this continuous cycle is important for several reasons:

- **Real-world Adaptation:** Offline evaluations cannot anticipate every possible input. Online monitoring ensures that real usage data continuously refines our understanding of performance.
- **Balanced Optimization:** It enables a holistic approach—optimizing not only accuracy but also latency, cost, and user satisfaction.
- **Risk Detection:** Early feedback from production highlights regressions, bias, or safety risks before they scale.
- **Test Data Enrichment:** We continuously transform real-world usage data (unstructured) into reusable, labeled evaluation datasets (structured), so our future offline testing better reflects what actually happens in production.
- **Sustained Improvement:** Most importantly, it keeps the product evolving as models, prompts, and user expectations shift over time.

Core Concepts of Evaluation in Langfuse

We will now explore the four core concepts of Evaluation as defined by Langfuse: **Scores, Evaluation Methods, Datasets, and Experiments.** These abstractions act as building blocks for both development-time (offline) and production-time (online) evaluation workflows. In practical terms, they allow us to define what we are measuring (Scores), how we are measuring it (Evaluation Methods), on what data (Datasets), and in what context (Experiments).

Scores

A **Score** in Langfuse is the **way of rating** how well our application or model performed on a specific task or interaction. Scores provide the measurable signal that teams use to track improvement (or regression). Because they are data objects in Langfuse, they can be filtered, aggregated, trended, and compared across versions or configurations. Scores tie the abstract notion of quality into concrete values that can be stored alongside the operational data of our application.

A Score can be tied to an individual trace or observation. We can also score the entire session of traces. **Each score can reference only one of these entities** that means we cannot score a trace and the observation under it separately.

Langfuse supports **numeric, categorical or boolean**(true/false, 0/1) types of scores. We can also create custom score configs to define the structure of our own scoring metric.

Experiments in Langfuse can also be scored for performance tracking.

Evaluation Methods

Evaluation Methods in Langfuse are the mechanisms by which scores are produced. In other words, an evaluation method is a function or tool that takes an object (a generation, a trace, or dataset item) and produces a score (or set of scores) according to some criterion. They define how we rate quality. Langfuse currently supports 3 evaluation methods:

- **LLM-as-a-Judge**: Uses another LLM to act as the evaluator, scoring outputs on dimensions such as hallucination, helpfulness, or accuracy.
- **Human Annotations**: Manual review of responses (or traces) by human annotators, yielding scores based on human judgments.
- **Custom Scores / Custom Methods**: If our domain has special requirements, we can implement our own evaluation logic via API/SDK.

In practice, we use a combination of these methods across the online and offline evaluation phases. We will see in later sections how to use each of these methods effectively.

Datasets

In Langfuse, a Dataset is a structured collection of examples (inputs and expected outputs) used primarily for offline evaluation. It acts as a test set or benchmark for our LLM application.

Datasets give us controlled conditions under which we can systematically compare model versions, prompt variants, or system changes. They serve as the grown truth side of evaluation. When we have expected outputs, we can more reliably measure functional correctness. They provide repeatability since every time we run the dataset, we are using the same benchmark, so that we can track regressions and improvements over time.

Langfuse is also very flexible in terms of how to create a Dataset. We can use the UI directly to create items manually or by uploading a CSV file. For developers, it is also possible to programmatically create datasets and items using the API/SDK.

Experiments

The final concept in evaluation is an Experiment. It is the process of executing our LLM application across a dataset under controlled conditions and optionally applying evaluation methods to collect scores. This concept allows us to compare different models / prompts / retrieval configurations side-by-side, track results, and measure impact.

We can run the same dataset under the same conditions, so results are comparable.

Experiments are essentially a bridge between the previous three concepts and help us operationalize evaluation workflow.

Summary of concepts covered so far:

Concept	Role in Evaluation Workflow
Scores	The measurable results / metrics we collect for each evaluation
Evaluation Methods	The mechanism by which we compute scores
Datasets	The structured set of inputs (and optionally expected outputs)
Experiments	The execution context: running our application across datasets + methods + capturing scores

Table 7.1: *Summary Table for Evaluation Concepts in Langfuse*

With this in mind, let us now prepare for running experiments by creating our first dataset in Langfuse.

Creating Our First Dataset in Langfuse

Our evaluation journey starts with the creation of a validation/test dataset. As defined earlier, a dataset in Langfuse is a structured set of example inputs (and ideally expected outputs) that our system will be tested on again and again to monitor performance, detect regressions, and measure improvements.

What Makes a Good Dataset

To get the most out of our experiments, it is important to have reliable items in our dataset. Consider the following qualities to create a truly useful dataset:

1. **Relevance to the Use Case**
    - The examples must reflect the real tasks our system is expected to handle. If we are building a support bot, include actual user questions rather than generic prompts.
    - Cover the types of interactions that matter most (common queries, rarely asked but critical support issues, domain-specific phrasing).
    - Avoid irrelevant generic items — they dilute focus and may give misleadingly optimistic evaluation.

2. **Diversity of Difficulty**
    - Standard ("happy path") cases where the system should succeed easily.
    - Edge cases and tricky scenarios — ambiguous queries, multi-step reasoning, rare domain terms.
    - Failure/negative cases — prompts where the system might struggle, so we can monitor improvement (or regression).
3. **Clear and Unambiguous Expected Outputs**
    - If we include expected outputs, they should be clearly defined so comparisons are meaningful. If we rely on semantic similarity rather than exact match, define how we will measure it.
    - For each item, ensure input and expected output are aligned and map to our evaluation methodology (for example, prompt variables match item keys).
    - This clarity prevents false positives/negatives in evaluation and improves reproducibility.
4. **Traceability to Real Usage**
    - Incorporate real production interactions, especially ones where the system failed or under-performed. These are valuable because they reflect actual user experience and domain challenges.
    - For example: pick a set of prompts that resulted in bad user feedback or high latency, augment them with expected output, and track them across versions.
    - This approach closes the loop between live feedback and offline evaluation.
5. **Maintainability and Versioning**
    - As our system changes (models, prompts, retrieval logic), the dataset should evolve too. We should add new items, archive outdated ones, and keep metadata to track when and why items changed.
    - Maintain a baseline version of the dataset so that we can track regressions.
6. **Sufficient Scale and Representativeness**
    - While we do not need thousands of items to begin, we do need enough variety to detect meaningful differences. A very small dataset with narrow coverage will miss many failures.
    - Ensure that the dataset represents the spectrum of inputs (different lengths, different user intents, different domain complexity) that we test.

7. **Linked Evaluation Context**
    - Each item should ideally carry metadata that places it in context – for example which prompt or model version it was created under, which business scenario it addresses, or tags such as "billing", "technical support", "escalation".
    - This helps you filter results later (such as "How did the system perform on billing-related questions after prompt update?").

Dataset Creation Using the UI/SDK

It is finally time to create our first dataset. The simplest way to start is using the UI. Datasets can be created by using the left navigation and clicking on **`Datasets`**. If we do not have any datasets yet, we should see a **`+ New dataset`** option.

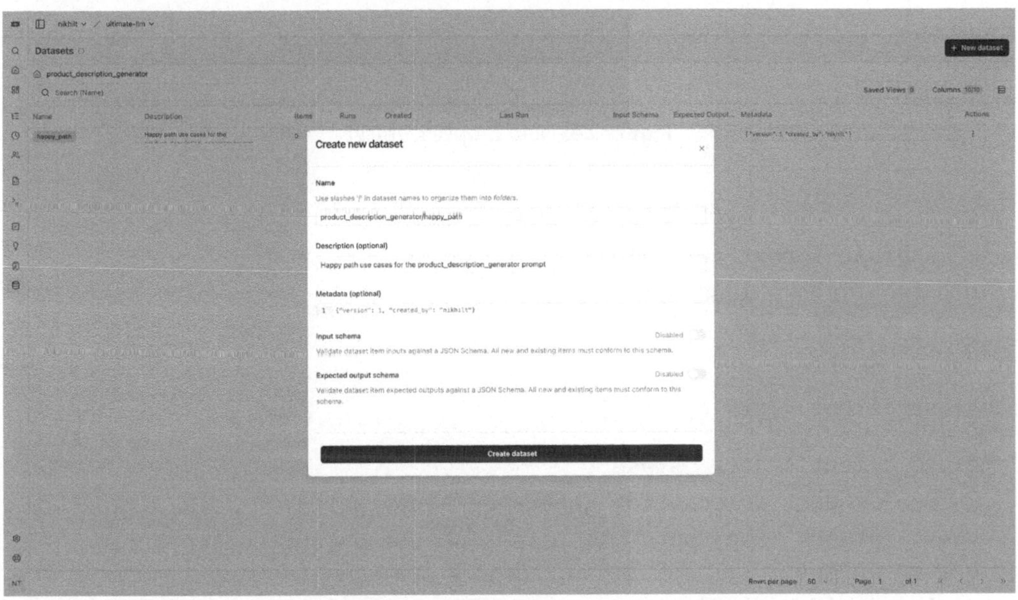

Figure 7.3: *Creating a New Dataset Using Langfuse UI*

To create a new dataset, we simply need a name. Adding a '/' in the name will organize the dataset in a folder which is encouraged to keep them organized. For this example, we will create a new dataset called "**`product_description_generator/happy_path`**" to test our **`product_description_generator`** prompt from the earlier chapter.

```
Write a compelling and concise product description for an e-commerce
listing.
Product Name: {{product_name}}
Key Features: {{features}}
Target Audience: {{audience}}
```

```
Write in a friendly, trustworthy tone. Limit your response to 90 words.
End with a short call to action.
```

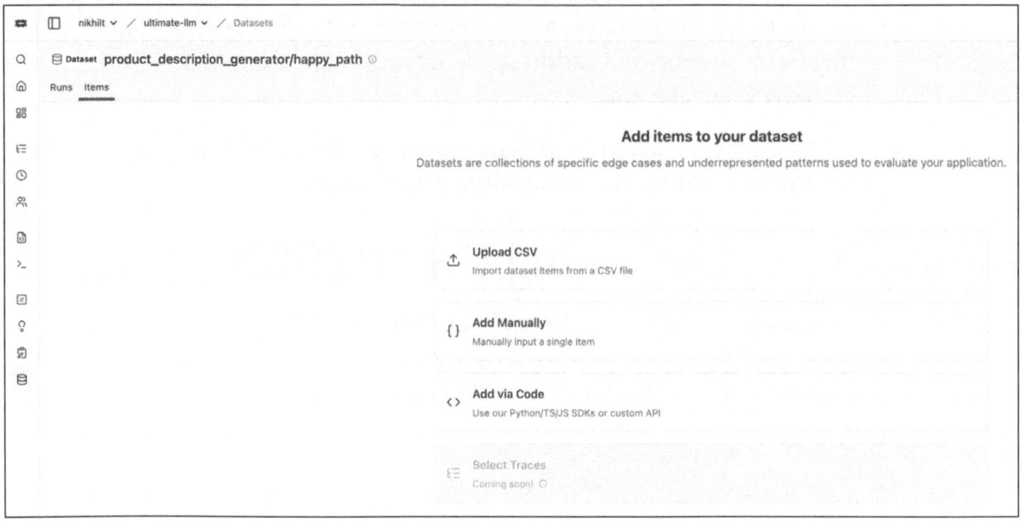

Figure 7.4: *New Empty Dataset*

The exact same dataset can also be created using the SDK:

```
from langfuse import get_client
from dotenv import load_dotenv

load_dotenv()

langfuse_client = get_client()

langfuse_client.create_dataset(
    name="product_description_generator/happy_path",
    description="Happy path use cases for the product_description_
generator prompt",
    metadata={"version": 1, "created_by": "nikhilt"},
)
```

There are several ways to add items to the dataset:

1. **Upload a CSV**: Each row in the CSV should have three columns: Input – for the input variables to the prompt. Expected output and Optional Metadata.
2. **Manually adding items**: This option can be used if you have few items and would like to add them one by one. This would also be the preferred way to add items to an existing dataset using the UI.
3. **Use the SDK**: We can write some code to add items to a dataset.

4. **Use existing traces:** Langfuse also allows us to use existing traces from production to be added to datasets. We will see later in the chapter on how we can do this.

For a dataset item input, the value should be a JSON containing key-value pairs for all the possible inputs to our prompt. The expected output can be a JSON or even a plain string.

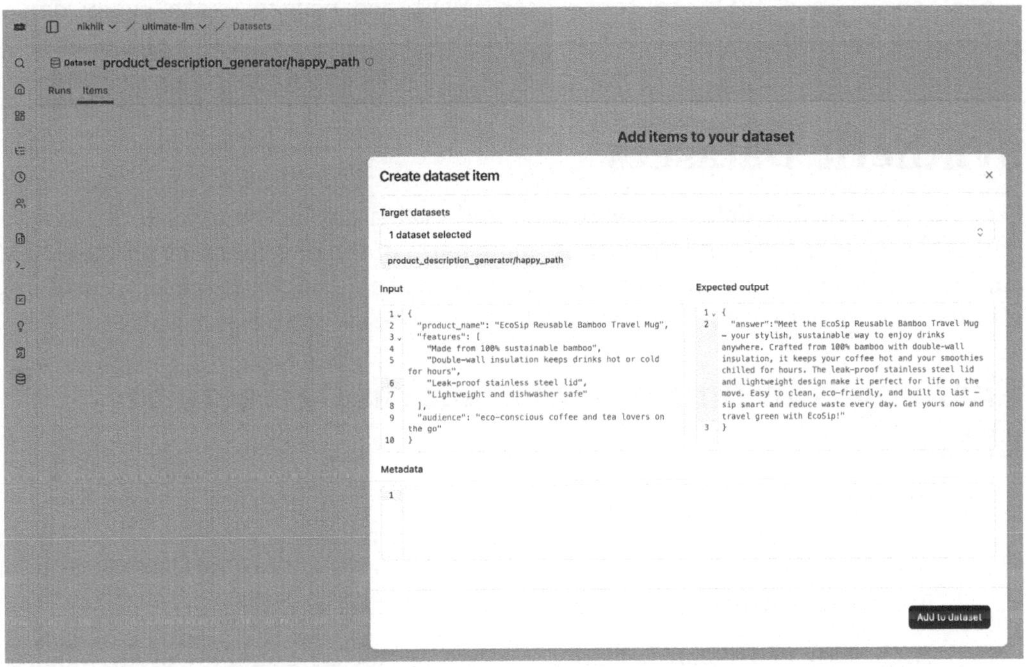

Figure 7.5: *Adding a New Item to the Dataset*

Currently the UI does not allow expected output to be a plain string. For plain string outputs, we need to use the SDK. Metadata should also be a JSON if used.

To add an item to the dataset, we can also use the SDK:

```
langfuse_client.create_dataset_item(
dataset_name="product_description_generator/happy_path",
    input={
        "product_name": "EcoSip Reusable Bamboo Travel Mug",
        "features": [
            "Made from 100% sustainable bamboo",
            "Double-wall insulation keeps drinks hot or cold for hours",
            "Leak-proof stainless steel lid",
            "Lightweight and dishwasher safe",
        ],
```

```
        "audience": "eco-conscious coffee and tea lovers on the go",
    },
expected_output= "Meet the EcoSip Reusable Bamboo Travel Mug – your
stylish, sustainable way to enjoy drinks anywhere. Crafted from 100%
bamboo with double-wall insulation, it keeps your coffee hot and your
smoothies chilled for hours. The leak-proof stainless steel lid and
lightweight design make it perfect for life on the move. Easy to clean,
eco-friendly, and built to last – sip smart and reduce waste every day.
Get yours now and travel green with EcoSip!"
)
```

Synthetic Datasets

Creating high-quality datasets for testing and evaluating LLM applications is often one of the most difficult and time-consuming parts of the development process. LLM applications operate on open-ended language tasks – summarization, reasoning, classification, generation where "ground truth" can be subjective and costly to define.

Challenges in Building Evaluation Datasets for LLMs

- **Ambiguity in Ground Truth:** Many LLM tasks have no single correct answer. For example, two different but equally good product descriptions may both meet the prompt requirements. Defining what "good" means requires human judgment, consistency, and clear evaluation criteria.
- **High Cost of Human Labeling:** Gathering labeled examples often requires expert reviewers or annotators who understand the context, tone, or domain. This process is slow, expensive, and hard to scale for large evaluation sets.
- **Data Privacy and Sensitivity:** Using real-world data especially customer conversations or support logs – raises privacy and compliance challenges. Such data must be anonymized or sanitized before reuse, adding complexity to dataset creation.
- **Limited Coverage of Edge Cases:** Manually created datasets tend to overrepresent common or easy examples and underrepresent the rare, tricky edge cases where LLMs often fail (for example, ambiguous questions, negations, or multi-step reasoning).
- **Rapid Model Evolution:** As prompts, model versions, and architectures evolve, previously built datasets may no longer reflect the latest requirements of the application. This makes continuous dataset upkeep difficult.

Synthetic datasets offer a scalable and flexible way to address many of these challenges. Rather than relying solely on manually collected examples, developers can use LLMs themselves – or other automated generation pipelines – to create synthetic input-output pairs that mimic real-world interactions. Synthetic datasets enable us to test LLM applications faster, safer, and at a much larger scale. We can rapidly generate thousands of diverse examples by adjusting prompts, parameters, and contexts, allowing us to explore how the model performs across different tones, domains, and edge cases. Once the generation pipeline is established, these datasets can be produced at low cost and updated continuously as the system evolves. Because the data is machine-generated, it remains safe and compliant, avoiding privacy issues common with real user data while still providing customizable ground truths for accurate evaluation.

We will see one example of how an LLM such as GPT can be used to generate datasets for our "**product_description_generator**" prompt evaluation. We will use the SDK to add these items to our dataset.

```
from langfuse import get_client
from langfuse.openai import openai
from dotenv import load_dotenv
import json

load_dotenv()

langfuse_client = get_client()

# System prompt for the GPT model to generate synthetic dataset examples
system_prompt = """
You are an AI assistant that generates high-quality synthetic dataset
examples for evaluating product description generation models.
Your goal is to produce structured dataset items based on the given
prompt template. Each dataset item should simulate a realistic
e-commerce scenario with diverse product categories, features, and
audiences.
Expected Output Format should be this JSON:
{
  "input": {
    "product_name": "...",
    "features": ["...", "...", "..."],
    "audience": "..."
  },
  "expected_output": "..."
}
"""

def generate_datatset_item(num_items=1):
    for i in range(num_items):
```

```
        # We require a structured JSON as the output from GPT
        completion = openai.chat.completions.create(
            model="gpt-4.1-mini",
            messages=[{"role": "system", "content": system_prompt}],
response_format={"type": "json_object"},
        )
dataset_item = json.loads(completion.choices[0].message.content)
        # For every dataset item, we create a new dataset item in
LangFuse
langfuse_client.create_dataset_item(
dataset_name="product_description_generator/happy_path",
            input=dataset_item["input"],
expected_output=dataset_item["expected_output"],
        )

generate_datatset_item(10)
```

After running this code, we will see ten dataset items in our dataset.

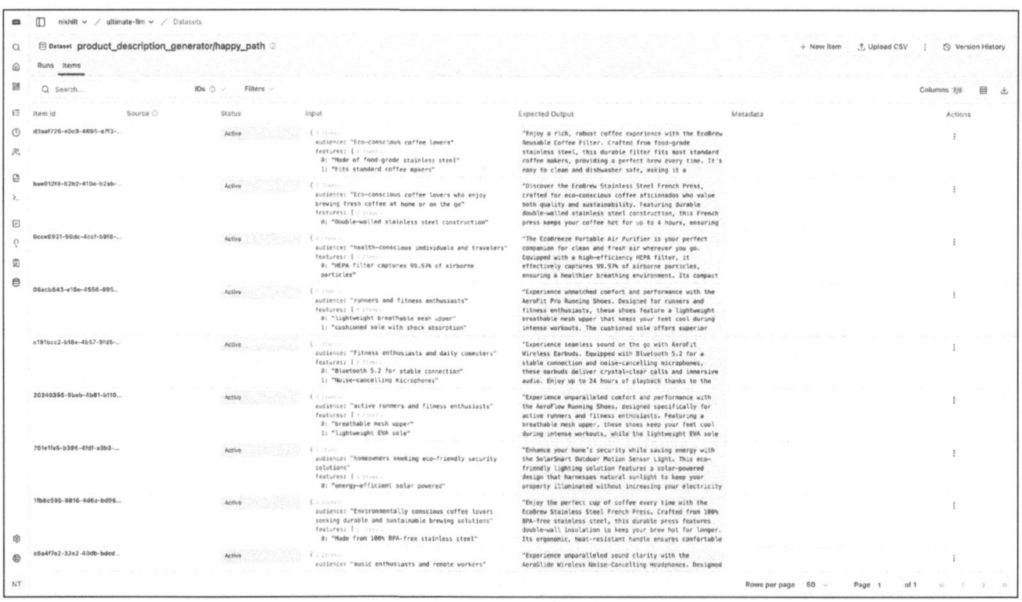

Figure 7.6: *Creating New Items Using Synthetic Dataset Creation*

There are many more ways to create synthetic datasets in Langfuse. Some of those ideas are available at **https://langfuse.com/guides/cookbook/example_synthetic_datasets**.

While synthetic datasets are an excellent way to accelerate the early stages of development, they should be viewed as a **starting point, not a substitute** for real-world data. They help us prototype quickly, identify weaknesses, and fine-tune prompts or scoring methods before deploying to production. However, as the application matures, it becomes essential to transition toward **real user interactions and authentic data samples** for evaluation. Real examples capture cases that synthetic data cannot fully reproduce, ensuring our evaluations truly reflect how the system performs in practice.

Automatic Trace Scoring Using LLM-as-a-Judge

The concept of **LLM-as-a-Judge** refers to leveraging one model to **evaluate and score the responses of another model** (or even itself) based on defined criteria such as accuracy, coherence, tone, or helpfulness. Instead of relying solely on human annotators, we use the reasoning and comprehension capabilities of an LLM to assess language outputs in a structured, scalable way. The model acts as an evaluator, interpreting both the prompt and the response, and then producing a judgment or score that reflects how well the output meets expectations. Using an LLM as a judge enables us to assess quality in a way that better mirrors **human judgment**.

As our application evolves, manual evaluations alone become impractical. Human reviews are expensive, time-consuming, and difficult to scale to thousands of interactions. An LLM-judge, on the other hand, can evaluate outputs in real time, offering immediate feedback on system performance. It allows us to evaluate continuously and adaptively, providing deeper insights into whether the model is improving or drifting over time.

Benefits of Using an LLM as a Judge

- **Scalable and Efficient Evaluation**: We can assess thousands of model outputs quickly without relying entirely on human reviewers. This makes large-scale evaluations feasible, allowing continuous monitoring of model quality.
- **Human-Like Judgment at Scale**: An LLM-judge can capture characteristics such as tone, clarity, relevance, or factual accuracy providing feedback that more closely reflects human perception of quality.
- **Consistency and Reproducibility**: By applying the same judging model across evaluations, we eliminate the variability and subjectivity common in human reviews. This ensures consistent and repeatable scoring over time.
- **Faster Iteration and Feedback Loops**: Using an LLM-judge accelerates our experimentation cycle. We can instantly evaluate new model versions or prompt designs, detect regressions early, and refine our system without waiting for manual annotations.

- **Responsible Evaluation**: We can design LLM judges to assess not only performance but also ethical and safety dimensions such as bias, inclusivity, or harmful content ensuring our evaluations align with both technical and social responsibility goals.

Langfuse integrates the LLM-as-a-judge approach directly into its evaluation workflow, allowing us to **automatically score traces** using model-based evaluators. Once configured, Langfuse can run an LLM to assess each recorded trace or output against defined criteria and assign a numerical or categorical score. This evaluation happens in the background so our application's performance is unaffected. We will now see how to set up an evaluator using this method.

Setting up an Evaluator

To set up an evaluator navigation to the `LLM-as-a-Judge` option from the left navigation in the UI. If there are no evaluators yet, we will see the `Create Evaluator` button.

Figure 7.7: *Choose a Default Model for the Evaluator*

Before an evaluator can be selected, we need to set up a default model for our project. To accomplish this, select the pencil icon located at the top right corner. **The default model is used for every evaluation by the automatic evaluators.** We can choose any configured model as the default one. Before using this feature, we need to set up an LLM Connection. Please refer to *Chapter 6, Prompt Management in Langfuse* to see how this can be done. **The chosen default model should support structured output and function calling.**

After setting up the default model, we can either choose one of the maintained evaluators of Langfuse or create our own. For the first example, we will choose an existing evaluator called **Hallucination** which can calculate a hallucination score for the trace.

Figure 7.8: *Setting up a New Evaluator for Hallucination*

An evaluator can be set up for either Traces, Observations or Experiments. If we want to have the same evaluator for both, we need to set up the evaluator twice. We will see later in the chapter how to set up an evaluator for experiments. When setting up for Traces, we can choose to run the evaluator for new traces only or even run the evaluation for existing past traces. Besides this, we can add filters to cherry pick only certain traces for running evaluations.

Since **LLM-as-a-Judge** technique is time consuming and incurs LLM costs per evaluation, we can sample the traces which will affect all future traces. For example, a value of 50% means only 50% of future traces will be evaluated with this evaluator. We can also add a delay time in seconds which will be the waiting time between when a trace is recorded and the evaluation begins. This is to ensure that the evaluation does not begin before the entire trace is recorded. We should set this to a higher value for long running traces.

The next step to configure is the **`Variable mapping`** between our trace and the prompt that will be used for the LLM evaluator call.

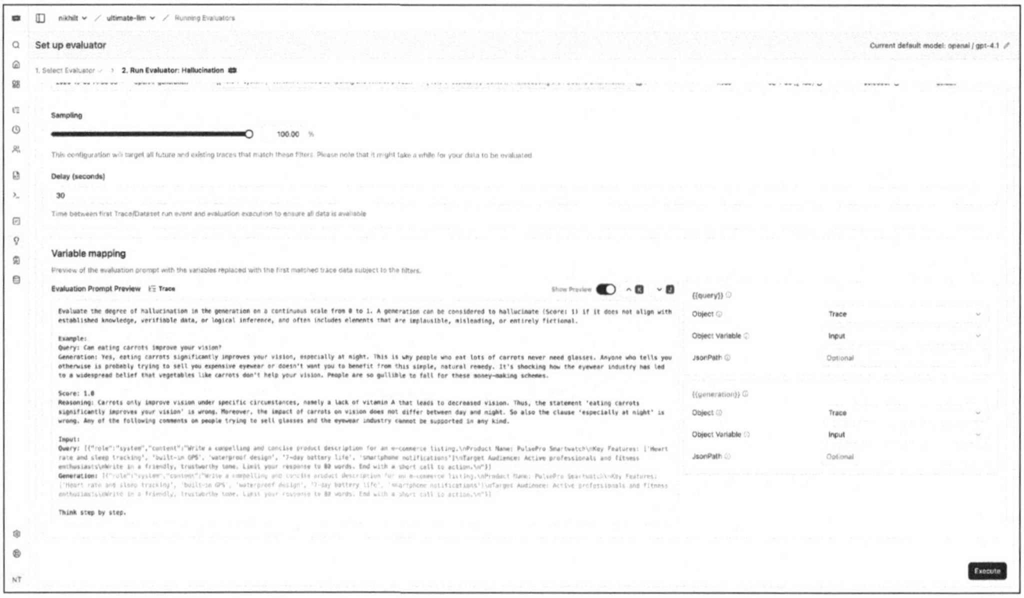

Figure 7.9: *Variable Mapping for the Evaluator*

For the maintained evaluators, we already have a default prompt that can be used directly without any modification. This prompt essentially explains our evaluator LLM on how to compute the score, in this case Hallucination. While this prompt works well enough for generic cases, we should update it before using it for a customized use case.

Langfuse allows us to use any part of the trace/observation as the variables in the prompt. In this example, we have 2 variables: **query** and **generation** which are the input and output of the trace. We also see the preview of the prompt including the variable mappings that will be sent to our evaluator. Using the K and J arrows, we can navigate to the previous or next trace to see the previews. For variable mappings, Langfuse supports **JsonPath** syntax to select only parts of the objects as variables. Once everything is setup, we can click **`Execute`** to complete the setup. After setting up an evaluator, we can go to the **LLM-as-a-Judge** page again to see the running evaluators.

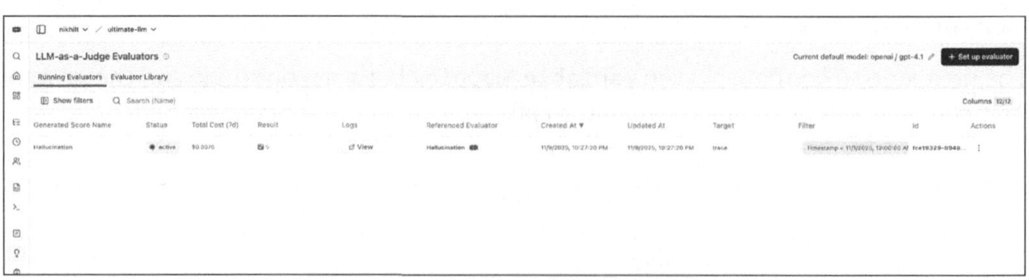

Figure 7.10: *List of Running Evaluators*

Since evaluators run in the background, it might be a while before the evaluations are completed. On this page we can see the running and completed evaluations and the total cost for the evaluations themselves.

Accessing Scores

After setting up the evaluators, Langfuse will automatically start collecting scores as and when the traces come in. There are several ways to access the scores for the evaluated traces.

Using the Scores Section

By navigating to the **Scores** section from the left navigation, we can see all calculated scores as a list including the Value of the score and the explanation for the evaluation under the Comment column.

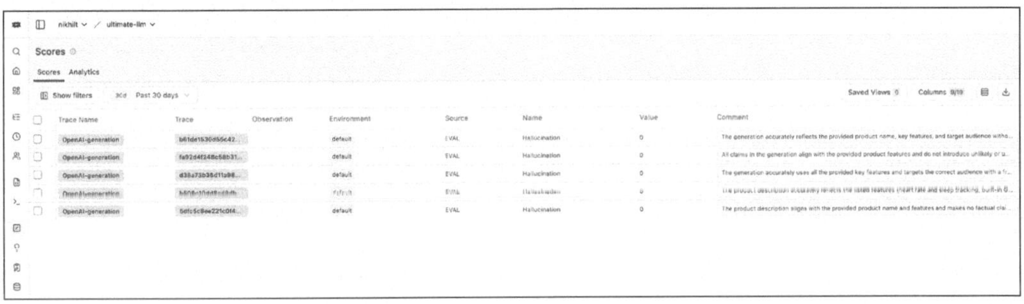

Figure 7.11: *Scores in Langfuse*

For every evaluation we can get a value and an explanation from the judge LLM on the score value. On this page, we can also filter scores and download them as a CSV file.

From the Traces Page

The next option to check the scores on a trace level is to navigate to the trace itself, either from the Scores page or the Traces page. On the individual trace, we can click the Scores tab to see all scores for the trace in a tabular format. We can use filters here as well or export the scores as a CSV file.

On the traces page, Scores also appear as a badge under the name of the trace. We can hover over the badge to see the explanation for the score and also navigate to the evaluation execution trace.

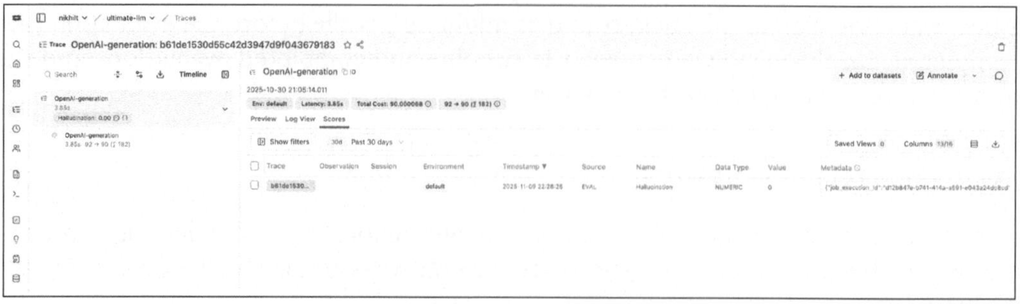

Figure 7.12: *Scores on a Trace Level*

The call made to the LLM judge itself can also be viewed as a trace on the Traces page. All evaluator traces have the environment as "**`langfuse-llm-as-a-judge`**" which can be used to filter these kinds of traces. These traces can then be viewed as a regular trace to check the reasoning and score value for the evaluation.

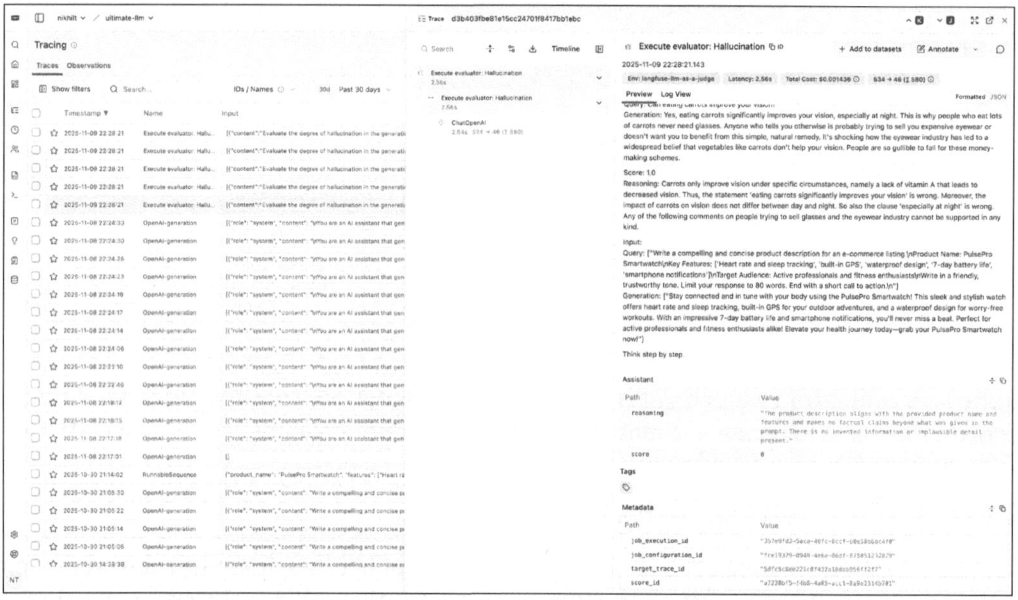

Figure 7.13: *Evaluation Trace*

This trace shows the exact call made to the judge and the response of the model including token usage, latency, and any errors that occurred during execution.

Custom Evaluators

Langfuse offers a huge list of built-in ready to use evaluators for the most common metrics used with LLMs. For some of the metrics, it uses the Ragas library **https://docs.ragas.io/en/stable/** to provide the evaluators by default.

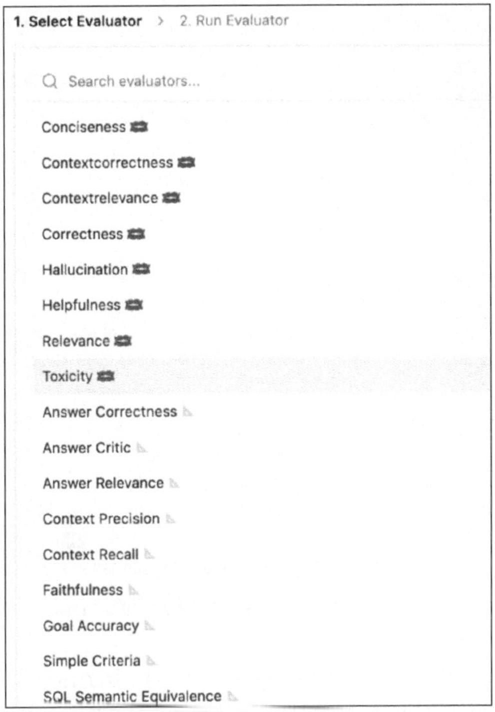

Figure 7.14: *Langfuse and Ragas Maintained Evaluators*

Even though this list is rich, we would sometimes want to create our own evaluator for the LLM as a judge method. The reasons could include:

- **Domain-Specific Criteria:** We may need to measure qualities unique to our application such as compliance with brand tone, legal accuracy, or domain expertise that generic evaluators cannot capture.
- **Custom Output Formats:** When our model generates structured outputs such as JSON, SQL, or code, a tailored evaluator ensures correctness, formatting, and adherence to required schemas.
- **Cost and Efficiency Optimization:** We update the prompts on evaluators to use lesser text, reducing cost and latency while keeping evaluations relevant and focused.
- **Multi-Metric Evaluation:** Some applications require assessing multiple aspects such as accuracy, tone, and clarity within a single run. A custom evaluator can combine these dimensions into one coherent scoring framework.
- **Edge-Case Evaluation:** Custom evaluators help us monitor unusual or low-frequency scenarios such as ambiguous queries or contradictory inputs.

To create a customer evaluator, we need to click on the `+ Create Custom Evaluator` button on the Set up evaluator page.

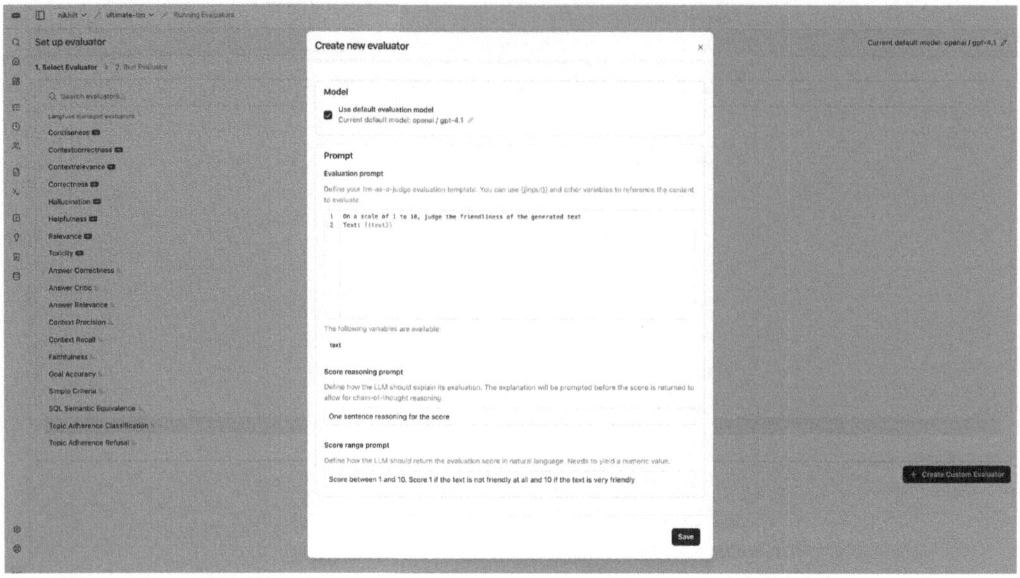

Figure 7.15: *Creating a Custom Evaluator in Langfuse*

Structurally, Custom Evaluators are the same as built-in ones. We need to have a name, the main prompt with variables and the scoring explanation and range prompts which are usually one or two sentences each. After saving this evaluator, it can be used in the same way as any other evaluator.

Manual Scoring

In evaluating the outputs of our LLM applications, automated metrics cannot replace human insight entirely. Manual scoring (also referred to as **Human Annotations**) allows us to bring human judgment into the loop, assessing domain-specific meanings that are difficult to automate reliably.

Human Annotations

Langfuse supports manual scoring via human annotation workflows that let teams collaboratively annotate traces, sessions, or individual observations with scores, forming a ground truth that can help broader evaluation strategies. There are many reasons why human scoring can be useful.

- **Understanding Context**: Human evaluators can recognize subtleties that automated scoring often misses. Manual scoring is used to accurately reflect important factors in evaluations, such as the effectiveness of customer-service responses, the clarity of product descriptions, and the cultural appropriateness of translations.

- **Building Trusted Benchmarks**: A manually reviewed dataset becomes a benchmark against which automated metrics can be calibrated. This helps align system-generated evaluations with human expectations and provides a trustworthy baseline for measuring future improvements.
- **Managing New or Evolving Scenarios**: When testing new use cases, such as new product categories, audiences, or languages, pre-defined evaluators may not yet exist. Human reviewers help bridge this gap, spotting errors or inconsistencies that automated systems may overlook during the early phases of model deployment.
- **Generating High-Quality Evaluation Data**: Manual annotations contribute to well-curated datasets used for regression testing and continuous evaluation. Because these scores reflect real human judgment, they ensure that future experiments test what truly matters to end users.

Getting Started with Annotations

Just like automated scoring, annotations can be added on a Trace, Observation or Session level. Before we can manually score objects, we need to define a score config which describes the score and defines its parameters such as data type and allowed values. To create a score config, we need to navigate to **`Settings`** and then choose **`Scores/Evaluation`**.

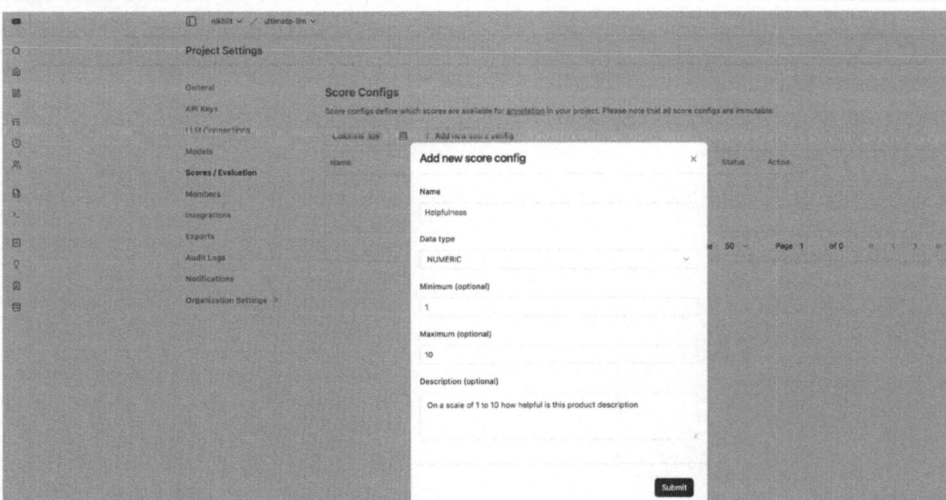

***Figure 7.16:** Adding a New Score Config*

In this example, we will add a new score config called "Helpfulness" which is a numeric score between 1 and 10. This score will be used by human annotators to rate the helpfulness of the generated product descriptions from our previous examples.

Other score types are **Categorical** where the values could be fixed labels or **Boolean** for a 0/1 or True/False type of score. We can create as many score configs as we like for the project. **Score Configs cannot be shared across projects** so if we need the same scores in a different project, we have to manual copy them.

After creating a score config, we also need to create something called an **Annotation Queue.** These queues help teams manage and organize human-review tasks at scale. We can group traces, sessions or observations into dedicated queues for review. These queues let us assign specific scoring criteria, track annotation progress, and distribute items among reviewers, making it easier to coordinate annotation efforts.

Advantages of using Annotation Queues in Langfuse:

- We can ensure **consistent scoring** across multiple reviewers by assigning specific score configurations and dimensions to each queue, which supports standardization of annotations.
- They provide **visibility into progress**, letting us monitor which items have been reviewed, by whom, and which items are still pending which enhances transparency.
- Annotation Queues support **scalable collaboration**, enabling multiple reviewers to work concurrently without conflicting annotations, which helps handle large batches more efficiently.
- Because items are batched in queues, we get a **better review throughput.** We can handle review cycles faster and feed annotated cases back into our evaluation pipeline more rapidly.

To create a queue, we can navigate to **Human Annotation** from the left navigation and then click `+ New queue`.

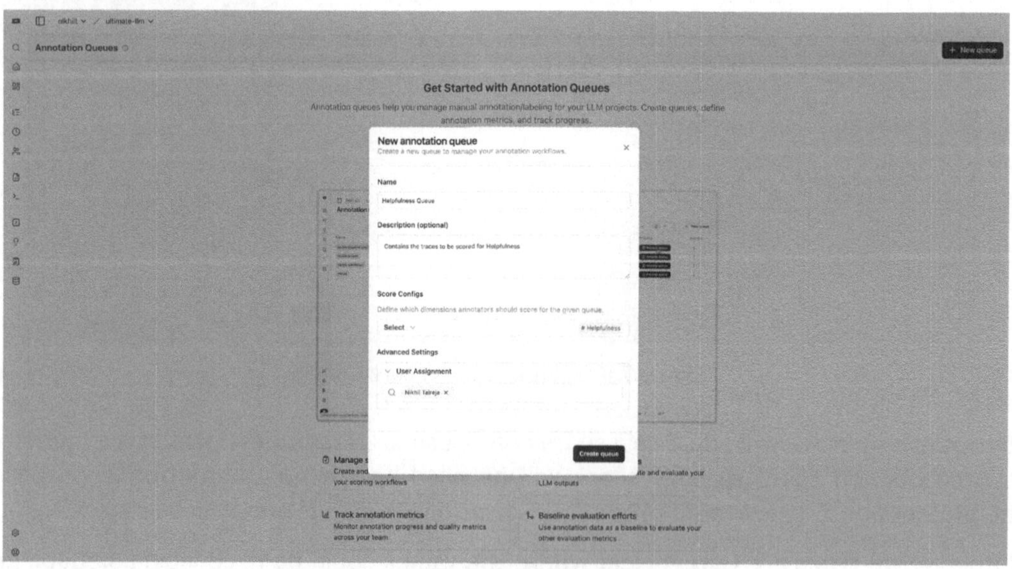

Figure 7.17: *Adding a New Annotation Queue*

For our example, we will create a queue to manage scoring for the product descriptions and use the score config we created above.

Adding Items to the Queue

Once we have a queue and the corresponding score config, we can start populating the queues with objects to score so that our human evaluators can start scoring them. There are several ways in which items can be added to a queue.

From the **`Tracing`** navigation, we can add individual traces to the queue using the option on the trace detail view. The option is on the top right corner next to the **`Annotate`** button.

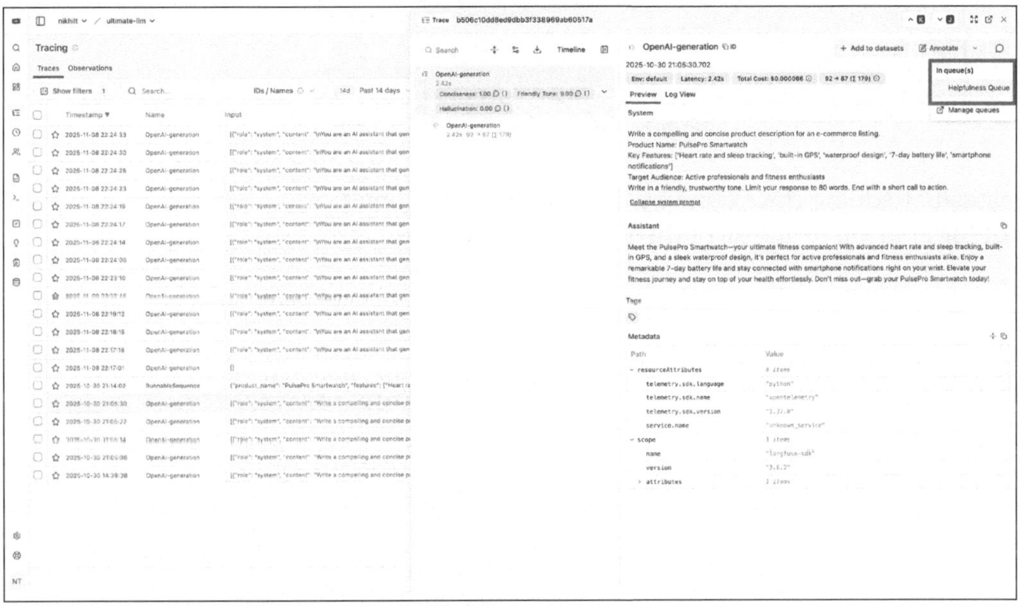

Figure 7.18: *Adding a Trace to an Annotation Queue*

On this view we can also directly annotate a Trace without adding it to a queue. We simply need to select the score config and can optionally add a comment. The newly added score will then appear along with the other scores for this trace.

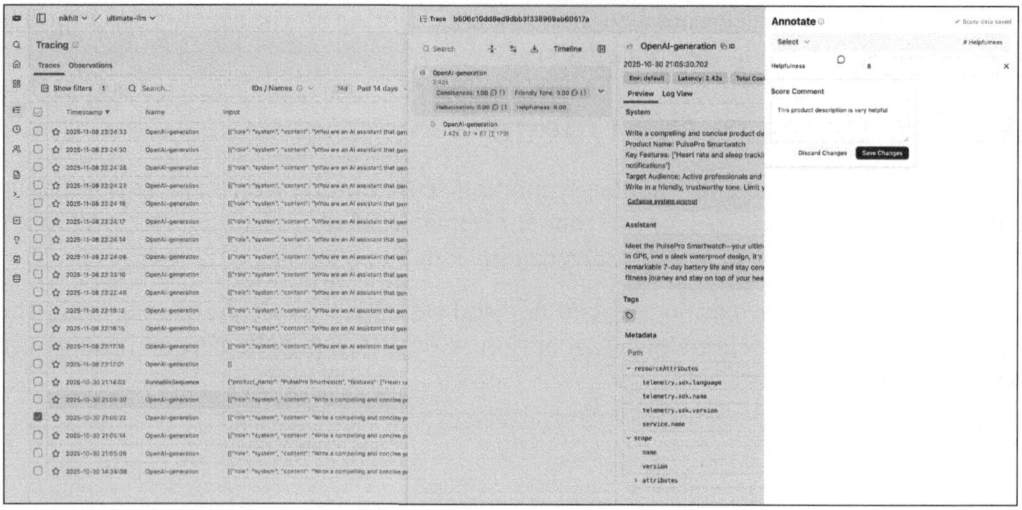

Figure 7.19: *Adding Score to a Trace*

Instead of adding traces one by one we can select multiple traces and then use the **`Actions`** button to add all of them to the queue.

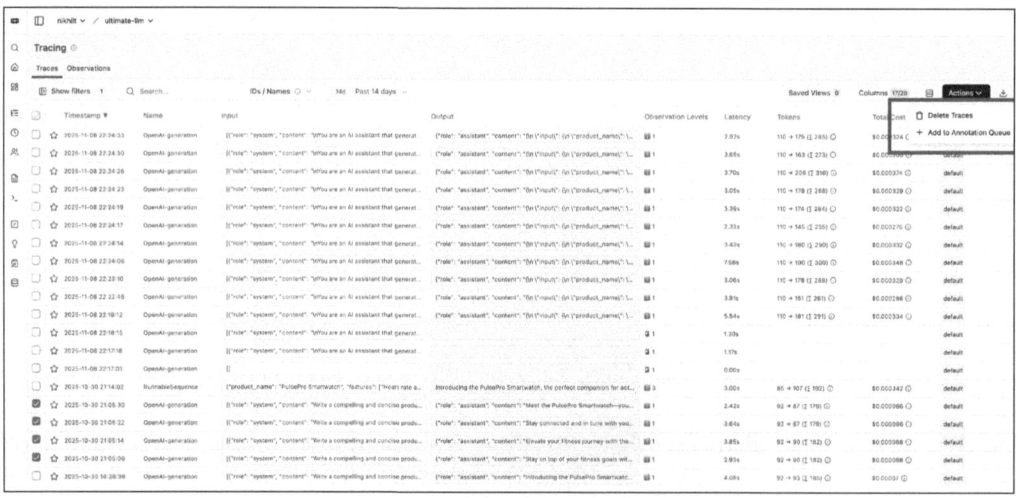

Figure 7.20: *Bulk Adding Traces to an Annotation Queue*

The above options also work for scoring individual **`Observations`** instead of Traces. We can also add objects for annotation from Experiment runs to score a side-by-side comparison of two experiments. We will see how to do this in the section on Prompt Evaluation. In the next section we will look at Custom Scores to see how we can score our objects with even more flexibility.

Custom Scores

In Langfuse, custom scores give us the flexibility to define and ingest our own evaluation metrics via API or SDK. These are score objects (Numeric, Categorical or Boolean) that we attach to traces, observations, sessions or dataset-run items. They can reflect whatever we care about for example: whether a generated JSON was valid, whether a response followed a required format, or whether a tool in an agent succeeded. Because custom scores are fully under our control, we can set up score configs we saw in the previous sections and ingest them from virtually any evaluation pipeline manual, automated, or rule based.

With LLM-as-a-Judge, we configure an LLM to evaluate outputs according to a metric (helpfulness, correctness, hallucination etc.) and assign scores accordingly. This approach works when we need scalable, human-style judgment with minimal manual effort. Custom scores shift the evaluation logic from an LLM to custom defined logic. Thus, custom scores give more control, but less built-in human-like nuance unless we build it ourselves.

Human Annotation on the other hand involves human reviewers assigning scores based on judgment, nuance, tone, and context especially useful for subjective qualities that automated systems struggle with. Custom scores may also represent human judgments, but they are not tied to a specific human-review workflow in the same way. They allow ingestion of any source (human or automated) into the scoring pipeline, not just human reviewers.

Custom scores become particularly valuable when we need fine-grained control over how evaluation is defined and measured. They allow us to encode our own rules, business logic, or validation checks directly into the scoring rather than relying on pre-built evaluators.

They are especially useful in the following cases:

- **Domain-Specific Requirements:** When our evaluation criteria are tied to the internal goals or operational standards of an application such as verifying compliance language, financial accuracy, or brand alignment custom scores let us represent those metrics exactly as needed.

- **Structured or Non-Textual Outputs:** Many LLM applications return data in formats such as JSON, SQL, or API responses. In such cases, we can use custom scores to programmatically validate structure, correctness, or successful execution, where language-based evaluation may fall short.

- **Integration with Existing Systems:** If we already collect metrics from downstream sources such as click-through rates, user satisfaction flags, or automated test results—these can be fed back into Langfuse as custom scores, enabling unified tracking alongside other evaluations.

- **Precision and Reproducibility:** By defining our own score schema, data types, and acceptable ranges, we ensure evaluations remain consistent over time. This makes it easier to compare model versions, measure progress, and trace changes in scoring logic.
- **Compliance and Transparency:** For teams operating in regulated or high-trust environments, custom scores offer full visibility into how evaluation decisions are made. Every rule or scoring criterion can be explicitly documented and aligned with organizational or legal standards.

Unlike the automated and manual scoring techniques, custom scoring is mostly done via the SDK/API. We will see some examples of how this can be done.

Example 1: Scoring a Trace Based on the Response of an External API Call

The easiest way to score a trace using this method is to add the score during ingestion of the trace. This way the trace and the score are immediately available on the UI when the method completes. This can also guarantee that scores are always available on our object.

Similar to the manual scoring technique, we should define a score config either via the project settings (which is the preferred way) or we can also create scores with the SDK directly.

```
from langfuse import get_client
from dotenv import load_dotenv
import requests

load_dotenv()

langfuse_client = get_client()

def get_api_success_score(status_code: int):
    return 1 if status_code == 200 else 0

def get_weather(city: str):
    """
    Fetch weather data for a given city using the wttr.in API.
    """
    with langfuse_client.start_as_current_span(name="get_weather") as
span:
        # Update the trace input
span.update_trace(input=city)
url = f"https://wttr.in/{city}?format=j1"
        try:
```

```
            response = requests.get(url, timeout=5)
response.raise_for_status()
            data = response.json()
        except Exception as e:
            print(f"API call failed for {city}: {e}")
        # Update trace output
span.update_trace(output=data)
        # Score the trace
span.score_trace(
            name="api_call_succeeded",
            value=get_api_success_score(response.status_code),
data_type="BOOLEAN",
        )

get_weather("London")
```

This will create a new Boolean type of score called **api_call_succeeded** which can then be used by other objects as well. Langfuse allows scoring the same object multiple times with the same score name and in this case, it will be stored as a multi-value list. This helps to get trends of a particular score on the same object.

In this example we have also created the score object itself in the code inside the **score_trace** method call. This is not the best practice because it does not enforce any constraint on how the score is captured. **For production use cases, we should also start with a score config and use it to score objects.**

Example 2: Check SQL Syntax

Imagine we are creating an LLM application that generates SQL queries based on the question of the user. We would like to know what percentage of questions result in a successful query execution.

For this example, we will create a score config called "SQL Execution Success" and then use the config ID in the **score_trace** call.

```
from langfuse import get_client
from dotenv import load_dotenv

load_dotenv()

langfuse_client = get_client()

def check_sql_execution(sql_query: str) -> float:
    try:
        # Run your query against your DB here
        return 1.0
```

```
    except Exception as e:
        print(f"SQL Error: {e} when running {sql_query}")
        return 0.0

def generate_sql(question: str):
    """
    Generate an SQL statement based on the given question.
    """
    with langfuse_client.start_as_current_span(name="generate_sql") as
span:
        # Update the trace input
span.update_trace(input=question)

        # Logic to generate SQL
generated_sql_query = """
        SELECT COUNT(*) AS total_orders
        FROM orders
        WHERE order_date>= DATE_TRUNC('month', CURRENT_DATE - INTERVAL
'1 month')
        AND order_date< DATE_TRUNC('month', CURRENT_DATE);
        """

        # Update trace output
span.update_trace(output=generated_sql_query)
        # Score the trace
span.score_trace(
            name="SQL Execution Success",
config_id="cmhxf7z9z0001qt07rta5bc7r",
            value=check_sql_execution(generated_sql_query),
        )

generate_sql(
    "How can I find the total number of orders placed by customers in the
last month?"
)
```

The **config_id** can be found under the **Score Configs** section of the Project Settings. It is important to note here that there is **no verification to match config_id and name** in the **score_trace** call. The **config_id** only ensures that the score follows the data type and the allowed values or numeric ranges mentioned in the config.

Custom scores can be viewed from the **Scores** tab on the left navigation.

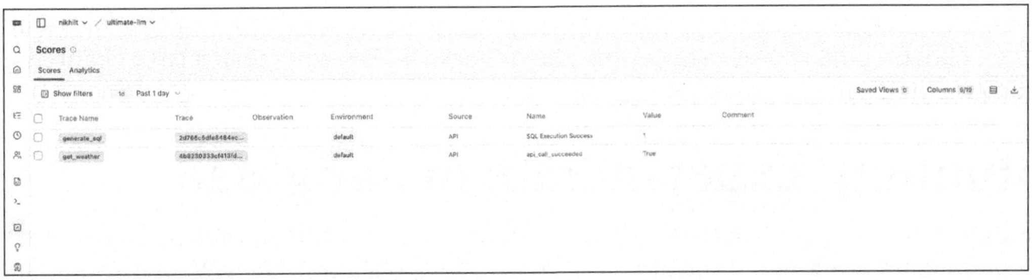

Figure 7.21: *Scores Page in Langfuse*

If a score is submitted without explicitly specifying a data type, Langfuse determines the type by examining the value itself. For categorical and Boolean scores, we can maintain both a string label and a numeric equivalent when relevant, even if only one form was provided.

Examples of automatic data type detection for custom scores:

Score Type	Input Value	Inferred data type	Validation Rules
Numeric	0.75, 42, -3.2	`NUMERIC` (if data type not set)	Automatically treated as numeric if no config is provided. Invalid if the value is non-numeric but the data type is NUMERIC.
Numeric with Config	0.5	`NUMERIC` (validated against config)	Must fall within allowed range or constraints defined in the Score Config.
Categorical	"correct", "partial", "wrong"	`CATEGORICAL`	Inferred as categorical if value is a string. If Score Config is set, numeric codes may also be accepted. Invalid if value type conflicts with config.
Categorical with Config	"high"	`CATEGORICAL`	Only allowed values from config are valid; the system may map strings to a numeric representation for reporting.
Boolean	True, False, 1, 0	`BOOLEAN`	If no config, numeric 1/0 or True/False are automatically interpreted as Boolean. Invalid if string "true"/ "false" is passed without proper type.
Boolean with Config	True	`BOOLEAN`	Must match the type and allowed values in the config; otherwise rejected.

Table 7.2: *Automatic Data Type Inference of a Custom Score in Langfuse*

In this section, we only covered adding custom scores to traces during ingestion. However, it may happen that we want to add custom scores to objects that were generated in the past. For automatic and human scoring this was very straightforward but for custom scoring this would involve programmatically retrieving the traces and then updating the scores using either the API or SDK. We will see in a later chapter on how to do this for already existing objects.

Running Experiments in Langfuse

So far in the chapter, we have laid the groundwork to run experiments in Langfuse. Experiments are a very crucial step in the LLM application lifecycle and something that we need to keep coming back to as we make changes to our application.

Experiments in Langfuse give us a structured way to test different versions of our prompts, models, or workflows against a dataset, and compare their outputs under the same conditions. This makes evaluation a repeatable, measurable process. There are many good reasons why we should run experiments for our application:

- **Controlled Comparison across Versions**: When we make changes such as modifying a prompt, switching model parameters, or updating business logic we need to make sure the change improves things. But without a test, we cannot know for sure. Running an experiment enables us to feed the same dataset through both the old and the new version and compare results in a consistent way. This gives transparency into whether the change leads to better, worse, or only marginally different outcomes.
- **Early Regression Detection and Continuous Improvement**: As systems evolve, prompts change, models update, and domain data shifts, there is a risk of regression. Experiments provide a safety check against regression. We can re-run our benchmark dataset whenever we make changes and watch for drop in quality. This helps ensure new versions do not degrade performance while we develop new features.
- **Making Data-Driven Decisions**: Rather than assuming a new prompt version is better, experiments let us objectively compare prompt versions using defined metrics. Over time, these quantitative results build into evidence that guides prompt development, model selection, and release decisions. It becomes possible to say with confidence that one version is better than another, not just by feeling, but by measurement.

Prompt Experiments

The first and the most common experiment in Langfuse is the Prompt Experiment. These experiments are triggered from the UI itself, and the main purpose is to compare prompt versions or LLM versions against a dataset.

Every experiment allows us to compare basic metrics such as token usage, cost and latency between different runs. To make experiments more meaningful, we should combine experimentation with one or more scoring techniques we have seen to really get full value from the outcome of the run. This step is optional in Langfuse, but highly recommended.

To run a Prompt experiment, we need to have:

1. **A Prompt:** This is the prompt we want to experiment with. Chapter 6 covered Prompt Management in detail where we learnt how to add and maintain our prompts in Langfuse.
2. **A Dataset:** Datasets need to be created against which the prompt will be run. A dataset can be used in an experiment only if the items are JSON objects with keys mapping all the variables in the prompt.
3. **LLM Connection:** This LLM connection is required to run the prompt with. LLM connections were also covered in *Chapter 6, Prompt Management in Langfuse.*
4. **LLM-as-a-Judge:** Prompt experiments work best with this scoring technique. Although Human Annotations and Custom Scores are also possible, they are not available by default for Prompt Experiments.

Once these pre-conditions are satisfied; we can navigate to our prompt from the **Prompts** navigation menu and start the experiment.

In this first example we will run an experiment on the **`product_description_generator`** prompt to compare responses between GPT 4.1 and GPT 4.1-mini models. For the comparison we will use three metrics: **Friendly Tone** which we created earlier and **Helpfulness** and **Conciseness** from the Langfuse built-in evaluators.

We start by selecting a prompt and a version. Model list will be available based on the LLM connections we have set up. In this step, we can also specify the JSON format for the expected output from the model.

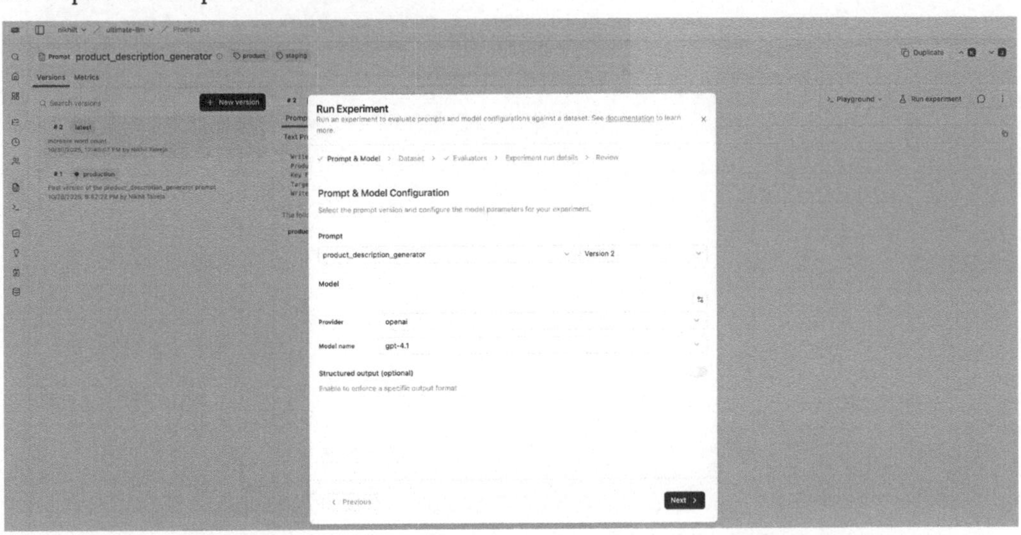

Figure 7.22: *Choosing a Prompt and Model for Our Experiment*

On the next screen we have to select the dataset for the experiment. Once we select the dataset, Langfuse will verify to see if every item in the dataset has the correct variables that are needed for the prompt. Incorrect dataset items will not be included in the experiment.

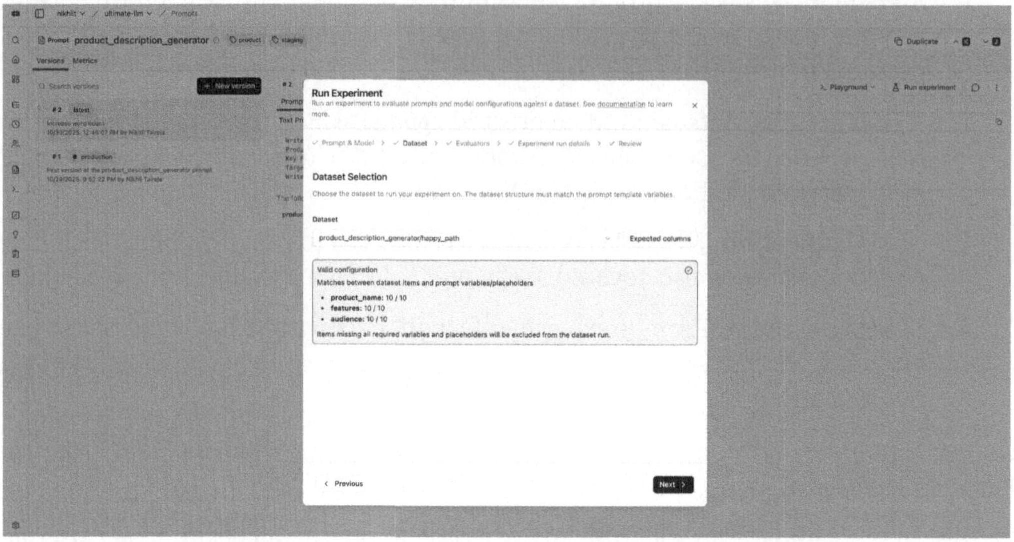

Figure 7.23: *Choosing a Dataset for the Experiment*

After the dataset, come the metrics/evaluators. This step is optional, but we should always try to have some evaluators for the run. In this example we have configured the three evaluators: **Friendly Tone**, **Helpfulness** and **Conciseness**.

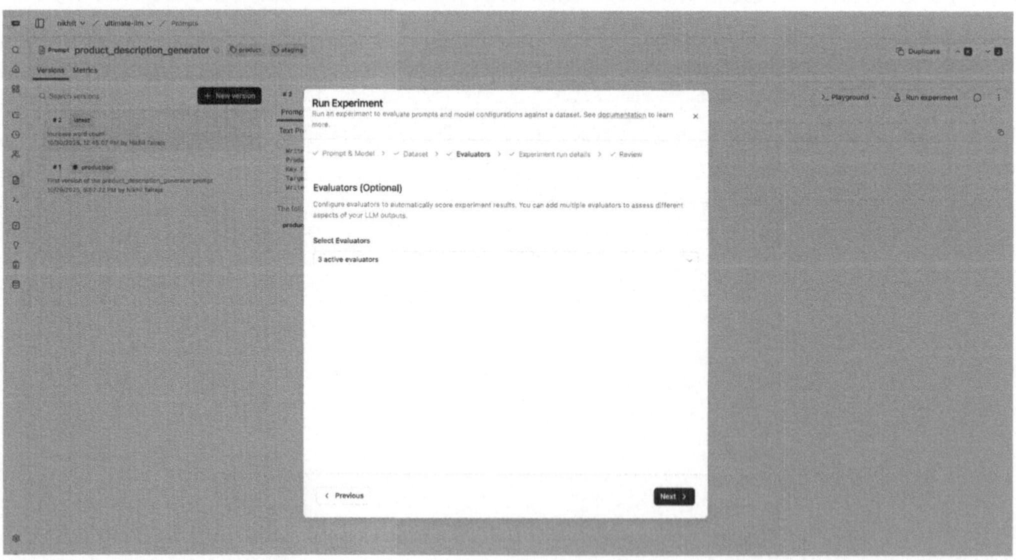

Figure 7.24: *Choose Evaluators for the Experiment*

On the next screen, we can give a meaningful name for the experiment and an optional description.

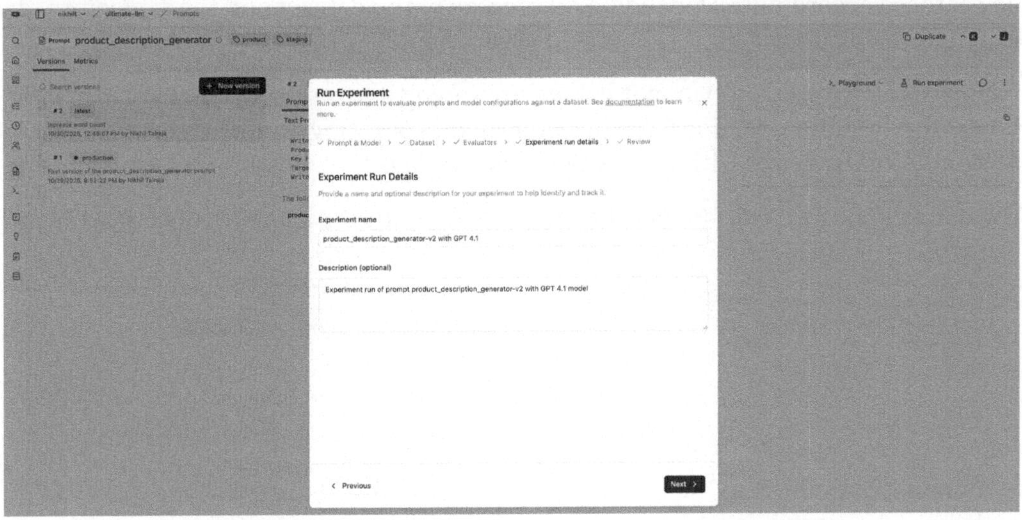

Figure 7.25: *Adding a Name and Description for the Experiment*

Finally, on the last page, we can preview all the inputs before starting the experiment. Langfuse also automatically generates a run name for every experiment run. This run name can later be used to fetch the run via the API/SDK.

We can also navigate back to the previous steps to change or correct any information.

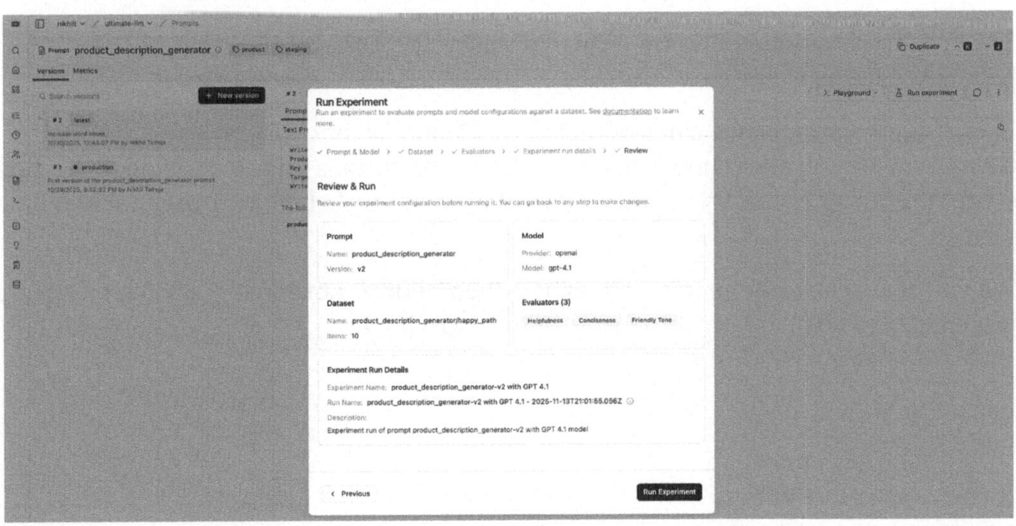

Figure 7.26: *Preview Experiment Inputs before Starting*

After clicking **`Run Experiment`**, Langfuse will start the experiment. For every dataset item, the prompt will be populated with the variables and then sent to the LLM we choose (in this case GPT 4.1). Every item run is also captured as a trace in Langfuse. If we have setup evaluators, those will also be run as separate traces and the scores will be captured accordingly. Depending on the size of the dataset and the evaluators, the experiment could take a few seconds to several minutes.

Langfuse is very efficient when it comes to running items or scoring them. Its event-based architecture combined with background processing can easily handle tens of thousands of item runs without any performance lags.

For our example, we will run another experiment with the same inputs but with GPT 4.1-mini.

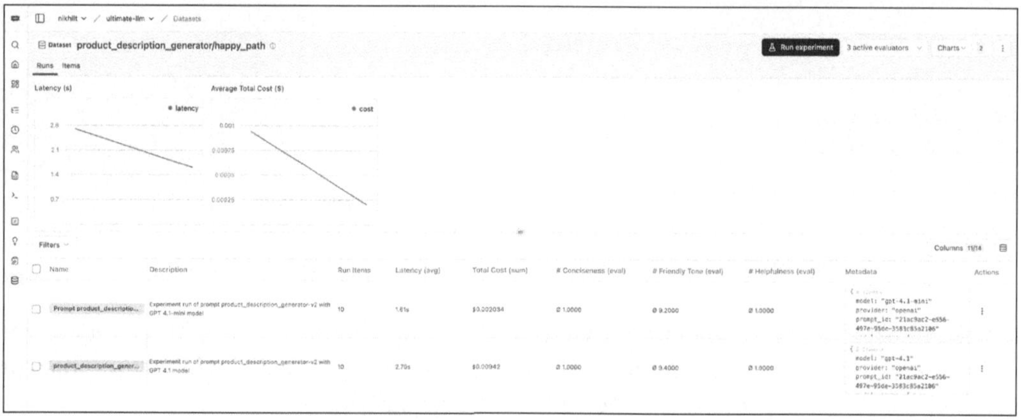

***Figure* 7.27:** *Experiment Comparisons*

The results of experiments are available under the **Datasets** section of the dataset being used in the experiment.

In our simple example we can see that GPT 4.1-mini is much faster and cheaper than GPT 4.1 and if we had to choose between these two options only, even though 4.1-mini scores 0.2 points less in Friendliness, it could be our ideal choice for the cost and time savings.

We can also select one or more runs and then choose **`Actions -> Compare`** to get a more detailed comparison of the runs of the experiment.

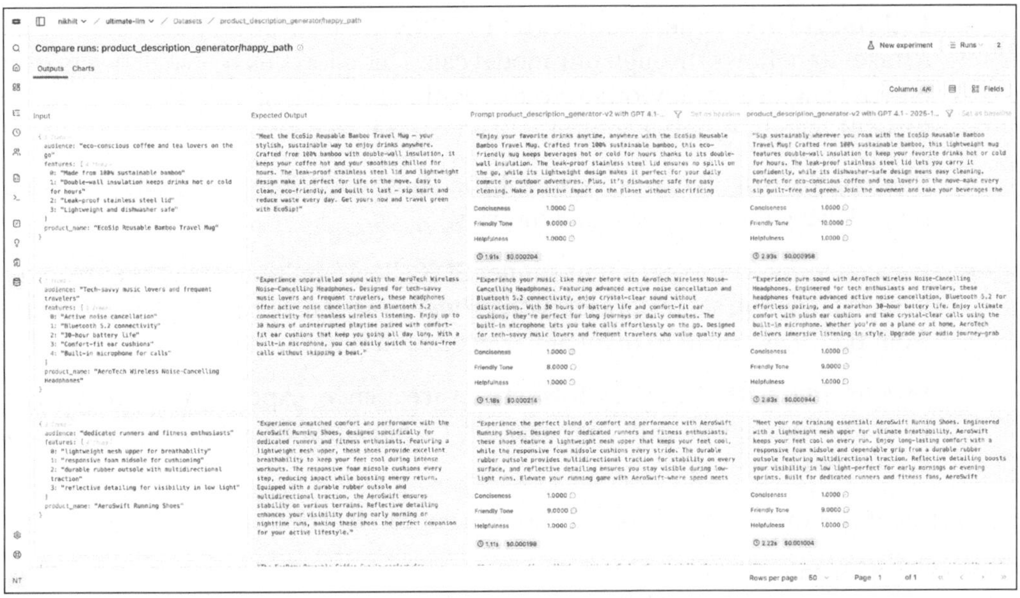

Figure 7.28: *Experiment Run Comparisons in Detail*

When running experiments like this, there a few potential pitfalls:

- Make sure every variable in the prompt matches a corresponding field in the dataset. A mismatch will omit the item from the experiment.
- Change only one major factor at a time (such as prompt wording or model version). When multiple variables are changed simultaneously, it becomes impossible to identify which one caused the improvement or regression.
- Large experiments especially those that run across multiple model versions or extensive datasets can quickly consume API tokens and budget. Even evaluations using LLM-as-a-Judge cost API tokens so this must be factored in when running the experiment.
- Prompt experiments are more suited for the Offline stage of development. When our application is live, we would want to run experiments on the real application and score based on Human Annotation or Custom Scores. How this can be done, is the subject for the next section.

Experiments Using the SDK

Experiments via the SDK offer far more control, reliability, and extensibility than running experiments directly in the UI. While the UI is ideal for quick comparisons or simple prompt tests, many of the limitations we have seen above can be overcome by programmatically running experiments and using real application outputs to compare prompt or model versions. Some features of experiments with SDK include:

- **Full control over experiment logic:** The SDK lets us explicitly define how each dataset item flows through our model call. This allows us to use datasets from either Langfuse or any other source without having strict requirements for variable matching between prompt and dataset items.
- **Custom Scoring:** Since we control the runs, each item run can be custom scored using our own logic and metrics.
- **Parallel Runs:** The experiment runner SDK allows multiple experiments to run in parallel on the same dataset with proper isolation. For prompt experiments from the UI, we need to manually trigger each run.
- **Integration with Existing Infrastructure:** Since experiments are written in code, you can plug in our existing CI pipelines analytics dashboards or structured validation logic.

To run a similar experiment like we saw above, we can use this code:

```
from langfuse import get_client
from dotenv import load_dotenv
from langfuse.openai import openai

load_dotenv()

langfuse_client = get_client()

# Define the dataset
 dataset = [
    {
        "input": {
            "audience": "Environmentally conscious coffee lovers",
            "features": [
                "Made from sustainable stainless steel",
                "Fits most standard coffee makers",
                "Easy to clean and dishwasher safe",
                "Reduces single-use paper waste",
                "Improves coffee flavor by preserving oils",
            ],
            "product_name": "EcoBrew Reusable Coffee Filter",
        }
    },
    {
        "input": {
            "audience": "Casual and professional runners",
            "features": [
                "Breathable mesh upper",
```

```
                "Lightweight EVA sole",
                "Reflective accents for night safety",
                "Arch support with memory foam insole",
            ],
            "product_name": "AeroSwift Running Shoes",
        }
    },
]

# Get the prompt from Langfuse
prompt = langfuse_client.get_prompt("product_description_generator")

# Define the logic to run each dataset item
def generate_product_description(*, item, **kwargs):
input_variables = item["input"]
    response = openai.chat.completions.create(
        model="gpt-4.1-mini",
        messages=[
            {
                "role": "system",
                "content": prompt.compile(
product_name=input_variables["product_name"],
                    features=input_variables["features"],
                    audience=input_variables["audience"],
                ),
            }
        ],
    )

    return response.choices[0].message.content

# Run the experiment on the dataset
result = langfuse_client.run_experiment(
    name="Prompt product_description_generator-v2 with GPT 4.1-mini",
    description="Experiment run of prompt product_description_
generator-v2 with GPT 4.1-mini model",
    data=dataset,
    task=generate_product_description,
)

print(result.format())
```

To run a local experiment, we need:

- **A Dataset**: Can be either local or an existing dataset from Langfuse.

- **The Task**: This is the method that is executed for every item, and should return the output from the application.

In this run, since we use local data, **no dataset item is created**, and only individual traces are generated. To generate dataset items and compare runs, we need to use existing datasets instead. This can be done by replacing the manual creation of dataset with:

```
dataset = langfuse.get_dataset("product_description_generator/happy_
path")
result = dataset.run_experiment(
    name="Prompt product_description_generator-v2 with GPT 4.1-mini",
    description="Experiment run of prompt product_description_
generator-v2 with GPT 4.1-mini model",
    task=generate_product_description,
)
```

Custom Evaluators

For experiments run via SDK, Langfuse gives the option to add custom defined evaluators or metrics on the individual **item level as well as on the run level.** This is useful when computing metrics for experiments requires application-level business logic or access to an external system or DB. In the example below we will run the experiment for our **`product_description_generator`** dataset and compute a simple metric called **`word_count`** on an item level and the **`max_word_count`** across the run level.

```
from langfuse import get_client
from dotenv import load_dotenv
from langfuse.openai import openai
from langfuse import Evaluation

load_dotenv()

langfuse_client = get_client()

# Define the dataset
dataset = langfuse_client.get_dataset("product_description_generator/
happy_path")

# Get the prompt from Langfuse
prompt = langfuse_client.get_prompt("product_description_generator")

# Define the logic to run each dataset item
def generate_product_description(*, item, **kwargs):
input_variables = item.input
```

```
    response = openai.chat.completions.create(
        model="gpt-4.1-mini",
        messages=[
            {
                "role": "system",
                "content": prompt.compile(
product_name=input_variables["product_name"],
                    features=input_variables["features"],
                    audience=input_variables["audience"],
                ),
            }
        ],
    )

    return response.choices[0].message.content

# Define an evaluator for each item
# This evaluator will input and the output of the item
def word_count(*, input, output, **kwargs):
    """Calculates the word count for the output"""
word_count = len(output.split())
    return Evaluation(
        name="word_count",
        value=word_count,
        comment=f"Response has {word_count} words",
    )

def max_word_count(*, item_results, **kwargs):
    """Finds the max word count across all items"""
    # item_results includes data about each item run in the experiment
    # We need to loop through every evaluation for each item to find the
word count
word_counts = [
eval.value
        for result in item_results
        for eval in result.evaluations
        if eval.name == "word_count"
    ]

    return Evaluation(
        name="max_word_count",
        value=max(word_counts),
        comment=f"The longest output is {max(word_counts)} words long",
```

```
    )

# Run the experiment on the dataset
result = dataset.run_experiment(
    name="Run level and item level evaluators",
    description="Experiment run to show the usage of run level and item
level evaluators",
    task=generate_product_description,
    # Item level evaluators
    evaluators=[word_count],
    # Run level evaluators
run_evaluators=[max_word_count],
)
```

We can use the **evaluators** or **run_evaluators** field to pass method references that compute or custom metric.

Run level and item level scores can be seen on the dataset

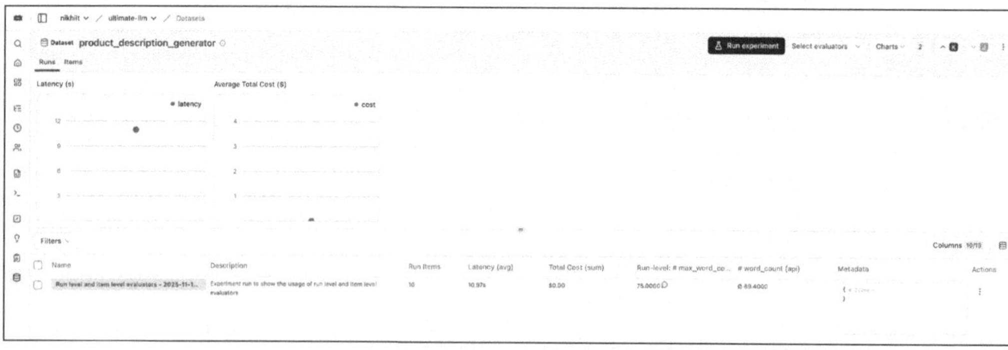

Figure 7.29: *Custom Metrics for SDK Experiments*

Having seen both types of experiments (Prompt and SDK) in Langfuse, here is a small guideline on when to use each of them:

- **Prompt Experiments**:
    - Trying a few new prompts quickly.
    - Comparing model versions.
    - Evaluating model parameters.
- **SDK Experiments**:
    - Running multi-step workflows.
    - Using real APIs or business logic for evaluation.
    - Running many experiments in parallel.

Conclusion

In this chapter, we have looked at the foundations of evaluating LLM applications. We explored the different features of evaluation in Langfuse ranging from automated scoring and LLM-as-a-judge methods to human annotation and custom scoring logic—and saw how each contributes uniquely to understanding application quality. We further examined the role of datasets, both real and synthetic, and learned how experiments in Langfuse help us compare prompts, models, and configurations in a controlled, repeatable way. Throughout the chapter, we emphasized the importance of combining quantitative signals with human judgment to create a well-rounded evaluation pipeline capable of catching regressions, validating improvements, and providing visibility into system behavior as it evolves. In the next chapter, we will see how to make sense of the metrics we have collected and turn them into insights via visualization capabilities in Langfuse.

References

- Evaluation in Langfuse – https://langfuse.com/docs/evaluation/overview
- Synthetic Datasets – https://langfuse.com/guides/cookbook/example_synthetic_datasets
- LLM as a judge in Langfuse – https://langfuse.com/docs/evaluation/evaluation-methods/llm-as-a-judge
- Scores Data Model in Langfuse – https://langfuse.com/docs/evaluation/evaluation-methods/data-model
- Datasets in Langfuse – https://langfuse.com/docs/evaluation/experiments/datasets
- Human Annotations in Langfuse – https://langfuse.com/docs/evaluation/evaluation-methods/annotation
- Custom Scores – https://langfuse.com/docs/evaluation/evaluation-methods/custom-scores
- Prompt Experiments – https://langfuse.com/docs/evaluation/experiments/experiments-via-ui
- Experiments with the SDK – https://langfuse.com/docs/evaluation/experiments/experiments-via-sdk

CHAPTER 8
Deriving Actionable Insights Using Langfuse Metrics

Introduction

In this chapter, we will explore how Langfuse dashboards and analytics help teams turn the data generated by their LLM applications into actionable insights. Building on traces, observations, and evaluation scores collected during runtime, metrics provide a structured way to analyze system behavior at scale. Using these metrics, teams can identify optimization opportunities such as reducing costs through prompt refinement, improving user satisfaction by addressing response quality issues, and mitigating reliability problems by monitoring error and performance trends. We also look at how metrics can be segmented by dimensions like model, prompt version, or user group, enabling deeper analysis across different slices of the system. This type of segmentation helps uncover patterns and trade-offs that are difficult to see when inspecting individual traces or evaluations in isolation.

Structure

In this chapter, we will cover the following topics:

- Score Analytics
    - Using Score Analytics
- Application Setup
- Dashboarding in Langfuse
    - Limitations of Custom Dashboards
- Accessing Metrics Programmatically
    - Metrics API
    - Querying via SDK

Score Analytics

In the previous chapter, we saw how to evaluate our LLM applications and generate different types of metrics and scores for our objects (Traces, Observations, and Sessions). These scores can be generated by either of the three techniques: **Human annotations**, **LLM-as-a-Judge evaluations,** or **Custom scores**. After accumulating this data over time through experiments or live traces it becomes natural to analyze the scores to inform development decisions and address issues in the application. This is where **Langfuse Score Analytics** becomes a crucial part of our evaluation workflow. It transforms scores into an organized, interactive analysis environment.

Score Analytics gives us ready-to-use analytical capabilities that enable us to:

- Quickly explore how scores are distributed.
- Compare two evaluation methods side-by-side.
- Assess consistency between judges.
- Identify outliers and mismatched assessments.
- Monitor quality changes over time.
- Pinpoint evaluation coverage gaps.

Score Analytics is accessible from `Scores -> Analytics` tab from the left navigation.

Figure 8.1: *The Score Analytics Feature of Langfuse*

This interface can be used for looking at the analytics of a single score or to compare two scores on the same object types (for example, observations). The key elements on this page are:

Feature	What It Tells Us
Basic Stats	Count, average, variability, dominant categories (for categorical scores).
Distribution Chart	How scores are spread out (clusters, skew, extremes).
Timeline Chart	Score trends and drifts over time.
Comparison Panel	(When two scores are selected) alignment and consistency.
Heatmaps or Confusion Matrices	Interaction between two scoring methods.

***Table 8.1**: Score Analytics Features*

One of the most valuable features is the ability to place **two scoring sources** side-by-side. These could be:

- Two different LLM judges (from two different LLMs);
- A human evaluation versus an automated score;
- Two versions of the same scoring rubric; and,
- Categorical versus a numeric score.

Comparisons can be made across any type of objects: Traces, Sessions, Observations, or Dataset Runs.

By doing so, we can measure how well one score aligns with another. Misalignment often points to:

- Inconsistent judge behavior.
- Ambiguously defined rubrics.
- Edge cases that confuse certain evaluators.
- Biases introduced after a new model or prompt release.
- Scoring methods drift apart over time.

This comparison can reveal several insights:

- **Correlation or Agreement Score**: Strength of the relationship between evaluators.
- **Error Metrics**: How far apart two numeric systems are, on an average.
- **Confusion Matrix (for Categorical Scores):** Whether evaluators disagree on certain classes.

- **Heatmap (for Numeric Pairings):** Where scores cluster and where mismatches occur.
- **Matched versus Full Distributions**: Whether one evaluator covers more data than the other.

Confusion matrices and Heatmaps only work when the metrics being compared are of the same type (categorical-categorical or numeric-numeric).

It should also be noted that high correlation between two evaluators does not validate the correctness of the evaluators themselves. It only means that the two evaluators agree with each other.

Score Analytics also includes time-series charts that show how scores behave across days, weeks, or months. This is especially useful for:

- Spotting silent regressions after deployment.
- Confirming quality improvements after prompt changes.
- Identifying evaluator drift (like a judge growing stricter).
- Observing anomalies caused by traffic spikes or unusual inputs.
- Tracking A/B test effects over time.

Sudden changes in trend lines often indicate:

- A new model being released;
- A modification to system prompts;
- Introduction of a new evaluation method;
- Shifts in user behavior; and,
- Data Pipeline changes.

At the time of writing, Score Analytics is a Beta feature and has the following limitations:

- Only two scores can be compared at once.
- Both scores must share the same underlying data type (numeric or categorical).
- Large datasets may be sampled for performance.

Using Score Analytics

The following are several real scenarios where Score Analytics helps us make decisions:

- **Validating Human-labeled Ground Truths:** If an automatic evaluator is supposed to mimic human feedback, we compare its scores against human labels. High alignment suggests we can safely rely on automated scoring for large-scale datasets.

- **Assessing Two LLM Judges:** Sometimes we test multiple LLMs to find the most consistent evaluator. A comparison chart can reveal which one produces more stable and interpretable judgments.
- **Investigating Quality Drops:** If recent scores dipped, Score Analytics helps us pinpoint when the decline started—and whether it aligns with a deployment, prompt update, or model change.
- **Studying Behavioral Trade-offs:** By comparing two scores, we can uncover correlations that lead to actionable improvements.
- **Detecting Unscored or Under-reviewed Cases:** Coverage gaps become obvious when one evaluator has far fewer entries. This helps us refine our scoring pipelines.

Application Setup

To make the best use of this chapter, we will create a small chatbot simulation application that is designed to answer questions about Langfuse. It is a simple GPT-based application without any RAG or tool usage since the idea is simply to generate enough scores to demonstrate the analytical features of Langfuse. The application will also simulate conversations between the chatbot and a real user using another LLM.

To make things realistic, the simulator will randomly ask an off-topic question to the chatbot to see how it responds to them. Eventually, we will generate a lot of traces in Langfuse and add scores for them using LLM-as-a-Judge.

We begin by loading environment variables and creating a Langfuse client instance. We also define two global parameters:

- **`MAX_TURNS`**: Number of user exchanges per conversation.
- **`N_CONVERSATIONS`**: Total number of conversations to simulate.

We can adjust these numbers based on the volume of traces we want to generate. If sampling is enabled, it can affect the number of traces that are recorded.

```
from dotenv import load_dotenv
from langfuse.openai import openai
from langfuse import get_client
import random
import uuid

load_dotenv()

# How many messages per conversation
MAX_TURNS = 10
N_CONVERSATIONS = 10

langfuse_client = get_client()
```

All prompts are retrieved directly from Langfuse.

```
# System prompts
chatbot_system_prompt = langfuse_client.get_prompt("langfuse_chatbot_
system_prompt")

simulator_system_prompt = langfuse_client.get_prompt("simulator_system_
prompt")

random_question_generator_prompt = langfuse_client.get_prompt(
    "random_question_generator_prompt"
)
```

The prompts are also pretty simple:

langfuse_chatbot_system_prompt : You are an expert assistant answering questions about Langfuse. Your goal is to give correct, structured, helpful, and concise answers. If a question is not about Langfuse, say so and don't answer.

simulator_system_prompt: You are simulating a curious user who wants to learn about Langfuse. You will ask questions, follow up naturally, refer to prior answers, and behave like a real human exploring a product. Do NOT answer questions—only ask them.

random_question_generator_prompt: You are a random question generator. Generate a random question not related to the conversation history Return only the question and nothing else.

```
def call_target_bot(conversation_history, session_id, user_id):
    chatbot_model = random.choice(["gpt-4.1-mini", "gpt-4.1"])
    response = openai.chat.completions.create(
        model=chatbot_model,
        messages=[{"role": "system", "content": chatbot_system_prompt.
prompt}, *conversation_history],
        name="langfuse-chatbot",
        metadata={"langfuse_session_id": session_id, "langfuse_user_id":
user_id},
        langfuse_prompt=chatbot_system_prompt,
    )
    return response.choices[0].message.content
```

Here, we send each conversation turn to our chatbot. This is the model whose performance we want to evaluate. The chatbot alternates between gpt-4.1-mini and gpt-4.1. This helps test how different model sizes perform across the same evaluation metrics. We send the entire turn-by-turn history to preserve context. **langfuse_**

session_id ties all messages from one simulated conversation together. **langfuse_user_id** allows us to test multi-user scenarios. Prompts are also linked to the traces using **langfuse_prompt=**

```
def get_user_question(conversation_history):
    simulator_prompt = random.choice([random_question_generator_prompt,
simulator_system_prompt])
    response = openai.chat.completions.create(
        model="gpt-4.1-mini",
        messages=[{"role": "system", "content": simulator_prompt.
prompt}, *conversation_history],
        name="question-generator",
        langfuse_prompt=simulator_prompt
    )
    return response.choices[0].message.content
```

User messages are created by the LLM. We randomly choose between a Langfuse-specific question and an off-topic question. Finally, we loop through the conversations:

```
def simulate_conversation(conv_id):
    print(f"\n=== Conversation {conv_id} ===")

    conversation_history = []
    # Generate a random session_id
    session_id = str(uuid.uuid4())
    # Choose a random user_id
    user_id = random.choice(["user_1", "user_2", "user_3"])

    # Continue the conversation
    for turn in range(MAX_TURNS):
        # simulated user query
        user_msg = get_user_question(conversation_history)
        conversation_history.append({"role": "user", "content": user_
msg})
        print(f"{user_id}:", user_msg)

        # chatbot replies
        bot_reply = call_target_bot(conversation_history, session_id,
user_id)
        conversation_history.append({"role": "assistant", "content":
bot_reply})
        print("Bot:", bot_reply)

if __name__ == "__main__":
```

```
    for i in range(N_CONVERSATIONS):
        simulate_conversation(i + 1)
        print("\n--- End Conversation ---\n")
```

Each conversation is generated step-by-step:

1. A new session ID is created.
2. A random user ID is chosen.
3. The simulator generates a user message based on previous turns.
4. The chatbot responds. This message is traced and scored by Langfuse.
5. Both messages are added to history, ensuring context grows naturally over time.

We will also set up the following **LLM-as-a-Judge Evaluators**

- **Chatbot Conciseness** based on the Conciseness in-built evaluator.
- **Chatbot Helpfulness** based on the Helpfulness in-built evaluator.
- **Chatbot Hallucination** built in evaluator.
- A custom metric called **Chatbot was off-topic** to evaluate if the chatbot answered a question that was not related to Langfuse.

This is the evaluation prompt used for the Chatbot was off topic evaluator:

```
You are a strict evaluator. Your job is to decide whether a chatbot made
a mistake by answering an off-topic question.

You will receive:
- A user message
- A chatbot message

Your task:

1. Decide if the user message is about Langfuse (the LLM engineering
platform).
   - If it mentions Langfuse features, tracing, prompts, evaluation,
metrics, dashboards, SDKs, or anything clearly related → it IS on-topic.
   - Everything else (general questions, unrelated tech, personal
topics, random topics) → off-topic.

2. If the user message is OFF-TOPIC:
      - If the chatbot ANSWERED the question → return "1" (incorrect
behavior)
      - If the chatbot REFUSED because it is off-topic → return "0"
(correct behavior)
```

```
3. If the user message is ON-TOPIC (about Langfuse):
      - Always return "0" (answering is correct)

Very important rules:
- A refusal must clearly say it cannot answer or that the question is
outside its domain.
- Ignore answer quality. Judge only topicality.
- Output MUST be exactly one character: "1" or "0". No words. No
punctuation.

Return only: 1 or 0.

User: {{user_message}}
Chatbot: {{assistant_message}}
```

Running the preceding program should generate enough traces for our use, and the LLM-as-Judge evaluators will automatically compute the metrics. Let us now revisit the Score Analytics section.

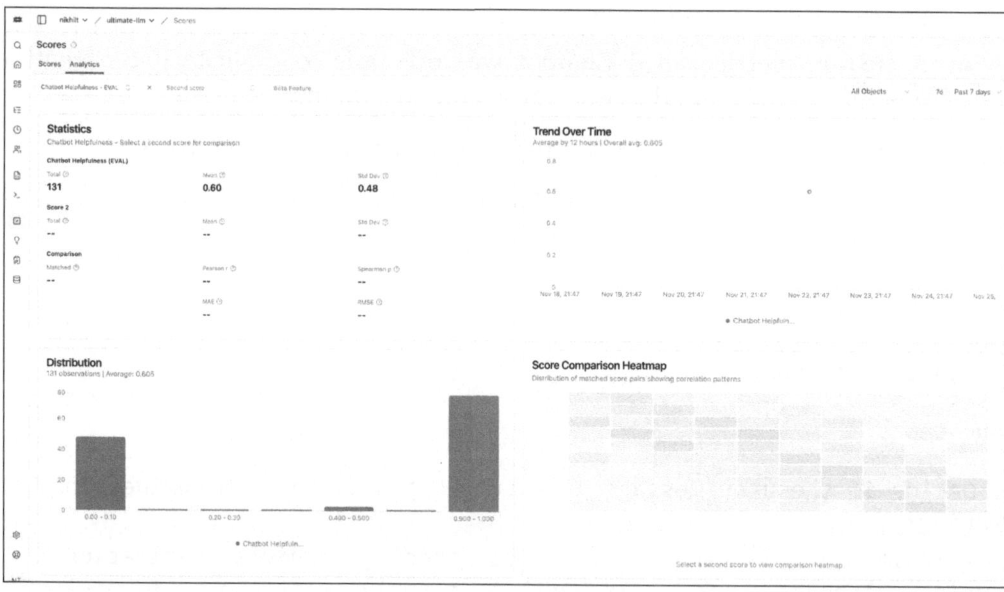

Figure 8.2: *Helpfulness Stats*

We can look at the statistics for each score individually or compare two scores to see the relationship between them. Here we can see that on average, our chatbot scores only 60% in Helpfulness, which may require deeper analysis into the reasoning of the evaluator to know the root cause.

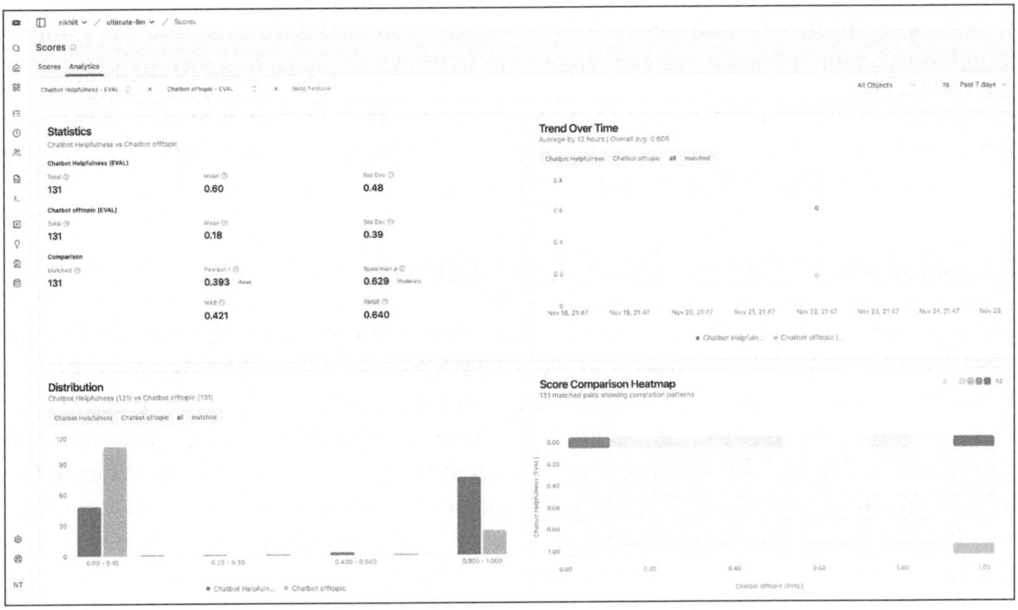

Figure 8.3: *Helpfulness versus Chatbot off-Topic*

On comparing Helpfulness with the off-topic metrics, we see that they are only loosely connected (Pearson r value of 0.4). This means when our chatbot gets an off-topic question, its helpfulness reduces, which is expected since it is not supposed to answer an off-topic question.

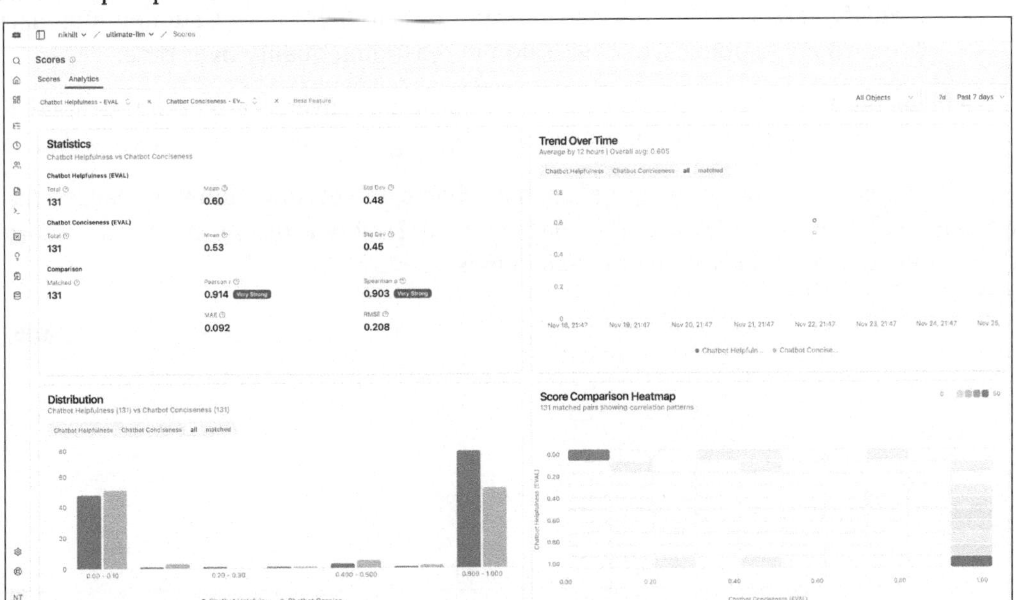

Figure 8.4: *Helpfulness versus Conciseness*

At the same time, we can see that Conciseness and Helpfulness are very highly correlated, which means a concise answer is also very likely to be more helpful.

These are just some of the examples of how Score Analytics can help uncover critical insights about our application. A more powerful feature to extract insights is using the Dashboard, which we will cover in the next section.

Dashboarding in Langfuse

Custom dashboards in Langfuse allow us to organize and visualize the metrics that are most relevant to our LLM application. These dashboards are built on the query system of Langfuse, which supports grouped aggregations and filtering across tracing data. This makes it possible to examine trends over time, compare behaviors across different user segments, or combine operational and quality metrics in one place. Whether we are monitoring how the application is performing or reviewing how changes impact user behavior, dashboards provide a structured way to interpret the data our system produces. These dashboards allow us to:

- **Centralize Key Metrics**: Bring all important KPIs, evaluation scores, latency, costs, and error types into a coherent view.
- **Customize Monitoring to Roles**: Product managers may focus on user experience scores, while engineers look at model performance or error spikes. Dashboards help us separate these perspectives clearly.
- **Identify Patterns Quickly**: We can spot dips in helpfulness, sudden increases in off-topic responses, or regression in reasoning quality over time.
- **Enable Repeatable Analysis**: Dashboards act as saved configurations. Instead of rebuilding filters or charts every time, we get consistent insights at a glance.

Each dashboard is made of "widgets" such as charts, tables, and summary cards—that we can configure to display exactly what we need. Dashboards can be accessed from the left navigation under the menu **`Dashboards`.**

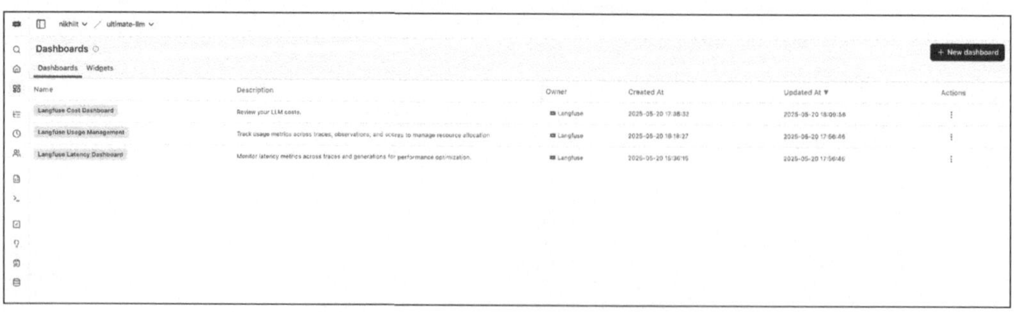

***Figure 8.5**: Dashboards in Langfuse*

By default, three dashboards are already pre-created in Langfuse, both in the cloud and the self-hosted version:

- **Langfuse Cost Dashboard:** Cost-related visualizations.
- **Langfuse Usage Management:** Usage metrics.
- **Langfuse Latency Dashboard:** Latency metrics.

These dashboards cannot be customized but contain a lot of useful visual components to access the most important information about our project at a glance. These curated dashboards can be cloned and customized to add our metrics as well.

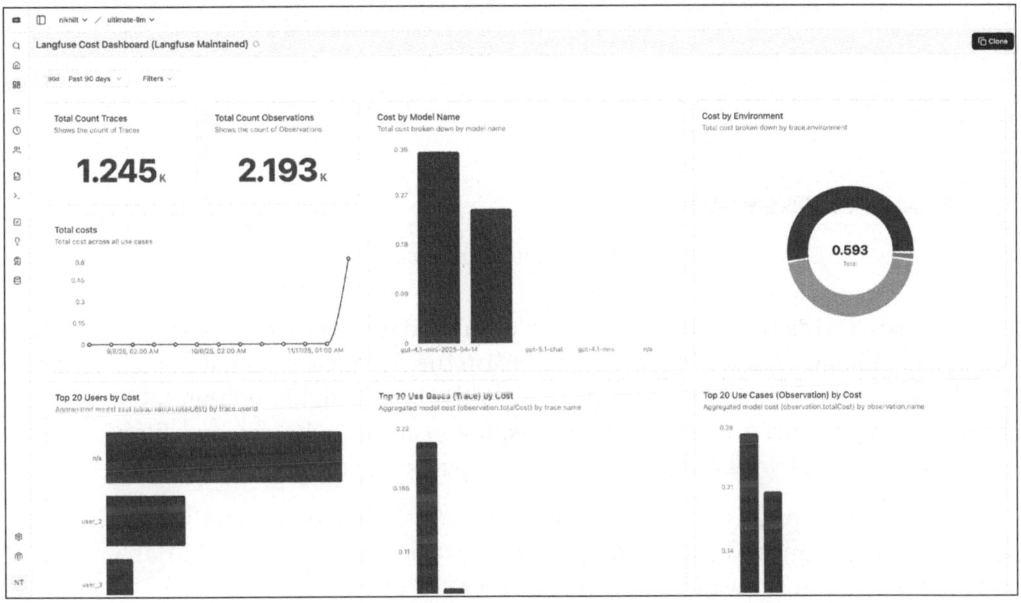

Figure 8.6: *Cost Dashboards in Langfuse*

To create a new Dashboard, we can use the **`+ New dashboard`** button.

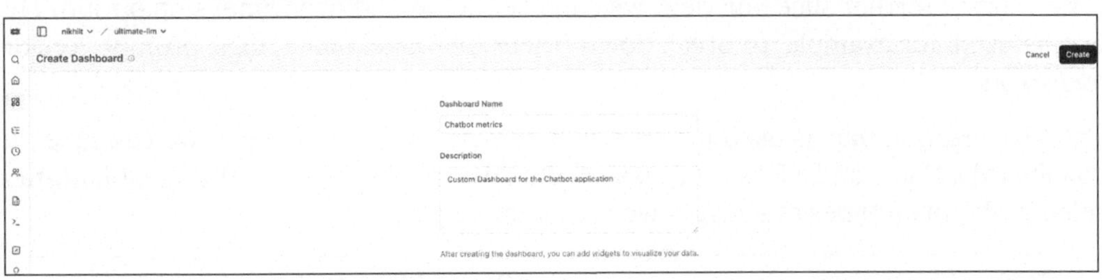

Figure 8.7: *Creating a New Dashboard*

To get the best out of dashboards, we should create our own Widgets, which are the individual visual elements in a dashboard. This can be done by clicking the **`Widgets`** tab and then clicking the **`+ New widget`** button.

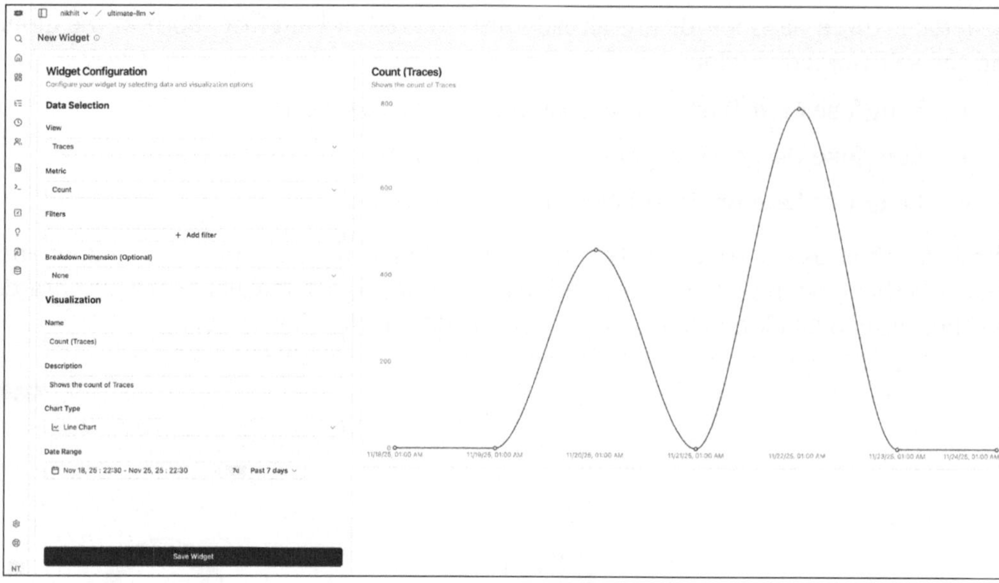

Figure 8.8: *Creating a New Widget*

In Langfuse, a **`widget`** is a single visualization or data-view component that we can add to a dashboard. Each widget is one "tile" on the dashboard, and it could be a chart, a table, a pivot, or any other data display. Widgets are highly configurable since we control the data source, the metric(s) to display, grouping/dimensions, filters, and the visualization style. Every widget has two main parts: the **`Data`** and the **`Visualization`.**

Within the Data, we can choose the main object (or View) for which the metric should be shown. This can be either, Traces, Observations, or Scores. Additionally, which metrics we want to show depends on the chosen View.

Optionally, we can apply filters over any of the attributes of the selected View, for example, Environment, Release version, Trace name, and so on.

If we want to further slice our view, we can use the Breakdown Dimension option. This can be used, for example, to break down traces by model name, tags, prompt version, and so on.

The Visualization part is used to customize the visual element. Here, we can give our dashboard a Name and a Description and select the chat type. As of the latest Langfuse release, the main types of widgets we can create include:

Widget Type	Use Case / When to Use
Line Chart / Time Series	Track how a metric evolves over time (for example, average latency, quality score trends).
Bar Chart (Vertical or Horizontal)	Compare metrics across categorical groups (for example, different models, users, features).

Widget Type	Use Case / When to Use
Histogram	Examine the distribution of a continuous metric (such as response latency, token counts, score values) — helps spot outliers or distribution shape.
Pie Chart	Show proportions or relative frequency among categories (e.g., share of responses per model, distribution of user types, fraction of off-topic violations).
Pivot Table	Multi-dimensional summary: cross-analyze two (or more) dimensions simultaneously (including quality score by model AND by user, or cost by feature AND time period).

Table 8.2: *Chart Types in Langfuse*

Here is an example of a **`Custom Dashboard`** showing the metrics for the **`Chatbot`** application.

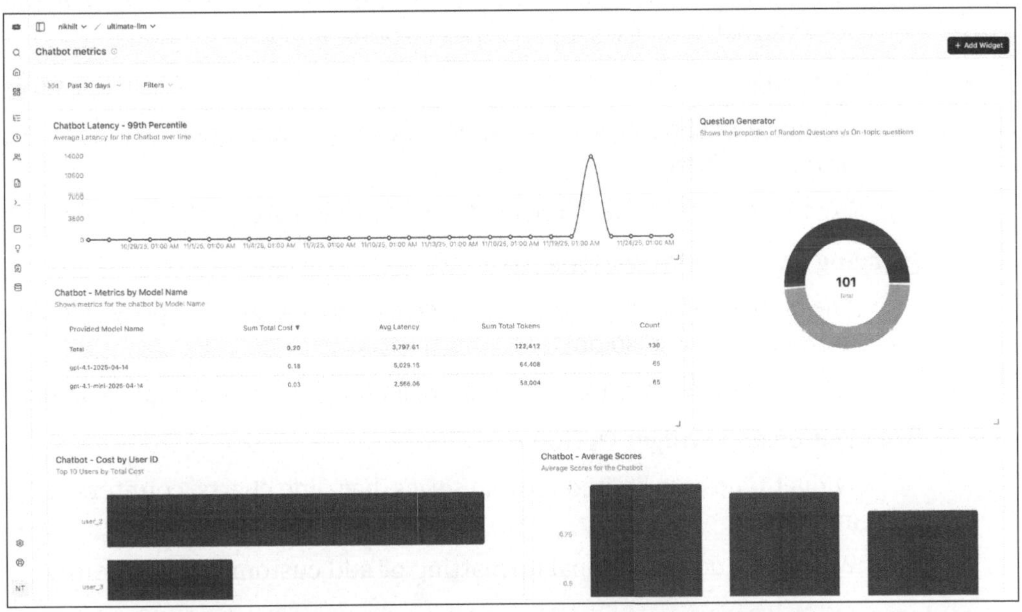

Figure 8.9: *Custom Dashboard for the Chatbot Application*

It has the following Widgets:

- Chatbot Latency (99th Percentile) showing model latency for the traces.
- Proportion of Random versus On-topic questions as a Pie Chart.
- Usage metrics broken by Model Name.
- Total cost by User ID.
- Average score values for Conciseness, Helpfulness, and Off-Topic responses.

As we can see, the number of possibilities of creating widgets is almost infinite, and we can customize these dashboards as per our monitoring needs.

Besides the features we have seen, we can also download the results from individual Widgets as CSV. To do this, we simply need to hover over the Widget and then click the Download button.

Limitations of Custom Dashboards

While the Custom Dashboards feature in Langfuse is very handy for creating some quick visualizations, it is not meant to be a full-scale Business Intelligence (BI) tool. For advanced analytics, there may be a need to have more customizations and data wrangling options. At the time of writing, Langfuse does not have support for the following features in Custom Dashboards:

- **Data Connectivity and Sources**
    - We can only visualize data from Langfuse, and there are no connectors for external databases, APIs, CSVs, or other application data.
- **Data Modeling**
    - Langfuse Dashboards do not support custom data models, dimensions, or relationships.
    - We cannot define calculated fields, custom measures, or transformations.
- **Querying and Transformations**
    - The number of aggregations is limited to what Langfuse exposes (counts, average, sum, and so on).
    - We cannot perform data cleaning, wrangling, or complex query logic.
- **Visualization and Widget Options**
    - Widget types are limited to time series, bar/line charts, counters/KPIs, and tables.
    - We cannot do conditional formatting or add custom colors/themes.
- **Interactivity**
    - Minimal interactivity (date filters, environment filters, tag filters).
    - No parameterized inputs or dynamic selectors.
- **Dashboard Customization and Layout**
    - Basic layout capabilities only; fixed grid with limited flexibility.
    - Cannot create multi-page dashboards or dashboard navigation flows.
- **Collaboration and Governance**
    - Versioning of dashboards is not possible.

- No granular role-based permissions (such as view versus edit at row/column level).
- **Exporting and Distribution**
    - Limited exporting options (for instance CSV for tables).
    - No option for PDF/Image export.
- **Limited Alerting / Automation**
    - Custom dashboards do not support threshold-based alerts (for example, notify when latency > X).
    - They do not integrate with on-call or incident management systems.

Due to these limitations, there may be situations where we would want to simply retrieve metrics data from Langfuse and use it in our own BI applications or any internal analytics stack we already rely on. This allows teams to combine Langfuse insights with broader business data, apply more advanced modeling or visualization techniques, and build dashboards with the flexibility and interactivity that dedicated BI tools provide.

Langfuse makes this data extraction possible by allowing us to access metrics/scores data programmatically, which we will cover in the next section.

Accessing Metrics Programmatically

As we saw earlier, there are some shortcomings of the dashboard options available in Langfuse, which would necessitate deriving metrics in another way. Langfuse makes this possible through its **Metrics API**. The Langfuse Metrics API provides a programmatic way to query aggregated analytics about our LLM application data from traces, model calls, evaluations, and related metadata. Instead of manually browsing dashboards, we can pull metrics results directly via an API call and integrate them into our own reporting tools or data pipelines.

Metrics API

With this API, we can group and filter data along many dimensions (which includes model name, user ID, session, prompt version, and environment) and retrieve a variety of measurements: counts of traces or observations, latencies, token or cost usage, and evaluation score distributions. Because it supports multiple views such as traces, observations, numeric scores, and categorical scores, the Metrics API gives us flexibility to build custom dashboards, export data for external BI tools, or drive automated reporting workflows based on real usage data.

Here is a simple code example on how to retrieve traces between two dates and aggregate them by name, showing the total count for each name:

```
from dotenv import load_dotenv
from langfuse import get_client

# To install pandas run pip install pandas
import pandas as pd

load_dotenv()
langfuse_client = get_client()

query = """
    {
        "view": "traces",
        "metrics": [{"measure": "count", "aggregation": "count"}],
        "dimensions": [{"field": "name"}],
        "fromTimestamp": "2025-11-01T00:00:00Z",
        "toTimestamp": "2025-11-30T00:00:00Z"
    }
"""

response = langfuse_client.api.metrics.metrics(query=query)
table = pd.DataFrame(response.dict()['data'])
print(table)
```

This will print a tabular structure with the results. The Metrics API offers all the possible options to derive data that we saw on the Custom Dashboard. The Data model for the API is extensive, but it can cover advanced needs for analytics quite easily. We will deep dive into every object of the API, but will cover the most important ones.

The Query object structure we saw earlier has the following fields:

Field	Type	Required?	Purpose / Meaning
`view`	string	Yes	Specifies which data view to query. Possible values: "traces", "observations", "scores-numeric", "scores-categorical" — determines whether you are querying at the trace-level, observation-level, or score-level.
`metrics`	array of metric objects	Yes	Defines which metrics to compute. Each metric object contains a measure (what to measure, e.g., "latency", "count", "totalCost", and so on) and an aggregation (how to aggregate: e.g., "sum", "avg", "p95", and so on).
`fromTimestamp`	string (ISO timestamp)	Yes	Start of time range to query (inclusive).

Field	Type	Required?	Purpose / Meaning
`toTimestamp`	string (ISO timestamp)	Yes	End of time range to query (inclusive).
`dimensions`	array of dimension objects	No	Allows grouping the results by certain fields, e.g., group by "name", "model", "userId", "environment", and so on. If omitted, results are aggregated globally across all items.
`filters`	array of filter objects	No	Provides filtering rules to restrict which data to include. Filters can be applied to metadata, string fields, numeric fields, and so on. Example: filter by userId, environment, tags, and custom metadata keys.
`timeDimension`	object	No	If provided, indicates that results should be grouped by time buckets (e.g., per hour, per day, per week). Example: { `"granularity": "day"` }. Useful for time-series analysis.
`orderBy`	array of ordering objects	No	Allows specifying the sorting order of the returned rows. Each ordering object typically references a field and direction (like ascending or descending).

***Table 8.3**: Query Object Structure for the Metrics API*

- **Metric Object:** Example: **`{ "measure": "latency", "aggregation": "p95" }`**. "Measure" selects the base metric; "aggregation" selects how to summarize (mean, percentile, count, sum, and so on).
- **Dimension Object:** Simplest form: **`{ "field": "name" }`**. Multiple dimensions allow multi-level grouping.
- **Filter Object:** Allows narrowing down data: for example, on metadata, numeric ranges, string matches, and so on. Example pattern includes fields such as column, operator, value, and optionally key when filtering on nested metadata.
- **Time Dimension:** Useful when you want metrics over time (such as daily averages, hourly counts, and so on) rather than a single aggregated value.

Here is another query to get aggregated metrics on a daily basis for all traces between two dates:

```
query = """
    {
        "view": "traces",
```

```
        "metrics": [
            { "measure": "count", "aggregation": "count" },
            { "measure": "latency", "aggregation": "avg" },
            { "measure": "totalTokens", "aggregation": "sum"},
            { "measure": "totalCost", "aggregation": "sum" }
        ],
        "dimensions": [],
        "timeDimension": {
            "granularity": "day"
        },
        "filters": [],
        "fromTimestamp": "2025-11-01T00:00:00Z",
        "toTimestamp": "2025-11-30T00:00:00Z"
    }
"""
```

Another advanced example to get average scores for our chatbot application.

```
query = """
    {
        "view": "scores-numeric",
        "metrics": [{"measure": "value", "aggregation": "avg"}],
        "dimensions": [{"field": "name"}],
        "filters": [
            {
                "column": "traceName",
                "operator": "contains",
                "key": "",
                "value": "langfuse-chatbot",
                "type": "string",
            }
        ],
        "fromTimestamp": "2025-11-01T00:00:00Z",
        "toTimestamp": "2025-11-30T00:00:00Z"
    }
"""
```

Even though the Metrics API gives us a flexible way to work with Langfuse analytics, the main inconvenience is that building effective queries requires familiarity with the underlying data model of Langfuse—views, dimensions, measures, and filter types—which can take some time to understand. Queries are however executed server side to improve performance which would make it an ideal choice for latency sensitive use cases. We will now see how we can also use the SDK to get metrics or scores programmatically.

Querying via SDK

While the Metrics API provides a structured way to retrieve aggregated analytics, it is not the only method available for accessing Langfuse data programmatically. Querying via the SDK offers a more flexible and direct alternative, especially for teams that prefer working with raw trace-level or observation-level data rather than pre-aggregated metrics.

Access to Raw Data Instead of Aggregates

The Metrics API is designed around aggregated queries: counts, averages, percentiles, grouped breakdowns, and time-series rollups. This is ideal when you already know the exact metric you want to compute.

The SDK, however, lets you pull the underlying trace, span, event, attachment, or score records directly, without requiring you to define a metrics query structure. This is useful when:

- You want to build your own custom aggregations.
- You need to join Langfuse data with data from your own systems.
- You want to inspect individual traces or evaluations for debugging or research.

In other words, the SDK allows you to handle data before any summarization occurs.

Supports Custom Filtering and Pagination

Where the Metrics API requires you to specify filters in terms of columns, operators, and types, the SDK often provides simpler filtering methods:

- Filtering by `traceId`, `userId`, `environment`, `name`.
- Searching by timestamp ranges.
- Paging through large collections of traces or observations.
- Applying metadata conditions that are easier to express directly.

This means you do not need to understand the full query object structure used by the Metrics API—you can fetch what you need, using more direct function calls.

Access to More Object Types

The Metrics API exposes only certain views: traces, observations, scores-numeric, and scores-categorical. Querying via SDK has broader coverage:

- Traces
- Observations
- Scores

- Prompts
- Datasets
- Sessions

This makes the SDK more suitable when our use case goes beyond metrics, for example, retrieving full traces for labeling, exporting your evaluation dataset, or inspecting prompt versions.

Querying via SDK is typically the better choice when:

- You want **raw trace or score data**, not metrics.
- You are building **custom aggregations** in your own code or BI system.
- You need to **debug** by inspecting full request/response logs.
- You want to create a **data export pipeline.**
- You prefer a more predictable, object-oriented way of interacting with data.

Here is an example of how to retrieve traces between two dates:

```
from dotenv import load_dotenv
from langfuse import get_client
from datetime import datetime

# To install pandas run pip install pandas
import pandas as pd

load_dotenv()

langfuse_client = get_client()

traces = langfuse_client.api.trace.list(
    limit=100,
    from_timestamp=datetime(2025, 11, 1),
    to_timestamp=datetime(2025, 11, 30)
)
records = [t.dict() for t in traces.data]
traces_df = pd.DataFrame(records)
```

This will return all the following fields of the traces:

Column	Description
`id`	Trace ID
`timestamp`	Trace Creation timestamp
`name`	Trace Name
`input`	Trace Input

Column	Description
`output`	Trace Output
`metadata`	Trace metadata
`tags`	Trace tags
`public`	Flag to indicate whether the Trace has a public link
`environment`	Langfuse environment
`htmlPath`	URL path of the trace
`latency`	Total latency of the trace
`totalCost`	Total cost for the trace
`observations`	List of linked Observation Ids
`scores`	List of linked Score Ids
`projectId`	Project Id to which the trace belongs
`bookmarked`	Flag to indicate whether the Trace has been bookmarked
`createdAt`	Timestamp when the trace was created
`updatedAt`	Timestamp when the trace was updated
`sessionId`	Session ID if the trace is linked to a session
`release`	Release name
`version`	Application version
`userId`	User ID if any user is linked to the trace
`externalId`	External ID, if any

Table 8.4: *Columns Returned for a Trace Using the SDK*

As we can see here, each trace record has a link to the underlying observations and scores, which we can fetch using the SDK as well.

As an advanced use case, let us try to fetch all scores for our chatbot between two dates, including the model's name and score values.

```
chatbot_traces = langfuse_client.api.trace.list(
    limit=100,
    from_timestamp=datetime(2025, 11, 1),
    to_timestamp=datetime(2025, 11, 30),
    name="langfuse-chatbot",
)
print(f"Fetched {len(chatbot_traces.data)} chatbot traces")

records = []
```

```
for t in chatbot_traces.data:
    # Loop through the observations
    for to in t.observations:
        observation_data = langfuse_client.api.observations.get(to)

        # Fetch ALL scores for the trace
        score_data = langfuse_client.api.score_v_2.get(trace_id=t.id).data

        # Create one record per score
        for s in score_data:
            record = {
                "trace_id": t.id,
                "model": observation_data.model,
                "score_name": s.name,
                "score_value": s.value,
            }
            records.append(record)

traces_df = pd.DataFrame(records)
```

The SDK-based approach is helpful when you need **exact, per-trace, and per-score details**, including the specific model used for each observation. However, it becomes **highly inefficient** because you must fetch traces, then fetch every observation, then fetch every score—often resulting in dozens of API calls per trace. It also requires handling the 100-trace pagination limit, making it slow and impractical for large time ranges.

In contrast, the Metrics API performs server-side aggregation, letting you query large datasets in a single request, but it does not provide raw, row-level data.

SDK versus Metrics API:

Aspect	SDK	Metrics API
Data Access	Full access to raw traces, observations, scores, and metadata.	Only aggregated metrics (counts, averages, percentiles, breakdowns).
Granularity	Row-level, per-trace, and per-score.	Aggregated over dimensions, time intervals, or filters.
Flexibility	Highly flexible: can implement custom joins, filtering, and transformations.	Limited to predefined measures, aggregations, and dimensions.
Performance	Slow for large datasets due to multiple API calls per trace/observation.	Fast for large datasets, server-side aggregation reduces overhead.
Pagination	Limited to 100 traces per request; requires manual paging.	No per-trace limit; a single query can cover large ranges.

Aspect	SDK	Metrics API
Ease of Use	Requires handling nested loops, joining, and data flattening.	Query structure needs understanding of metrics, dimensions, and filters.
Best Use Case	Debugging, exporting raw data, building custom pipelines, or analyzing specific traces.	Trend analysis, BI dashboards, cost/latency monitoring, and high-level reporting.
Limitations	Inefficient at scale, complex to maintain, risk of duplicate rows if loops are not structured correctly.	Cannot access raw trace-level data or custom observation details.

Table 8.5: *SDK versus Metrics API Comparison*

Conclusion

In this chapter, we have looked at how Langfuse helps teams get actionable insights from LLM applications. We covered Score Analytics for checking model performance, discussed how dashboards make monitoring easier, and compared ways to access data via the Metrics API or SDK. Each method has its strengths—whether you need detailed trace-level data or big-picture trends. The Metrics API should be preferred for scale, while the SDK access should be used for inspection and enrichment workflows. Langfuse gives teams flexible tools for monitoring, troubleshooting, and improving their applications. In the next chapter, we will look at the Administration features in Langfuse to add access level security and an introduction to the concept of Guardrails and how Langfuse can help integrate them in our applications.

References

- Metrics in Langfuse –
  https://langfuse.com/docs/metrics/overview
- Score Analytics in Langfuse –
  https://langfuse.com/docs/evaluation/evaluation-methods/score-analytics
- Custom Dashboards in Langfuse –
  https://langfuse.com/docs/metrics/features/custom-dashboards
- Langfuse metrics API –
  https://langfuse.com/docs/metrics/features/metrics-api
- Query via SDK –
  https://langfuse.com/docs/api-and-data-platform/features/query-via-sdk

CHAPTER 9

Administration, LLM Security, and Guardrails

Introduction

This chapter covers how Langfuse supports administrators and teams in managing access, ensuring compliance, and enforcing guardrails that keep LLM systems safe and reliable. We will explore the importance of Role-Based Access Control (RBAC), secure handling of API keys and tokens, and integration with existing enterprise identity systems. On the guardrails side, we will learn strategies to prevent toxic, biased, or unsafe outputs from propagating to end-users. This includes content filtering, response validation, and monitoring for prompt injections.

Structure

In this chapter, we will cover the following topics:

- Role-Based Access Control (RBAC) in Langfuse
    - Supported Authentication Modes
    - Enterprise SSO: Integration and Enforcement
    - Environment Variables for Authentication and SSO (Self-Hosted version)
    - Role-Based Access Control (RBAC)
- Admin features in Langfuse
    - Audit logs
    - Data Deletion
    - Data Retention
    - Spend Alerts
- LLM Security and Guardrails
- Using a Guardrail with Langfuse

Role-Based Access Control (RBAC) in Langfuse

Whether we run Langfuse in the cloud or self-host it, authentication is the first line of security. It ensures that only verified users and systems can access the observability and logging data of our LLM applications. Poor or weak authentication undermines all higher-level controls (authorization, auditing, and encryption).

Langfuse offers flexible authentication options that integrate cleanly with enterprise identity systems, while preserving security and operational simplicity.

Supported Authentication Modes

Langfuse supports multiple authentication strategies — from simple email/password login to enterprise-grade SSO integrations. At a high level:

Mode	When It is Useful / What It Provides
Email + Password (default, for quick start / small teams)	Good for small teams or internal evaluation; minimal setup overhead.
Social Logins (which includes Google, GitHub, Microsoft Azure AD)	Useful when we want to leverage existing accounts — good for informal teams or dev-only deployments.
Enterprise SSO via OIDC / OAuth2 / SAML-like flows	Essential for production / corporate environments, especially when integrating with identity providers like Okta, Keycloak, Azure AD, JumpCloud, or enterprise GitHub accounts.

***Table 9.1**: Supported Authentication Methods in Langfuse*

If we self-host Langfuse, we get full control over which modes to enable by enabling email/password or social login or disabling them and relying solely on SSO. There may be some differences in supported authentication methods between self-hosted and the cloud version.

Enterprise SSO: Integration and Enforcement

Using Single-Sing-on (SSO) significantly reduces friction for users in organizations that already manage identity centrally and helps enforce corporate security standards:

- Langfuse supports standard identity protocols (OIDC / OAuth2 / SAML equivalents) so that Langfuse acts as a "service provider," delegating authentication to our IdP (Identity Provider).

- At the time of writing, Langfuse supports "IdP-initiated" SSO flows meaning users can start login directly from the dashboard of their identity provider (such as Okta, Azure AD). This simplifies onboarding and reduces user friction.
- For self-hosted deployments, configuration is via environment variables. We covered environment variables in *Chapter* 4, *Introduction to Langfuse*. A full list of which environment variables to set based on our IdP is available at:

  `https://langfuse.com/self-hosting/security/authentication-and-sso#sso`
- Optionally, we can enforce that sign-in must happen via SSO (disabling email/password or social login), by whitelisting certain domains. This helps ensure that only users from the organization's domain (or approved identity domain) can sign up or log in.

Environment Variables for Authentication and Self-Hosted Version (SSO)

The following table groups the environment variables that influence authentication behavior and SSO integration when we self-host Langfuse:

Variable	Description	Default
`NEXTAUTH_URL`	Public URL used to generate auth redirects and callbacks. Must match the address users access to avoid SSO failures.	**None** (must be set for SSO)
`AUTH_SESSION_MAX_AGE`	Maximum session lifetime in minutes; controls how long users remain logged in before a new authentication cycle is required.	**43200** (≈ 30 days)
`AUTH_DISABLE_SIGNUP`	Disallows new user sign-ups; useful when access is managed only through invitations or an IdP.	**false**
`AUTH_DISABLE_USERNAME_PASSWORD`	Removes built-in email/password login so that only SSO or other providers are used.	**false**
`AUTH_DOMAINS_WITH_SSO_ENFORCEMENT`	Comma-separated list of email domains that must authenticate through SSO only.	**None**
`AUTH_HTTP_PROXY / AUTH_HTTPS_PROXY`	Proxy settings for outbound communication with identity providers, required in networks with enforced outbound proxies.	**None**

***Table 9.2**: Configuration Variables for Authentication and SSO in Langfuse*

Role-Based Access Control (RBAC)

Access control determines who can do what inside our Langfuse deployment. Now that we've established how users authenticate, we need to define how those authenticated identities interact with the system. RBAC provides an organized method for assigning permissions, minimizing potential damage, and preventing unintended or unauthorized actions in shared environments where several people manage the same instance.

As we have seen in earlier chapters, in Langfuse we work with *Organizations* and *Projects*. These are also the two scopes in which permissions apply. An organization is the top-level container; projects sit underneath it. Certain actions only make sense at one of these levels, so the model separates responsibilities cleanly.

When multiple teams or developers use Langfuse, we must ensure a few things:

- Users should see only the projects they are meant to interact with.
- Operational tasks like deleting data, editing settings, or managing access should not be available to someone who only needs to view traces.
- Admin-level oversight must be limited to a small group so that misconfigurations or destructive actions cannot happen by accident.
- CI jobs, backend services, and automation tooling must operate under predictable, least-privilege principles.

RBAC supports this by mapping users to roles, and roles to allowed actions. This makes access predictable and reviewable.

We can access project and organization roles by choosing **`Settings`** on the left navigation and then selecting **`Members`**.

From the same page, organization settings can be accessed by clicking **`Organization Settings`**.

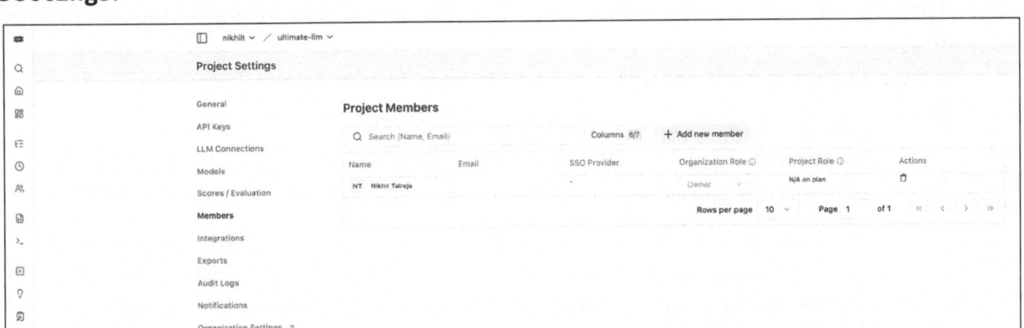

***Figure 9.1**: Managing Project Members in Langfuse*

To add a new member to the project, click the **`+ Add new member`** button.

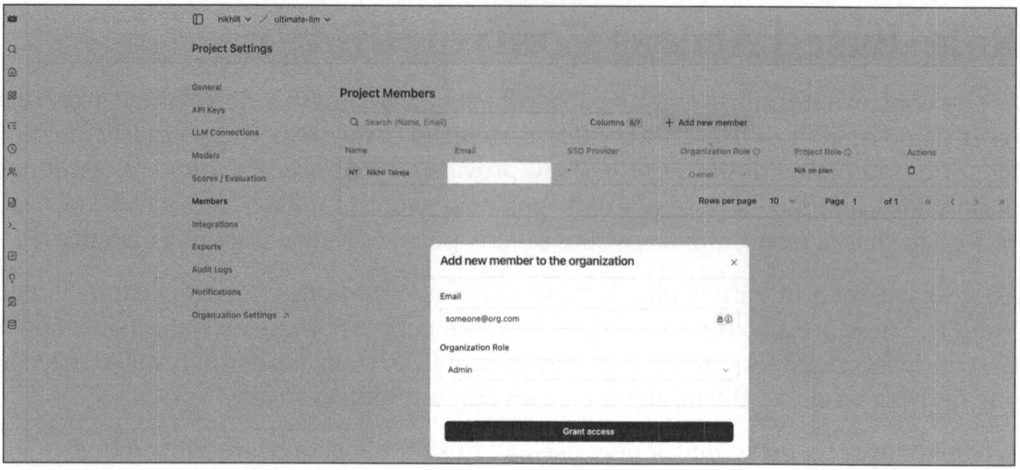

***Figure* 9.2**: *Adding a New Member to the Project*

The RBAC Model: Organizations and Projects

Across a Langfuse instance, we have two RBAC layers:

1. **Organization Layer:** This governs global membership, admin privileges, and the creation or deletion of projects.
2. **Project Layer:** It governs interaction with traces, evaluations, datasets, and other project-specific assets.

The same user may have different roles in different projects and may or may not have elevated rights at the organization level.

Organization Roles

The organization roles determine who can manage membership and structural configuration.

Role	What the role can do
Org Admin	Can invite and remove members, create or delete projects, manage billing (if applicable), and view all projects. We rely on this role for top-level governance.
Org Member	Can join and access projects they are assigned to but cannot modify organization-wide settings. This is appropriate for most internal users.

***Table* 9.3**: *Organization Level Roles in Langfuse*

Project Roles

Project roles govern operational work within a single project. These are more granular because they reflect the day-to-day actions inside Langfuse.

Role	What the role can do
Project Admin	Full control over project settings, tokens, datasets, prompt versions, evaluations, and member assignments. We rely on this role for people who maintain the observability setup.
Editor	Can modify project data, create evaluations, update prompts, and interact with datasets – but cannot change membership or delete the entire project. Most developers fit here.
Viewer	Can inspect traces, metrics, prompts, and related information but cannot create or modify anything. Ideal for read-only access, audits, demos, and non-technical stakeholders.

Table 9.4: *Project Level Roles in Langfuse*

Note that Project level roles are only available in Pro and Enterprise versions of Langfuse. Even for self-hosted versions, the Enterprise add-on needs to be purchased separately for project level RBAC.

By default, users will have the role they are assigned on the organization level, and this cannot be over-ridden in projects. The table here shows each and every permission which is available to different roles in Langfuse. The acronym **CRUD** is used to denote Create Read Update and Delete permissions.

Functionality	Permission	Owner	Admin	Member	Viewer
API Keys	`apiKeys:CUD`	✓	✓		
	`apiKeys:read`	✓	✓	✓	
Annotation Queues	`annotationQueueAssignments:CUD`	✓	✓		
	`annotationQueueAssignments:read`	✓	✓	✓	
	`annotationQueues:CUD`	✓	✓	✓	
	`annotationQueues:read`	✓	✓	✓	✓
Audit Logs	`auditLogs:read`	✓	✓		
Automations	`automations:CUD`	✓	✓		
	`automations:read`	✓	✓	✓	✓
Comments	`comments:CUD`	✓	✓	✓	
	`comments:read`	✓	✓	✓	✓

Functionality	Permission	Owner	Admin	Member	Viewer
Dashboards	`dashboards:CUD`	✓	✓	✓	
	`dashboards:read`	✓	✓	✓	✓
Datasets	`datasets:CUD`	✓	✓	✓	
Evaluations	`evalDefaultModel:CUD`	✓	✓	✓	
	`evalDefaultModel:read`	✓	✓	✓	✓
	`evalJob:CUD`	✓	✓	✓	
	`evalJob:read`	✓	✓	✓	✓
	`evalJobExecution:read`	✓	✓	✓	✓
	`evalTemplate:CUD`	✓	✓	✓	
	`evalTemplate:read`	✓	✓	✓	✓
Exports	`batchExports:create`	✓	✓	✓	
	`batchExports:read`	✓	✓	✓	
Integrations	`integrations:CRUD`	✓	✓		
LLM API Keys	`llmApiKeys:create`	✓	✓		
	`llmApiKeys:delete`	✓	✓		
	`llmApiKeys:read`	✓	✓	✓	✓
	`llmApiKeys:update`	✓	✓		
LLM Schemas	`llmSchemas:CUD`	✓	✓		
	`llmSchemas:read`	✓	✓	✓	✓
LLM Tools	`llmTools:CUD`	✓	✓		
	`llmTools:read`	✓	✓	✓	✓
Model Config	`models:CUD`	✓	✓		
Objects	`objects:bookmark`	✓	✓	✓	
	`objects:publish`	✓	✓	✓	
	`objects:tag`	✓	✓	✓	
Project	`project:delete`	✓			
	`project:read`	✓	✓	✓	✓
	`project:update`	✓	✓		
Project Members	`projectMembers:CUD`	✓	✓		
	`projectMembers:read`	✓	✓	✓	
Prompt Experiments	`promptExperiments:CUD`	✓	✓	✓	
	`promptExperiments:read`	✓	✓	✓	✓

Functionality	Permission	Owner	Admin	Member	Viewer
Prompts	`promptProtectedLabels:CUD`	✓	✓		
	`prompts:CUD`	✓	✓	✓	
	`prompts:read`	✓	✓	✓	✓
Scores	`scoreConfigs:CUD`	✓	✓	✓	
	`scoreConfigs:read`	✓	✓	✓	✓
	`scores:CUD`	✓	✓	✓	
Table View Presets	`TableViewPresets:CUD`	✓	✓	✓	
	`TableViewPresets:read`	✓	✓	✓	✓
Traces	`traces:delete`	✓	✓		

Table 9.5: *Role and Permissions Matrix in Langfuse*

Transferring Projects between Organizations

Transferring a project between organizations is a controlled operation reserved for users who hold the **`projects:transfer_organization`** permission. When we initiate a transfer, the project is detached from its current organization and attached to the target one, where access will depend on the roles defined there. The move does not alter or discard any project data such as traces, evaluations, prompts, settings, and API keys all remain intact. Aside from access management being reset under the new organization, the project continues operating normally. All functionalities, including logging and prompt workflows, remain uninterrupted throughout the transfer.

Admin Features in Langfuse

When managing Langfuse across large-scale internal teams or distributed production settings, robust administrative controls are crucial for ensuring operational effectiveness. The admin features offer us three foundational capabilities: a comprehensive **audit trail** that logs every significant action (who did what, when and where), robust **data deletion** mechanisms to remove traces or entire projects when needed, and configurable **data-retention** policies that allow us to define how long traces, evaluations, scores, and media assets persist. Together, these tools give us control over data lifecycle, accountability over changes, and the ability to comply with privacy or storage constraints all without compromising ongoing operations, observability, or historical context.

Audit Logs

In team, organizational, or enterprise settings where Langfuse is used, it is essential to maintain oversight of all modifications, particularly when multiple users, services, or

API keys interact with the same projects. Audit logs give us visibility into all changes that happen on the project level by recording every significant action taken in the system, along with metadata that lets us trace it back to the responsible identity.

At a minimum, each audit-log entry captures:

- **Who**: The user or the API key that initiated the action.
- **What**: The specific action (like create, update, delete) on a resource.
- **When**: An exact timestamp.
- **Where**: The organization and project context in which the action occurred.
- **Before / After State**: For updates, the complete resource state before and after modification – stored as JSON. This gives us full context of what changed.

These immutable records form a comprehensive audit trail suited for security reviews, compliance requirements, forensic investigation after incidents, or accountability in collaborative environments.

Viewing and Navigating Logs

Audit logs are available under Project Settings (Enterprise / Self-hosted Enterprise versions only) and users with the **`auditLogs:read`** permission typically project admins or owners can browse the complete history of actions.

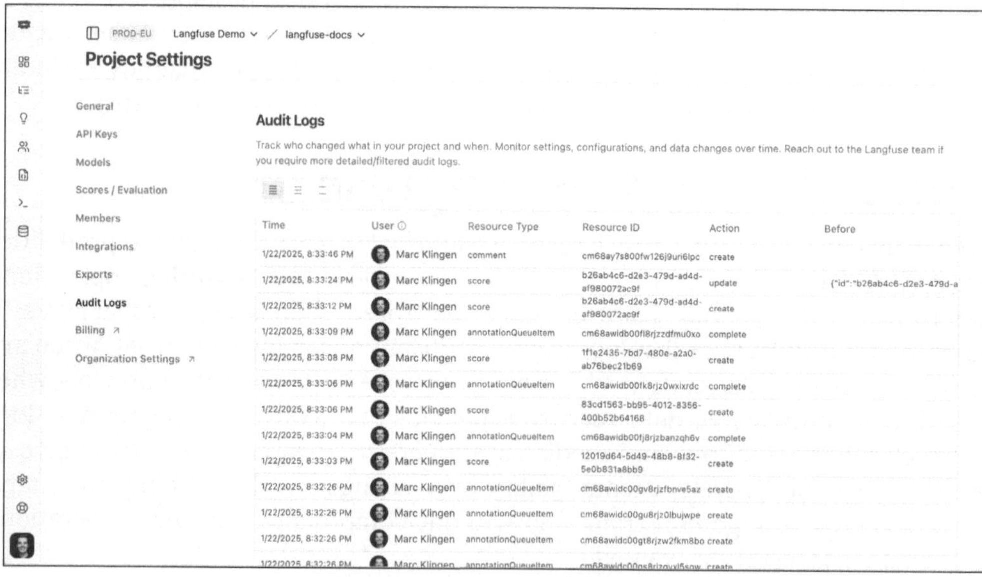

Figure 9.3: Audit Logs in Langfuse
(Source: *https://langfuse.com/docs/administration/audit-logs*)

From this page we can:

- Filter by time window (date ranges);
- Filter by project activities; and,
- Paginate through large result sets efficiently.

This makes it practical to investigate when something unexpected happens – for example, who deleted a dataset, or when an API key was rotated.

We can export audit-log data from the UI (or via batch export in self-hosted Enterprise) into downloadable formats that enable offline analysis, integration with external compliance tooling, or long-term archival. That export capability is especially useful if we want to push logs into a custom reporting pipeline.

Langfuse tracks a wide variety of resource types and operations. Among them:

- Project-Level Actions (create, update, delete, transfer);
- API Keys and LLM API Keys (create, delete, update);
- Datasets and Dataset Items (create, update, delete);
- Evaluations – Jobs, templates, runs (create, update, delete);
- Prompt operations – creation, deletion, promotion, label/tags changes, updates;
- Comments, annotations, dashboards, and other UI-level entities (create, delete, update); and,
- Trace/bookmark/publish/delete operations, session or blob storage integrations, and more.

Because update events include full "before" and "after" state snapshots, we can always reconstruct exactly what changed – critical for traceability when many actors or services are involved. Audit entries clearly distinguish between:

- **User-Initiated Actions** (via UI, by a logged-in user), and
- **Programmatic Actions** (via API keys).

Each log record embeds the identity source (user ID or API key ID), the organization and project context, and the role the actor had at the moment of the action.

That means we know not only what changed but who did it, when, and in which organizational context. This level of metadata is essential for security audits, compliance reviews, or debugging mistakes and misconfigurations after the fact. We rely on audit logs whenever we need to:

- Investigate unexpected changes. This includes a dataset or prompt that vanishes, API keys revoked, or settings adjusted.

- Meet compliance or regulatory requirements, where we must demonstrate a tamper-evident history of changes.
- Run security reviews or forensic analyses after incidents (similar to unauthorized access, or credential compromise).
- Provide accountability in large teams or multi-tenant environments – especially when many developers, data engineers, or automation bots interact with the same instance.
- Archive a long-term history of changes outside Langfuse (via export) for audits or external oversight.

Data Deletion

Langfuse accumulates data rapidly, including traces, evaluations, scores, observations, and prompts. In certain circumstances, it is necessary to delete specific portions of this data, such as erroneous traces, outdated experiments, obsolete projects, or user information for privacy and compliance purposes. Langfuse offers multiple deletion operations designed to facilitate the safe and intentional removal of data as needed. We can remove data at various scopes:

- A **single trace** which is useful when a trace was created by mistake.
- A **batch of traces**, selected via the UI or API for cleaning up multiple unwanted traces.
- All traces matching a **query filter** for example, delete everything before a certain date or matching certain metadata.
- An entire **project** including all its data, settings, associated keys and metadata.
- For cloud/self-hosted deployments: an **organization** when it contains no projects.
- A **user account** containing user data, useful for privacy or account cleanup. (Cloud and self-hosted have slightly different procedures).

We might choose to delete data in scenarios such as:

- Mistaken or test traces created during development require cleaning them up once real data flows begin.
- Privacy-sensitive data or PII accidentally captured in traces / observations, requiring removal for compliance.
- Cleanup after a project is deprecated or replaced.
- Periodic housekeeping, especially in long-running environments, to keep storage usage manageable.

- User-requested deletion (in cloud deployments), if a user wants their historical data removed.
- Because deletions are irrevocable, we must confirm carefully and ensure we have backups (if needed) or that no required data is lost.

The easiest way to delete traces is from the **Traces** page. We can delete a single trace or a batch of traces which are either selected manually or by using query filters on the traces page.

We need to keep in mind the following before deleting traces:

- For trace deletion, related entities (like scores, observations tied to that trace) are also removed. That ensures we do not leave orphaned records.
- Most deletion operations are executed quickly, but trace removals may take time; Langfuse schedules a background task to purge trace data from the warehouse. Typical deletion completes within minutes, but the system may take up to ~15 minutes, and there is **no explicit confirmation**. To verify deletion, we need to manually re-query the data.

Figure 9.4: *Deleting Traces in Langfuse*

To delete traces, we can select the traces using the checkboxes and then under **`Actions`** select **`Delete Traces`**.

To delete a project, go to the **`Settings`** page and choose **`Delete Project`** in the **`Danger Zone`** section.

***Figure 9.5**: Deleting a Project in Langfuse*

Deleting a project or an organization triggers immediate revocation of all associated API keys and schedules full cleanup of all data tied to that project. This action is irreversible and should be used with caution.

Deleting traces or a project does not automatically affect configurations or metadata outside the data itself (except revoking API keys on project deletion). For example:

- Project settings (names, descriptions, configurations) are removed only when deleting the project, not when deleting traces.
- Other projects or organizational metadata remain intact when traces are deleted.
- For self-hosted users, deletion routines rely on the backend; if there are lingering problems (like in data cleanup), manual verification or cleanup may be needed.

Data Retention

While manual deletion lets us remove specific data when needed, it does not address the steady accumulation of traces, observations, scores, and other data that builds up during normal operation. In long-running projects, this growth can fill storage and slow down queries if left unchecked. To prevent that, Langfuse supports project-level data retention where we define how long event data should remain available, and anything older than that window is automatically purged. This gives us a predictable, ongoing cleanup mechanism that complements manual deletion and keeps the system performant over time.

- Retention is set at the project level: each project defines a retention window (in number of days).
- The minimum allowed retention period is 3 days.
- If no retention period is configured, Langfuse retains event data indefinitely (default behavior).
- Project owners or administrators can change this setting via the Project Settings from the UI (or via the Projects API).

The retention policy applies only to the main objects in Langfuse. Once data for any of these entities is older than the configured retention period, it becomes eligible for deletion.

Object Type	Timestamp Field Checked
Traces	`timestamp`
Observations	`start_time`
Scores	`timestamp`
Media Assets	`created_at`

Table 9.6*: Data Retention Timestamp Fields for Different Objects*

The deletion process is as follows:

- Every night, Langfuse scans for records older than the retention threshold and deletes them.
- This purge is irreversible and once deleted, the data cannot be recovered.
- Because deletion is independent of references, we may end up with dangling references: for example, a dataset run in Langfuse might point to a trace that has since been purged.

If we run the self-hosted version and use external blob or object storage (like S3) for media assets, we must ensure that the service account / IAM role used by Langfuse has permission to delete objects (such as **`s3:DeleteObject`** on the relevant buckets). Without this permission, retention-triggered cleanups of media assets may fail silently.

Also, if the storage bucket is versioned, the delete operations of Langfuse only remove the "current" version (that is the delete is recorded at the API level). Old versions or delete markers must be cleaned up manually or via lifecycle rules configured in the storage backend.

We rely on retention policies in several common operational scenarios:

- **Storage Management:** As trace volume grows (especially in high-traffic production systems), retention helps control storage costs and prevents indefinite growth.

- **Performance Maintenance:** Reducing amount of historical data improves query and UI response times especially when UI or analytics dashboards scan over large time windows.
- **Privacy and Compliance Needs:** For sensitive data (like user messages, PII), we can automatically purge old records after a set period, aiding compliance with regulations or internal data-handling policies.
- **Operational Hygiene:** Retention offers a "set-and-forget" cleanup strategy since once configured, we do not need to manually remember to delete old traces.

Similar to project level RBAC, *data retention feature is only available in Pro and Enterprise versions of Langfuse. For self-hosted versions, the Enterprise add-on needs to be purchased separately for the data retention feature.*

Spend Alerts

With Spend Alerts enabled, we can define a monetary threshold for the spending of our organization. Once total charges including base fees, usage-based fees, discounts, and taxes exceed that threshold, Langfuse will send an email notification to alert organization admins or owners.

The Spend Alerts feature is only available on the **`Core`**, **`Pro`** and **`Enterprise`** versions. It can be configured under the **`Billing`** option of the organization's Settings page.

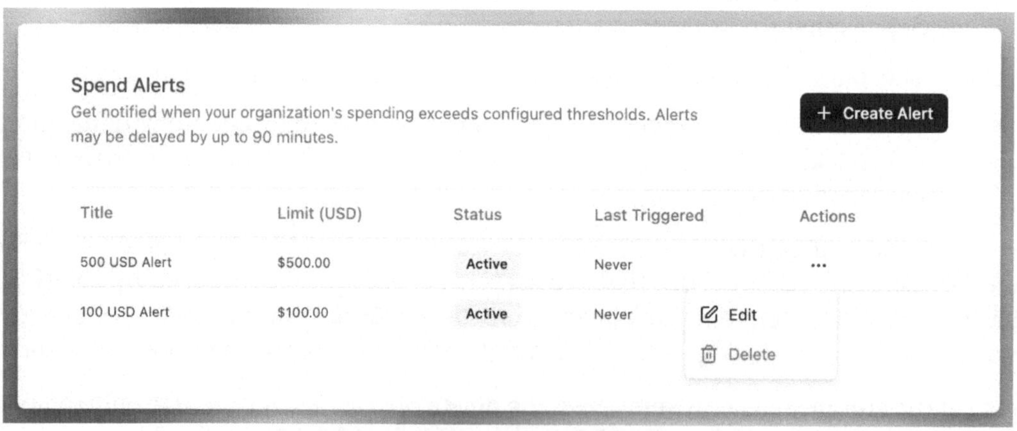

Figure 9.6: *Spend Alerts in Langfuse*
(Source: https://langfuse.com/docs/administration/spend-alerts)

Spend Alerts in Langfuse operate through a straightforward mechanism:

- Alert thresholds are configured in the billing currency of the organization.
- Spend is periodically evaluated (every 60–90 minutes) to check if the threshold is exceeded.

- Notifications are sent only once per billing cycle per alert.
- Emails go to members with "Owner" or "Admin" roles in that organization.

We use spend alerts when:

- We want to keep spending under control, especially in environments with variable workload or bursty traffic.
- We run shared or multi-team projects and need guardrails against runaway costs.
- We want visibility into billing spikes and granular cost oversight without manually reviewing invoices or dashboards.

LLM Security and Guardrails

When we expose our LLM applications to real users or external systems, we must assume that the model can receive malformed inputs, adversarial prompts, or sensitive data. Without safeguards, an application may reveal internal information, produce inappropriate or unsafe outputs, or mis-handle private content. Guardrails address this by placing checks around the model like validating or transforming inputs, filtering outputs, enforcing access restrictions, and monitoring how the system behaves over time.

Common guardrail components include input validation, output moderation, policy-based constraints, and clear access boundaries. These controls help limit the impact of prompt injection attempts, unintentional data leakage, or misuse of model outputs. They also provide a structure for compliance requirements when dealing with regulated or sensitive information.

Langfuse fits into this picture by giving us the operational context needed to apply and evaluate these controls. Audit logs allow us to trace who triggered a model call and what changed in the system. RBAC helps restrict access to sensitive projects and API keys. Retention and deletion rules ensure that historical prompts, traces, or outputs do not persist longer than necessary. And because Langfuse captures detailed traces of model inputs and outputs, we can review how guardrails respond in practice, detect recurring failure modes, and adjust our policies accordingly. While guardrails themselves must be implemented in the application layer, Langfuse provides the observability, accountability, and data-lifecycle mechanisms necessary to maintain and iterate on a secure LLM deployment.

Guardrails in Practice

Guardrails become meaningful only when they are applied consistently at run time. Most applications define a clear sequence of steps around the model call: validate the input, apply security checks, redact or transform sensitive content, generate the model output, and optionally apply additional checks before returning a response.

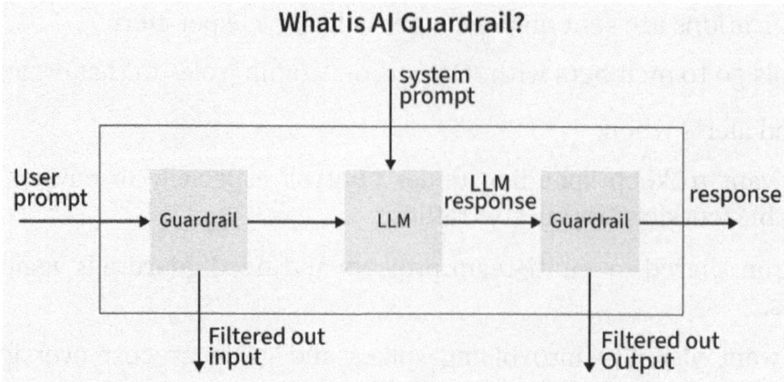

Figure 9.7: *Basic Structure of a Guardrail in LLMs*
(Source: https://www.geeksforgeeks.org/artificial-intelligence/what-are-ai-guardrails/)

This structure keeps control around the model, even when the model itself cannot enforce constraints. A range of open-source and commercial libraries can assist with implementing run-time checks in LLM systems. Although they differ in design, they address similar categories of risk:

- They can block or modify user prompts before they reach the model if the prompt appears adversarial, off-topic, or intended to circumvent system instructions.
- They can redact PII before sending a request to the model and re-inject the original data in the final response.
- They can evaluate prompts or model outputs at run time for toxicity, safety, relevance, or other constraints and suppress or alter output if needed.

These tools reduce the amount of custom rule-writing required, but they still benefit from observability to verify that they perform as intended. We will not cover LLM security or Guardrails in detail since it is not the main subject of the book. Readers are encouraged to learn more about this crucial topic from other sources to help them understand the concepts around security and guardrailing in the context of LLM applications.

Using a Guardrail with Langfuse

Guardrails are effective only if we can verify their behavior. Langfuse provides the visibility needed to assess whether our run-time checks are functioning correctly and where gaps remain. By tracing the full lifecycle of a request, Langfuse allows us to review:

- Which validation or filtering steps were applied.
- How the input changed before reaching the model.

- How long each step took,
- Whether the guardrail produced a block, modification, or score.

This helps diagnose security issues, understand unexpected behavior, and verify that filtering logic is executed consistently. By attributing security-related scores (toxicity, safety, PII presence, jailbreak likelihood and so on), we can track these metrics over time. This gives us early signals if certain risks increase or if a recent change weakens our protections.

We can evaluate the effectiveness of security tools through the two evaluation techniques we have seen earlier:

- **Human Annotations**
    - Teams can manually label a subset of production traces as a ground truth baseline.
    - Scores produced by guardrail libraries can then be compared against these labels to measure accuracy and detect blind spots.
- **LLM-as-a-Judge**
    - Using automated LLM-as-a-Judge evaluations we can periodically scan traces for toxicity or sensitivity.
    - This provides an audit of the guardrail pipeline, identifying gaps without relying solely on real-time checks.

In the following example, we walk through a practical workflow for applying run-time guardrails to an LLM-powered code-review assistant. The idea is straightforward: before the model processes any user request, we run a lightweight security check that looks for common risks such as leaked secrets or toxic language. Depending on the outcome, the request is either blocked, redacted, or allowed to proceed. Throughout this workflow, we use Langfuse to record each step like guardrail decisions, model inputs, model outputs, and trace-level scores so we can later analyze how the system behaved, verify that guardrails triggered correctly, and monitor overall safety patterns in production.

```
import re
from typing import Dict, Any
from langfuse import get_client
from langfuse.openai import openai
from dotenv import load_dotenv

load_dotenv()
langfuse_client = get_client()
```

For our guardrail we have a simple method that checks for certain toxic keywords or secrets which should not be present in the text.

```
TOXIC_WORDS = {"idiot", "stupid", "hate"}
SECRET_PATTERNS = [
    re.compile(r"sk-[A-Za-z0-9]{20,}"),  # API-key like strings
    re.compile(r"AKIA[0-9A-Z]{16}"),  # AWS-style key
    re.compile(r"\b\d{16}\b"),  # 16-digit number
]

def run_guardrail(prompt: str) -> Dict[str, Any]:
    """
    Synchronous guardrail example:
      - flags toxicity via keyword search
      - flags and redacts potential secrets via regex
      - returns whether the request is allowed, redacted prompt,
reasons, and scores
    Real deployments should call specialized libraries
    and treat this function as a placeholder that demonstrates how to
record results.
    """
    reasons = []
    toxicity = 0.0
    secret_risk = 0.0

    lowered = prompt.lower()
    if any(w in lowered for w in TOXIC_WORDS):
        toxicity = 0.8
        reasons.append("toxic_language")

    redacted = prompt
    for pattern in SECRET_PATTERNS:
        if pattern.search(prompt):
            secret_risk = max(secret_risk, 0.9)
            reasons.append("possible_secret")
            redacted = pattern.sub("[REDACTED]", redacted)

    # block when toxicity exceeds thresholds
    allowed = not toxicity > 0.7
    if not reasons:
        reasons.append("clean")

    return {
        "allowed": allowed,
        "redacted_prompt": redacted,
        "reasons": reasons,
```

```
        "scores": {
            "toxicity": toxicity,
            "secret_risk": secret_risk,
        },
    }
```

Next, we have a helper method which runs the entire flow:

1. **Start a root trace** to capture the overall request and metadata.
2. **Run the guardrail check** to detect toxicity or leaked secrets and record the result.
3. **Block or continue** based on the guardrail decision.
4. **Call the LLM** (if allowed), using the redacted prompt and logging the generation step.
5. **Finalize the trace** with the chosen reply and guardrail outcome.

```
def handle_code_review(user_id: str, user_prompt: str) -> str:
    """
    Guarded code-review helper.
    Returns:
      - the assistant reply (or block message)
      - a dict with trace-relevant metadata useful for tests or
assertions
    """
    with langfuse_client.start_as_current_observation(
        as_type="chain",
        name="code-review-session",
        input={"user_id": user_id, "user_prompt": user_prompt},
        metadata={"feature": "code_review_guarded"},
    ) as root:
        # 1) Guardrail step
        with langfuse_client.start_as_current_observation(
            as_type="guardrail",
            name="secret-and-toxicity-check",
            input={"user_prompt": user_prompt},
        ) as guard_obs:
            guard_result = run_guardrail(user_prompt)
            guard_obs.update(output=guard_result)

        # expose guard scores on the trace so we can analyze later
        root.score_trace(
            name="guard_toxicity",
```

```
            value=guard_result["scores"]["toxicity"],
            data_type="NUMERIC",
        )
        root.score_trace(
            name="guard_secret_risk",
            value=guard_result["scores"]["secret_risk"],
            data_type="NUMERIC",
        )
        # If guardrail blocks, update root and return early (no LLM call)
        if not guard_result["allowed"]:
            blocked_reply = (
                "I can't help with this request because it seems to
contain "
                "sensitive or unsafe information. Please remove secrets
or "
                "abusive language and try again."
            )
            root.update(output={"reply": blocked_reply, "blocked_by_
guardrail": True})
            return blocked_reply

        # 2) LLM generation for the actual code review
        system_prompt = (
            "You are a careful senior engineer. Review the user's code
for "
            "correctness, readability, and security. Never repeat
secrets."
        )

        messages = [
            {"role": "system", "content": system_prompt},
            {
                "role": "user",
                "content": guard_result["redacted_prompt"],
            },
        ]

        with langfuse_client.start_as_current_observation(
            as_type="generation",
            name="code-review-llm",
            model="gpt-4o-mini",
            input=messages,
            model_parameters={"temperature": 0.3},
```

```
        ) as gen_obs:
            completion = openai.chat.completions.create(
                model="gpt-4o-mini",
                messages=messages,
                temperature=0.3,
            )
            answer = completion.choices[0].message.content or ""
            gen_obs.update(output=answer)

        # 3) final response on root observation
        root.update(
            output={
                "reply": answer,
                "blocked_by_guardrail": False,
            }
        )

        return answer
```

To simulate this flow, we can run some example code reviews.

```
SIMULATIONS = [
    (
        "clean-user",
        "Please review the following Flask snippet and suggest security 
improvements:\n\n"
        "from flask import Flask\napp = Flask(__name__)\n\n@app.
route('/')\ndef index():\n    return 'ok'\n",
    ),
    (
        "secret-leak",
        "Help me review this code. I accidentally pasted my AWS key 
AKIA1234567890ABCDEF. "
        "How to store this properly?\n\n"
        "from flask import Flask\napp = Flask(__name__)\n",
    ),
    (
        "toxic-request",
        "You're an idiot. Fix my code and make it not stupid: \n\
nprint('hello')\n",
    ),
    (
        "borderline-redactable",
        "I used placeholder card 4111111111111111 while testing billing. "
```

```
        "Please ensure we don't log card numbers and suggest safe
storage.\n\napp code...\n",
    ),
]
if __name__ == "__main__":
    for case_name, prompt in SIMULATIONS:
        print(f"Simulation: {case_name}")
        answer = handle_code_review(user_id=f"sim-{case_name}", user_
prompt=prompt)
        print("Code review output:\n", answer)
```

This is a summary of how our guardrails will be applied in each of the four cases:

Example Name	What the Prompt Contains	Guardrail Action	LLM Call	Expected Outcome
Clean Request	Normal code, no sensitive content	Marked clean	Yes	Full review response
Secret-Leak Request	AWS key / secret-like patterns	**Redact secret**, allow	Yes	Safe review based on redacted prompt
Toxic Request	Abusive/toxic language	**Block**	No	Safe fallback message to user
Borderline Redactable	Secret text that looks like a credit card number	**Redact pattern**, allow	Yes	Normal review with redacted input

***Table 9.7**: Guardrail Actions for the Simulated Scenarios*

We can see in the trace that for toxic content, the request is simply blocked.

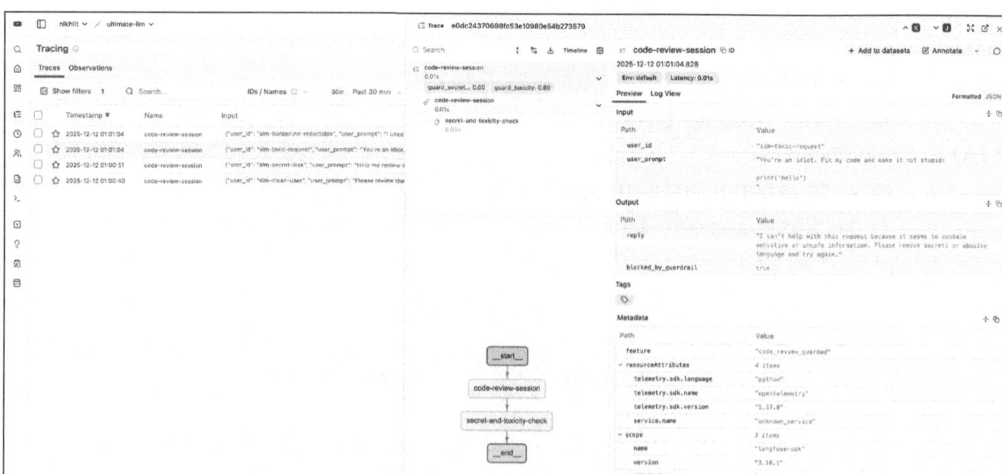

***Figure 9.8:** Example of Guardrail Blocking in a Trace*

Clean requests are allowed to proceed as normal and when secret patterns are detected in the code to be reviewed, they are redacted and the redacted content is sent to the LLM.

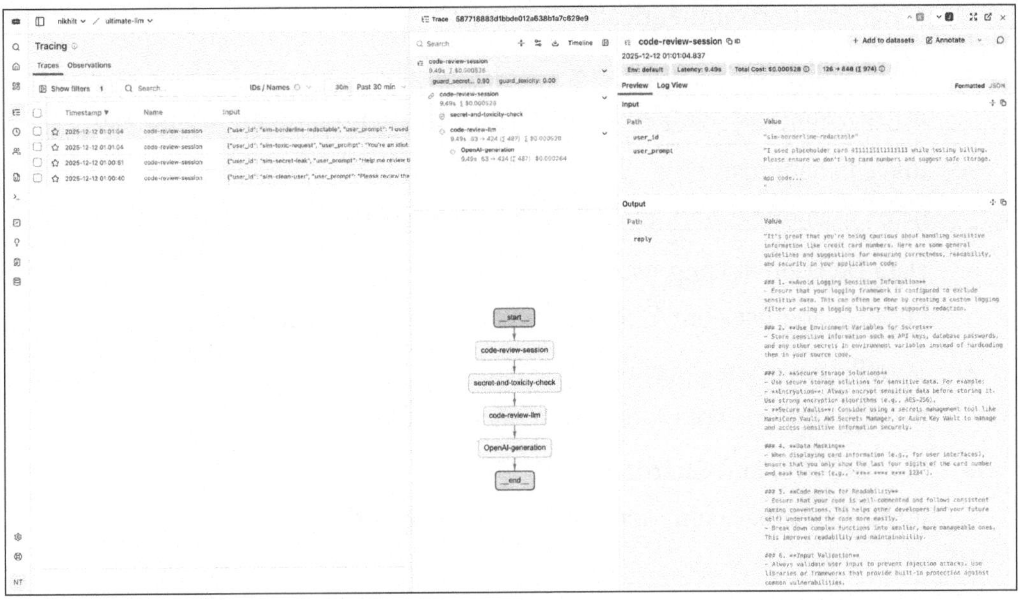

Figure 9.9: *Example of Guardrail Redacting Secret Text in a Prompt*

This example shows a minimal blueprint, and there are many ways to extend it. A natural next step is to integrate real security libraries, or custom classifiers instead of simple keyword and regex checks. We can also add output-side guardrails to inspect the response of the model before returning it to the user.

Conclusion

In this chapter, we have seen the essential administrative and security features Langfuse offers to support safe, compliant, and reliable LLM observability. We explored the importance of Role-Based Access Control (RBAC) for managing permissions at both organizational and project levels, as well as flexible authentication options including enterprise SSO integration and environment variable configuration for self-hosted environments. The chapter detailed key admin features such as audit logs for tracking actions, data deletion and retention mechanisms, and spend alerts for cost oversight. We also looked at how Langfuse helps implement and assess guardrails that protect against toxic language, secret leaks, and unsafe outputs. In the next chapter, we will look at some of the best practices that we can follow when using Langfuse for production-ready applications.

References

- Authentication and SSO in Langfuse - https://langfuse.com/docs/administration/authentication-and-sso
- SSO Configuration variables – https://langfuse.com/self-hosting/security/authentication-and-sso
- RBAC in Langfuse – https://langfuse.com/docs/administration/rbac
- Data Deletion in Langfuse – https://langfuse.com/docs/administration/data-deletion
- Data Retention in Langfuse – https://langfuse.com/docs/administration/data-retention
- LLM Security and Guardrails – https://langfuse.com/docs/security-and-guardrails

CHAPTER 10
Langfuse Best Practices

Introduction

This chapter summarizes the key best practices for getting the most out of Langfuse in LLM workflows. It provides short, actionable guidelines and lightweight code snippets to help teams set up reliable traces, organize projects efficiently, and maintain high-quality evaluation data. We will gradually learn practical techniques to make Langfuse integrations cleaner, dashboards more meaningful, and evaluations more reproducible.

Structure

In this chapter, we will cover the following topics:

- Best Practices for Langfuse
    - Separate Organizations and Projects
    - Choose a Sampling Rate
    - Structure Traces and Spans
    - Managing Prompts
    - Standardizing Datasets and Evaluations
    - Dashboards

Best Practices for Langfuse

By now we have seen how to use Langfuse for our LLM applications and how its core features like traces, prompts, datasets, and evaluations fit into a typical LLM application lifecycle. In practical applications, the effectiveness of Langfuse is determined more by the working practices and routines that teams establish than by its individual capabilities.

This chapter focuses on some conventions that tend to emerge naturally when teams use Langfuse at scale, for e.g. consistent ways of structuring traces, disciplined prompt versioning, clear separation between environments, stable evaluation datasets, and dashboards that highlight meaningful patterns. These are not mandatory rules but practices that help teams keep LLM observability consistent, maintainable, and reproducible.

The sections that follow outline these recommendations with brief code examples where appropriate. The objective is to provide supplementary guidance that aligns with official documentation, incorporating insights from experienced users to ensure that Langfuse implementations remain reliable over time.

Separate Organizations and Projects

Although Langfuse allows a single organization to host multiple projects, many teams find it valuable to create multiple organizations even inside one company. This may seem unnecessary at first, especially when permissions and roles already exist at the project level (at least for Enterprise users). However, separating work into distinct organizations solves a set of problems that become more noticeable as development scales. The separation of organizations in Langfuse could vary depending on the teams but some of the ways to do this could be:

- **By Product line:**
  - Search and Recommendations
  - Customer Support
  - Seller Tools
  - Catalog and Content Generation
- **By Business Vertical:**
  - Marketplace Operations
  - Logistics and Fulfillment
  - Payments and Fraud Detection
  - Advertising and Merchandising
- **By Team or Function**:
  - R&D / Prototyping
  - Core LLM Platform Team
  - Production Applications
  - Quality Assurance

- **By Security Boundary or Compliance Requirement:**
    - Payments / PCI-Related Workflows
    - Identity and Authentication Systems
    - User-Generated Content Moderation

For Langfuse deployments where project based RBAC is not available, separating projects by organizations could help in limiting user access to only the projects they should be allowed to access. However, over-fragmentation of projects could also complicate analytics so project separation should make sense in the context of the team.

Choose a Sampling Rate

In Langfuse, the default behavior is to collect every trace. In many environments especially during early development this makes sense. However, as traffic grows, capturing all traces can lead to very large volumes of data, many of which may provide little incremental insight. We have seen in *Chapter 5 - Observability in Langfuse* that Langfuse supports client-side trace sampling, which allows us to control the proportion of traces the SDK actually sends to the backend. There are two ways to set sampling rate.

```
from langfuse import Langfuse
import os
# Setting the environment variable
os.environ["LANGFUSE_SAMPLE_RATE"] = "0.5"
# Constructor parameter when initializing
langfuse = Langfuse(sample_rate=0.5)
```

Adjusting `LANGFUSE_SAMPLE_RATE` is a useful best practice for high-traffic systems because it lets teams balance trace volume with utility. For example, during routine production operation a lower sample rate can reduce noise and cost while still preserving a representative view of system behavior. During targeted investigations such as performance debugging or prompt experiments it can be temporarily raised to collect more complete data. Setting the rate via an environment variable also keeps sampling configuration external to application logic, making it easy to change without code releases.

Structuring Traces and Spans

To recap some basic concepts, Langfuse structures observability data into a hierarchy of traces, observations, and optionally sessions. A trace represents a complete interaction or request in our application and contains one or more observations, which correspond to individual steps (like model calls or retrievals) within that interaction. Sessions group related traces for example, all traces in a multi-turn conversation.

Langfuse's SDK offers **three main ways** to create spans and traces. Each approach has trade-offs between convenience and control:

Observe Decorators

We use the `@observe()` decorator to trace function execution automatically. Langfuse captures the inputs, outputs, runtime, and errors as a span of the function.

When to Use:

- When we want minimal manual instrumentation.
- For higher-level business functions (like service handlers) where we care about entire function behaviors.
- Best suited for synchronous functions.

```
from langfuse import observe
from langfuse.openai import openai
from dotenv import load_dotenv

load_dotenv()

@observe(name="generate_product_answer")
def answer_question(question: str):
    # LLM call inside the observed function
    result = openai.chat.completions.create(
        model="gpt-4o-mini",
        messages=[{"role": "user", "content": question}],
    )
    return result.choices[0].message.content

response = answer_question("What is the return policy for electronics?")
print(response)
```

Context Managers

For finer control, we use context managers to mark specific sections of code as observations. We explicitly name and type them, and we can nest them as needed.

When to Use:

- When structuring complex flows with multiple nested steps.
- When we want precise control over start/end semantics or observation metadata.

```
from langfuse import get_client
from openai import OpenAI
from dotenv import load_dotenv
```

```
load_dotenv()

openai_client = OpenAI()
langfuse_client = get_client()

def answer_question(question: str):
    with langfuse_client.start_as_current_observation(
        as_type="span", name="answer_question"
    ) as main_span:
        main_span.update(input=question)
        # Step 1: Retrieve context
        with langfuse_client.start_as_current_observation(
            as_type="retriever", name="retrieve_context"
        ) as retrieval_span:
            context_docs = ["doc about returns", "doc about electronics policy"]
            retrieval_span.update(output=context_docs)
        # Step 2: Compose prompt
        with langfuse_client.start_as_current_observation(
            as_type="span", name="compose_prompt"
        ) as compose_span:
            prompt = (
                "User question: What is the return policy?\n"
                f"Context: {context_docs}\n"
                "Provide a concise answer."
            )
            compose_span.update(output=prompt)
        # Step 3: Generate response
        with langfuse_client.start_as_current_observation(
            name="llm_generation", as_type="generation"
        ) as gen_span:
            response = openai_client.chat.completions.create(
                model="gpt-4o-mini",
                messages=[{"role": "user", "content": prompt}],
            )
            gen_span.update(output=response.choices[0].message.content)
        main_span.update(output=response.choices[0].message.content)

answer_question("What is the return policy for electronics?")
```

Manual Observations

For the utmost control, we can create spans and observations explicitly by invoking low-level SDK methods.

When to Use:

- When tracing events that do not fit naturally into a decorator or context manager pattern.
- For custom instrumentation in frameworks that do not support the other modes.

Manual instrumentation requires more codes but gives us full control over attributes and timing.

Method	Ease of Use	Control	Typical Use Case
Decorator	*High*	Medium	Quick instrumentation of discrete functions
Context Manager	Medium	*High*	Structured tracing of logical steps or nested blocks
Manual Observations	Low	*Highest*	Custom workflows and non-standard event types

Table 10.1: *Choosing the Right Approach to Send Traces to Langfuse*

Use Observation Types

We also saw in *Chapter 5, Observability in Langfuse*, how Langfuse supports a set of specific observation types that convey the semantic role of each operation in our LLM workflow for example, whether something is a model generation, a retriever call, a tool invocation, or an evaluator function. The observation types include ***event, span, generation, agent, tool, chain, retriever, evaluator, embedding, and guardrail***. Using these types consistently is a best practice because it makes our traces self-describing and easier to filter or group when exploring data in dashboards or when querying via the API.

Langfuse supports setting observation types both automatically (namely via agent framework integrations) and manually (by specifying `as_type` when creating an observation). By choosing the correct type for each observation such as *generation* for a model call, *retriever* for a vector search, or *tool* for an external HTTP request we make our data more actionable and our dashboards more informative. As a refresher, Langfuse supports the following types of observations when using the SDK:

- **Event** is the root observation type under which all other observations are nested. These are automatically created for each trace.
- **Span** are the individual time sliced blocks within an event.
- **Generation** represents the observation which generates an output for an LLM call.
- **Agent** observation can be used when calling an AI Agent within a trace/span.
- **Tool** represents a tool call used mostly in connection with agents.

- **Chain** mostly synonymous with LangChain can include different steps which go into the entire chain of a LangChain call.
- **Retriever** mostly used in RAG applications, represents the data retrieval steps, such as a call to a vector store or a database.
- **Evaluator** can be used for a step within a trace which returns a metric or a score.
- **Embedding** for calls to generate embeddings.
- **Guardrail** for guardrailing or security steps.

Use Tags and Metadata Effectively

Tags and metadata help us add meaningful structure to traces and observations in Langfuse. When used consistently, they make filtering, debugging, and organizing much easier even as applications grow more complex. Tags give us lightweight categorization, while metadata provides more detailed, structured context. The following table summarizes how we should use each.

	Purpose	Best Practices
Tags	Simple labels for categorizing traces/observations.	Use short, descriptive tags; apply them early so they propagate; tag traces consistently for reliable filtering.
Metadata	Structured key-value context attached to traces/observations.	Keep keys/values concise; propagate important metadata early in the trace; use metadata for attributes we may query or segment later.

***Table 10.2**: Best Practices for Tags and Metadata*

Managing Prompts

In *Chapter 6, Prompt Management in Langfuse*, we looked at the Prompt Management features of Langfuse. Langfuse provides a controlled environment where prompts can be versioned, labeled, grouped, and safely deployed. These practices help us maintain clarity as prompts change, experiment systematically, and ensure reproducibility when analyzing model behavior.

- **Centralize Prompts Instead of Hardcoding Them:** Keeping prompts inside application code makes updates risky and time consuming. By storing prompts in Langfuse, we gain version history, auditing, and the ability to test variations without a redeploy.
- **Use Versioning and Labels to Control Deployments:** Every time we update a prompt in Langfuse, a new version is created. Labels (for example, *production*,

staging, experiment-A) let us bind application environments to the prompt versions they should use.

- **Organize Prompts with Folder-Like Naming:** Using slash (/) in prompt names creates a structure for browsing and maintenance of prompts, especially in large applications.
- **Use Prompt config to Bundle Model Parameters with the Prompt:** Prompts often depend on consistent model settings temperature, max tokens, or whether the output must follow a schema. Rather than managing these values separately in code, we can attach them directly to the prompt version.
- **Link Prompts to Traces for Better Analysis:** When we tie prompt versions to Langfuse traces, we gain the ability to inspect how a specific version performs over time and its latency, cost, failure patterns, or evaluation scores.

```
from langfuse import get_client
from dotenv import load_dotenv
from langfuse.openai import openai

load_dotenv()

langfuse_client = get_client()

# Retrieve the default prompt version (label="production")
prompt = langfuse_client.get_prompt("product_description_generator")

def generate_product_description(product_name: str, features: list[str],
audience):
    # Pass variable values to the prompt
    prompt_content = prompt.compile(
        product_name=product_name, features=features, audience=audience
    )
    # Retrieve config from the prompt and use it in the call to openai
    config = prompt.config
    completion = openai.chat.completions.create(
        model=config.get("model", "gpt-4.1-mini"),
        messages=[{"role": "system", "content": prompt_content}],
        temperature=config.get("temperature", 0.1),
        max_tokens=config.get("max_tokens", 200),
        top_p=config.get("top_p", 1),
        # Link the generation to the prompt
        langfuse_prompt=prompt,
    )
    return completion.choices[0].message.content
```

- **Combine UI Editing with Code-Based Integration:** The Langfuse UI is ideal for editing, reviewing, and documenting prompts. The SDK ensures that our application consistently fetches the correct prompt version defined by our deployment strategy. This hybrid workflow lets non-engineers contribute to prompt iteration while engineering teams maintain strict, version-controlled integration.

Standardizing Datasets and Evaluations

Creating Datasets and running LLM evaluations is one of the key features in Langfuse. We saw how this works in detail in *Chapter 7, Evaluating LLMs in Langfuse.* Standardizing how datasets and evaluations are created and used helps teams compare changes reliably and track performance over time.

- **Include Expected Outputs Where Possible**: Including a ground truth value in our dataset enables automatic scoring and meaningful comparison between runs. This becomes crucial when evaluating prompt changes, model swaps, or logic modifications.
- **Keep Datasets Representative**: Cover common "happy path" cases, edge cases, and important failure modes. A dataset that reflects real usage patterns gives us better visibility into regressions or improvements than one limited to simple inputs.
- **Profile Test Coverage Explicitly**: Where possible, annotate or tag dataset items with metadata indicating difficulty, category, or source. These tags help segment evaluation results and diagnose issue clusters more quickly.
- **Run Experiments Consistently via SDK or UI**: Langfuse supports dataset experiments through both SDK and UI. Choosing one consistent approach allows us to compare experiment runs easily and reuse the same dataset definitions.

Some more standard best practices include:

Practice	How it Helps
Central Dataset Definitions	Avoid duplication; every experiment should run against the same standard list of test cases.
Separate Datasets by Domain	This keeps evaluations targeted (e.g., support queries vs. transactional queries).
Automate Evaluator Logic	Whether using a custom evaluator or an LLM-as-a-judge, automated scoring scales better than manual checks.
Version Datasets Over Time	Freeze dataset definitions per major release to ensure like-for-like comparisons.

***Table 10.3**: How Teams Typically Standardize Workflows*

One of the most effective ways to improve LLM quality over time is to systematically convert real production usage into structured evaluation datasets. The high-level steps to achieve this are:

Step 1: Capture Production Interactions

Trace production interactions consistently, including inputs, outputs, prompt versions, model configuration, and key metadata such as latency and cost.

Step 2: Select Representative and Problematic Cases

Identify production examples that indicate success, failure, or edge behavior such as repeated user rephrasing, negative feedback, or known failure modes.

Step 3: Label and Annotate Examples

Review selected interactions and assign quality labels, which includes correctness, relevance, and safety. This converts raw traces into labeled evaluation data.

Step 4: Curate Evaluation Datasets

Group annotated examples into datasets with a clear purpose, such as regression testing or coverage of specific intents.

Step 5: Define and Apply Evaluation Criteria

Establish consistent scoring methods—automated, human, or both so results can be compared across runs.

Step 6: Reuse Datasets for Regression Testing

Re-run the same datasets whenever prompts, models, or pipelines change to detect regressions and measure improvements.

We will see in the next chapter an example of how to convert captured observations directly into Dataset items.

Dashboards

We already covered in *Chapter 8, Deriving Actionable Insights using Langfuse Metrics*, how metrics and dashboards work in Langfuse and in this section we will see some best practices that focus on how to use them effectively in practice. In Langfuse, dashboards are most valuable when they support concrete decisions rather than simply reporting activity. This means prioritizing metrics that explain system behavior and change over time, and combining quality, performance, and cost signals in ways that make trade-offs visible.

Begin with Well-Defined Questions

A common oversight is designing dashboards that simply replicate all the metrics tracked by Langfuse. Instead, we should begin by defining the questions the dashboard is meant to answer for example, whether a new prompt improved quality, whether latency is drifting, or whether costs increased after a model change. Dashboards built around questions tend to stay relevant, while dashboards built around data tend to become less useful over time.

The curated dashboards of Langfuse provide a useful starting point, as they focus on common concerns such as latency, cost, and usage. These can then be extended or adapted as requirements become clearer. Effective dashboards emphasize a small number of high-signal metrics:

- **Quality metrics**, such as evaluation scores or user feedback trends.
- **Performance metrics**, including latency and error rates.
- **Cost metrics**, such as token usage and spend by model or prompt version.
- **Volume metrics**, including request and session counts.

Use Dimensions to Provide Context

Metrics without context are difficult to interpret. Langfuse supports grouping and filtering metrics by dimensions such as environment, model, prompt version, trace name, tags, and metadata. Using these dimensions consistently allows dashboards to answer more nuanced questions, such as whether a latency increase affects all prompts or only a specific workflow.

As a best practice, dashboards should almost always include at least one contextual breakdown rather than relying on global averages.

Combine Quality, Performance, and Cost in the Same View

LLM systems often involve trade-offs. A prompt change that improves quality may increase latency or cost, while a model switch that reduces cost may impact accuracy. Langfuse custom dashboards make it possible to place these metrics side by side, helping teams evaluate changes holistically rather than optimizing in isolation. This combined view is especially valuable during experiments and rollouts, where unintended side effects are easy to miss.

In practice, the most effective Langfuse dashboards are those that remain intentionally simple, reflect real decision-making needs, and stay closely tied to the evaluation and observability workflows already in place.

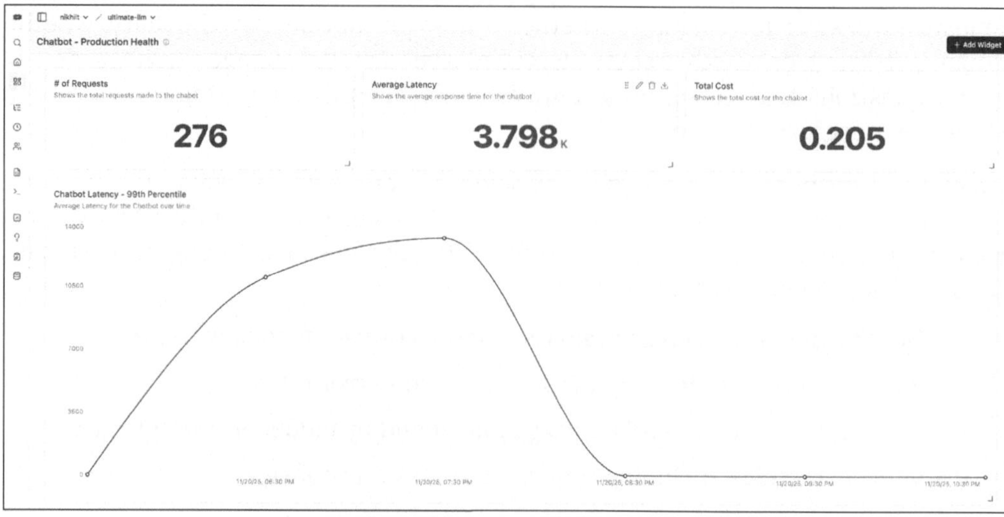

***Figure 10.1**: Example of a Dashboard Showing Only Key Metrics*

Use Clear Names for Dashboards and Widgets

Dashboard and widget titles should describe the question they answer, not just the metric they display. Names like "Prompt v2 Quality vs Cost" or "Production Latency (p95)" are more effective than generic labels such as "Latency Chart" or "Scores over Time". Clear naming reduces misinterpretation, makes dashboards easier to navigate as their number grows, and helps non-authors understand what decisions a dashboard is meant to support.

Conclusion

This chapter presented practical guidelines for leveraging Langfuse effectively at scale. It addressed essential aspects such as managing access, implementing sampling strategies, and establishing clear trace and span structures. The chapter also covered selecting appropriate observation types, utilizing tags and metadata, versioning prompts, and transforming production traces into curated evaluation datasets. Additionally, best practices for designing informative dashboards were reviewed. Collectively, these approaches foster transparency, facilitate meaningful experimentation, and enable reliable detection of changes within our LLM systems. As we come closer to the end of the book, the next and final chapter will cover practical examples on how to use Langfuse for the most common type of LLM applications. The chapter will be a handy ready to use playbook for readers who want to get started with integrating Langfuse in their new or even existing applications.

References

- Sampling in Langfuse – https://langfuse.com/docs/observability/features/sampling
- Langfuse Data Model – https://langfuse.com/docs/observability/data-model
- Getting Started with Langfuse- https://langfuse.com/docs/observability/get-started
- Observation types in Langfuse – https://langfuse.com/docs/observability/features/observation-types
- Tags in Langfuse – https://langfuse.com/docs/observability/features/tags
- Metadata in Langfuse – https://langfuse.com/docs/observability/features/metadata
- Prompt Management in Langfuse – https://langfuse.com/docs/prompt-management/overview
- Evaluations in Langfuse – https://langfuse.com/docs/evaluation/overview
- Datasets in Langfuse – https://langfuse.com/docs/evaluation/experiments/datasets
- Custom Dashboards in Langfuse – https://langfuse.com/docs/metrics/features/custom-dashboards

CHAPTER 11
Langfuse Playbooks

Introduction

This chapter brings the concepts we have seen in the book so far together through a series of hands-on playbooks, each focused on applying Langfuse features in realistic LLM workflows. Starting with a minimal integration, we progress through complex scenarios such as prompt iteration, Retrieval-Augmented Generation (RAG), Agentic Orchestration, Bias/Hallucination Monitoring, and Cost Optimization. Each example is presented with runnable code snippets, plus a list showing the Langfuse concepts or features covered in the playbook. For non-technical users, a no-code playbook illustrates how prompt iteration and evaluation can be done entirely from the Langfuse UI.

Structure

In this chapter, we will cover the following playbooks:

- Langfuse Integration with OpenAI + LangChain
- Retrieval-Augmented Generation (RAG) in Langfuse
- Agentic Workflow with LangChain
- Hallucination and Bias Monitoring
- Detecting and Responding to Model Drift
- Cost Optimization via Model Routing
- No-Code Playbook: Prompt Iteration for a Summarization Task

Langfuse Integration with OpenAI + LangChain

Our first playbook covers one of the most widely used integrations with Langfuse: OpenAI + LangChain. We briefly introduced LangChain in *Chapter 1, Introduction to*

Large Language Models and Monitoring, and have used it for some of the examples in the book. LangChain is a framework for building LLM-powered applications by composing prompts, models, and logic into **chains**. Instead of treating the LLM as a single black-box call, LangChain encourages us to think in steps formed as a chain: prompt construction → model execution → output parsing → downstream logic.

We will need to install the following dependencies:

```
# pip install langfuse langchain langchain_openai
```

Like the previous code examples, we also need to set the following environment variables:

OPENAI_API_KEY, **LANGFUSE_SECRET_KEY**, **LANGFUSE_PUBLIC_KEY**, and **LANGFUSE_HOST**

In this example, we will see a very simple Customer Support query automation system that can generate automated replies to the query of the customer based on a two-stage resolution process:

1. **Research Stage:** Analyzes the issue of the customer and extracts key facts/causes.
2. **Response Stage**: Crafts an empathetic, region-aware reply using the research.

We start by importing the necessary classes and setting up Langfuse client as well as the LangChain callback handler.

```
from dotenv import load_dotenv
from langfuse import propagate_attributes, Langfuse
from langchain_core.prompts import ChatPromptTemplate
from langchain_core.output_parsers import StrOutputParser
from langchain.chat_models import init_chat_model
from langfuse.langchain import CallbackHandler
import os

# Load environment variables
load_dotenv()

# Check if environment variables are set for Langfus
print("LANGFUSE_HOST =", os.getenv("LANGFUSE_HOST"))
print("LANGFUSE_PUBLIC_KEY starts with =", (os.getenv("LANGFUSE_PUBLIC_
KEY") or "")[:3])
print("LANGFUSE_SECRET_KEY set =", bool(os.getenv("LANGFUSE_SECRET_
KEY")))

# Create the Langfuse client and LangChain callback handler
langfuse_client = Langfuse(
```

```
    release="1.0.0"
)
langfuse_handler = CallbackHandler()
```

Next, we create the two chains, which will use prompts and model config directly from Langfuse.

```
# ===========================================================================
# STAGE 1: Issue Research (Analyzes customer problem)
# ===========================================================================
research_prompt = langfuse_client.get_prompt(
    "support/research_prompt", type="chat", label="production"
)
research_prompt_template = ChatPromptTemplate.from_messages(
    research_prompt.get_langchain_prompt()
)
research_model = init_chat_model(
    research_prompt.config["model_name"],
    model_provider=research_prompt.config["model_provider"],
)
research_chain = research_prompt_template | research_model |
StrOutputParser()

# ===========================================================================
# STAGE 2: Response Generation (Creates customer-facing reply)
# ===========================================================================
response_prompt = langfuse_client.get_prompt(
    "support/response_prompt", type="chat", label="production"
)
response_prompt_template = ChatPromptTemplate.from_messages(
    response_prompt.get_langchain_prompt()
)
response_model = init_chat_model(
    response_prompt.config["model_name"],
    model_provider=response_prompt.config["model_provider"],
)
response_chain = response_prompt_template | response_model |
StrOutputParser()
```

We will use very simple chat-based prompts for this example:

`support/research_prompt`:

```
System: You are an expert customer care representative. Research this
```

```
customer issue thoroughly and provide key facts, potential causes, and
solutions.
User: {{query}}
```

support/response_prompt:

```
System: Based on this research: {{research}}
Generate a helpful, empathetic response to: {{query}}
Include: resolution steps, escalation if needed, and follow-up
questions. Ensure response is culturally sensitive for {{region}}.
```

We will also use the same model config for now in both the prompts:

```
{
    "model_name": "gpt-4.1",
    "model_provider": "openai"
}
```

The entire business logic is encapsulated in the following method:

```
def handle_customer_query(ticket: dict, user_id: str = None):
    """
    Handles customer support ticket
    Args:
        ticket: Dict containing 'query', 'region', 'priority', 'product'
        user_id: For user-level analytics
    """
    # Create root trace capturing full support session
    with langfuse_client.start_as_current_observation(
        as_type="span",
        name="customer-support-session"
    ) as session_span:
        # Update tags and user_id for the trace
        with propagate_attributes(
            user_id=user_id,
            tags=[
                "prod",
                "support-v2",
                f"priority-{ticket.get('priority', 'medium')}",
            ],
        ):
            session_span.update(
                input=ticket,
                metadata={
                    "region": ticket.get("region", "global"),
                    "team": "support",
```

```
            "feature": "ai-ticket-resolution",
        }
    )
    try:
        # STAGE 1: Research customer's issue
        research_inputs = {"query": ticket["query"]}
        research_output = research_chain.invoke(
            research_inputs,
            config={
                "callbacks": [langfuse_handler],
                "run_name": "ticket-research",
            },
        )
        # STAGE 2: Generate empathetic response using research
        response_inputs = {
            **research_inputs,
            "research": research_output,
            "region": ticket.get("region", "global"),
        }
        final_response = response_chain.invoke(
            response_inputs,
            config={
                "callbacks": [langfuse_handler],
                "run_name": "ticket-response",
            },
        )
        session_span.update(
            output=final_response,
        )
        return final_response
    except Exception as e:
        session_span.update(
            output={"error": str(e)},
            level="ERROR",
            metadata={"error_type": type(e).__name__},
        )
        raise
```

This method orchestrates the complete customer support workflow with full observability. Here is what each key part does, step by step:

1. **Root Trace Creation (Lines 8–12)**

```
with langfuse_client.start_as_current_observation(
    as_type="span",
    name="customer-support-session"
) as session_span:
```

This creates a **parent trace** in Langfuse that wraps the entire support session. Every child operation (research, response) nests under this trace.

2. **Global Tags and Context (Lines 14–20)**

```
with propagate_attributes(
     user_id=user_id,
     tags=[
         "prod",
         "support-v2",
         f"priority-{ticket.get('priority', 'medium')}",
     ],
 ):
```

It applies **session-wide labels** that automatically flow to all nested spans. It further helps in filtering traces by tags like priority.

3. **Session Metadata (Lines 21–27)**

```
session_span.update(
        input=ticket,
        metadata={
            "region": ticket.get("region", "global"),
            "team": "support",
            "feature": "ai-ticket-resolution",
        }
    )
```

This stores ticket details as searchable metadata.

4. **Stage 1: Research (Lines 32-38)**

```
research_output = research_chain.invoke(
            research_inputs,
            config={
                "callbacks": [langfuse_handler],
                "run_name": "ticket-research",
            },
        )
```

Runs the research chain and calls the LLM to generate research data for the supplied ticket information. This trace is automatically traced as a child span named "**`ticket-research`**". The output from this chain is then passed to the next stage.

5. **Stage 2: Response (Lines 43-49)**

```
final_response = response_chain.invoke(
                    response_inputs,
                    config={
                        "callbacks": [langfuse_handler],
                        "run_name": "ticket-response",
                    },
                )
```

It feeds research from the first LLM call into response generation, which is traced as "ticket-response".

To run this example, we can use the following inputs:

```
support_ticket = {
    "query": "My AquaTrack subscription renewal failed twice. Support chat is unresponsive.",
    "region": "IN",
    "priority": "high",
}

response = handle_customer_query(support_ticket, user_id="u768075")
print("Customer Response:", response)
```

This is how the trace should look like in the Dashboard after we execute this example.

Figure 11.1: *Example of OpenAI + LangChain Integration in Langfuse*

Langfuse features covered:

- Prompt Management
- Trace Tags and Metadata
- Full Session Tracing
- Callback Handler for LangChain
- Custom Names for Spans (Using the **"run_name"** Config Parameter)
- Error Tracing
- User Tracking

In the next playbook, we will see how we can convert this example into a more realistic query resolution system using Retrieval-Augmented Generation (RAG). In production applications, LLMs will rely on external information to answer customer queries. RAG is one of the methods where we can leverage static documentation to enhance the context of the LLM. This entire RAG flow can also be traced in Langfuse with features such as observation types and the Retrieval chains of LangChain, which help orchestrate RAG-based chains.

Retrieval-Augmented Generation (RAG) in Langfuse

We briefly introduced RAG in *Chapter 2, LLM Monitoring Principles and Metrics*. RAG is used by LLMs to connect to external knowledge sources to provide a more accurate, context-specific, and factually grounded response, reducing the risk of the model hallucinating.

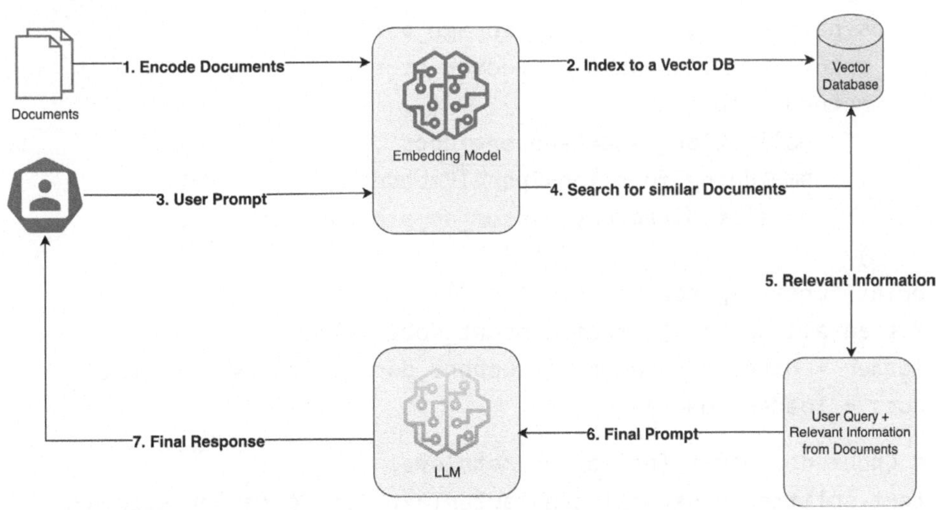

Figure 11.2: *Retrieval-Augmented Generation*

One of the key components in RAG is the Vector DB, which stores the embeddings of the external knowledge (in our example, we will use static documents). When a query is made to the LLM, using similarity search, relevant documents are retrieved from the vector DB and added as content to the prompt. This allows the LLM to give a better answer to the support query of the customer.

We will use RAG to replace the research chain from our previous example to use the support documents of the company as a knowledge base rather than doing random research on the customer's issue. To implement RAG, we need to include these extra imports first.

```
from langchain_community.document_loaders import DirectoryLoader
from langchain_text_splitters import RecursiveCharacterTextSplitter
from langchain_openai import OpenAIEmbeddings
from langchain_chroma import Chroma
from langchain_core.runnables import RunnablePassthrough, RunnableLambda
import os
```

To keep the Vector DB simple, we will use Chroma Vector DB, which is a fast in-memory vector DB that can store embeddings on local disk as well.

```
# ==========================================================================
# RAG SETUP: Load, chunk, embed, and index support documents
# ==========================================================================
vector_db_storage_dir = "./chroma_db"

def setup_rag_index():
    """Create an InMemory vector store from ./support_docs/ folder (run
only once)"""
    if os.path.exists(vector_db_storage_dir):
        print("Loading existing vector store")
        return Chroma(
            collection_name="support_docs",
            embedding_function=OpenAIEmbeddings(),
            persist_directory=vector_db_storage_dir,
        )
    print("Creating new vector store")
    # Load all documents from support_docs folder
    loader = DirectoryLoader("./support_docs/", glob="**/*.txt")
    docs = loader.load()

    # Chunk documents for better retrieval
    text_splitter = RecursiveCharacterTextSplitter(chunk_size=500,
chunk_overlap=50)
```

```
    splits = text_splitter.split_documents(docs)

    # Create embeddings and vector store
    vectordb = Chroma.from_documents(
        documents=splits,
        embedding=OpenAIEmbeddings(),
        persist_directory=vector_db_storage_dir,
    )
    return vectordb

# Initialize RAG index
rag_index = setup_rag_index()
retriever = rag_index.as_retriever(
    # Retrieve top 2 relevant docs
    search_kwargs={"k": 2}
)
```

Step 1. Vector Store Location Definition (Lines 5–6)

```
vector_db_storage_dir = "./chroma_db"
```

It defines the **persistent storage location** for the vector database on disk. This directory allows embeddings to be reused across application restarts, instead of being recomputed every time.

Step 2. Existing Vector Store Detection (Lines 10–17)

```
if os.path.exists(vector_db_storage_dir):
    print("Loading existing vector store")
    return Chroma(
        collection_name="support_docs",
        embedding_function=OpenAIEmbeddings(),
        persist_directory=vector_db_storage_dir,
    )
```

This checks whether a previously built Chroma index already exists.

Step 3. Document Loading from Knowledge Base (Lines 20–22)

```
loader = DirectoryLoader("./support_docs/", glob="**/*.txt")
docs = loader.load()
```

It loads all support documents from a local folder into memory. This acts as the **knowledge source** for the RAG system.

Step 4. Document Chunking Strategy (Lines 25–27)

```
text_splitter = RecursiveCharacterTextSplitter(
```

```
        chunk_size=500,
        chunk_overlap=50
    )
    splits = text_splitter.split_documents(docs)
```

This splits long documents into smaller, overlapping chunks to improve retrieval quality. Smaller chunks ensure more precise semantic matches and overlap preserves context across chunk boundaries. **`RecursiveCharacterTextSplitter`** avoids breaking sentences unnaturally This step has a major impact on answer accuracy.

Step 5. Embedding and Vector Index Creation (Lines 30-34)

```
    vectordb = Chroma.from_documents(
        documents=splits,
        embedding=OpenAIEmbeddings(),
        persist_directory=vector_db_storage_dir,
    )
```

It converts text chunks into embeddings and stores them in Chroma. Each chunk then becomes a vector and is stored persistently on disk. This is the core of the RAG retrieval layer.

Step 6. RAG Initialization (Lines 38-44)

```
    rag_index = setup_rag_index()
    retriever = rag_index.as_retriever(
        search_kwargs={"k": 2}
    )
```

This wraps the vector store in a retriever interface used by LangChain. k=2 limits retrieval to the two most relevant chunks. This component directly controls how much knowledge is injected into the LLM.

We will create some dummy support docs in a local directory called "**`support_docs`**" which contains text files that act as a knowledge base for the customer support team of the company. The sample texts will be available to the readers on the official GitHub page of the book. As an example, one of the support document looks like this:

```
Title: Subscription Renewal Failures - AquaTrack

When a subscription renewal for AquaTrack fails, the most common reasons
are: expired card, insufficient funds, or bank blocking the transaction.
Ask the customer to confirm if their card details or billing address
recently changed.

If the payment failed twice in a row, advise the customer to update
their payment method in the billing portal and try again. If they use a
corporate card, suggest contacting their bank or finance team to approve
recurring charges to AquaTrack.
```

```
For high-priority accounts, keep service active for a brief grace period
while they resolve the issue. Clearly communicate the grace period and
what happens if payment is not completed.
```

Our RAG retrieval logic will choose two of the most relevant documents based on the query of the customer to enhance the context of the LLM.

The response chain from the earlier example needs to be altered as well:

```
response_chain = (
    {
        "context": RunnableLambda(lambda x: x["query"]) | retriever,
        "query": RunnableLambda(lambda x: x["query"]),
        "region": RunnableLambda(lambda x: x["region"]),
    }
    | RunnablePassthrough.assign(
        research=RunnableLambda(
            lambda x: "\n\n".join(doc.page_content for doc in
x["context"])
        )
    )
    | response_prompt_template
    | response_model
    | StrOutputParser()
)
```

We can then remove the research part from the **handle_customer_query** method:

```
def handle_customer_query(ticket: dict, user_id: str = None):
    """
    Handles customer support ticket
    Args:
        ticket: Dict containing 'query', 'region', 'priority', 'product'
        user_id: For user-level analytics
    """
    # Create root trace capturing full support session
    with langfuse_client.start_as_current_observation(
        as_type="span",
        name="customer-support-session"
    ) as session_span:
        # Update tags and user_id for the trace
        with propagate_attributes(
            user_id=user_id,
            tags=[
```

```
            "prod",
            "support-v2",
            f"priority-{ticket.get('priority', 'medium')}",
        ],
    ):
        session_span.update(
            input=ticket,
            metadata={
                "region": ticket.get("region", "global"),
                "team": "support",
                "feature": "ai-ticket-resolution",
            },
        )
        try:
            # Generate response using RAG research
            final_response = response_chain.invoke(
                {
                    "query": ticket["query"],
                    "region": ticket.get("region", "global"),
                },
                config={
                    "callbacks": [langfuse_handler],
                    "run_name": "ticket-response",
                },
            )

            session_span.update(
                output=final_response,
            )

            return final_response

        except Exception as e:
            session_span.update(
                output={"error": str(e)},
                level="ERROR",
                metadata={"error_type": type(e).__name__},
            )
            raise
```

This is how the trace should look like in Langfuse:

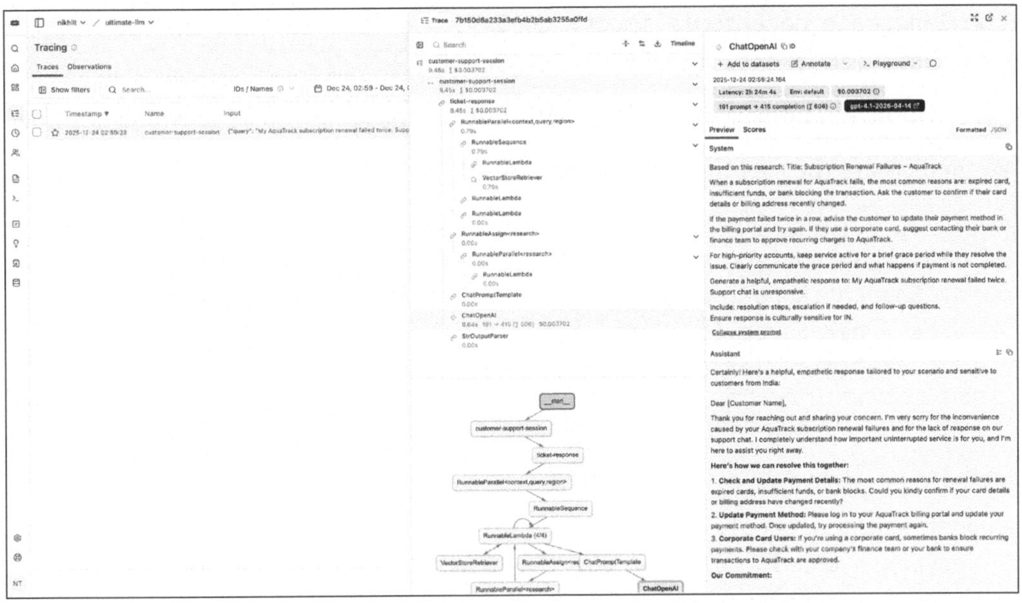

Figure 11.3: *RAG Based Trace in Langfuse*

As we can see in the LLM call, the research part of the prompt is retrieved from the support documents we have used. Also notice how Langfuse automatically detects the observation called **`VectorStoreRetriever`**, and marks it as observation type "**`Retriever`**".

Additional Langfuse features covered:

- Observation types

In the next playbook, we will add agentic capabilities to this example. Instead of using plain LLM's we will create a small agent that will use tools to answer the query of the customer and will be able to think step by step in order to arrive at an answer.

Agentic Workflow with LangChain

We talked about LangChain in *Chapter 4, Introduction to Langfuse*. LangChain is an orchestration framework that can be used to build a variety of LLM based applications. An Agent created using LangChain, requires two main components: A model (any supported LLM) and tools which are basically functions that the agent can use. We will modify the RAG based example from above to create a basic AI agent that has access to a single tool that can be used to query support documents from our previously created vector database.

First, we import the required classes from LangChain:

```
from langchain_core.tools import tool
from langchain.agents import create_agent
```

The creation and initialization of the RAG index is the same as the previous example.

We then create the tool that can be used by our agent:

```
@tool
def search_support_docs(query: str) -> str:
    """Search support documentation for relevant information."""
    docs = retriever.invoke(query)
    return "\n\n".join([doc.page_content for doc in docs])
```

In LangChain, tools are simple methods that just need to be annotated with **`@tool`**.

Similarly, an agent can be created using:

```
support_agent = create_agent(
    response_model,
    tools=[search_support_docs],
)
```

An agent created this way, replaces the **`response_chain`** we created in the previous example.

Agents created in LangChain can automatically figure out if a tool should be invoked based on the documentation provided in the method. Hence, it is important to add precise documentation to the method and its parameters.

The last difference is in the invoking of the agent.

```
def handle_customer_query(ticket: dict, user_id: str = None):
    """
    Handles customer support ticket
    Args:
        ticket: Dict containing 'query', 'region', 'priority', 'product'
        user_id: For user-level analytics
    """
    # Create root trace capturing full support session
    with langfuse_client.start_as_current_observation(
        as_type="span", name="customer-support-session"
    ) as session_span:
        # Update tags and user_id for the trace
        with propagate_attributes(
            user_id=user_id,
```

```
            tags=[
                "prod",
                "support-v2",
                f"priority-{ticket.get('priority', 'medium')}",
            ],
        ):
            session_span.update(
                input=ticket,
                metadata={
                    "region": ticket.get("region", "global"),
                    "team": "support",
                    "feature": "ai-ticket-resolution",
                },
            )
            try:
                # Invoke agent with conversation state
                config = {
                    "callbacks": [langfuse_handler],
                    "run_name": "agent-response",
                }

                # Agent input as HumanMessage
                input_message = {
                    "messages": [
                        HumanMessage(
                            content=f"Customer query: {ticket['query']}\
nRegion: {ticket.get('region', 'global')}"
                        )
                    ]
                }

                # Stream agent execution (or use .invoke() for single
response)
                for chunk in support_agent.stream(
                    input_message, config, stream_mode="values"
                ):
                    last_message = chunk["messages"][-1]
                    if isinstance(last_message, AIMessage):
                        session_span.update(output=last_message.content)
                        print("Agent:", last_message.content)

                session_span.update(
                    output=last_message.content,
```

```
            )
            return last_message.content

        except Exception as e:
            session_span.update(
                output={"error": str(e)},
                level="ERROR",
                metadata={"error_type": type(e).__name__},
            )
            raise
```

We can use the same inputs to invoke the agent:

```
support_ticket = {
    "query": "My AquaTrack subscription renewal failed twice. Support
chat is unresponsive.",
    "region": "IN",
    "priority": "high",
}

response = handle_customer_query(support_ticket, user_id="u768075")
print("Customer Response:", response)
```

After executing this code, the trace should appear in Langfuse.

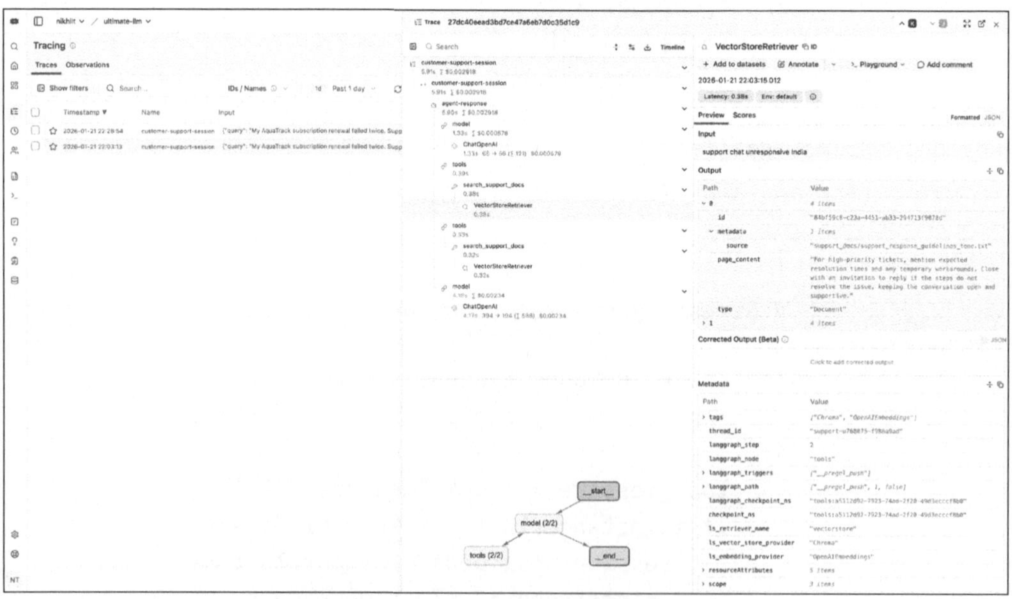

Figure 11.4: *Agent Based RAG Trace in Langfuse*

The trace also clearly shows tool usage done by the Agent. It calls the tools twice, once for the statement "`My AquaTrack subscription renewal failed twice`" and another time for "`Support chat is unresponsive.`"

In the next example, we will look at how we can detect Bias and Hallucination in Langfuse.

Hallucination and Bias Monitoring

Hallucinations in LLM applications are not random. They tend to occur at specific points in the system when context is missing, retrieval fails, prompts are ambiguous, or models are forced to answer beyond their knowledge. Effective hallucination monitoring is therefore not about catching every incorrect statement, but about **understanding when and where hallucinations occur**, so that targeted mitigations can be applied. This makes hallucination monitoring an observability problem.

A common misconception is that hallucinations are a flaw in language models. In practice, hallucinations usually indicate a different problem, such as:

- Missing or irrelevant retrieved context
- Overly permissive prompts (statements such as "always answer")
- Incorrect routing or tool selection

By knowing where hallucination occurs in the system, we can figure out how to prevent it.

In the example we saw previously, a hallucination would occur if the agent either retrieves the wrong support documentation (or none at all) and tries to answer the question based on this faulty retrieval step. In this case, knowing if the correct context was retrieved can help us monitor hallucination in the responses of our application.

For applications where context retrieval is crucial, we can use the **`Contextrelevance`** evaluator of Langfuse from the **LLM-as-a-Judge** feature. This evaluates whether or not a "**`relevant`**" context was retrieved for the LLM to be able to answer a user query. After setting it up in Langfuse for our customer support example, it should look something like this:

Figure 11.5: *Context Relevance Monitoring to Detect Hallucinations*

This evaluator uses the inbuilt observation type `Retriever` to extract context and will now automatically generate context relevance scores for traces. A low value here would indicate hallucination. This kind of an evaluator can be complimented with another user feedback loop to find co-relations between context relevance scores and user feedback. Low user feedback for traces with low context relevance score confirms hallucination in the model's responses.

Since hallucination can only be detected relative to a reference, another way to detect it would be using the **Human Annotation** feature in Langfuse. This is useful in cases where references or contexts are not part of traces for some reason and therefore, automatic evaluation is not possible. Human evaluators can then score traces to detect responses that are not factual or plausible in the context of the application.

Similar to the evaluator we set up here, an evaluator for tool usage can also be created to make sure the correct tools were invoked to retrieve context. If our application uses tools from LangChain or any other framework, Langfuse can detect those observations as tool calls and then we can run evaluation on those observation types. Invoking wrong tools is one of the common reasons why hallucinations may occur.

Sometimes prompt instructions can also cause the model to hallucinate. Bad prompt engineering does not cause hallucinations directly but creates conditions where hallucination is the most compliant behavior.

How Bad Prompt Engineering Leads to Hallucinations

- **Forcing an Answer Under Uncertainty**

  Example: Answer the question of the user as completely as possible.

  When required to answer despite missing information, the model fills gaps with invented details instead of expressing uncertainty.

- **Unclear Knowledge Boundaries**

  Example: Based on the following research, answer the question.

  Without explicitly restricting the model to the provided context, it may mix retrieved content with general knowledge, producing unsupported claims.

- **Overconfidence in Tone Instructions**

  Example: Provide a confident and authoritative response.

  Tone constraints override uncertainty, causing speculative or incomplete information to be stated as fact.

- **Rigid or Exhaustive Output Requirements**

  Example: List all the steps of the refund process.

  If the full process is not present in the context, the model invents plausible steps to satisfy the required structure.

- **Missing Failure or Fallback Behavior**

  Example: Generate a resolution plan for the issue.

  When no valid resolution exists and failure behavior is undefined, the model hallucinates one rather than asking for clarification or escalating.

By managing prompts in Langfuse, we can make sure instructions that may cause hallucinations are not present in the prompt.

Another Langfuse feature that can come in handy to monitor hallucinations is **Datasets.** Curated datasets provide a way to understand when and where hallucinations occur in our application, enabling prevention rather than reactive fixes. We can create datasets containing inputs that are known or suspected to trigger hallucinations such as edge cases, ambiguous requests, or scenarios with incomplete information. Responses can be evaluated for unsupported claims, overconfidence, or fabrication using Human Annotations or LLM-as-a Judge.

Because dataset runs in Langfuse are linked to prompts and models, hallucinations can be correlated with specific changes such as prompt updates, model upgrades, or routing logic.

Monitoring Bias Using Langfuse

We covered bias monitoring and detection in detail in *Chapter* 3. We also saw some best practices to detect and avoid bias in our applications.

Best Practice	Example
Prompt and Context Design	• Instead of "Describe a typical nurse," use "Describe a nurse, avoiding stereotypes. • Add "Use inclusive language" when asking for job descriptions. • Provide balanced context in a travel prompt: "Suggest destinations across different budget ranges."
Monitoring Outputs for Bias	• Flag when the model defaults to male pronouns for "doctor" or "engineer". • Detect summaries that consistently highlight Western sources but ignore others. • Benchmark by asking "Describe a leader" or "Describe a family" periodically to catch stereotype drift.
Human-in-the-Loop	• Route financial planning answers to review when income levels differ significantly across user queries. • Sample outputs from customer support bots to check tone differences between regions. • Include evaluators from multiple cultures to spot subtle bias in product recommendations.
Transparency	• Add disclaimers such as "This is AI-generated and may reflect biases". • Add a "Report response" button for users to flag biased or unfair content.

***Table 11.1**: Summary of Best Practices to Deal with Bias*

Unlike hallucinations, bias is not usually obvious in isolation. Bias in LLM systems rarely appears as a single incorrect response. Instead, it emerges as **systematic differences in behavior across users, contexts, or groups**. Because of this, bias cannot be reliably detected by inspecting individual outputs.

Since bias is a segmented issue, it is necessary to capture groups/segments with traces. In Langfuse, this can easily be done using tags or metadata. Relevant attributes include:

- User region or language
- Product or feature area
- Request type or priority

- System configuration (prompt version, model)

Next, we should use Evaluations (manual or automatic) to quantify qualitative differences. Bias often can be detected through qualitative signals:

- Tone and Empathy
- Willingness to help or escalate
- Politeness or Directness

By using these evaluation scores, subjective aspects become measurable. Over time, differences in these scores across groups can indicate potential bias.

In Langfuse, we can break down our monitoring dashboards by tags and then reliably detect if a particular score is skewed against an attribute. For example, low empathy for a particular user region. Here is a handy checklist to ensure that bias monitoring is in place for our application.

1. **Context and Attribute Capture**
    - Are relevant user and request attributes captured at runtime (for example, region, language, product, priority) using metadata or tags?
    - Are these attributes consistently propagated to all traces and evaluations?
    - Are sensitive attributes handled carefully and only included when justified?
2. **Clear Behavioral Signals**
    - Do we track qualitative scores such as empathy, helpfulness, politeness, or refusal?
    - Are these scores recorded as structured scores rather than free-text comments?
    - Are the scoring criteria consistent across evaluators or models?
3. **Segment Comparison**
    - Are metrics compared across meaningful segments (for example, region versus region, language versus language)?
    - Do dashboards highlight gaps rather than absolute scores?
    - Are comparisons statistically meaningful (enough samples per segment)?
4. **Prompt and Model Change Tracking**
    - Are prompt versions and model versions logged with each trace?
    - Do we review bias-related metrics after prompt or model changes?
    - Are regressions flagged before or shortly after release?

5. **Curated Bias Evaluation Sets**
    - Do we maintain curated datasets that represent different user groups or contexts?
    - Are these datasets replayed regularly or before major releases?
    - Are bias evaluations attached to dataset runs, not just live traffic?
6. **Human Review and Escalation**
    - Are suspicious bias signals reviewed by humans before conclusions are drawn?
    - Is there a defined escalation path when bias indicators cross thresholds?

Detecting and Responding to Model Drift

In *Chapter* 3, we introduced drift as a gradual change in behavior to our system triggered by external changes to the environment. We also covered the definitions of the different types of drifts we can encounter:

- **Data Drift** which is caused by changes to inputs over time.
- **Prompt Drift** when users change their phrasing of queries.
- **Feedback Drift** for change in ratings or satisfaction patterns.
- **Usage Drift** happens when the purpose for which the system is being used changes over time.
- **Knowledge Drift** when facts or correctness shifts over time.

In the same chapter, we also listed down the ways in which Langfuse features can help detect these drifts. Now we can finally elaborate on how this can be practically implemented.

Drift detection requires groundwork from the beginning of the life of the system so that it is detectable since day 1. Before drift can be detected, a baseline must exist. This baseline represents what normal looks like for the system when it is behaving as expected:

- Capturing distributions of inputs (length, topics, and so on);
- Recording quality metrics (evaluation scores, user feedback); and,
- Logging latency, cost, and usage patterns.

In practice this means:

- We are already logging traces in Langfuse.
- We attach metadata/tags (region, task type, prompt version, model, and so on) to traces.

- We capture evaluations or feedback where possible.

We can use the following table as a guideline to lay the foundational work:

Drift Type	Langfuse Features to Use	What to Log	Example Dashboard Widgets	What Drift Looks Like
Data Drift	Traces Metadata Tags Dashboards	Input text Input length, Topic labels	Average / p95 input length over time Top keywords or topics by week	New topics appear Terminology shifts Inputs get longer or more complex
Prompt Drift	Prompt Management Traces Metadata Tags	Prompt length Formatting style Instruction patterns	Average prompt length by week/ month Quality score by prompt cohort	Users change how they phrase requests Longer, more directive prompts
Feedback Drift	Scores Evaluations Dashboards	User Ratings Evaluator Scores User Comments	Average feedback score over time Feedback by release version	Gradual decline in satisfaction Specific tasks degrade first
Usage Drift	User Sessions Tags Latency and Token usage	Session length Task labels Token usage	Avg session length Token usage per session (p95)	System used for new purposes Longer, more expensive sessions
Knowledge Drift	Datasets Experiments	Ground Truth for responses	Accuracy on benchmark dataset Answer change rate for fixed prompts	Answers to the same questions change Factual accuracy degrades

***Table 11.2**: Langfuse Features by Type of Drift Detection*

How We Can Use This Table:

- **Build one dashboard per drift type** using the suggested widgets.
- **Review periodically** for slow-moving trends.
- **Compare pre- and post-release** to catch regressions.
- **Use curated datasets** to validate fixes before production.

After we set up our system to effectively use Langfuse, we need to also prepare for the eventuality in case drift shows up.

What to Do When We See Drift

The most common types of drift when observed, can be triaged with some of these first actions:

Observed Signal	Likely Root Cause	First Action
Input length increases	Usage drift or Prompt drift	Review if newer inputs are being received.
Feedback drops, usage stable	Prompt or Knowledge drift	Sample low-score traces.
Feedback drops after release	Regression	Roll back or hotfix.
Token usage spikes	Usage drift	Audit User Sessions for time and token usage.
Answer inconsistency	Knowledge drift	Refresh benchmarks for the system.

***Table 11.3**: Some First Responses to Different Drift Types*

It could also happen that what looks like drift is short term noise. In these cases, it might be helpful to not take immediate action if the spikes in trends last only for a short time. If the trend persists for a longer time, use segmented dashboards before moving to fix or change something.

Defining clear ownerships on the types of drift could also help mitigate the problem. Not every type of drift can be fixed by the tech teams. Understanding the underlying reasons for drift is key to finding a resolution.

In the next section, we will look at how Langfuse can help with cost optimization to choose the best model for a balanced cost to performance ratio.

Cost Optimization via Model Routing

Although Langfuse cannot directly route models for us, it can help us implement a routing logic in our system based on the available data in traces to make an informed decision about which model to use for a particular query. By storing information about model usage, cost and evaluation scores, Langfuse allows us to orchestrate LLM calls to the most suitable model within our application. In this section, we will focus on cost optimization (without compromising on quality) and see how to use the cheapest model for an incoming query.

In this example, we will assume that our system can potentially use two or more different LLMs where cost per request differs between the options. To achieve cost optimization in Langfuse, we can follow these steps:

Identify Low-Risk Requests That do not Need the Expensive Model

By **tagging traces** and tracking quality metrics per tag, Langfuse reveals where:

- Output quality is consistently high

- Hallucination and error rates are low
- User feedback is stable

This helps us identify candidate requests that can be routed to the cheaper model.

Compare Model Quality versus Cost Using Experiments

If experimental datasets with ground truths are available, we can already run experiments to see which requests could be served by the cheaper model already. These experiments can help implement data driven routing decisions in our application already. For example, "If Model B is 60% cheaper with only a 3% quality drop for task X", we can safely route calls for this task to Model B.

This approach requires that we have enough validation data to prove our **claim** and continuous monitoring is available in production to detect variations between experiments and real usage.

If this is not an option, we need to collect traces from our application before implementing any routing logic.

Define Routing Rules in the Application

Once we understand where cheaper models could be used, we define routing rules inside our applications, such as:

- Route complex queries to high-end models.
- Route short, repetitive queries to cheaper models.
- Escalate to stronger models when scores drop.

Langfuse can provide the historical evidence that these rules are safe based on past usage.

After routing is deployed, use Langfuse to monitor:

- Cost per request
- Quality scores per routed model
- Feedback differences across routing paths

Although tag-based routing may be simple to implement, it comes with some drawbacks.

- **Tag Quality Becomes a Single Point of Failure:** Routing decisions are only as good as the tags. If tags are incorrectly assigned, then the routing becomes ineffective.

- **Routing Rules Do Not Adapt Automatically:** Routing logic is static and needs to be updated manually in the application as user behavior changes or when prompts evolve. This requires us to update our routing assumptions.
- **Low Returns at Small Scale:** Routing complexity has overhead If request volume is low, cost differences between models are small or quality requirements are uniformly high. In this case routing adds complexity without meaningful benefit.
- **Not Suitable for Every Request:** When correctness and safety are primary goals, we may not want to do routing at all. Requests which include legal advice, medical recommendations or financial decisions are more suited to a reliable model without trying to optimize cost.

In the last example of this chapter, we will look at a no-code example of how Langfuse can help with iterating over different prompt versions or models before deciding on the perfect candidate for our application.

No-Code Playbook: Prompt Iteration for a Summarization Task

This playbook demonstrates how anyone can actively participate in prompt development using Langfuse. The focus is on **prompt iteration**, not infrastructure, and relies entirely on the **Playground** feature of Langfuse rather than code.

The task used throughout this playbook is **text summarization**, a common use case that clearly exposes trade-offs between model choice, prompt clarity, and output quality.

This playbook assumes:

- No curated validation dataset exists yet to run Experiments.
- The goal is to find a **strong starting prompt.**
- Multiple models will be tested to understand quality-cost trade-offs.
- All experimentation happens manually in the Langfuse Playground.

The quality of a prompt frequently influences whether an LLM feature is perceived as effective or inconsistent. However, prompt iteration is frequently tightly coupled with engineering workflows, limiting input from the people who best understand the task domain.

Using Langfuse Playground enables:

- Fast iteration without deployments
- Direct involvement of non-engineers

- Side-by-side comparison of prompts and models
- Traceability of what worked and why

We will follow a step-by-step approach to this problem so that it is easily repeatable for other kinds of tasks as well.

Step 1: Define the Goal Clearly

Before opening the Playground, we must agree on what a good result would look like. For summarization, this usually includes decisions like:

- Should the summary be short or detailed?
- Is the tone neutral, instructional, or conversational?
- Should opinions or interpretations be avoided?
- Is the summary for internal users or customers?

This goal acts as a north star during iteration and prevents subjective opinions later.

Step 2: Prepare a Small Set of Representative Inputs

Since no curated dataset exists yet, we can start with 1-3 real examples that reflect typical usage.

These examples should:

- Vary slightly in length and complexity;
- Come from real or realistic data; and,
- Include at least one "hard" example.

These inputs will be manually pasted into the Playground during testing.

Step 3: Create an Initial Baseline Prompt

The goal of the baseline prompt is to provide a reference point against which improvements can be measured.

In our example, we will use a very simple initial version.

System Prompt:

```
You are a helpful assistant that summarizes text.
```

User Prompt:

```
Summarize the following text:
{{input_text}}
```

Save the initial prompt in Langfuse to be used in the Playground later.

Step 4: Test across Multiple Models in the Playground

Langfuse Playground allows switching models while keeping the prompt constant.

At this stage:

- Run the same input through 2–3 different models.
- Observe differences in verbosity, tone, and faithfulness.

Check against some basic requirements:

- Does the model invent details?
- Is the summary too long or too shallow?
- Is important information dropped?

Step 5: Refine the Prompts

Based on the observations from Step 4, start refining the prompts. After each change:

- Rerun the same examples.
- Compare outputs side by side.
- Discuss whether the change improved consistency.

We can choose to refine only the system prompt or both system and user prompts depending on the use case. Usually, we refine the system prompt first and once it looks stable, we can refine the user prompt to guide the model on the structure of the response.

To begin, we add our initial prompt to Langfuse. Then from the Playground menu option click on **`Fresh Playground`.**

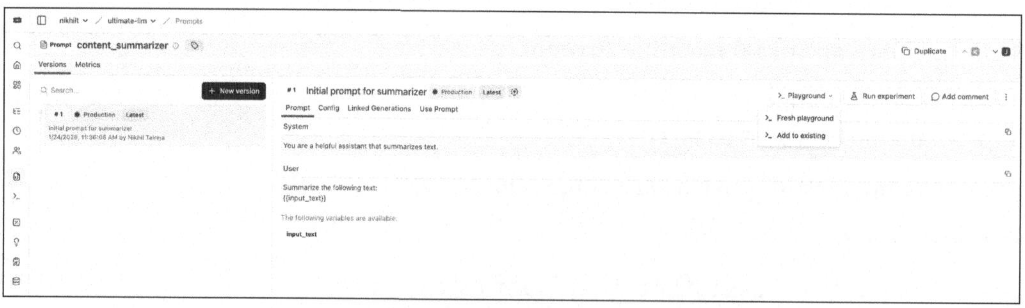

Figure 11.6: *Opening a Prompt in the Playground*

This will open the prompt in the Playground. As the next step, we will use one of our sample texts to iterate the same prompt over 3 different models. To keep things simple, we will assume that we have the following goal: **Our application needs to summarize customer tickets to include the main highlights so that it can be escalated to the respective team as quickly as possible.**

```
I contacted support last Thursday because my subscription renewal
failed, and I couldn't access the premium features anymore. The chatbot
kept repeating the same message, so I eventually emailed support. I did
receive an automated response saying someone would get back to me within
24 hours, but that hasn't happened yet. I've been using the product for
over a year and this is the first time I've had an issue like this. Other
than that, I've generally been happy with the service.
```

After the prompt opens in the playground, we simply need to add our text in the **Variables** section.

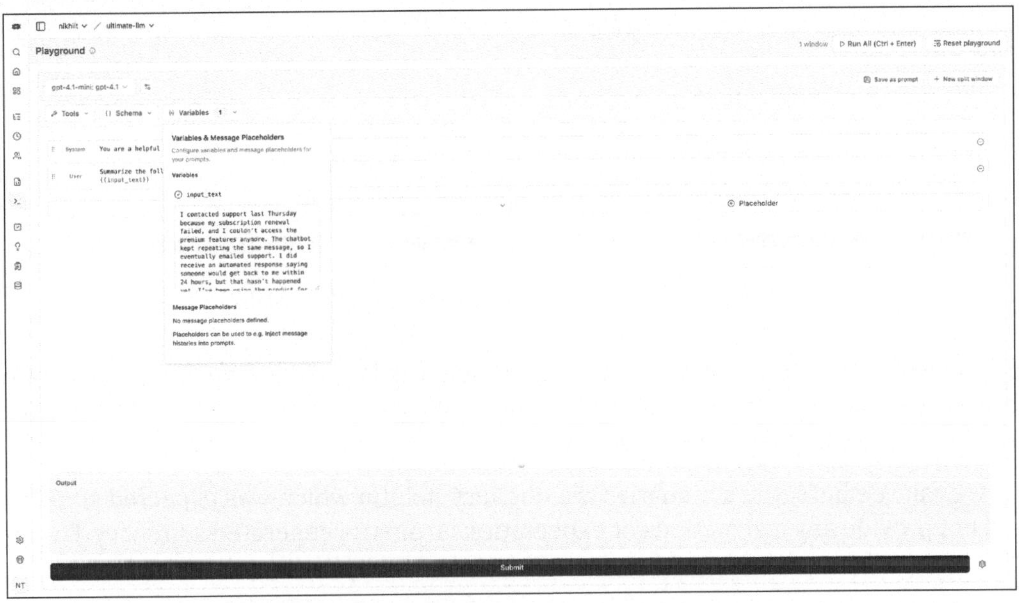

Figure 11.7: *Adding Variables to the Prompt*

We will test 3 basic models from OpenAI: GPT 4.1, GPT 4.1-mini and GPT 4.1-nano. To add more models to the same window we can click the **`+ New split window`** button two more times to have a total of 3 prompt windows open. The prompt and variables are automatically copied over to the new windows.

We will select the model version from the drop down and after that click on the **`Run All`** button on the top right. This will simultaneously execute all the three requests using the respective models and generate the outputs.

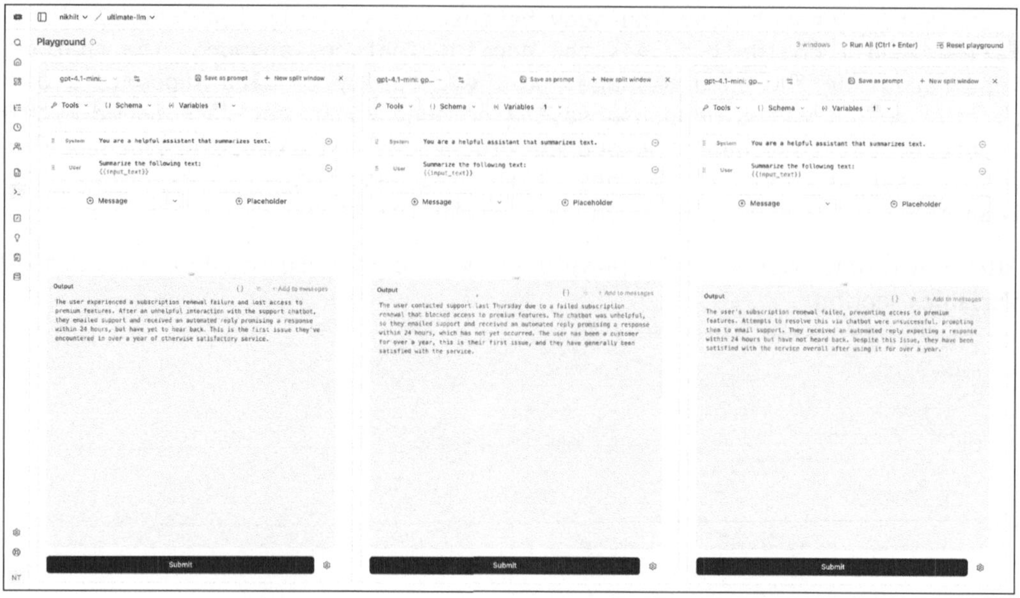

Figure 11.8: *Testing a Prompt with Multiple Models*

It is important to note that these executions from the Playground **do not generate any traces**. That is why it is not possible to run evaluations such as Human Annotations and LLM-as-a-Judge on these responses.

As we can see here, the summaries are not very helpful which was expected since we did not provide any instructions or expectations from the generated summary. For the next iteration, we will use a refined version of the prompt.

```
You summarize customer support tickets so they can be quickly understood
by internal teams.
Focus on the main issue, any important context, and what is blocking the
customer.
Keep the summary concise and factual.
Do not add assumptions or solutions that are not mentioned in the
ticket.
```

The best way to do this is to remove the split windows and keep only the first one. Copy/edit the prompt in the one window and then click the **`+ New split window`** again which will automatically copy the new prompt to the windows. We need to reselect the model version from the drop down and then click the **`Run All`** button.

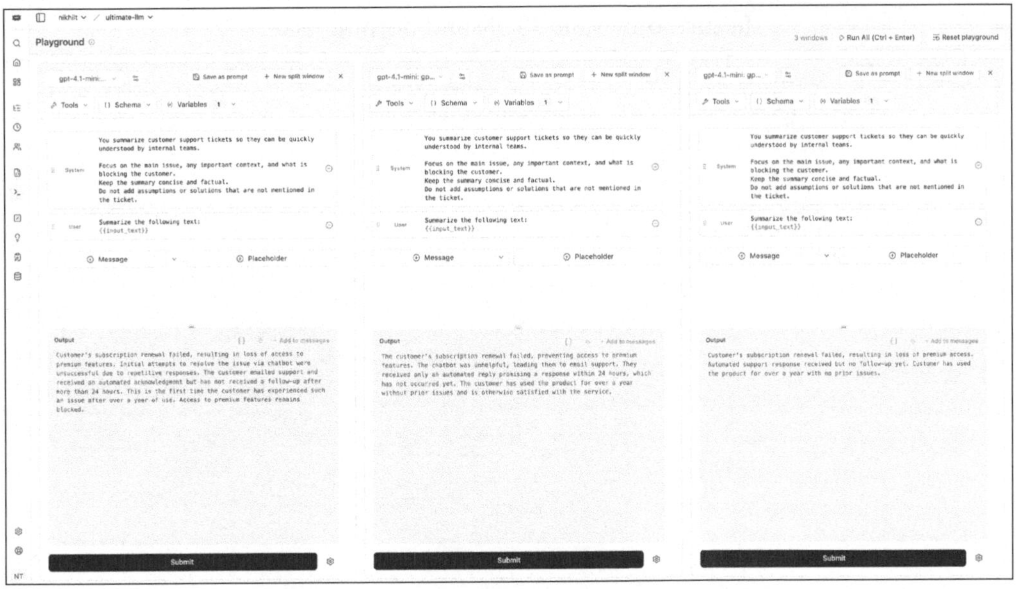

Figure 11.9: *Testing a Refined Version of the Prompt*

This time we can see that results are much better and GPT 4.1 nano seems to have an edge when it comes to understanding the instruction on being concise and focusing on the main issue.

For the next iteration, we will refine the prompt to have a fixed structured response instead. Since the goal is to find the responsible team, it would help if responses were predictable and information is easy to locate in the final response of the model. We will also enforce a limit on the number of sentences to make sure the summaries are not too verbose.

```
You summarize customer support tickets for internal escalation.
Return the summary in valid JSON using the exact structure below:
{
  "issue": "",
  "context": "",
  "blocker": ""
}
Guidelines:
- "issue": the main problem the customer is facing.
- "context": relevant background needed to understand the issue.
- "blocker": what is preventing resolution or why escalation is needed.
Each field should be one concise sentence.
Do not add information that is not explicitly mentioned in the ticket.
If the information for a field is missing, leave the value as an empty
string.
```

Return only valid JSON and nothing else.

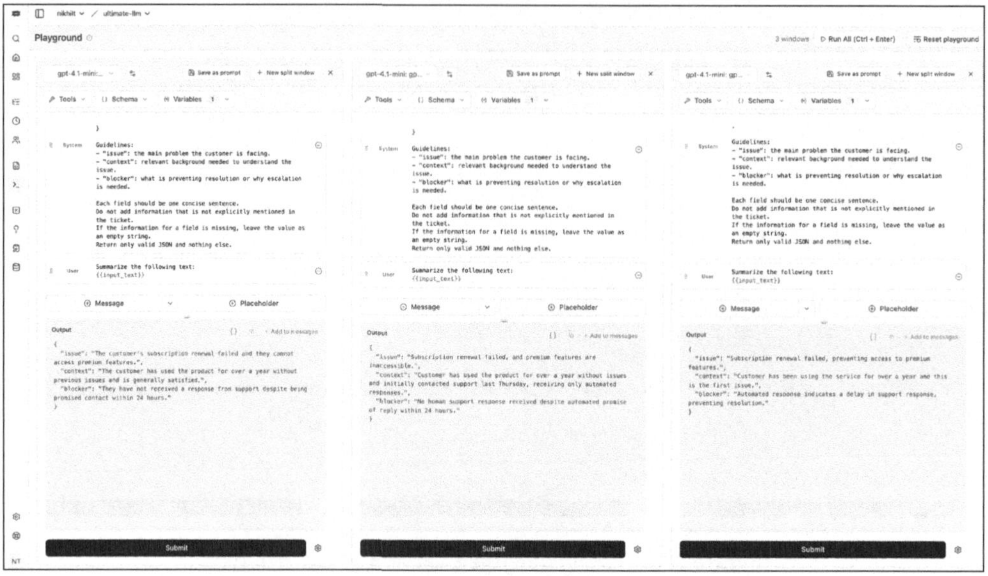

Figure 11.10: *Adding More Instructions to Our Prompt*

By forcing JSON outputs, we make the summary more predictable and structured. This also contextualizes the response and makes it usable for downstream systems which may rely on a fixed set of values for the different fields. If we are satisfied with the response, we can save the prompt as a new prompt or even as a new version of the existing prompt.

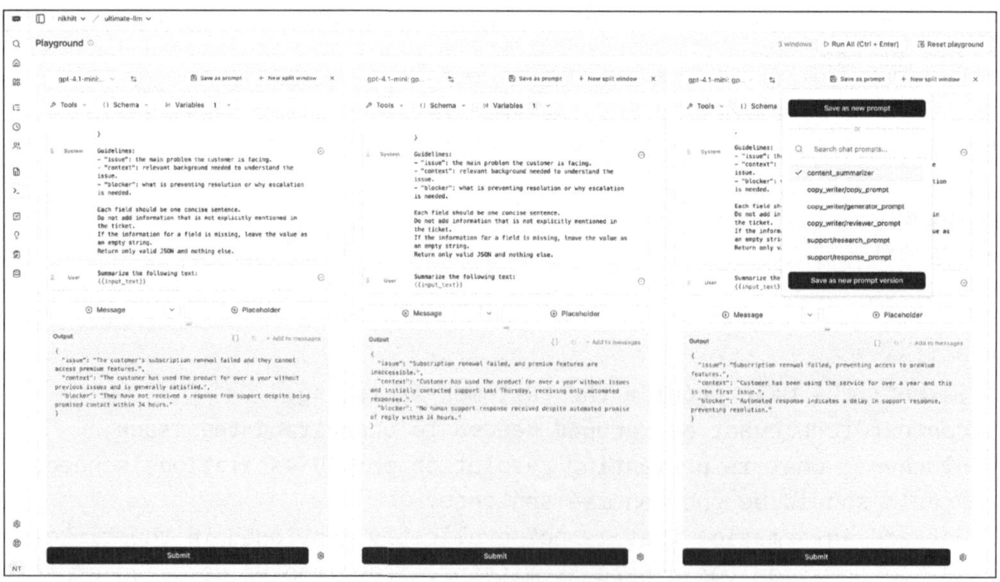

Figure 11.11: *Saving a New Prompt Version from the Playground*

Although this prompt may not be the final version, this iterative process can help teams quickly converge on a prompt that is fit for purpose, reveal model-specific strengths and limitations, and establish a shared understanding of what "good" looks like before any engineering effort or automation is introduced.

Conclusion

This chapter brings together practical playbooks demonstrating how Langfuse can be integrated into real-world LLM workflows for improved observability, evaluation, and optimization. Starting with foundational integrations using OpenAI and LangChain, it explores advanced topics such as Retrieval-Augmented Generation (RAG), agentic workflows, and robust monitoring for hallucinations and bias. The chapter emphasizes best practices for drift detection, cost optimization via model routing, and the importance of structured evaluations using both automated and human-in-the-loop methods. A special focus is given to enabling non-technical users through Langfuse's no-code Playground for prompt iteration. Through step-by-step guides and concrete examples, readers learn to design, monitor, and refine LLM applications, ensuring transparency, reliability, and adaptability as systems evolve. The playbooks empower teams to collaborate efficiently and proactively respond to challenges, establishing Langfuse as a key tool for building trustworthy, scalable AI solutions. With this chapter we are moving near towards the end of the book. In the next and the last chapter, we shall recapitulate our learning and look at a roadmap that the readers can follow to continue with their Langfuse journey.

References

- Langfuse integration with LangChain - https://langfuse.com/integrations/frameworks/langchain
- Build a RAG agent with LangChain - https://docs.langchain.com/oss/python/langchain/rag
- Langfuse Environment variables - https://langfuse.com/self-hosting/configuration

CHAPTER 12
Putting It All Together

Introduction

This concluding chapter brings the book full circle. We will be recapitulating the journey from understanding Large Language Models (LLMs) and their challenges, to introducing Langfuse as a monitoring and observability layer, and exploring its capabilities across deployment, prompt management, drift detection, metrics analysis, security, and administration. Along the way, we have observed both theoretical underpinnings and hands-on playbooks, illustrating how Langfuse supports reliable, cost-effective, and responsible LLM applications in real-world settings. Finally, the chapter offers a forward-looking view: where the monitoring ecosystem is headed, how Langfuse might evolve alongside agentic AI, and why observability will only grow in importance as models become more complex. We will also look at some recommendations for further learning, community resources for Langfuse, and advanced tooling to deepen our expertise.

Structure

In this chapter, we will cover the following:

- A Recap of the Key Themes of the Book
- Putting Theory into Practice
- Looking Ahead: Langfuse Roadmap
    - How to Use the Roadmap
    - Impact of Joining ClickHouse
- The Future of LLM Engineering and Observability

A Recap of the Key Themes of the Book

In *Chapter 1, Introduction to Large Language Models and Monitoring*, we introduced LLMs by looking at them within the historical evolution of Natural Language Processing, from early rule-based systems to modern Transformer-based architectures. We examined how LLMs work at a conceptual level, including tokenization, embeddings, attention mechanisms, and layered representations. The chapter established that LLM outputs are probabilistic and non-deterministic, which distinguishes LLM-based systems from traditional software. We additionally explored common industry use cases and identified the core challenges of deploying LLMs in production, such as hallucinations, performance constraints, cost escalation, and ethical risks. Finally, we had also outlined the LLM application lifecycle and introduced the core tooling stack used throughout the book, thereby, setting the foundation for a monitoring-first perspective.

In *Chapter 2, LLM Monitoring Principles*, we shifted our focus from models to systems by introducing the foundational principles of LLM monitoring and observability. We clarified the distinction between monitoring and observability and explained why both are necessary for understanding LLM behavior in production. We introduced traces and spans as the structural units that capture end-to-end request execution, highlighting the need to include LLM-specific context such as prompts, retrieved documents, and generated outputs. We adapted Site Reliability Engineering (SRE) concepts to LLM applications, showing how Service Level Indicators, Service Level Objectives, and error budgets can be extended to cover semantic reliability, safety, and output quality. The chapter also established key monitoring principles, including semantic-layer monitoring, user feedback integration, drift detection, and balancing cost, performance, and quality metrics.

In *Chapter 3, Detecting Model Drift and Bias in LLMs*, we took the path to examine model drift and bias as long-term risks in LLM-based systems. We gradually explained how drift can arise not only from model updates but also from changes in data sources, retrieval corpora, user behavior, and prompt evolution. We had discussed different forms of drift, including data drift, behavioral drift, and quality drift, and emphasized why static evaluation is insufficient in production environments. The chapter also addressed bias and fairness concerns, showing how LLMs can reproduce or amplify biases present in training data or retrieval sources. We highlighted the role of continuous monitoring and evaluation in detecting these issues early and mitigating their impact over time.

In *Chapter 4, Introduction to Langfuse*, we focused on instrumentation and the practical aspects of capturing observability data from LLM applications. We showed how to record traces, observations, and metadata in a structured way so that system behavior can be analyzed retrospectively. The chapter demonstrated how instrumentation enables visibility into latency bottlenecks, cost drivers, prompt effectiveness, and failure modes. Our discussion primarily emphasized upon the fact that high-quality observability data is a prerequisite for meaningful evaluation and monitoring, and that incomplete or inconsistent logging severely limits the ability to diagnose issues in production.

In *Chapter 5, Observability in Langfuse*, we not only focused on observability in Langfuse,but also on how traces and observations form the foundation for understanding LLM application behavior. We further showed how to instrument applications to capture end-to-end execution paths, including prompt construction, model generations, retrieval steps, and tool calls. The chapter explained how metadata, tags, and user identifiers enable meaningful segmentation and analysis of production traffic. We also examined how the observation types of Langfuse help classify different stages of an LLM workflow, making complex systems easy to debug. Overall, we established Langfuse as the central layer that connects raw execution data with higher-level monitoring, evaluation, and operational insight.

In *Chapter 6, Prompt Management in Langfuse*, we explored Prompt Management. We discussed why prompts should be versioned, tested, and evaluated in the same way as code. The chapter showed how prompt changes can significantly affect output quality, cost, and safety, making uncontrolled prompt updates a major source of production instability. We positioned prompt observability and prompt-level metrics as essential tools for controlled iteration and reproducibility.

In *Chapter 7, Evaluating LLMs in Langfuse*, we examined how LLMs can be evaluated systematically using Langfuse. We introduced evaluation as a continuous process rather than a one-time validation step, covering both automated methods and human-in-the-loop reviews. We showed how evaluation scores can be attached directly to traces, prompts, and model versions, enabling objective comparison across experiments and production traffic. The chapter also demonstrated how LLM-as-a-judge, datasets, and manual annotations can be combined to measure qualities such as correctness, relevance, and hallucination.

In *Chapter 8, Deriving Actionable Insights Using Langfuse Metrics*, we had focused on deriving actionable insights from Langfuse metrics and dashboards. We showed how raw traces and evaluations can be transformed into aggregated metrics that reveal trends in quality, latency, cost, and user behavior. The chapter emphasized designing dashboards around decisions rather than data volume, using clear naming and focused widgets to highlight regressions, trade-offs, and improvement opportunities. We also discussed segmenting metrics by attributes such as model version, prompt, or user cohort to uncover hidden patterns.

In *Chapter 9, Administration, LLM Security and Guardrails*, we addressed administration, security, and guardrails for LLM applications. We examined how access control, environment separation, and configuration management help operate LLM systems safely at scale. The chapter introduced guardrails as structured mechanisms to constrain model behavior, covering input validation, output filtering, and policy enforcement to reduce risks such as prompt injection, unsafe content, and data leakage. We also discussed auditing and governance practices, showing how Langfuse supports visibility into sensitive operations through traces and metadata.

In *Chapter 10, Langfuse Best Practices*, we aimed to consolidate the lessons from earlier chapters into a set of best practices for operating LLM applications in production. We emphasized the importance of clear naming conventions for traces, metrics, prompts, and dashboards to ensure shared understanding across teams. We highlighted the need to align monitoring with decision-making by focusing on actionable metrics rather than raw volume. The chapter reinforced treating prompts as versioned artifacts, combining automated and human evaluation, and reviewing dashboards regularly to detect regressions early.

Finally, in *Chapter 11, Langfuse Playbooks*, we targeted to apply the monitoring and evaluation concepts from earlier chapters through a set of practical Langfuse playbooks. We demonstrated how observability is implemented in real LLM workflows, starting from a basic OpenAI and LangChain integration and extending to Retrieval-Augmented Generation, agentic systems, hallucination and bias monitoring, drift detection, and cost optimization through model routing. The chapter emphasized how traces, evaluations, metadata, and dashboards make complex system behavior understandable and measurable. We also showed how prompt iteration can be performed without code using the Langfuse Playground, enabling structured experimentation and broader collaboration before production deployment.

Here is also a summary table with the key topics covered in each of the chapters:

No.	Title (Short)	Key Topics and Keywords
1	**Introduction to Large Language Models and Monitoring**	LLM basics, Transformers, tokenization, embeddings, attention, use cases, deployment challenges, hallucination, latency, cost, token usage, correctness, relevance, completeness, LLM lifecycle, OpenAI SDK, LangChain, Langfuse
2	**LLM Monitoring Principles**	Monitoring vs observability, traces & spans, semantic monitoring, SRE for LLMs, SLIs/SLOs, error budgets, user feedback, drift detection, safety metrics, monitoring dimensions (functional, non-functional, ethical)
3	**Detecting Model Drift and Bias in LLMs**	Data drift, prompt drift, feedback drift, usage drift, knowledge drift, bias detection, fairness, segmentation, qualitative evaluation, long-term reliability
4	**Introduction to Langfuse**	Langfuse architecture, core concepts, traces, observations, projects, environments, SDKs, integrations, UI overview, basic setup

No.	Title (Short)	Key Topics and Keywords
5	**Observability in Langfuse**	Traces, observations, observation types, metadata conventions, tagging strategies, workflow visibility, and debugging complex LLM pipelines
6	**Prompt Management in Langfuse**	Prompt versioning, prompt storage, prompt deployment, reproducibility, controlled iteration, prompt comparison, prompt as code
7	**Evaluating LLMs in Langfuse**	Datasets, experiments, LLM-as-a-judge, human annotations, correctness, hallucination, relevance, completeness, automated vs human evaluation
8	**Deriving Actionable Insights Using Langfuse Metrics**	Aggregated metrics, dashboards, trend analysis, segmentation, quality vs cost vs latency trade-offs, naming conventions, decision-driven dashboards
9	**Administration, LLM Security and Guardrails**	Access control, environments, governance, prompt injection, output filtering, PII, safety policies, guardrails, auditing, compliance
10	**Langfuse Best Practices**	Operational discipline, naming standards, prompt versioning, dashboard hygiene, regression detection, evaluation workflows, continuous improvement
11	**Langfuse Playbooks**	OpenAI + LangChain integration, RAG, agents, hallucination monitoring, bias monitoring, drift response, model routing, cost optimization, no-code Playground, prompt iteration

Table 12.1: *Summary of the Key Concepts Covered in Each of the Chapters*

Putting Theory into Practice

After reading this book, we are well-positioned not only to use Langfuse but to actively **engage with it as a platform, an open-source project, and a community**. The ideas covered so far become most valuable when they are applied, tested, shared, and refined in real-world settings. This section outlines concrete ways we can get involved with Langfuse, regardless of whether we are engineers, ML practitioners, product owners, or technical leaders.

A natural first step is to **start using Langfuse with an existing or experimental LLM application**. We can begin by integrating Langfuse into a small workflow such as a chatbot, summarization pipeline, or internal tool and instrumenting basic traces. This allows us to observe prompts, model calls, latency, token usage, and outputs in one place. Even minimal integration immediately surfaces insights about system behavior that are otherwise difficult to reason about, making Langfuse a practical learning environment rather than just a theoretical concept.

We can then **experiment with Langfuse in a local or self-hosted setup**. Because Langfuse is open source, it can be run locally or deployed in private infrastructure. This is particularly valuable for teams working in regulated environments or those who want full control over data and configuration. Running Langfuse locally encourages deeper exploration of its architecture, data model, and extensibility, and helps bridge the gap between understanding how Langfuse works and understanding why it was designed the way it was.

Once basic usage is established, we can **apply Langfuse to iterative improvement workflows**. This includes using prompt management to version and compare prompts, running evaluations on curated datasets, and setting up dashboards to monitor trends over time. By replaying real traces, testing alternative prompts, or comparing models under the same conditions, we can directly practice the experimentation and evaluation techniques described earlier in the book. These hands-on iterations reinforce the idea that quality, cost, and reliability are measurable properties, not subjective opinions.

Beyond individual experimentation, we can **use Langfuse as a collaboration layer** within teams. Engineers can share traces with product managers, domain experts, or stakeholders to review model behavior together. Non-engineers can contribute by annotating outputs, iterating on prompts in the Playground, or defining what "good" looks like for specific tasks. This collaborative usage is often where Langfuse has the most impact, as it aligns technical implementation with real-world expectations and domain knowledge.

For someone who wants to go further can **engage with Langfuse as an open-source project**. This can start simply by reading the source code, reviewing documentation, or following discussions to understand how features evolve.

The official GitHub page for Langfuse: **https://github.com/langfuse/langfuse**

More active involvement might include reporting bugs, suggesting improvements, or contributing documentation based on practical experience. For technically inclined users, contributing code, whether fixing small issues or adding integrations, provides an opportunity to shape the platform while deepening their own understanding of LLM observability.

Another important way to get involved is to **apply Langfuse in different domains and share learnings**. The monitoring patterns described in this book apply across use cases, but each domain, such as customer support, finance, healthcare, internal tooling, and research, introduces unique constraints and metrics. By applying Langfuse in varied contexts and reflecting on what works and what does not, we contribute to a growing body of shared best practices around LLM monitoring. These insights often surface through blog posts, talks, internal write-ups, or community discussions.

We can also **participate in shaping evaluation and monitoring standards**. As LLM systems mature, the industry is still converging on how to measure quality, safety, and reliability consistently. By experimenting with evaluators, defining custom metrics, and testing different monitoring strategies, we can help refine what good monitoring looks like in practice. Langfuse provides the tooling, but the standards emerge from how practitioners use it.

For teams planning to scale LLM usage, Langfuse can become a **central operational system**. We can use it to define internal guidelines around prompt changes, model upgrades, cost controls, and release validation. Over time, this leads to repeatable processes where new features or experiments are introduced with evidence rather than risk. Engaging Langfuse at this level means treating it as part of the production infrastructure, not just a debugging tool.

Finally, we can **stay engaged with the Langfuse ecosystem as it evolves**. LLM tooling, models, and usage patterns change rapidly, and Langfuse continues to adapt alongside them. By staying connected through updates, discussions, or continued experimentation, we ensure that their monitoring practices evolve with the systems they operate. This ongoing engagement reinforces the central message of the book: **reliable LLM systems are not built once, but continuously shaped through observation, measurement, and learning.**

Looking Ahead: Langfuse Roadmap

The Langfuse roadmap is intended as a living, high-level guide to the ongoing evolution of the platform. Instead of just listing features, it guides users on how Langfuse will develop and meet new needs in LLM observability, evaluation, and production engineering. The roadmap is open to everyone. It shows where things are heading, welcomes ideas, and shares plans, but doesn't set exact dates or specific tasks.

The roadmap organizes work around domains rather than individual tasks. These domains reflect the aspects of LLM application engineering that evolve most rapidly and where ongoing innovation has the greatest impact. For users, the roadmap provides context about where Langfuse's development energy is focused, how different components relate to each other, and how to anticipate support for new patterns and use cases.

The roadmap is available at: **https://langfuse.com/docs/roadmap**

How to Use the Roadmap

For readers of this book, the roadmap functions as a **reference framework** to help connect the concepts discussed earlier with how the platform will support them. It can be used in several practical ways:

1. **Tracking Progress over Time:** As Langfuse releases new versions, we can compare actual evolution with the thematic direction on the roadmap to understand how platform capabilities are maturing.

2. **Planning Adoption:** Teams that are planning to adopt or scale Langfuse can align their internal milestones, such as onboarding, experimentation workflows, or governance controls, with broader platform investments.
3. **Aligning Expectations:** When thinking about long-term observability needs (such as multi-tenant governance, advanced evaluation metrics, or real-time alerting), the roadmap helps set realistic expectations about when and how support might evolve.
4. **Influencing Priorities:** Because Langfuse publishes the roadmap publicly and solicits community input, users are empowered to shape future direction by raising issues or voting on ideas. This democratizes product evolution and ensures that priorities reflect real usage patterns across the industry.

Impact of Joining ClickHouse

A major organizational milestone occurred in early 2026: **Langfuse was acquired by ClickHouse**, a company known for its real-time analytics database and data infrastructure offerings. ClickHouse is also the primary analytical database used in Langfuse to store transactional data such as traces, costs, token usage, and so on. The acquisition was announced jointly by both teams, and it underscores two strategic points:

- Langfuse will **remain open source and self-hostable**, with no planned changes to licensing or core product usage. Langfuse Cloud will continue to operate with the same behavior and support commitments as before the acquisition.
- The acquisition enables accelerated progress on the public roadmap by combining Thc domain expertise of Langfuse in LLM observability with the infrastructure resources and engineering scale of ClickHouse. Specifically, the expanded engineering capacity is intended to improve performance, enterprise-grade compliance, documentation, and overall product polish, advancing goals that were already part of the roadmap of Langfuse prior to the acquisition.

Langfuse had already adopted ClickHouse as its core storage layer in a prior platform release, migrating from earlier architectures to harness the analytical performance and scalability of ClickHouse. The formal acquisition solidifies this technical alignment and establishes a deeper integration between the LLM observability workflows of Langfuse and the data capabilities of ClickHouse.

The Future of LLM Engineering and Observability

As we look ahead, the practice of engineering systems powered by LLMs is poised to become more structured, rigorous, and deeply integrated into standard software development lifecycles. One of the defining trends of this evolution is the central role that **observability** will play in making complex AI behavior transparent, measurable, and governable.

We have already seen how traditional metric and logging approaches are insufficient because LLM systems produce non-deterministic outputs and often involve layered processes such as retrieval, reasoning, and agent behavior. As generative AI features become embedded across products from conversational chatbots to autonomous agents, the need for rich observability tools will only intensify.

A robust LLM observability approach captures structured traces that unify prompts, model responses, token usage, latency, and system metadata. This enables teams to diagnose quality issues, attribute cost, track drift, and debug complex interaction chains in ways that were previously opaque. Tools in this space have evolved rapidly in response to these needs, and engineers will increasingly rely on observability as a **foundation for quality assurance and operational confidence** rather than an optional add-on.

The recent acquisition of Langfuse by ClickHouse underscores this shift. The strategic investment of ClickHouse reflects the growing recognition that LLM observability is fundamentally a **data problem** requiring high-performance analytics to support scale and responsiveness in AI systems. By combining the open-source platform of Langfuse for LLM observability with the capabilities of ClickHouse in real-time analytics and large-scale data processing, the broader ecosystem is signaling that observability will be a core infrastructural layer in future AI stacks.

Looking forward, several trends will shape the landscape of LLM engineering:

- **Formalization of Engineering Practices:** As with DevOps and MLOps, LLM engineering will develop standardized workflows for versioning prompts, defining evaluation criteria, automating regression tests, and performing trace-based performance checks. Observability data will be integrated into continuous integration and continuous delivery (CI/CD) pipelines, enabling automated quality gates and evidence-based deployments.
- **Observability for Autonomous and Agentic Workflows:** Complex AI systems, which use chains of reasoning and agentic models, introduce additional observability challenges. Such systems have intermediate reasoning steps and dynamic tool usage that must be made visible for debugging and governance. Research into hybrid observability techniques for multi-agent and hybrid semantic/system tracing suggests that future tooling will need to capture both high-level intent and low-level execution contexts simultaneously to be effective.
- **Expanded Evaluation Dimensions:** Beyond correctness and performance, evaluation frameworks will routinely measure safety, bias, reliability, and user

experience. Observability platforms will increasingly integrate structured evaluation results, enabling teams to track quality across multiple axes and over time.

- **Governance, Compliance, and Transparency:** As LLM systems are used in regulated domains, observability will be central to meeting compliance and audit requirements. Transparent records of system behavior, including prompt versions, evaluation outcomes, and drift metrics, will be essential for both internal governance and external reporting.
- **Data-Driven Optimization:** Operational observability will inform optimization strategies such as adaptive routing, cost-performance trade-offs, and workload segmentation across model families. With rich time-series and trace data, teams will be able to justify architectural decisions based on empirical evidence rather than intuition.

In conclusion, **observability will be an essential aspect of future LLM engineering**, enabling developers not only to *see* what their systems are doing, but to reason about *why* they behave as they do, and to *act* on those insights with confidence. As models become more complex and enter mission-critical roles, this foundational capability will be indispensable for building trustworthy, maintainable, and scalable AI systems.

References

- What is LLM Observability and LLM Monitoring? –
  https://langfuse.com/faq/all/llm-observability
- ClickHouse welcomes Langfuse –
  https://clickhouse.com/blog/clickhouse-acquires-langfuse-open-source-llm-observability
- Observability in Large Language Models: A Framework for Real-Time Applications
  https://www.ijlrp.com/papers/2024/12/1319.pdf
- LLM observability tools: Monitoring, debugging, and improving AI systems -
  https://medium.com/online-inference/llm-observability-tools-monitoring-debugging-and-improving-ai-systems-5af769796266

Index

D

E

P

Q

R

S

T

U

V

W